Analytical Chemistry in Archaeology

An introductory manual that explains the basic concepts of chemistry behind scientific analytical techniques and that reviews their application to archaeology. It explains key terminology, outlines the procedures to be followed in order to produce good data, and describes the function of the basic instrumentation required to carry out those procedures. The manual contains chapters on the basic chemistry and physics necessary to understand the techniques used in analytical chemistry, with more detailed chapters on atomic absorption, inductively coupled plasma emission spectroscopy, neutron activation analysis, X-ray fluorescence, electron microscopy, infrared and Raman spectroscopy, and mass spectrometry. Each chapter describes the operation of the instruments, some hints on the practicalities, and a review of the application of the technique to archaeology, including some case studies. With guides to further reading on the topic, it is an essential tool for practitioners, researchers, and advanced students alike.

MARK POLLARD is Edward Hall Professor of Archaeological Science, Research Laboratory for Archaeology and the History of Art, University of Oxford.

CATHY BATT is Senior Lecturer in Archaeological Sciences, University of Bradford.

BEN STERN is Lecturer in Archaeological Sciences, University of Bradford.

SUZANNE M. M. YOUNG is NASA Researcher and Lecturer in Chemistry at Tufts University.

CAMBRIDGE MANUALS IN ARCHAEOLOGY

General Editor
Graeme Barker, *University of Cambridge*

Advisory Editors
Elizabeth Slater, *University of Liverpool*
Peter Bogucki, *Princeton University*

Books in the series
Pottery in Archaeology, Clive Orton, Paul Tyers, and Alan Vince
Vertebrate Taphonomy, R. Lee Lyman
Photography in Archaeology and Conservation, 2nd edn, Peter G. Dorrell
Alluvial Geoarchaeology, A.G. Brown
Shells, Cheryl Claasen
Zooarchaeology, Elizabeth J. Reitz and Elizabeth S. Wing
Sampling in Archaeology, Clive Orton
Excavation, Steve Roskams
Teeth, 2nd edn, Simon Hillson
Lithics, 2nd edn, William Andrefsky Jr.
Geographical Information Systems in Archaeology, James Conolly and Mark Lake
Demography in Archaeology, Andrew Chamberlain
Analytical Chemistry in Archaeology, A.M. Pollard, C.M. Batt, B. Stern,
    and S.M.M. Young

Cambridge Manuals in Archaeology is a series of reference handbooks
designed for an international audience of upper-level undergraduate
and graduate students, and professional archaeologists and archaeological
scientists in universities, museums, research laboratories, and field units.
Each book includes a survey of current archaeological practice alongside
essential reference material on contemporary techniques and methodology.

ANALYTICAL CHEMISTRY IN ARCHAEOLOGY

A.M. Pollard
Research Laboratory for Archaeology and the History of Art,
University of Oxford, UK

C.M. Batt and B. Stern
Department of Archaeological Sciences,
University of Bradford, UK

S.M.M. Young
NASA Researcher, Department of Chemistry, Tufts University,
Medford, Massachusetts, USA

CAMBRIDGE
UNIVERSITY PRESS

CAMBRIDGE UNIVERSITY PRESS
Cambridge, New York, Melbourne, Madrid, Cape Town, Singapore, São Paulo
Delhi, Dubai, Tokyo, Mexico City

Cambridge University Press
The Edinburgh Building, Cambridge CB2 8RU, UK

Published in the United States of America by Cambridge University Press, New York

www.cambridge.org
Information on this title: www.cambridge.org/9780521655729

First published 2007
Reprinted 2011

Printed in the United Kingdom at the University Press, Cambridge

A catalogue record for this publication is available from the British Library

ISBN 978-0-521-65209-4 Hardback
ISBN 978-0-521-65572-9 Paperback

CONTENTS

v

FIGURES

ix

TABLES

PREFACE

The purpose of this book is to provide an introduction to the applications of analytical chemistry to archaeology. The intended audience is advanced students of archaeology, who may not have all of the required background in chemistry and physics, but who need either to carry out analytical procedures, or to use the results of such analyses in their studies. The book is presented in three parts. The first is intended to contextualize analytical chemistry for students of archaeology – it illustrates some of the archaeological questions which have been addressed, at least in part, by chemical analysis, and also chronicles some of the long history of interaction between chemistry and archaeology. Additionally, it introduces chemistry as a scientific discipline, and gives a brief historical introduction to the art and science of analytical chemistry.

The second part consists of seven chapters, which present a range of analytical techniques that have found archaeological application, grouped by their underlying scientific principles (absorption/emission of visible light, absorption of infrared, etc.). Each chapter describes the principles and instrumentation of the methods in some detail, using mathematics where this amplifies a point. The majority of each chapter, however, is devoted to reviewing the applications of the techniques to archaeology. We do not pretend that these application reviews are comprehensive, although we do hope that there are enough relevant references to allow the interested reader to find her or his way into the subject in some depth. We have also tried to be critical (without engaging in too much controversy), since the role of a good teacher is to instill a sense of enthusiastic but critical enquiry! Nor can we pretend that the topics covered in these chapters are exhaustive in terms of describing all of the analytical methods that have been, or could profitably be, applied to serious questions in archaeology. The critical reader will no doubt point out that her or his favorite application (e.g., NMR, thermal methods, etc.) is missing. All that we can say is that we have attempted to deal with those methods that have contributed the most over the years to archaeological chemistry. Perhaps more attention could usefully have been applied to a detailed analysis of how chemical data has been used in archaeology, especially when hindsight suggests that this has been unhelpful. It is a matter of some debate as to whether it is worse to carry out superb chemistry in support of trivial or meaningless archaeology, or to address substantial issues in archaeology with bad chemistry. That, however, could fill another book!

In order for the intended audience of students to become "informed customers" or, better still, trainee practitioners, we present in the final part some of the basic science necessary to appreciate the principles and practice underlying modern analytical chemistry. We hope that this basic science is presented in such a way that it might be useful for students of other applied chemistry disciplines, such as environmental chemistry or forensic chemistry, and even that students of chemistry might find some interest in the applications of archaeological chemistry.

Chapters 10 and 11 introduce basic concepts in chemistry, including atomic theory and molecular bonding, since these are necessary to understand the principles of spectrometry, and an introduction to organic chemistry. Chapter 12 discusses some basic physics, including wave motion and the interaction of electromagnetic waves with solid matter. Chapter 13 is an introduction to some of the practicalities of analytical chemistry, including how to make up standard solutions, how to calibrate analytical instruments, and how to calculate such important parameters as the minimum detectable level of an analyte, and how to estimate errors. We also outline quality assurance protocols, and good practice in laboratory safety. Much of this material has been used in teaching the underlying maths, physics, and chemistry on the BSc in Archaeological Science at the University of Bradford, in the hope that these students will go on to become more than "intelligent consumers" of analytical chemistry. It is gratifying to see that a number of ex-students have, indeed, contributed significantly to the literature of archaeological chemistry.

In this background material, we have taken a decidedly historical approach to the development of the subject, and have, where possible, made reference to the original publications. It is surprising and slightly distressing to see how much misinformation is propagated through the modern literature because of a lack of acquaintance with the primary sources. We have also made use of the underlying mathematics where it (hopefully) clarifies the narrative. Not only does this give the student the opportunity to develop a quantitative approach to her or his work, but it also gives the reader the opportunity to appreciate the underlying beauty of the structure of science.

This book has been an embarrassing number of years in gestation. We are grateful for the patience of Cambridge University Press during this process. We are also grateful to a large number of individuals, without whom such a work could not have been completed (including, of course, Newton's Giants!). In particular, we are grateful to Dr Janet Montgomery, who helped to collate some of the text and sought out references, and to Judy Watson, who constructed the figures. All errors are, of course, our own.

PART I

THE ROLE OF ANALYTICAL CHEMISTRY IN ARCHAEOLOGY

ARCHAEOLOGY AND ANALYTICAL CHEMISTRY

This chapter aims to place the role of analytical chemistry into its archaeological context. It is a common fallacy that archaeology is about things – objects, monuments, landscapes. It is not: archaeology is about people. In a leading introductory text, Renfrew and Bahn (1996: 17) state that "archaeology is concerned with the full range of past human experience – how people organized themselves into social groups and exploited their surroundings; what they ate, made, and believed; how they communicated and why their societies changed". In the same volume, archaeology is called "the past tense of cultural anthropology" (Renfrew and Bahn 1996: 11), but it differs from anthropology in one crucial and obvious respect – in archaeology it is impossible to interview the subjects of study, or to observe them directly in their everyday life. Archaeology therefore operates at a very different level of detail when compared to anthropology. Inferences about past societies are made from the material evidence recovered by archaeological excavation – sometimes in the form of surviving artifacts or structures (i.e., the deliberate products of human activity), but also from associated evidence such as insect remains, from which environmental and ecological information can be derived. Sometimes it is the soils and sediments of the archaeological deposit itself – their nature and stratigraphy – which provide the evidence, or add information by providing a context. Hence the often acrimonious debate about the effects of looting or the undisciplined use of metal detectors, where objects are removed from their contexts without proper recording. It is always the case that information is lost, sometimes totally, when an object is removed from its archaeological context without proper recording.

Although archaeology is a historical discipline, in that its aim is to reconstruct events in the past, it is not the same as history. If history is reconstructing the past from written sources, then 99.9% of humanity's five million years or more of global evolution is beyond the reach of history. Even in historic times, where written records exist, there is still a distinctive role for archaeology. Documentary evidence often provides evidence for "big events" – famous people, battles and invasions, religious dogma, and the history of states – but such written sources are inevitably biased. History is written by the literate, and usually by the victorious. We do not have to look far into our own recent history to realize that it can obscure the past as well as illuminate it. In contrast, archaeology is generally the unwritten story of the unnamed common people – the everyday story of how they lived and died.

At the heart of archaeology is the process of reconstructing past events from material remains. It is this focus on material evidence that creates the need for scientific approaches to the past. Since every archaeological excavation might be thought of as an unrepeatable scientific experiment (in the sense of a data-gathering exercise that can only be done once), there is a practical and moral requirement to extract the maximum possible information from the generally mundane collection of bones, stone tools, shards of broken pots, corroded metalwork, and biological assemblages that constitute the vast bulk of archaeological finds. Trade routes are inferred from fragments of broken glass or pottery manufactured in one place but found in another. The economies of ancient cities are reconstructed from a study of the animal bones found on midden tips. In this respect, archaeology has much in common with modern forensic science – events, chronologies, relationships, and motives are reconstructed from the careful and detailed study of a wide range of material evidence. In order to set the scene, it is instructive to challenge new students in the study of the science of archaeology to name a scientific discipline that has no relevance to modern-day archaeology. One can easily go through the scientific alphabet, from astronomy to zoology, and find many obvious applications. It is possible, of course, to carry out the same exercise in the social sciences, and also in engineering and medical sciences. Since the subject of study in archaeology is the whole of human history, it is not surprising that few (if any) academic disciplines exist that have no relevance or application to archaeology. It is inherently an interdisciplinary subject.

There are a number of more or less comprehensive published histories of scientific analysis applied to the study of past peoples and materials. Caley (1949, 1951, 1967) summarizes the early applications of chemistry to archaeology, and a review paper by Trigger (1988) gives a general overview of the relationship between archaeology and the physical and biological sciences. A collection of recent scientific studies, largely relating to museum objects, including dating, authenticity, and studies of metalwork, ceramics, and glass, can be found in the edited volume of Bowman (1991), and Henderson (2000) provides an overview of the information derived from scientific studies of a similar range of inorganic archaeological materials. Many conference proceedings (especially those entitled *Archaeological Chemistry*, produced by the American Chemical Society [Beck (1974), Carter (1978), Lambert (1984), Allen (1989), Orna (1996), Jakes (2002)], and also the published proceedings of the *International Archaeometry Symposia* [see website]) contain a very wide range of chemical studies in archaeology. Of the several books covering the chemical aspects of archaeological science, Goffer (1980) gives a very broad introduction to archaeological chemistry, covering basic analytical chemistry, the materials used in antiquity, and the decay and restoration of archaeological materials. More recent publications include Pollard and Heron (1996), which gives a basic introduction to instrumental chemical analysis followed by seven chapters of case studies, and Lambert (1997), which has eight chapters, each one based on the study of a particular archaeological material. The "standard works" on science in archaeology include Brothwell and Higgs (1963, 1969), Ciliberto and Spoto (2000), and Brothwell and Pollard (2001), but earlier general works such as the eight volume *A History of Technology* (Singer 1954–84), *Thorpe's Dictionary of Applied Chemistry* in twelve volumes (Thorpe and Whiteley 1937–56), and the monumental *Science and Civilisation in China* (Needham 1954–2004) contain, amongst much else, masses of information derived from chemical studies of archaeological material.

1.1 The history of analytical chemistry in archaeology

For the reasons given above, there is a strong moral and practical requirement to extract the maximum information from the material remains recovered during archaeological investigation. Of prime importance in this endeavor is the application of analytical chemistry, now taken to mean instrumental methods of chemical analysis for the detection and quantification of the inorganic elements, but also including a vast array of methods of organic analysis, and (more recently) techniques for the measurement of isotopic abundances for a range of elements. The long history of the relationship between archaeology and chemistry has been described in detail elsewhere (Caley 1951, 1967; Pollard and Heron 1996). Much of this history has focused around the use of analytical chemistry to identify the constituents of archaeological artifacts. Initially this stemmed out of a curiosity to find out what these objects were made from, but, very quickly, more sophisticated questions were asked – most notably relating to *provenance* (or, in the US, *provenience*, but see below). The term here is used to describe the observation of a systematic relationship between the chemical composition of an artifact (most often using trace elements, present at less than 0.1% by weight) and the chemical characteristics of one or more of the raw materials involved in its manufacture. This contrasts sharply with the use of the same term in art history, where it is taken to mean the find spot of an object, or more generally its whole curatorial history. In fact, a recent North American textbook on geoarchaeology has used the term *provenience* for find spot, and *provenance* for the process of discovering the source of raw materials (Rapp and Hill 1998, 134). Although this is an elegant solution to a terminological inexactitude, it has not yet been universally adopted, at least in Europe. Since provenance has been such a dominant theme in archaeological chemistry, further consideration is given below to the theory of provenance studies.

The history of analytical chemistry itself has relied extensively on the contributions of great scientists such as Martin Heinrich Klaproth (1743–1817), and it is gratifying to see how many of these pioneers considered archaeological material as a suitable subject for study. Following a successful career as a pharmacist, Klaproth devoted himself to the chemical analysis of minerals from all over the world. He is credited with the discovery of three new elements – uranium, zirconium, and cerium – and the naming of the elements titanium, strontium, and tellurium, isolated by others but sent to him for confirmation. His collected works were published in five volumes from 1795 to 1810, under the title *Beiträge zur chemischen Kenntniss der Mineralkörper*, to which a sixth (*Chemische Abhandlungen gemischten Inhalts*) was added in 1815. In addition to these monumental contributions to mineralogical chemistry, Klaproth determined gravimetrically the approximate composition of six Greek and nine Roman copper alloy coins, a number of other metal objects, and a few pieces of Roman glass. Gravimetry is the determination of an element through the measurement of the weight of an insoluble product of a definite chemical reaction involving that element, and was the principal tool of quantitative analytical chemistry until the development of instrumental techniques in the early twentieth century. His paper entitled *Memoire de numismatique docimastique* was presented to the Royal Academy of Sciences and Belles-Lettres of Berlin on July 9, 1795, and published in 1798. He first had to devise workable quantitative schemes for the analysis of copper alloys and glass; the former scheme has been studied in detail by Caley (1949). He was appointed Professor at the Artillery Officer Academy in Berlin, and in 1809 became the first Professor of Chemistry at the newly created University of Berlin.

Humphry Davy (1778–1829), discoverer of nitrous oxide (N_2O, or "laughing gas", subsequently used as a dental anaesthetic and today as a general pain-killer), identifier of the chemical nature of chlorine gas, and inventor of the miner's safety lamp, also played a part in developing archaeological chemistry. In 1815, he read a paper to the Royal Society concerning the chemical analysis of ancient pigments collected by himself in "the ruins of the baths of Livia, and the remains of other palaces and baths of ancient Rome, and in the ruins of Pompeii" (Davy 1815). In a series of letters reported by others in the journal *Archaeologia*, Michael Faraday (1791–1867), the discoverer of electromagnetic induction, showed that he had studied a wide range of archaeological material, including a copper alloy coin, glass, and various fluids (*Archaeologia* XXV 13–17 1835), enameled bronze, glass, fuel residue, food residue, and oil (analyzed by tasting, which is no longer the preferred method!: *Archaeologia* XXVI 306–10 1836), and Roman lead glaze pottery (*Archaeologia* XXXII 452 1847). One of the first wet chemical investigations of ancient ceramics (Athenian pottery from the Boston Museum of Fine Arts) was carried out at Harvard and published in the *American Chemical Journal* by Theodore William Richards (1895). Many other eminent chemists of the nineteenth century (including Kekulé, Berzelius, and Berthelot) all contributed to the growing knowledge of the chemical composition of ancient materials. Undoubtedly, their archaeological interests were minor compared to their overall contribution to chemistry, but it is instructive to see how these great scientists included the analysis of archaeological objects as part of their process of discovery.

The appearance of the first appendices of chemical analyses in a major archaeological report represents the earliest systematic collaboration between archaeology and chemistry. Examples include the analysis of four Assyrian bronzes and a sample of glass in Austen Henry Layard's *Discoveries in the Ruins of Nineveh and Babylon* (1853), and Heinrich Schliemann's *Mycenae* (1878). So distinguished was this latter publication that William Gladstone, the British Prime Minister of the day, wrote the preface. The scientific reports in both of these publications were overseen by John Percy (1817–89), a metallurgist at the Royal School of Mines in London. Percy also wrote four major volumes on metallurgy, which included significant sections on the early production and use of metals (Percy 1861, 1864, 1870, and 1875). Because of his first-hand experience of metallurgical processes now lost, these books remain important sources even today. The analysis of metal objects from Mycenae showed the extensive use of native gold and both copper and bronze, which was used predominantly for weapons. Percy wrote in a letter to Schliemann dated August 10, 1877 that "Some of the results are, I think, both novel and important, in a metallurgical as well as archaeological point of view" (quoted in Pollard and Heron 1996: 6).

Toward the end of the nineteenth century, chemical analyses became more common in excavation reports, and new questions, beyond the simple ones of identification and determination of manufacturing technology, began to be asked. In 1892, Carnot published a series of three papers that suggested that fluorine uptake in buried bone might be used to provide an indication of the age of the bone (Carnot 1892a, 1892b, 1892c), preempting by nearly 100 years the current interest in the chemical interaction between bone and the burial environment. Fluorine uptake was heavily relied upon, together with the determination of increased uranium and decreased nitrogen, during the investigation of the infamous "Piltdown Man" (Weiner *et al.* 1953–6, Oakley 1969). This methodology became known as the "FUN method of dating" (fluorine, uranium, and nitrogen) when applied to fossil bone (Oakley 1963). Subsequently such methods have been shown to be strongly environmentally dependent, and only useful, if at all, for providing relative dating evidence.

The development of instrumental measurement techniques during the 1920s and 1930s such as optical emission spectroscopy (OES; see Section 3.1) gave new analytical methods, which were subsequently applied to archaeological chemistry. The principal research aim at the time was to understand the technology of ancient bronze metalwork, especially in terms of identifying the sequence of alloys used during the European Bronze Age. Huge programs of metal analyses were initiated in Britain and Germany, which led to substantial publications of analytical data (e.g., Otto and Witter 1952, Junghans *et al.* 1960, 1968–74, Caley 1964: see Section 3.5). Unfortunately, there is often an inverse relationship between the size and scope of an analytical project and its archaeological usefulness – perhaps because large size leads to a lack of focus, or simply that size leads inevitably to complexity and, consequently, uncertainty. For whatever reason, these monumental projects (and others like them) have had little lasting influence on modern thinking in archaeometallurgy, and have slipped into semi-obscurity.

As a result of the rapid scientific and technological advances precipitated by the Second World War, the immediate postwar years witnessed a wider range of analytical techniques being deployed in the study of the past, including X-ray analysis and electron microscopy (Chapter 5), neutron activation analysis (Chapter 6), and mass spectrometry (Chapter 8). Materials other than metal, such as faience beads and ceramics, were subjected to large-scale analytical programmes. Faience, an artificial high temperature siliceous material, was first produced in the Near East, and during the second millennium BC it was distributed widely across prehistoric Europe as far as England and Scotland. In 1956, Stone and Thomas used OES to "find some trace element, existent only in minute quantities, which might serve to distinguish between the quartz or sand and the alkalis used in the manufacture of faience and glassy faience in Egypt and in specimens found elsewhere in Europe" (Stone and Thomas 1956: 68). This study represents a clear example of the use of chemical criteria to establish provenance: to determine whether faience beads recovered from sites in Britain were of local manufacture, or imported from Egypt or the eastern Mediterranean. This question was of great archaeological significance, because for many years it had generally been assumed that significant technological innovations originated in the east and had diffused westwards – a theory termed *diffusionism* in archaeological literature, and encapsulated in the phrase *ex Oriente lux* (a term associated with Montelius (1899), but in circulation before then). Although the initial OES results were equivocal, the data were subsequently reevaluated by Newton and Renfrew (1970), who suggested a local origin for the beads on the basis of the levels of tin, aluminium, and magnesium. This conclusion was supported by a subsequent reanalysis of most of the beads using neutron activation analysis (NAA) by Aspinall *et al.* (1972).

During the late 1950s and early 1960s, the diffusionist archaeological philosophies of the 1930s were replaced by radical new theoretical approaches in anthropology and the social sciences. This became known as "New Archaeology", and represented an explicit effort to explain past human action rather than simply to describe it. The philosophy of science played a significant role in providing the terminology for this more statistical and quantitative approach to archaeology (see Trigger 1989). This New Archaeology reinvigorated research into prehistoric trade and exchange. The movement of population, via invasion or diffusion of peoples, was no longer seen as the principal instigator of cultural change. Instead, internal processes within society were emphasized, although evidence for "contact" arising from exchange of artifacts and natural materials (as proxy indicators for the transmission of ideas) was seen as an important factor and one in which chemical analysis of artifacts and raw materials might be useful. This increased interest in the distribution of materials initiated a "golden era" in *archaeometry* (a term coined in the 1950s by Christopher Hawkes in Oxford) as a wide range of scientific techniques were employed in the hope of chemically characterizing certain rock types, such as obsidian and marble, as well as ceramics, metals, glass, and natural materials, such as amber (see Pollard and Heron 1996). These characterization studies were aimed at "the documentation of culture contact on the basis of hard evidence, rather than on supposed similarities of form" (Renfrew 1979). Quantitative chemical data formed part of the basis of this "hard evidence", which made it necessary for archaeologists to become familiar with the tools and practice of analytical chemistry, as well as the quantitative manipulation of large amounts of analytical data.

Until recently, the applications of analytical chemistry to archaeology focused primarily on inorganic artifacts – the most obviously durable objects in the archaeological record – or occasionally on geological organic materials such as amber and jet. Increasing attention has been directed over the past few decades towards biological materials – starting with natural products such as waxes and resins, but extending to accidental survivals such as food residues, and, above all, human remains, including bone, protein, lipids, and, most recently of all, DNA (Jones 2001). Perhaps surprisingly, the preservation of a wide range of biomolecules has now been demonstrated in a number of archaeological contexts. This is probably due to two main factors: the increasing sensitivity of the analytical instrumentation brought to bear on such samples, and the increasing willingness to look for surviving material in the first place.

It has been shown over the years that, to be of lasting interpretative value, chemical analysis in archaeology needs to be more than a descriptive exercise that simply documents the composition of ancient materials. This is often much more difficult than producing the primary analytical data; as DeAtley and Bishop (1991: 371) have pointed out, no analytical technique has "built-in interpretative value for archaeological investigations; the links between physical properties of objects and human behaviour producing the variations in physical states of artefacts must always be evaluated." There has been a constant call from within the parent discipline for meaningful scientific data, which address real current problems in archaeology and articulate with modern archaeological theories. This demand for relevance in the application of scientific analyses in archaeology, although self-evidently reasonable, must be qualified by two caveats – firstly, the concept of what is meaningful in archaeology will change as archaeology itself evolves, and secondly, the fact that analytical data on archaeological artifacts may be of relevance to disciplines other than archaeology. An example of the latter is the use of stable isotope measurements on wood recovered from archaeological sites to reconstruct past climatic conditions. On the former, Trigger (1988: 1) states that "archaeologists have asked different questions at different periods. Some of these questions have encouraged close relations with the biological and physical sciences, while other equally important ones have discouraged them." Only a close relationship between those generating the analytical data and those considering the archaeological problems (ideally, of course, so close that they are encircled by the same cranium) can ensure that costly data does not languish forever in the unopened appendices of archaeological publications.

1.2   Basic archaeological questions

This short introduction has identified the origins of many of the issues addressed by the application of analytical chemistry to archaeology. They can be divided, somewhat arbitrarily, into those projects which use chemical methods to address specific questions of direct interest to archaeology, and those projects which attempt to understand the processes acting upon archaeological material before, during, and after burial. The latter category can and often does address specific issues in archaeology (such as site formation processes), but is perhaps of more general (as opposed to site-specific) interest.

Identification

Perhaps the simplest archaeological question that can be answered by chemical means is "what is this object made from?". The chemical identity of many archaeological artifacts may be uncertain for a number of reasons. Simply, it may be too small, corroded, or dirty to be identified by eye. Alternatively, it may be made of a material that cannot be identified visually, or by the use of simple tests. An example might be a metal object made of a silvery-colored metal, such as a coin. It may be "pure" silver (in practice, a silver alloy containing more than about 95% silver), or it could be a silver-rich alloy that still has a silver appearance (silver coins with up to 30% copper can still look silvery, in which case the precise composition may well carry information about coinage debasement, which in turn relates to economic history). It may also be an alloy designed to look like silver, but contain little or no precious metal, such as "nickel silver" (cupronickel alloys, such as are used in modern "silver" coinage). It could equally be a coin with a silver surface but a base metal core, such as is produced by plating, or chemical methods of surface enrichment (or as a result of electrochemical corrosion in the ground). Conceivably, it could consist of some more exotic silvery metal, such as platinum, but this would excite great interest if identified in a European context prior to the mid eighteenth century AD since this metal was supposedly unknown in Europe before that date.

Thus, even the simple identification of a material may have important ramifications (expanded upon below), but none of these possibilities could be absolutely confirmed by visual examination alone. Chemical analysis (or chemical analysis combined with physical examination, in some cases) is necessary to identify the true nature of the material. In general, to answer this basic question, the required levels of analysis are relatively simple, subject to the usual constraints posed by archaeological materials (primarily the need to be as nearly as possible "non-destructive"). Consequently, one preferred technique for many years has been X-ray fluorescence (XRF), because of its nondestructive nature (providing the sample can fit into a sample chamber), its restricted sample preparation requirements, and its simultaneous multi-element capability (see Chapter 5). During the 1960s an air path machine was developed in Oxford specifically to allow the nondestructive analysis of larger museum objects (Hall 1960), and since then a portable hand-held XRF system has been produced for use on museum displays or at an archaeological excavation, as well as for geological purposes (Williams-Thorpe *et al.* 1999).

Identification of organic materials in archaeological contexts can pose more problems. The identification of amorphous organic residues (either visible or occluded in another matrix) is addressed in Chapter 7. An example of a situation where the identification of the organically-derived raw material used to manufacture artifacts is important is the discrimination between jet, shale, and various forms of coal. Up until 30 years ago, the classification of small pieces of jewellery made from various black materials was carried out by eye using a number of simple criteria, such as color and physical properties (Pollard *et al.* 1981). Although there is little difficulty when applying these simple techniques to geological hand specimens, the small size of most archaeological finds and the nature of the destructive sampling required for thin sectioning or even streak testing often renders such judgments difficult to make, if not impossible. Such identifications are, however, rather important because of the restricted number of geological sources of jet when compared to other related materials. In the British Bronze Age, for example, if a piece of jet is identified in a Wessex burial context in southern England, then it is automatically taken as evidence of trading links with Whitby on the north-eastern coast of England (approximately 400 km distant), since this is the nearest significant source of jet in England. Other similar materials, such as shales and the various workable types of coal, are more widely distributed. Analytical work, initially by neutron activation analysis (NAA) and then using XRF, showed that inorganic composition could be used to partially discriminate between these sources, and showed also that many of the original attributions were likely to be incorrect (Bussell *et al.* 1981). Subsequent work has refined the procedures (Hunter *et al.* 1993), and most recently organic mass spectrometry using pyrolysis–gas chromatography–mass spectrometry (Py–GC–MS) has made further progress in characterizing such material (Watts *et al.* 1999). Hindsight suggests that, given the organic nature of such materials, the use of organic techniques of analysis might have yielded an earlier and more convincing solution to the problem, but the approach taken reflects the trajectory of analytical work in archaeology, starting as it does largely from the study of inorganic materials.

The postulate of provenance

As noted above, many of the early large-scale analytical projects in archaeology examined ancient metal objects, initially with a view to understanding their composition and the technology needed to produce the artifacts. Very quickly, however, other more directly relevant archaeological questions emerged. In the mid 1850s, according to Harbottle (1990), the Austrian scholar Jan Erazim Wocel had suggested that correlations in chemical composition could be used to provenance (i.e., identify the source of) archaeological materials, and even to provide relative dates for their manufacture and use. During the 1840s, C. C. T. C. Göbel, a chemist at the University of Dorpat in Estonia, began a study of large numbers of copper alloy artifacts from the Baltic region, comparing the compositions of those recovered from excavations with known artifacts of prehistoric, Greek and Roman origin. He concluded that the artifacts were probably Roman in origin. The French mineralogist Damour was one of the first to propose explicitly that the geographical source of archaeological artifacts could be determined scientifically: "mineralogy and chemistry must make known the characteristics and composition of the artefacts unearthed" (Damour 1865). He applied this to a study of prehistoric "Celtic" stone axes, particularly of jade, which is not known to occur in Europe. By comparing French jade axes to geological samples from all over the world, he was able to "cast new light on the migratory movements of people of prehistoric times". He was, however, suitably cautious in his interpretation. When he discovered that the closest chemical match for a particular axe was with New Zealand jade, he concluded that it was necessary to analyze many more samples from Asia before concluding that there was indeed no source nearer than New Zealand.

The work of Otto Helm, an apothecary from Gdansk, Poland, to provenance amber towards the end of the nineteenth century constitutes one of the earliest fully systematic applications of the natural sciences in archaeology. He had a specific archaeological problem in mind – that of determining the geographical source of over 2000 amber beads excavated by Schliemann at Mycenae. In the English translation of the excavation monograph, Schliemann (1878) noted that "It will, of course, for ever remain a secret to us whether this amber is derived from the coast of the Baltic or from Italy, where it is found in several places, but particularly on the east coast of Sicily." A full account of the investigations made and the success claimed by Helm, along with the eventual shortcomings, has been compiled by Curt Beck (1986) who in the 1960s published, with his co-workers, the results of some 500 analyses using infrared (IR) spectroscopy that demonstrated for the first time successful discrimination between Baltic and non-Baltic European fossil resins (Beck *et al.* 1964, 1965). As a result of this work (see Section 4.4), it is possible to state that the vast majority of prehistoric European amber does derive from amber originating in the Baltic coastal region.

Interestingly, therefore, the idea that chemical composition might indicate raw material source appears in archaeology to be many years in advance of the same idea in geochemistry. The quantitative study of the partitioning behavior of the elements between iron-rich and silicate-rich phases in the Earth's crust was carried out in the first half of the twentieth century, giving a much better understanding of the chemical behavior of the elements in geological systems, and resulting in the geochemical classification of the elements as *lithophile* and *siderophile*. Much of this early work was summarized by Goldschmidt in his seminal work on geochemistry (1954). It was really not until this theoretical basis had been established that the concept of chemical provenance using trace elements acquired currency in geochemistry, almost 100 years after the idea had emerged in archaeology. A possible explanation for this is the fact that the idea of provenance (based on stylistic or other visual characteristics) has a long history in archaeology, going back to at least the eighteenth century (Trigger 1989). In the absence of any scientific means of dating artifacts in museum and private collections, a great deal of attention was paid to the observation of stylistic development within particular classes of artifacts, and the search for "parallels" in other collections, some of which might, hopefully, be associated with dateable material such as coins or inscriptions. These effectively gave a relative chronology for a particular set of objects, and allowed proposals to be made about where certain objects might have originated, if they were deemed to be "exotic", or "imports". It is not surprising, therefore, that in the early chemical studies, but more particularly with the advent in the 1920s of instrumental methods of analysis, the composition of an object was added to the list of characteristics that might be used to indicate either the "provenance" of the object, or the position of an object in some evolutionary sequence of form or decoration. Thus were born the great ambitious programs of analytical studies of ancient artifacts, perhaps typified by the SAM program (Studien zu den Anfangen der Metallurgie) for the analysis of European Bronze Age metalwork during the 1950s, described above and in Section 3.5. Although lacking the underpinning geochemical theory provided by Goldschmidt and others at about the same time, it appears that (some would say "for once") archaeology can be shown to have developed a methodological framework subsequently used elsewhere, rather than simply borrowing existing techniques from other disciplines.

With all of this work, scientific analysis progressed beyond the generation of analytical data on single specimens to, as stated by Harbottle (1982: 14), "establishing a group chemical property." In this major review of chemical characterization studies in archaeology, Harbottle lists a wide range of materials that have been studied analytically, but reminded practitioners that:

... with a very few exceptions, you cannot unequivocally source anything. What you can do is characterize the object, or better, groups of similar objects found in a site or archaeological zone by mineralogical, thermoluminescent, density, hardness, chemical, and other tests, and also characterize the equivalent source materials, if they are available, and look for similarities to generate attributions. A careful job of chemical characterisation, plus a little numerical taxonomy and some auxiliary archaeological and/or stylistic information, will often do something almost as useful: it will produce groupings of artefacts that make archaeological sense. This, rather than absolute proof of origin, will often necessarily be the goal.

This statement strictly applies only to those materials that are chemically unaltered as a result of extraction and fashioning into objects, or as a result of burial – most obviously, natural stone such as obsidian, jade, and marble. When flakes of obsidian are removed from a core, the bulk composition of the artifact is unaltered from the source material (assuming the material is chemically homogeneous in the first place), although changes may occur over archaeological time periods as a result of groundwater interaction (such as the growth of a *hydration layer*). However, in the case of pyrosynthetic materials such as ceramics, metals, and glass, production may bring about significant changes in the composition of the finished artifact. The whole question of provenance then becomes a much more complex issue, as discussed by Cherry and Knapp (1991), Tite (1991), and Wilson and Pollard (2001), amongst others.

Harbottle (1982) usefully defines several terms in the context of archaeological characterization studies:

- *source* – "the ultimate starting point" – the clay bed, the obsidian flow, mine of flint or copper or marble quarry, which is the natural deposit of a material. It is where one goes to procure and thus initiate the chain of processing and/or distribution.

- *production centre* – the manufacturing workshop, which may bear no geographical relationship to the source, and may be regional rather than locationally specific.
- *provenance* – can mean where something is found, but in characterization studies should be restricted to source, production centre or origin.
- *local and imported* – local is "near or associated with the production centre", although the geographical scale of what is local may vary with the rarity of the material. Imported is that which is not local.

The term *origin* is often used synonymously with both *source* and *production centre*, but is less specific than either.

The assumption that scientific provenancing is possible depends upon a number of prerequisites, which can be stated as follows, using the above definitions:

- *characterizability* – the object contains a characteristic chemical or isotopic signal that is unique to a particular source, or at least unique in the context of the potential sources available at the time in question;
- *uniqueness* – this source is sufficiently geographically unique to be archaeologically meaningful, as opposed to a particular geological sedimentary environment, which may occur widely;
- *predictability* – the signal to be detected should either be accidental and unaffected by human processing, in which case it can be predicted from the variation in the source material, or, if it is affected by anthropogenic processing, then this should be sufficiently predictable to allow its effect to be calculated;
- *measurability* – the analytical procedures employed have sufficient accuracy and precision to distinguish between the different sources, and
- *stability* – any postdepositional alteration to the material should be negligible, or at least predictable.

These are stringent requirements, which are often not fully met in practice. In particular, the requirement of predictability is often not achievable at all in the case of synthetic materials. In the case of ceramics, for example, it is rarely possible to match the finished product with a single clay bed, for many reasons, including:

- clays are often extremely inhomogeneous, and the ingenuity of the potter is in blending clays (and nonplastic inclusions) to give the correct physical properties for the desired vessel;
- clays are almost always processed and refined to remove coarse particles, which will alter the chemical composition in a manner only broadly predictable;
- firing affects the mineralogical and chemical composition of clays, again in a way that is only partially predictable from the thermal properties of clay minerals and the volatility of the constituents.

For these and other reasons, it has become commonplace to compare fired ceramic material with fired ceramic material assumed to be representative of a particular production centre. Material of "assumed provenance" can be used, but, for preference, "kiln wasters" are often used as comparative material. These are vessels that have failed in the firing for some reason, and have been dumped close to the kiln (it is assumed that nobody would transport such useless material over any distance). Although ideal in terms of contextual security, wasters are, by definition, products that have failed in the kiln for some reason, and therefore may be chemically atypical of the kiln's production if failure is related to faulty preparation. This introduces a further complexity into the chain of archaeological inference.

The influence of the high-temperature processing, particularly of reduction processes in metalworking, on trace element composition of the finished product have long been the source of debate and experimentation. It appears obvious to conclude that the trace element composition of a piece of smelted metal depends on a number of factors, only one of which is the trace element composition of the ore(s) used. Other factors will include the reduction technology employed (temperature, redox, heating cycle), and the degree of beneficiation and mineralogical purity of the ore(s) used. Thus changes observed in the composition of finished metal objects may be the result of changes in ore source, as desired in provenance studies, but may also represent changes in processing technology, or at least be influenced by such changes. Further complications arise in the provenance of metals as a result of the possibility of recycling of scrap metal. Many authors concede this as a theoretical complication, and then proceed to ignore it in their subsequent inferences. Arguments have been made that if a particular group of objects shows tight clustering in some chemical or isotopic measurements, then this must indicate that they are made from "primary" metal, since the composition must reflect that of a single ore source, which is assumed (probably erroneously) to have a coherent composition. This need not be so. Indeed, it is possible that it reflects exactly the opposite – extensive mixing and recycling.

Given all of these potential complications in the inference of source from analytical data derived from manufactured materials, a fruitful line of thinking has developed, based not on the desire to produce some *absolute* statement about the source of some particular manufactured product, but on the observation that in the archaeological context it is *change* that is important. After all, in the Early Bronze Age, for example, where chronological uncertainty might amount to a few tens or even hundreds of years, do we have enough understanding of the social organization of extractive and subsequent exchange processes to actually use the information that a piece of metal was made from ore deriving from this particular mine, rather than one of similar mineralogy 5 km away? The analytical data can unequivocally indicate when a particular characteristic in a product (e.g., a trace element concentration, or an isotopic ratio) changes relative to the precision of the measurement, since this is what is directly measured. Rather than simply infer that this is due to a change in the exploitation of the source material, it may be more realistic in complex societies to infer that there has been some change in the pattern of production and/or circulation – perhaps a change in raw material source, but also equally possibly a change in the pattern of mixing or smelting of raw materials from different sources, or a change in the recycling strategy. Such an observation is no less archaeologically valuable than that which is attempted if a simple geographical conclusion is reached – indeed, given that it probably reflects the reality of the complexity of the ancient trading patterns, it may actually be a more valid and important conclusion.

It is undoubtedly overstating the case to say that all traditional forms of scientific provenance studies have been addressing the wrong question. A knowledge of the exploitation of particular raw material sources is certainly of great interest, but perhaps reflects an overly simplistic model of trade and exchange in complex society. With some notable exceptions, the attempts to pin down raw material sources to explicit geographical locations, especially in the case of lead and silver in the prehistoric Mediterranean, have led to endless controversy (Pollard in press a: see Section 8.5). One of the more distressing aspects of this Utopian approach to sourcing has been the accompanying demand for constantly improving analytical sensitivity. It is implicitly assumed that increasing analytical sensitivity will automatically lead to improved archaeological interpretability. Self-evidently, this is not necessarily so.

Scientific characterization studies remain an important research area in archaeology, utilizing a range of trace element compositions as determined by increasingly sensitive analytical instrumentation, but now also including biomarker compositions and isotopic measurements on an increasing range of materials. Perhaps most successful over the years has been the chemical characterization of ceramics, the majority of which have been carried out by neutron activation analysis (NAA) (Neff 1992: see Section 6.3). Despite the sophistication of the analytical techniques, the fundamental limitations of the process must, however, be remembered. In order to be successful, the project requires carefully chosen samples to answer a well-constructed archaeological question, which in turn must be securely based on an appropriate archaeological model of the situation. Even if the archaeological side of the problem is well defined, there remain limitations as to what can be achieved. It has to be assumed that the range of possible sources tested for a particular material represent all of the potential sources, and conversely ones that were not available in antiquity have been omitted, since these will distort any numerical analysis. Since the method is essentially one of elimination ("X could not have come from Y, but is similar to Z"), there is always the possibility that similarity does not equate with congruity.

Manufacturing technology, date, and authenticity
Another subset of questions that can be meaningfully addressed via chemical analysis relates to the determination of the technology used to

produce an object, as outlined above. Often manufacturing technology can be adequately determined by careful visual and microscopic examination of the object, although experience has shown that laboratory or field simulations of ancient technologies are essential in order to fully understand ancient technologies, and can reveal some unexpected results (Coles 1979). Occasionally, however, chemical analyses are required, either of the object itself, or sometimes of the waste material from the process, such as the vast quantities of vitreous slag produced during iron manufacture. In this case a knowledge of the purity of the iron produced, the composition of the waste slag, and the composition of any residual slag included in the metal can be combined to give an understanding of the general nature of the technology involved (e.g., bloomery or blast furnace), as well as a more detailed knowledge of the operating conditions of the process (Thomas and Young 1999).

Given the increasing interest in our recent industrial heritage (*industrial archaeology*), and the resulting pressures to extend the legal protection and public explanation of its monuments, it is becoming more important to improve our understanding of the manufacturing processes employed, some of which, even from our very recent past, are now all but forgotten. Experience has shown that even contemporary literary and patent evidence cannot always be taken as reliable, as has been shown by studies of the post-Medieval European brass industry (Pollard and Heron 1996, 205). The traditional method for the manufacture of brass is known the "calamine process", introduced on a large scale into Europe by the Romans. This procedure is carried out in a sealed crucible, in which small lumps of copper metal are mixed with "calamine" (taken to be zinc carbonate or the roasted form, zinc oxide) and heated with charcoal. The zinc vapor is absorbed by the copper before it melts, therefore producing brass by a solid–vapor reaction. The more modern process is called the direct process, and involves mixing metallic zinc with molten copper. Because of thermodynamic restrictions in the calamine process, the maximum uptake of zinc into the brass alloy appears to be limited to around 28–30%, whereas the direct process can be used to give any desired alloy of copper and zinc. Thus the chemical analysis of a brass object can be used to give an indication of the process by which it was made, and also some idea of date – European brass with more than about 30% zinc is taken to be a product of the direct process, and therefore implicitly to date to some time after the introduction of that process into Europe. Extensive analyses of well-dated objects including scientific instruments and coinage has shown, however, that the British patent to manufacture brass by the direct process, taken out in 1738, was done so some time after the actual introduction of the process into western Europe, probably around 1650.

This (admittedly crude) analytical test to distinguish between manufacturing processes for brass is obviously somewhat limited, since it cannot distinguish between calamine brass and brass made by the direct process but containing less than 30% Zn. There has been some interest in recent years over the possibility that certain high temperature anthropogenic metal producing processes might introduce measurable isotopic fractionation into the product (Budd *et al.* 1995a). Early interest concentrated on lead, and more recently on copper (Gale *et al.* 1999), but theoretical studies and experimental observations on zinc have demonstrated for the first time that anthropogenic processes in brass manufacture might introduce sufficient differential isotopic fractionation of the zinc to allow the processing methodology to be distinguished (Budd *et al.* 1999). If verified by higher precision measurements, this observation has not only archaeological significance, but also wider implications for environmental geochemical monitoring.

The example of brass illustrates how the determination of manufacturing technology (by chemical or perhaps isotopic analysis) can also give a rough indication of the date of manufacture. More specifically, it gives an indication of a date before which a particular object could not have been manufactured, providing our understanding of the appropriate ancient technology is accurate and complete. This leads directly into the complex and controversial field of authentication of ancient objects, in which chemical analysis plays a large role. Thus any European brass object shown by analysis to contain more than 30% Zn must be dated to some time after the introduction of the direct process into Europe (remembering the uncertainty in the actual dates involved). This might be an extremely important consideration when judging the authenticity of a potentially valuable brass object. Perhaps the most famous example of brass authentication is that of the "Drake Plate", so called because it was said to have been left by Sir Francis Drake to claim the San Francisco Bay area in the name of Queen Elizabeth I of England, and dated to June 17, 1579. Analysis of the plate (Hedges 1979) by X-ray fluorescence showed it to have a very high zinc content (around 35%), with very few impurities above 0.05%. This was quite unlike any other brass analyzed from the Elizabethan period, which typically had around 20% zinc and between 0.5% and 1% each of tin and lead. It was therefore adjudged unlikely to be of Elizabethan manufacture (a view supported by the fact the it had a thickness consistent with the No. 8 American Wire Gage standard used in the 1930s, when the plate first appeared). In fact, European brass was imported into North America from the first half of the seventeenth century, and there have been a number of very successful analytical studies using the composition of such objects to map relationships between native North Americans and the early European traders (Hancock *et al.* 1999a).

A wide range of archaeological materials have been subjected to scientific authenticity studies (Fleming 1975). Where possible, this takes the form of a direct determination of the date of the object, such as by radiocarbon dating for organic materials (the most famous example of which is undoubtedly the Shroud of Turin – Damon *et al.* 1989) or thermoluminescence analysis for ceramics and the casting cores of cast objects. For metal objects in particular, it has of necessity taken the form of chemical analysis and comparison with reliably dated objects from the same period. Coins have been particularly subjected to such studies, since the variations in fineness for precious metal coinage can give a reasonably reliable calibration curve by which to date or authenticate other coins, but also because the fineness of the precious metals in circulation can give a great deal of information about the economic conditions prevalent at the time (e.g., Metcalf and Schweizer 1971). Authenticity has been a particular concern for all the major museums in the world, and most have facilities for carrying out a number of tests similar to those described here in advance of making any acquisition.

Considerably more questionable, however, is the situation with respect to the commercial trade in antiquities, where access to scientific laboratories willing to carry out authentication on objects of undefined provenance has been partially blamed for encouraging the uncontrolled looting of some of the richest archaeological sites in the world (Chippindale 1991). This view has been contested by some, but it is undoubtedly the case that looting continues unabated, particularly in areas of conflict such as Iraq. The 1970 UNESCO Convention on the Means of Prohibiting and Preventing the Illicit Import, Export and Transfer of Ownership of Cultural Property is an international agreement designed to protect cultural objects by controlling their trade and also to provide a means by which governments can co-operate to recover stolen cultural objects. With the signing of this convention it is now the case that few if any reputable scientific laboratories in universities carry out commercial authenticity testing for the art market. The Illicit Antiquities Research Centre in the McDonald Institute for Archaeological Research, University of Cambridge, UK, provides a comprehensive and up-to-date website relating to the trade in illicit antiquities (http://www.mcdonald.cam. ac.uk/IARC/home.htm).

Chemical analysis of human remains
The voluminous and still growing literature on bone chemical investigations generated during the last three decades represents one of the significant growth areas of archaeological analytical chemistry (e.g., Price 1989a, Lambert and Grupe 1993, Sandford 1993a, Pate 1994, Ambrose and Katzenberg 2000, Cox and Mays 2000). Quantitative analysis of inorganic trace elements (such as strontium, barium, zinc, and lead) incorporated into

bone mineral, and, more recently, in teeth and hair, has been used to address questions of diet, nutrition, status, pathology, and mobility. Similar inferences have been made through measurement of light stable isotope ratios of carbon and nitrogen in bone and dental collagen and other noncollageneous proteins, and the carbon isotope composition of bone and dental carbonate (Section 8.5).

The recognition of the likelihood of significant compositional and mineralogical alteration during long-term burial (termed *diagenesis*) has, however, brought about a reevaluation of inorganic bone chemical investigations. Early on in the study of bone chemistry it became apparent that inorganic trace element studies in bone were potentially bedeviled by postmortem diagenetic effects, the magnitude and significance of which have been extensively debated (Hancock *et al.* 1989, Price 1989b, Radoserich 1993, Sandford 1993b, Burton *et al.* 1999). Isotopic studies have been analytically far less controversial and, for Holocene material at least, appear to avoid most of the diagenetic problems encountered with trace elements (Nelson *et al.* 1986). There are several reviews of dietary reconstruction using isotopic measurements on bone collagen (DeNiro 1987, Schwarcz and Schoeninger 1991, van der Merwe 1992, Ambrose 1993), bone lipid (Stott *et al.* 1999) and bone and dental carbonate (Ambrose and Norr 1993). Most authors have concluded that if some collagen survives in a molecularly recognizable form, then the isotopic signal measured on this collagen is unchanged from that which would have been measured in vivo. The length of *post mortem* time that collagen may be expected to survive is difficult to predict, but is affected by factors such as temperature, extremes of pH, the presence of organic acids, and the presence of any damage to the collagen structure itself. According to Collins *et al.* (2002), however, the thermal history of the sample (the integrated time-temperature history) is the key factor influencing survival. It is to be expected, therefore, that in hotter temperature regimes the likelihood of collagen survival for more than a few tens of thousands of years is low. This is why researchers interested in the evolution of hominid diets have resorted to isotopic measurements on carbon in dental enamel carbonates, which do appear to survive unaltered for longer (Sponheimer *et al.* 2005).

The willingness to interpret trace element data in bone without considering the possibility of post-mortem alteration has been termed a triumph of hope over reality, and makes for an interesting case study in archaeological chemistry. The issue is not the quality of the measurements, but the meaning of the data. It is now widely accepted that trace element concentrations in biological tissue are highly susceptible to a wide range of postdepositional alterations including exchange between ions in the soil solution and the biological mineral (e.g., Lambert *et al.* 1984a, Radosevich 1993, Burton and Price 2000). The onus of proof is on the analyst to demonstrate that the analytical data are not geochemical artifacts that are more likely reflecting the complex interaction between bone and the burial environment than any dietary or other signal which may have accumulated during life. Recently, attempts have been made to model this interaction using commercial geochemical modeling packages, with enough success to suggest that this is a fruitful line for further research into this complex problem (Wilson 2004).

It has been demonstrated conclusively that the chemical study of the protein and mineral fraction of archaeological bone and teeth can reveal information on diet, health, social organization, and human mobility, providing that our knowledge of living bone metabolism is adequate, and that we can account for the changes that may occur during burial. Both of these factors provide significant scientific challenges to archaeological chemists.

Organic analysis in archaeology
It has been shown above that the analysis of organic materials – especially amber – played a significant role in the development of archaeological chemistry in the nineteenth century. During the "golden age", however, archaeological chemists paid more attention to the analysis of inorganic artifacts – both natural stone and synthetic materials (ceramics, metals, glass, and glazes). This is partly because these are the most obviously durable artifacts in the archaeological record, but it also reflects the rapid rate of development of instrumental methods for inorganic analysis. In recent years, however, attention has returned to organic materials, including natural products (such as waxes and resins), accidental survivals (such as food residues), and, above all, human remains, including bone, protein, lipids, and DNA. The methodology for this work has been imported not only from chemistry, biochemistry, and molecular biology, but also from organic geochemistry, which has grown from a discipline interested in the chemical origins of oil and coal into one which studies the short-term alteration and long-term survival of a very wide range of biomolecules (Engel and Macko 1993).

It used to be thought that the survival of organic remains was only to be expected in a limited number of unusual preservational environments, such as extreme aridity, cold, or waterlogging, or as a result of deliberate action such as mummification. With more sensitive analytical techniques, however, the preservation of a wide range of biomolecules has now been demonstrated in a much wider range of far less exceptional archaeological contexts.

Most organic archaeological residues exist as amorphous biological remains in the archaeological record, but since they lack the macroscopic cellular structure present in seeds, wood, leather, or pollen they cannot be recognized by traditional microscopic techniques. Typical residues include food deposits surviving (either visibly on the surface, or invisibly absorbed into the fabric) in pottery containers used for cooking, storing, or serving solids and liquids; gums and resins used for hafting, sealing, or gluing; the balms in the wrappings of mummified bodies; and traces of colouring dyes impregnating ancient textiles. The sorts of questions asked of organic remains are very similar to those asked of inorganic materials – what are they? how were they made? where do they come from? what date are they? They are, however, particularly interesting from the perspective of asking the question, what was it used for? – a question which traditional chemical approaches have rarely been able to address. This is especially relevant in the case of organic residues on ceramics, where it is often the residue that can directly inform on use, more successfully than the traditional indirect approach using form or ethnographic parallel. The suggested survival of recognizable protein residues (including blood, which has allegedly been identified to species) on stone tool surfaces (Loy 1983, Loy and Dixon 1998) offers the tantalizing possibility of directly characterizing artifact use and identifying the utilization of particular animal resources. These results, however, remain deeply contentious and generally poorly replicated (Smith and Wilson 2001).

Early organic analyses in archaeology relied on finding a few compounds in an archaeological residue which were present in modern examples of the likely original material, and making identifications based on these similarities. Thus, a large number of claims have been made for the identification of products that would not now be accepted, because they are insufficiently specific to define the material. The most effective approach is molecular analysis – ideally, the presence of a specific unique compound or known quantitative distribution of compounds in an unknown sample is matched with a contemporary natural substance. This is known as the *molecular marker* approach, but even this is not without problems on ancient samples since many compounds are widely distributed in a range of natural materials, and the composition of an ancient residue may have changed significantly during use and burial. Molecular markers often belong to the compound class known as *lipids*, a heterogeneous group of molecules that includes fats and oils.

The potential for the preservation of lipids is relatively high since by definition they are hydrophobic and not susceptible to hydrolysis by water, unlike most amino acids and DNA. A wide range of fatty acids, sterols, acylglycerols, and wax esters have been identified in visible surface debris on pottery fragments or as residues absorbed into the permeable ceramic matrix. Isolation of lipids from these matrices is achieved by solvent extraction of powdered samples and analysis is often by the powerful and sensitive technique of combined gas chromatography–mass spectrometry (GC–MS: see Section 8.4). This approach has been successfully used for the identification of ancient lipid residues, contributing to the study of artifact use patterns and food consumption (Heron and Evershed 1993). Despite their relative stability, lipids often undergo alteration, and sometimes it is only possible to conclude that an unspecified animal or plant lipid is present. In some circumstances, specific sources can be identified, such as the cooking of leafy vegetables (e.g., cabbage) in ancient pottery indicated by the presence of long-chain waxy compounds from epicuticular waxes of plants (Evershed *et al.* 1991). The relatively recent coupling of gas chromatography with isotope ratio mass spectrometry (GC–C–IRMS) has enabled the measurement of the carbon and nitrogen isotope ratios on single compounds within complex mixtures (termed *compound specific* isotope determinations). This has shown great promise in further differentiating the source of ancient lipid residues, such as discriminating ruminant from nonruminant animal fats in cooking vessels (Evershed *et al.* 1997a). The ability to identify lipids characteristic of dairy products (as opposed to meat) has allowed the history of dairying to be charted from the Neolithic in the British Isles (Copley *et al.* 2005a, 2005b, 2005c), complementing the evidence provided by traditional methods such as the study of animal bones and of pottery shapes.

Lipids can also be used to study the decay processes associated with human and other remains, in order to understand the sequence of events around death, deposition, and preservation. Studies include those of preserved soft tissue from peat-buried bog bodies and soft-tissue remains in permafrost. Even without post-mortem contamination, not all of the lipids extracted from buried bodies are endogenous to living healthy humans. A recent study of lipids in archaeological bone from human remains recovered from the eighteenth to nineteenth century AD burial ground at Newcastle Infirmary (UK) revealed mycolic acid lipid biomarkers resulting from tuberculosis (TB). The authors reported the chemical identification of TB in 5 out of 21 individuals, which agrees well with the documented level of tuberculosis among infirmary patients (27.1%). However, none of the rib samples had the characteristic lesions associated with TB, indicating that TB would not have been diagnosed without the molecular study (Gernaey *et al.* 1999).

Food lipids are not the only source of amorphous organic residues. Higher plant resins and their heated derivatives (wood tar and pitch) served as sealants and adhesives, perfumes, caulking materials, and embalming substances. The use of a tar derived from heating birch bark has been demonstrated in prehistoric Europe from the early Holocene onwards (Aveling and Heron 1998). This tar served as a ubiquitous hafting adhesive for attaching stone tools to handles of wood, bone, or antler. Birch bark tar is also the source of chewing "gums" excavated from bog sites of Mesolithic date in southern Scandinavia. Recent historical evidence suggests that chewing tar may have played a role in dental hygiene and in treating throat disorders. Beeswax has been identified on a pottery vessel dating to the fourth millennium BC in Europe and provides some of the earliest evidence for the collection of wax and, by association, presumably honey (Heron *et al.* 1994). The value of lipid molecules as indicators of specific human activities has been demonstrated by the persistence in soils and sediments of biomarkers of fecal material. Ratios of certain biomarkers (α- and β-stanols) and the relative abundance of others (bile acids) show that it is possible to provide an indication of the animal donor to the archaeological record (Bull *et al.* 1999).

Biomarkers from plant extracts with psychoactive properties have also been reported. For example, lactones from the intoxicating drink kava have been identified in residues adhering to pottery fragments from Fiji (Hocart *et al.* 1993). Traces of another intoxicant, wine, have been discovered by means of chemical "spot tests" for tartaric acid, supported by infrared spectroscopy, ultra violet/visible spectroscopy, and high pressure liquid chromatography (HPLC). Positive results have been reported on a shard from a Neolithic jar (5400–5000 BC) with a thin yellowish deposit from the site of Hajji Firuz Tepe in the Zagros mountains, Iran (McGovern *et al.* 1996). Systematic investigations have also been undertaken on bituminous substances (Connan 1999). Bitumens were widely used in the Near and Middle East in antiquity, serving as glue, waterproofing material, building mortar, medicinal agents, and, in Ancient Egypt, as a mummification ingredient from 1000 BC to 400 AD. It has proved possible to identify molecular and isotopic characteristics of bitumen, which enables archaeological finds to be assigned to a particular source (Connan *et al.* 1992).

1.3 Questions of process

Analytical chemistry has also been used to address questions that do not relate directly to archaeological interpretation, but which nevertheless have importance for understanding the processes that act upon the archaeological record and the materials within it. Of particular interest in this context is the concept of *preservation in situ*. Archaeology is a key component of the tourist industry in many countries. Consequently, there is a growing need to manage the preservation and presentation of the archaeological resource in the face of increasing pressure from development and natural processes such as coastal erosion and climate change. Up until quite recently, most national bodies with responsibility for protecting archaeological heritage have operated a policy of *preservation by record* when archaeological remains were threatened by development. In effect this meant that the archaeological site was completely excavated and recorded before destruction, resulting in many very large-scale excavations during the 1970s and 1980s such as Coppergate in York. As well as resulting in the destruction of the physical remains, it is an expensive and slow process to fully excavate a large site, and produces several tons of material requiring study and storage. Consequently, a new policy has been adopted in many countries, focusing on the concept of *preservation in situ*. This requires that any development on archaeologically sensitive sites must ensure that damage to the known archaeology is minimized by designing the whole development to be as nonintrusive as possible. This includes taking steps such as locating piles and other load-bearing structures away from features, and designing subsurface structures around existing archaeology. The basic assumption is that by minimizing the direct damage the majority of the archaeology is preserved for future generations to study. A related concept is preservation by reburial, in which previously excavated archaeological structures are reburied rather than preserved above ground by constant maintenance interventions. This strategy is being used to protect some of the more vulnerable buildings of the Puebloan culture between AD 850 and 1250 in Chaco Canyon, New Mexico. Here the assumption is that reburial will recreate the original burial environment, and therefore continue the preservation conditions that prevailed before excavation.

The problem with both of these approaches is that the fundamental science that is necessary to understand the interaction between archaeological deposits and the burial environment is currently poorly understood, and is certainly insufficient to predict how these deposits might change in response to external forcing. A wealth of relevant practical experience has been built up, but, at best, the scientific underpinning for the policy is empirical. Quantitative prediction is necessary to aid risk assessment, and in particular to evaluate the damaging effects of changes in soil/groundwater conditions and soil chemistry following a disturbance (such as excavation, reburial, or major construction). Conservation strategies for artifacts and heritage management plans for subsurface and standing monuments therefore need explicit knowledge of degradative processes.

Degradative processes (diagenesis)
Most material that enters the archaeological record degrades until it ceases to be a macroscopically recognizable entity. If this were not so, then the world would be littered with the bones and other physical remains of our ancestors, and all the creatures that have ever lived! Molecular evidence may remain, but for all intents and purposes the objects have disappeared. Exceptions to this general rule constitute the material evidence upon which archaeological inference is based – the exception, then, rather than the norm. Some materials, such as stone, almost always survive degradative processes (although they may succumb to other physical processes such as translocation or frost shatter). Others, such as skin, hair, and organic fabrics, only survive in exceptional circumstances such as extremes of cold or dryness. Many materials, such as metals, glass, and some of the more resistant organic materials such as amber, will undergo some degradation, but are likely to

survive for a considerable time in a recognizable and recoverable form. Biological hard tissue (e.g., bone, teeth, horn, shell) undergoes particularly complex patterns of degradation because of its composite nature, but in general (apart from particularly resistant tissue such as enamel) should not be expected to survive for more than a few thousand or tens of thousands of years (Collins *et al.* 2002).

Chemical and biological degradation processes are part of a wider phenomenon, which is termed *taphonomy*, originally defined as the process of transition of a biological organism from the biosphere to the lithosphere (Efremov 1940). It includes all natural and anthropogenic processes that create death assemblages before deposition, as well as those chemical, physical, and biological processes that act on the assemblage after deposition (these are often termed *diagenetic* processes). It is also possible, archaeologically speaking, to conceive of the postdepositional "taphonomy" of nonbiotic material, e.g., metal and ceramic artifacts, since they too experience change as a result of environmental interaction (Wilson and Pollard 2002), although this goes well beyond the original definition. Analytical chemistry has a fundamental role to play in helping to understand some of the major aspects of taphonomic change. Some processes are likely to be primarily chemical in nature, such as the electrochemical corrosion of a metal object in an aqueous environment (McNeil and Selwyn 2001), although even here microbiological mediation is likely to be important (Little *et al.* 1991). Some processes are structural, such as mineralogical changes taking place in ceramics as a result of interaction with groundwater (Freestone 2001). Others, such as the degradation of organic materials, may be largely biological (Cronyn 2001), although chemical hydrolysis may also have an important role. Whatever the driving force, however, analytical chemistry is essential as a means of measuring, monitoring, modeling, and verifying these processes.

It is useful to think of diagenesis in thermodynamic terms. An object, once it reaches its "final depositional environment", seeks to reach equilibrium with its environmental conditions, with the net rate of change slowing down as equilibrium is approached. This gives rise to the concept of an object being "stable" in its burial environment (providing, of course, the equilibrium position is one of survival rather than complete loss). Strictly speaking, it is only metastable, since any alteration to that environment through natural (e.g., climate change) or anthropogenic (e.g., excavation) agency will cause the object to move towards a new position of equilibrium, resulting in further change. The cautious use of the term "final depositional environment" is deliberate, since although the physical location of a buried object might be fixed over archaeological time, it is unlikely that the local physical, chemical, or biological conditions will be constant over a similar timescale (particularly if this includes major climatic fluctuations). Thus an object might be expected to experience a sequence of metastable conditions throughout its postdepositional and postexcavational existence. We can visualize this history as a series of *diagenetic trajectories* or *pathways*. In a stable burial environment, the diagenetic pathway is in principle predetermined by the nature of the object and of the burial environment, and the interaction between them. This trajectory might lead to perfect preservation or complete destruction, but more often to some intermediary state. If the burial conditions change, the object will set off on a new trajectory, but always towards a more altered state (in other words, as entropy dictates, it cannot spontaneously recover its original state). Naturally, the complexity of the real burial environment makes these simplistic views rather difficult to interpret in practice. In particular, the concept of noncommutativity is important – the order in which things happen can have an influence on the final outcome (e.g., the sequence of insect or microbial colonization on a carcass can drastically affect the rate of decay). Overall, the situation is similar to the familiar conflict in chemistry between thermodynamics (generally well understood) determining which reactions are possible and kinetics (generally less well understood) determining which of these reactions will actually happen.

Material–environment interactions

The objective of understanding degradative (diagenetic) processes is to improve our knowledge of the factors that control the preservation of archaeological evidence in the burial environment. Once an object is buried, the potential for survival is governed by the interaction (chemical, physical, and biological) of the material with its depositional environment. It is, however, likely that the history of the object before "burial" will also have a significant influence on the trajectory of the postdepositional processes. In the case of biological material, this predepositional history might be the dominant factor in dictating the long-term fate of the object. For example, the survival of animal bone might well be dictated largely by the length of surface exposure of the carcass before burial. It is felt by many that the long-term fate of biological material is in fact determined by what happens in the first few days and weeks after death. This results in a temporal continuum between what happens in the short term (perhaps over a few months to years), a knowledge of which may have forensic interest, the behavior of archaeological deposits (a few tens of years up to tens of thousand), and ultimately to material of geological and paleobiological interest (hundreds of thousands to millions of years).

There is, however, little systematic understanding of the factors that control preservation for the wide range of materials encountered archaeologically, and virtually nothing in the way of predictive models. Soil pH (crudely speaking, acidity: see Section 13.1) and Eh (redox potential, or oxidation state, or, equally crudely, oxygen availability) are often referred to as the "master variables" in the consideration of soil chemistry (Pollard 1998a) and are thought to be the main controlling parameters. However, their measurement in the field is not always easy or even possible because of fluctuating conditions, particularly when above the water table. Moreover, the chemical composition of the soil water is a complex interaction of the mineralogical, organic, and atmospheric composition of the soil, further complicated by speciation, redox, and solubility factors within the soil solution (Lindsay 1979). Again, direct measurement in the field is often difficult, since the very act of collecting and measuring the water might alter the complex equilibria within it. Nevertheless, knowledge of such factors is vital for understanding the chemical environment of buried archaeological objects. In response to these practical difficulties, a whole family of groundwater geochemical modeling programs has been developed over the last 30 years (Jenne 1979). These allow speciation to be calculated for given total ion concentrations under specified conditions and the modeling of the behavior of particular mineral species in contact with waters of specified chemistry, enabling the stabilities of such systems and their responses to environmental change to be predicted.

Although it seems clear that this approach has a great deal to offer, geochemical modeling has, to date, rarely been used in archaeological research. There are probably several reasons for this, but an obvious one is the difficulty in setting up the conceptual models appropriate for studying archaeological processes, since this is not the purpose for which the programs were developed. A related problem is the lack of published thermodynamic data for some of the reactions needed. The potential use of geochemical models in the study of bone diagenesis has been actively promoted (Pollard 1995) for some time but only preliminary studies of the inorganic phase have yet been carried out (Wilson 2004). Hydrological modeling of the bone–water system has received more attention (Hedges and Millard 1995) and preliminary applications of these models to the uptake of uranium into bone from groundwater have met with some success (Millard and Hedges 1996), enabling more precise dates to be produced by uranium-series dating of bone (Pike *et al.* 2002).

The investigation of archaeological copper (Thomas 1990) and lead (Edwards 1996) corrosion has been carried out using very simple thermo-dynamic modeling packages. Modeling packages have advanced significantly since these early applications, with current models capable of handling many geochemical processes simultaneously, and microbially mediated processes can now also be tentatively investigated (e.g., Bethke 2003). This software has been used to correctly simulate dynamic laboratory experiments and field observations relating to the influence of agrochemicals on the rate of corrosion of buried metal (Wilson *et al.* in press). Practical experience now suggests that a fruitful way of studying complex material–environment interaction systems (such as those encountered in archaeology) is to combine long-term field experiments with laboratory microcosm studies (which can be better controlled than field studies), and then using geochemical modeling to interpret the resulting data. It would appear that a more holistic understanding of the geochemical aspects of diagenesis is achievable using such an approach.

Conservation science

Conservation in an archaeological context means the investigation, stabilization, and, in some cases, reconstruction of the entire spectrum of archaeological materials. As a profession, however, conservation is taken to include all materials that might be put into a museum, such as ethnographic material and objects of industrial and military interest, as well as more conventional museum exhibits. The term "conservation science" has emerged in recent years to denote a subdiscipline of conservation, which includes the characterization of the constituent materials and production techniques of archaeological objects, the study and understanding of decay processes, and the study and evaluation of conservation products and techniques (Tennant 1993). It also includes issues surrounding the environmental monitoring of display conditions, impact of visitor numbers, and the like (Cronyn 1990). Chemistry is generally at the heart of the conservation process, since the first step in conservation is to stabilize the object by preventing any further degradation. This requires an understanding of the composition of the object itself, and also the mechanisms by which such objects degrade, which usually requires chemical and microstructural analysis, and the identification of corrosion products.

In the museum context, nondestructive (or quasi-nondestructive) techniques such as X-ray fluorescence (XRF) (Chapter 5) are often preferred for the analysis of inorganic objects, although microanalysis by laser ablation–inductively coupled plasma–mass spectrometry (LA–ICP–MS) (Chapter 9) is growing in importance, since the ablation craters are virtually invisible to the naked eye. Raman and infrared spectroscopy (Chapter 4) are now being used for structural information and the identification of corrosion products to complement X-ray diffraction (Section 5.4).

2

AN INTRODUCTION TO ANALYTICAL CHEMISTRY

This chapter gives a short introduction for aspiring archaeological chemists to the science of chemistry – its principal divisions, some basic definitions of atoms, molecules and mixtures, and the use of symbols for chemical compounds and reactions. This chapter is intended to provide enough information to allow the reader to understand the background of the material presented in Chapters 3 to 9, with more detail being reserved for Chapters 10 to 13. This material is covered more fully in any of the multitude of introductory general chemistry texts, such as Atkins and Beren (1992), or Cotton *et al.* (1995) for inorganic chemistry, Atkins (2001) for physical chemistry, and Brown (2000) for organic chemistry. The subfield of analytical chemistry is then described in more detail, including a brief history of its development. Again, there are several introductory texts to modern instrumental methods of chemical analysis, including Ewing (1985, 1997), Christian (1994), and Skoog *et al.* (1998).

2.1 What is chemistry?

Organic, inorganic, and physical chemistry

The simple dictionary definition of chemistry is the "science of elements and their laws of combination and behaviour" (Little Oxford Dictionary), or "1. Branch of science dealing with the elements and compounds they form and the reactions they undergo. 2. Chemical composition and properties of a substance" (Pocket Oxford Dictionary). More elaborately, it is given in the Oxford English Dictionary (1989) as "the branch of physical science and research, which deals with the several elementary substances, or forms of matter, of which all bodies are composed, the laws that regulate the combination of these elements in the formation of compound bodies, and the various phenomena that accompany their exposure to diverse physical conditions." Interestingly, the following gloss is added: "Chemistry is thus at once a science and an art; the latter, called *applied* or *practical chemistry*, is that referred to by earlier authors and explained in early dictionaries."

The "science of the elements and compounds" can be construed as the branch of chemistry that describes the composition and properties (both chemical and physical, e.g., melting points) of all of the known elements and compounds. The "reactions they undergo" describes how elements combine to form compounds, and how different compounds can react together – in other words, it is the study of chemical change, but it also embodies an attempt to explain (which therefore confers the ability to predict) these reactions in terms of why and how they happen. It is therefore much more than an observational subject.

Traditionally, chemistry has been divided into *organic, inorganic,* and *physical* chemistry, although the further subdivision of chemistry continues at an ever-increasing rate. All sorts of other subdivisions (e.g., co-ordination chemistry, which combines organic and inorganic compounds) are possible, as well as the linkage of chemistry with other areas of science, such as pharmaceutical chemistry, forensic chemistry, and, perhaps most recently, archaeological chemistry. It used to be thought that "organic chemistry" comprised the study of animal and plant products, whilst "inorganic chemistry" was the study of those elements and compounds of inorganic origin. From at least the seventeenth century it had been believed that the formation of organic compounds required the influence of nature's "vital force" – the theory of "vitalism". The vitalist theory was epitomized in literature in 1816, when Mary Shelley wrote of Frankenstein's monster, which required "galvanic forces" (i.e., electricity) to bring it to life. Berzelius had shown by 1814 that Dalton's laws of simple combinations also applied to organic compounds, but even Berzelius was reluctant to relinquish the concept of vitality. This simple division of chemistry was finally shown to be inappropriate in 1828 when Wöhler succeeded in producing urea (an organic substance found in urine, formula H_2NCONH_2, modern name carbamide) from the inorganic substance ammonium cyanate (NH_4NCO), thus demonstrating that the "vital force" was not necessary to produce organic compounds. *Organic chemistry* is now more generally defined as the chemistry of compounds that contain carbon. *Inorganic chemistry* is the study of all other elements and compounds (including carbonates – compounds containing the CO_3^{2-} group, but which are considered to be inorganic). *Physical chemistry* includes a study of the structure of atoms, molecules, and compounds, which leads to a knowledge of the energetics of such entities, which in turn forms the basis of an understanding of how and why chemical reactions occur.

Atoms, elements, and molecules
At this stage, it is necessary to introduce some basic definitions. An *atom* is now regarded as the basic building block of matter, at least from a chemical standpoint – physicists insist on finding an apparently endless number of exotic subatomic particles, which have, however, little impact on the practical world. The original concept of the atom is credited to the Greek philosopher Democritus in the fifth century BC, who speculated that all matter is made up of a common ground substance, which is itself made up of small indivisible particles which he called atoms. These differ from one another only in form and size. In this model, chemical change was thought to be the

result of separation and recombination of these atoms – a view not too far removed from the current concept of the atom, apart from its indivisibility. After many centuries, this view was replaced by an alternative model, which saw matter as being composed of the *four elements* – air, earth, fire, and water – which were at the heart of the alchemical view of nature. It was not until 1789 that the French chemist Lavoisier reinstated the atom as the fundamental unit of matter in his book *Elements of Chemistry.*

We now know that the atom is indeed divisible, being composed of more fundamental particles. A simplified, but still useful, model of the atom attributable to the physicist Bohr is given in Section 10.2. This envisages the atom as a miniature "solar system", with the position of the sun at the center being occupied by the *nucleus*, and the orbiting planets being subatomic particles called *electrons*. The nucleus itself is composed of at least two different kinds of subatomic particles. (A full treatment of nuclear structure is beyond the scope of this book.) These are called *protons* and *neutrons*, and the number of positively charged protons governs the chemical identity of the atom, as described in Section 10.5. The number of electrically neutral neutrons in the nucleus defines the particular *isotope*. Atoms of the same element can often have a different number of neutrons in the nucleus, i.e., can exist as a number of different isotopes. An *element* is a pure substance made up only of atoms that are identical in chemical character, and which cannot be decomposed into simpler substances by chemical means. Elements are given chemical symbols, which are unique to each element. Thus the symbol "Na" denotes sodium, which is defined on the atomic scale as being made up of only atoms containing 11 protons in the nucleus. The chemical symbols often derive from the classical name for the element (Ringnes 1989). Some are relatively obvious and familiar, such as "Cu" for the metal copper, from the Latin name *cuprum* for the island of Cyprus, which was an important source of copper. Others are less obvious, but equally familiar, such as "Pb" for lead, which derives from the Latin name *plumbum*. Some, for elements only recently discovered, may be more obscure, such as "Lr" for lawrencium, discovered in 1961 in Berkeley, California, and named after Ernest Lawrence, the inventor of the cyclotron. A complete list of chemical symbols and names of the elements is given in Appendix VI. Almost all introductory chemistry texts give details of the nuclear constitution of the elements. A useful recent addition is the "WebElements" website (http://www.webelements.com), which gives a great deal of valuable and up-to-date information.

Compounds and mixtures

As noted above, an element is a substance that contains only one kind of atom (although it may contain different isotopes of that element). There are 91 elements known to occur in nature, and yet there are many thousands of inorganic compounds, and several millions of organic compounds. Clearly, there is more to chemistry than the elements themselves. Atoms can combine to form *molecules*. Many of the elements, especially those which normally occur as gases, exist not as atoms, but as molecules, where two or more atoms of the same kind have combined to form a stable molecule, such as oxygen, which occurs as the diatomic molecule O_2. This is chemical shorthand to signify that two individual atoms of oxygen (symbol O) have combined to form the molecule O_2, where the subscript after the chemical symbol gives the number of atoms involved. When two atoms of different elements combine to form a stable molecule, then a *compound* is formed, which may have totally different chemical characteristics and physical properties from the parent atoms. Thus, when the highly reactive metal sodium (Na) combines with the green, toxic gas chlorine (symbol Cl), then the result is a white crystalline powder called sodium chloride, and given the formula NaCl, but otherwise known as common or table salt.

There are rules that guide the way in which the various elements can combine, which were most elegantly expressed by John Dalton (1766–1844) in his *New System of Chemical Philosophy*, published in three volumes between 1808 and 1827. Here he explained the theory of the *Law of Multiple Proportions*, which formed the basis of his atomic theory, as follows:

i every element is made up of homogeneous atoms whose weight is constant, and

ii chemical compounds are formed by the union of the atoms of different elements in the simplest numerical proportions.

These simple numerical proportions are now known to be governed by a property of the elements known as *valency*, which in turn is a consequence of the structure of the atom, as discussed Chapter 11.

These atoms, molecules, and compounds manifest themselves to us as *matter*, and it is conventional to consider that there are three *states of matter*, solid, liquid, and gas. (Although this in itself is a simplification: a fourth state, *plasma*, entails the splitting of neutral atoms into highly energetic ionic components, and liquids and gases are often better thought of as a single state termed *fluid*.) These conventional states are sometimes indicated in chemical formulae by the addition of a subscript; solid $_{(s)}$, liquid $_{(l)}$, gas $_{(g)}$, and $_{(aq)}$ for solutions in water. Matter may be composed of pure elements, such as yellow sulfur (symbol S), pure compounds (such as common salt, NaCl), or as *mixtures* of compounds, such as most natural rocks. The difference between a mixture and a compound is an important one. Pure common salt, although it is made up of two elements combined, and although in quantity it is composed of a myriad of tiny particles (*crystals*), is still a compound. It has well-defined physical properties such as melting point, density, etc., and cannot be separated by physical means into anything more fundamental. There is also a fixed relationship between the proportions of the constituent elements in the compound – one atom of sodium is always combined with one atom of chlorine. This fixed relationship between the constituents of a compound is called the *stoichiometry* of the compound. If common salt were mixed with sugar, however, then the result would be a *mixture*. It has no well-defined physical properties, nor is there a fixed relationship between the amounts of sugar and salt present. Furthermore, the two constituents could, in principle, be separated by physical means – perhaps by visual observation of crystal shape (*morphology*) using a microscope, or by selectively dissolving out one component.

The above is an example of a *heterogeneous mixture*, since the composition of the mixture is not uniform throughout. The alternative, a *homogeneous mixture*, is also called a *solution*, but this does not necessarily need to imply that it is in the liquid state. Salt dissolved in water yields a homogeneous liquid which we recognize as a solution. It is a mixture, because the properties of the solution depend on the amount of salt added to the water – they do not have to be in fixed proportions to each other. Many metal alloys, however, are also solutions, but they are *solid solutions*. For example, steel is an alloy of iron (symbol Fe) with small amounts of carbon (C) added. It is a homogeneous mixture rather than a compound because, again, there is no fixed ratio between the Fe and the C added, and the properties of the alloy depend strongly on the amount of C present. It is sometimes difficult, in fact, to distinguish between a pure substance and a mixture. It is not obvious to the eye that steel is a mixture, whereas iron is a pure element. One relatively simple test is to observe the behavior of the material when heated. When a pure substance melts (or, in the case of a liquid, boils) the behavior is characteristic. The temperature of the material stays constant whilst the melting (or boiling) takes place. The material is said to be undergoing a *phase change*, and, for a pure substance, this takes place at a fixed and well-defined temperature (the melting or boiling point), and requires a fixed amount of heat energy to effect the change per unit mass of material (the *latent heat*). Mixtures, however, usually undergo phase transitions over a range of temperatures, and the temperature of the material will change as the solid melts or the liquid boils, and thus, in general, they can be easily distinguished.

Chemical terminology

Understanding chemistry requires above all a knowledge of the language used. The preceding section introduced one of the basic shorthand systems used in chemistry – the use of a symbol, usually one or two letters, to denote the elements. Symbols can be used in text as synonyms for the element, in discussion of nuclear structure as representation of a single atom of the element, or in equations as a fixed measure (such as the *mole* – see Section 2.3

below) of an element. Context dictates the interpretation. When dealing with compounds, a chemical formula composed of atomic symbols (e.g., "NaCl") can refer to a single molecule or to the stoichiometry of the compound. Most often the latter is the case. In this case, the crystal structure is made up of alternating Na and Cl entities in a cubic array (called the *lattice*), in such a way that the average composition over the structure is an equal number of Na and Cl units (see Figure 11.3 in Chapter 11.)

Many chemical compounds were given names (descriptive, contextual, or tributary) before pure substances were known. These are the *common names*. Now, with more than 20 million compounds known, a defined system, referencing exact composition, is used internationally. The arbiter for terminology in chemistry is IUPAC – the International Union for Pure and Applied Chemistry. It is IUPAC who, for example, has defined the term "sulfate" to be the correct designation for compounds containing the SO_4^{2-} group, rather than the more familiar (at least in the UK) "sulphate". In ionic compounds (see Section 11.1), *cations* (positively charged species) are both listed first in the chemical formula and named first. *Anions* (negatively charged species) are listed and named last, using the root of the name (usually) with the suffix "-ide." So, for example, in NaCl, where the positively charged species Na^+ is ionically bound to a negative Cl^-, the correct name is sodium chloride. Common names, such as "table salt" for sodium chloride, still survive, but should not be used in scientific contexts, for the same reasons (i.e., specificity and clarity) that Latin names are used in biology in preference to common names for the description of plants and animals.

In circumstances where an element can form more than one type of cation (*variable valency*), a capital Roman numeral is parenthetically inserted after the name of the cation to indicate its charge (or *oxidation state*). Iron(II) sulfate indicates $FeSO_4$, where the Fe ion has a charge of 2^+, rather than the alternative Fe^{3+}. Previously the suffix "-ic" indicated the higher oxidation state, and "-ous" indicated the lower, e.g., ferric and ferrous, rather than iron(III) and iron(II) respectively. However, some elements with variable valency can have more than two oxidation states, and thus Roman numeral nomenclature is clearest. When a compound, often in the crystalline state, is associated with water (H_2O), the term "hydrate" preceded by a Greek prefix, indicating how many water molecules are present, follows the inorganic name, e.g., $FeSO_4.7H_2O$ is iron(II) sulfate heptahydrate.

Systematic and traditional names exist in abundance in organic chemistry. Many familiar names, such as chloroform (an organic solvent), have been replaced by names that more accurately reflect the structure of the molecule – in this case, trichloromethane ($CHCl_3$). This conveys the fact that the structure of chloroform is the same as that of methane (CH_4 – a tetrahedral arrangement of four hydrogens around a central carbon), but with three of the hydrogens substituted by chlorine. Systematic names are undoubtedly much more useful than the older nomenclature, but can become cumbersome, such as the renaming of citric acid to 2-hydroxy-1,2,3-propanetricarboxylic acid. It is certainly true that the systematic name allows the trained chemist to write down the chemical formula for the molecule (in this case $HOC(COOH)(CH_2COOH)_2$) from the name alone (see Section 11.5), but it is also understandable if some of the common names tend to survive in all but the most rigorous of chemical literature. As well as some recent texts on the subject (e.g., Leigh *et al.* 1998, Thurlow 1998), the Merck Index produced and updated annually (and available electronically: http://library. dialog.com/bluesheets/html/bl0304.html) is a useful source of reference. Another resource for nomenclature, formulas, structure, physical properties, and also valuable safety information are the sales catalogs produced annually (and often distributed for free) by the major chemical companies, e.g., Aldrich and Sigma.

Before leaving the question of terminology, it is worth emphasizing the link between chemical formula and chemical structure, which is implicit in the above. For example, the formula "$CaCO_3$" refers to calcium carbonate, the dominant constituent of limestone rocks. It would be extremely confusing to use the formula "O_3CaC" to represent calcium carbonate, not only because of our familiarity with the conventional notation, but also because the normal notation carries with it structural information that helps emphasize the integrity of the carbonate (CO_3) group, and the fact that the oxygen atoms are linked to the carbon and not directly to the calcium. It also implies that during the bonding process the calcium atom has become the doubly positive charged calcium *ion* Ca^{2+} and that the carbonate group has two negative charges on it (CO_3^{2-}). The situation is even more acute in the field of organic chemistry. We could, for example, have written the formula for citric acid given above as $C_6H_8O_7$. This contains the same number of carbon, hydrogen, and oxygen atoms, but gives no structural information. With a little practice, the structural formula for citric acid can be used to draw the molecule (and vice versa). The structure, nomenclature, and representation of organic compounds are discussed further in Section 11.5.

The most precise use of chemical notation is that involved in the writing of equations to represent chemical reactions. These are often very simple (or at least, can appear so), but contain much additional subliminal information. The ability to write an equation to quantitatively represent a chemical reaction is one of the great beauties of chemistry, and depends on a number of important concepts. One of the earliest is the *Law of Conservation of Mass*, first stated by Antoine-Laurent Lavoisier (1743–94) in his antiphlogistic *Traité élémentaire de chimie, présenté dans un ordre nouveau et d'après les découvertes modernes* in 1789 – "in any chemical reaction the total mass of the products is always equal to the mass of the reactants". Having led Lavoisier to discover oxygen, this law was found to be true providing that all the reactants and products are accounted for, especially in reactions in which gases take part or are evolved. This idea of conservation of mass can be extrapolated to state that *matter can neither be created nor destroyed in a chemical reaction*. This is a fundamental practical guide, but one which, in the light of the relativistic theories developed in the early twentieth century, is misleading at the subatomic particle level. Every chemical reaction is accompanied by the evolution or absorption of energy, and this energy change can affect the mass of the reactants and products, since it has been demonstrated that mass and energy are interchangeable – a relationship encapsulated by Einstein in his famous $E = mc^2$, where E is energy, *m* is mass, and *c* is a constant identified as the velocity of light in a vacuum. Such considerations are, however, practically speaking negligible and well removed from the realm of experience of analytical chemists.

Other important concepts are those of the Law of Constant Composition and the Law of Reciprocal Proportions, unified by Dalton in his Atomic Theory, as noted above. These relate to the ratios by weight in which the elements combine. It was shown, for example, that water (H_2O) is always formed by hydrogen and oxygen combining in the weight ratio of 1:8 – i.e., 1 gram of hydrogen for every 8 grams of oxygen. These observations formed the basis of the concept of *equivalent weights*, which are defined in terms of the masses of individual elements which combine with 8.0000 parts by mass of oxygen. Thus the equivalent weight of hydrogen is 1. The *gram-equivalent* of an element is its equivalent weight expressed in grams, and one liter (cubic decimeter) of solution that contains the gram-equivalent of an element is known as a *normal* solution, signified as 1N. The subject of different systems for recording the strengths of solutions is dealt with below, but the *normality* of a solution, based on the system of equivalent weights, is still important because of the tendency of the American literature to retain the system. In European literature, the concept of equivalency has largely been replaced by that of *molarity*, based on the definition of the *mole*. The mole is defined in terms of the *molecular weight* of a compound, and is also further discussed below.

2.2   Analytical chemistry

Analytical chemistry is that branch of chemistry which deals with the qualitative or quantitative determination of one or more constituents in an unknown material. Ewing (1985: 1) defines it as "the science and art of determining the composition of materials in terms of the elements or compounds contained in them". Many would regard analytical chemistry as the cornerstone of chemistry itself, since the ability to identify and quantify chemical constituents underpins the theoretical and practical advancement of other areas of chemistry. Analytical chemistry can itself be subdivided in many ways. An important one is the difference between *qualitative* and *quantitative* analysis. Qualitative analysis is when a particular element or compound is simply determined to be present or not in a particular sample. Quantitative analysis attempts to attach a number to the level at which something is present. This can be *fully quantitative*, if a more or less precise estimate is made of the concentration of a particular component, or *semiquantitative* if the estimate is categorical, or "ballpark". Different circumstances demand different levels of quantitation, and a great deal of the art of chemical analysis revolves around knowing how precise an analytical estimate needs to be before a particular question can be answered, or, conversely, what are the limitations of inference that can be made from an analytical estimate of stated precision.

Most modern analytical chemistry involves the use of dedicated instrumentation of some sort, justifying the title *instrumental chemical analysis*. This contrasts with older approaches, such as spot tests, gravimetric analysis, volumetric analysis, or colorimetric analysis, in which relatively simple instruments are used (if at all). In *spot tests*, for example, the presence of a particular element or compound is confirmed if a particular reagent is applied and a particular color develops, or an identifiable gas is given off (Feigl 1954). The intensity of the reaction, as gauged by the depth of color developed or the vigor of gaseous evolution, can often be used to partly quantify the concentration of the *analyte* (the element or compound being looked for). In general, such tests are most often used qualitatively. It is, however, a common modern trait to regard such methods as inherently less reliable and less sensitive than those which rely on expensive instrumentation. This is fallacious, and often leads to inappropriate and grossly overexpensive methods being applied to situations in which a few test tubes and a bottle of hydrochloric acid would provide a perfectly adequate answer. That is not to say that modern analytical methods are not far superior in terms of speed of throughput, multielement capability, and analytical sensitivity, but just occasionally (particularly in archaeology) the combination of simple methods, chemical knowledge, and good laboratory skills can still prove worthwhile. Unfortunately, it is becoming a lost art, seldom taught in universities, as it requires a great deal of specialized knowledge (e.g., see Svehla 1996). The majority of chemical analysis now relies upon sophisticated instrumentation and the ubiquitous computer.

A brief history of analytical chemistry
Many chemical processes of undoubted antiquity, such as dyeing, soapmaking, and various metallurgical skills, must have required the ability to identify the correct raw materials or ingredients, and thus represent the application of an early form of analytical chemistry. It is likely, however, that this took the form of experience rather than direct analysis, in much the same way as a skilled mineralogist can identify hundreds of mineral species by eye, using indicators such as color, shape, mode of occurrence, and mineral associations, without resorting directly to chemical or structural analytical procedures. The earliest analytical test that we know of is that used to

measure the purity of gold, which was certainly in use by the third millennium BC in the Near East (Oddy 1983). One method, known as *fire assay* or *cupellation* involves heating an alloy containing gold with lead until the mixture is molten, and then blowing off the oxidizable lead as litharge, which will take with it any baser metals, including silver. The weight of the resulting refined gold, when compared to the original weight of alloy, is a measure of the gold purity of the alloy. This is an early use of the principle of *gravimetric analysis* – determination by weighing. Another technique of great antiquity is the use of the *touchstone*, a slab of black stone, probably slate, upon which the gold alloy is scratched. The purity of the gold is assessed by observing the color of the streak; this process is described by some as the oldest *colorimetric* method of analysis (Oddy 1986).

Several authors (e.g., Szabadváry 1966) have described various analytical procedures that have been deciphered from the writings of the alchemists. This literature is of great value and interest, but presents a contradictory philosophy to the modern mind. The goal of the "great work" of alchemy was to convert base metal into gold by repeated processing, designed to remove the base "sulfurous" element from the metal, which was conceived of as being made up of varying proportions of idealized "mercury" and "sulfur". Many alchemical authors were quite clear that "alchemical gold" was fundamentally different from "true gold". The resemblance was only one of color. Since tests for gold were well established by the early Middle Ages in the Old World, it appears strange to us that such contradictions were tolerated and even encouraged. It is perhaps only a reminder that the modern "scientific" view of the world is relatively recent and is, by no means, a universal philosophy.

Analytical chemistry entered a more recognizable form during the early nineteenth century, by which time the atomistic ideas reintroduced by Lavoisier had begun to have a significant effect on chemistry. A considerable impetus for the development of inorganic analytical chemistry was the desire to identify minerals, e.g., Wilhelm August Lampadius' (1772–1842) *Handbuch zur Chemischen Analyse der Mineralkörper*, published in Freiberg in 1801, which, along with subsequent works concerned with the analysis of minerals by scientists such as Martin Heinrich Klaproth (1743–1817) and Jöns Jakob Berzelius (1779–1848), established classical qualitative inorganic analysis much as it is today. This process culminated in the emergence of what is probably the first "modern" textbook of qualitative inorganic analysis published by Carl Remegius Fresenius (1818–97) in 1841 (*Anleitung zur qualitativen chemischen Analyse)*. A quantitative textbook followed in 1845. There were 17 German editions of the former by the author's death. It was translated shortly after the first edition into English, French, Italian, Dutch, Spanish, Hungarian, Chinese, and Russian. The first English edition (translated by J. Lloyd Bullock) was called *Elementary*

Instruction in Chemical Analysis and was published in 1843. This set the standards for the systematic analysis of all the known metal oxides, using the following recommended equipment (quoted from Szabadváry 1966: 171):

> *A spirit burner ..., blow-pipe, one platinum crucible, one platinum sheet and 3– 4 platinum wires, a test tube stand with 10–12 test tubes, several beakers and flasks, one porcelain dish and a pair of porcelain crucibles, several glass filter funnels in various sizes, a wash-bottle, several rods and watch glasses, one agate mortar, several iron spoons, a pair of steel or brass pincers, a filtration stand made of wood and one iron tripod stand.*

Such a tool kit and the rigorous step-by-step analytical procedure devised to go with it are probably familiar to those who did microchemical analysis as part of their school or university chemistry course up to about 30 or 40 years ago. Since Fresenius went on to found the journal *Zeitschrift für analytische Chemie* in 1862, he can certainly be regarded as the founder of modern analytical chemistry. The twentieth century equivalent of Fresenius' volumes (which were reprinted through to 1921) are still very useful handbooks published by Arthur Israel Vogel (1905–66), starting with *A Textbook of Qualitative Chemical Analysis* (1937), last republished as *Vogel's Textbook of Micro- and Semimicro- Qualitative Inorganic Analysis* by Svehla (1996). This was followed by *A Textbook of Quantitative Inorganic Analysis* (1939), most recently republished as *Vogel's Textbook of Quantitative Chemical Analysis*, edited by Jeffrey (1989).

The routine techniques of "classical" analytical chemistry – weighing, measuring gas and liquid volumes, observing color changes in solution, etc. – gave way at the beginning of the twentieth century to an inexorable increase in the use of instrumental methods. Initially, these were based on the emission and absorption of light by atoms, as described in Chapter 3. Isaac Newton (1642–1727) had shown in 1666 that light can be separated into its component wavelengths using a large prism ("Light it self is a heterogeneous mixture of differently refrangible rays": Newton 1671–2). The use of color to identify compounds of the alkali metals (sodium and potassium) by heating in a flame was, according to Partington (1961–70: Vol. 2:727), first reported by Andreas Sigismund Marggraf (1709–82) in 1758–9 – the origins of flame photometry. Julius Plücker, in 1858, observed the characteristic wavelengths arising from electronic transitions in the orbital structure of atoms, in gaseous hydrogen, using one of the first gas discharge (cathode ray) tubes (see Section 12.3). The first instrument to use these observations was the spectroscope of Kirchoff and Bunsen, which, in 1860, elevated "spectrum analysis" to the level of a branch of analytical chemistry (Chapter 3). Considerable instrumental improvements have been made, but spectroscopy, as such, changed little in principle until the last 30 years. This change followed the work of A. J. Dempster (1918) in the USA and F. W. Aston

(1920) in England, who independently built the first mass spectrographs to measure the isotopic abundances of the elements (Chapter 8). In the late 1970s a number of researchers perfected the instrumentation for using mass spectrometric detectors to enhance the sensitivity and performance of a wide range of analytical instruments, including the various types of optical spectroscopies, which has resulted in the wide range of so-called "hyphenated techniques" we see today, such as ICP–MS, GC–MS, etc., as discussed in Chapters 8 and 9.

There can be no doubt that instrumental methods of analysis have revolutionized analytical chemistry, in terms of increased sensitivity, more rapid throughput, multielement capability, computerized calibration, and data handling, etc. There is a cost, too, of course – increased capital expenditure, increased instrumental complexity, and, above all, the current tendency to believe implicitly the output of a computer. Just because a machine gives an analysis to 12 places of decimals doesn't mean that it is true (see Chapter 13)!

2.3   Special considerations in the analysis of archaeological material

For all investigations by analytical chemistry, the limitations imposed by archaeological samples can be considerable. For the most part, archaeological materials are now analyzed on factory-standard equipment – sometimes on a machine dedicated to archaeological research, but often on a multipurpose instrument. In this sense, archaeological materials are no different from any other environmental or geological samples that require analysis. In other ways, however, archaeological material can pose special problems from the analyst. Restrictions are often placed on sampling, either by physical limitations or by consideration of aesthetic value. Typically the resulting samples can be far from ideal from the analytical point of view – small, fragmentary, and (particularly in the case of biological samples) often considerably degraded. They are likely to be contaminated in some way during burial, and after recovery (postexcavation) may suffer further contamination due to storage media, handling, or airborne particles. Samples taken from museum material, which was collected some time ago, may have been subjected to unknown conservation, restoration, or fumigation procedures. The ubiquitous problem of degradation and contamination, although not insoluble, makes archaeological chemistry a challenging field, and usually not one which can be regarded as just another routine analytical application.

Parallels have been drawn between archaeological and forensic chemistry (Heron 1996), since the forensic chemist often has to deal with similarly small and degraded samples. In many ways, there is a close relationship between the two. Both derive evidence from samples obtained from a controlled recovery situation, and both attempt to reconstruct patterns of human behavior from material evidence. In both cases too, the samples are often unique, and often far from ideal from an analytical point of view. Attempts have been made over the last decade or so to draw together the two disciplines of archaeology and forensic science (Hunter *et al.* 1997) and an examination of the analytical literature on both subjects reveals some evidence of crossfertilization, particularly in the area of forensic anthropology – the physical and biochemical study of human remains. There is less evidence, however, of interaction in the area of inorganic analysis and interpretation, which is unfortunate, since the problems are often similar – e.g., the matching of the glass from a broken car headlight to a database of manufacturers' glass compositions, and the matching of Roman glass to source material in the Levant. It would seem, therefore, that there is room for further co-operation.

PART II

THE APPLICATION OF ANALYTICAL CHEMISTRY TO ARCHAEOLOGY

3

ELEMENTAL ANALYSIS BY ABSORPTION AND EMISSION SPECTROSCOPIES IN THE VISIBLE AND ULTRAVIOLET

This chapter reviews some of the most common techniques used to analyze a wide range of inorganic materials. The techniques are all based on the emission or absorption of radiation in the visible or ultraviolet region of the electromagnetic spectrum. The full background to these techniques is set out in Chapter 12, as are the principles underlying the quantification of the methods (the Beer–Lambert law). The first technique described (OES) is now obsolete, and in archaeology was replaced in the 1980s by atomic absorption. This, in turn, has been largely superseded by another emission technique, but this time using an inductively coupled plasma (ICP) torch to achieve a higher temperature. This chapter explains the use of ICP excitation as a source for emission spectroscopy (ICP–AES, sometimes termed ICP–OES). A discussion of the use of ICP excitation as an ion source for mass spectroscopy (ICP–MS) is deferred to Chapter 9, following a general discussion of mass spectrometry (Chapter 8). Section 3.4 gives an overview of the comparative performance of this family of techniques, in terms of minimum detectable levels (defined in full in Section 13.4) across the periodic table. More detailed information on atomic absorption spectroscopy (AAS) can be found in Price (1972), Varma (1985), Haswell (1991), and on ICP–AES in Golightly and Montaser (1992), Boss and Fredeen (1999), Nölte (2003), and Thompson and Walsh (2003).

3.1 Optical emission spectroscopy (OES)

Optical emission spectroscopy, as originally carried out with a spark source and photographic recording, is now of historical interest only, but is worth including because replacement of the source with an ICP torch and better detection has given a new generation of emission spectrometers, as described below. It was also one of the first instrumental techniques to be widely used to analyze metallurgical, geological, and archaeological samples, and there is, therefore, much OES data still in the archaeological literature. Some of the difficulties of using these "legacy" data are discussed in Section 3.5 below.

The original OES instruments, dating from the 1930s but used consistently from the 1950s, used a spark source to excite the emission spectrum, which usually consisted of a graphite cup as one electrode, and a graphite rod as the other. The sample (solid or liquid) was placed inside the cup and the graphite rod lowered until it was close to the cup. The sample was then vaporized by applying a high voltage across the two electrodes, which caused a spark to "jump" across the gap. The energy of the spark was sufficient to promote some outer electrons in the sample atoms to excited states, which then relaxed (virtually instantaneously) back to the ground state and emitted light of a wavelength characteristic of that particular atom (explained in more detail in Section 10.4). The resultant emitted light was resolved into its different wavelength components using a large quartz prism or, in later models, a diffraction grating, and recorded on a single photographic plate. Although this introduces serious reproducibility issues (from differences in the development process of the plate), it does have the advantage of recording all emission lines simultaneously, which could lead to the identification of unexpected elements in the sample. Later instruments used a number of fixed photomultiplier tubes sited at the correct angle from the diffraction grating for a particular emission line of one element, thus giving simultaneous information about a fixed (but limited) number of elements (in the same way as modern ICP–AES: see below). Quantitative information was obtained from the photographic plate using a scanning densitometer, which measured the intensity (darkening) of each emission line. The instrument was calibrated by measuring known standards as the sample, and constructing a calibration curve of emission intensity against concentration for each element to be measured.

One advantage of the OES system using a photographic plate was that all elements present in the sample could be detected, even if they were not known to be present, since the plate simultaneously records the emission spectrum of all elements in the sample. Given the complexity of elemental emission spectra, however, in practice the number of elements that could be determined from a single plate was usually no more than 20. The principal disadvantage of the OES system was the poor reproducibility of the excitation conditions and the development conditions of the photographic plate, both leading to poor precision and accuracy and a relatively poor minimum detectable level. The use of an "internal spike" (a known quantity of an element otherwise not present in the sample – often lithium: see Section 13.3) could be used to reduce these problems, resulting in minimum detectable levels (MDLs) as low as 0.001% (10 ppm) in a solid sample of 10 mg in the best cases. Precisions, however, were usually quoted as being between 5% and 25% for major and minor elements.

3.2   Atomic absorption spectroscopy (AAS)

Atomic absorption completely replaced OES in archaeological chemistry during the 1980s, and differs from it in a number of ways. Firstly, it is primarily a solution-based technique, therefore requiring solid samples to be dissolved prior to analysis. Secondly, it is based on the absorption of light by atomized samples in a flame, in contrast to OES which is based on emission. Because of this, AAS requires a source of light that has a wavelength characteristic of the element which is being analyzed – consequently, it can usually only determine one element at a time. It is, therefore, a sequential analytical technique, in that all standards and samples to be measured are analyzed for one element, then the light source is changed, and the standards and samples are reanalyzed for the second element, and so on. It has now largely been superseded in most applications by inductively coupled plasma techniques, although it still has some advantages over these for specific elements in particular circumstances. More recent developments in AAS (described below) can give sensitivity comparable to or better than ICP techniques for some elements, and it is still the method of choice for the analysis of some elements in particular matrices (often biomedical applications).

The liquid sample is drawn up by capillary action into the instrument, and aspirated into the flame where it is decomposed from a molecular to an elemental form. Light of a wavelength characteristic of the element to be measured is passed through the flame, and the atoms in the flame quantitatively absorb some of the light, becoming excited in the process. By comparing the intensity of the light before and after passage through the flame, and applying the Beer–Lambert law (Section 12.4), it is possible to calculate the concentration of analyte atoms in the flame, and hence in the solution. This is then converted into an estimate of the concentration of that element in the original solid sample, using the known weight of the sample in the solution.

For light elements, the absorption/emission behavior in the flame can easily be understood in terms of the energy level diagrams (explained in Section 10.4). For Na, for example, the most intense lines are the doublet at 589.0 and 589.6 nm (see Section 12.3), arising from $3p_{3/2} \rightarrow 3s$ and $3p_{1/2} \rightarrow 3s$ transitions respectively (remembering that p orbitals are split due to spin–orbit coupling). This wavelength is in the yellow-orange region of the spectrum, and gives rise to the characteristic orange glow of sodium vapor street lights. Because it has the same electronic orbital configuration as Na, the energy level diagram for the singly charged Mg^+ ion is similar (although the energies are different), but as the number of electrons outside the closed shells increase, the energy level diagrams (and hence the emission/absorption spectra) become more complex. For two outer electrons (e.g., atomic Mg, which has two $3s$ electrons), singlet and triplet states exist, corresponding to paired outer electrons (antiparallel) or unpaired (parallel) spins. As the number of outer electrons increases, the splitting increases. In general, the complexity of the absorption/emission spectrum increases with increasing valency and increasing atomic number (e.g., Li has 30 absorption/emission lines in the ultraviolet and visible region of the spectrum; Cs has 645, and Fe has 4757). However, not all lines are excited during the analysis, because of the relatively low temperature of the flame. Atomic emission/absorption lines have a natural line width of $\sim 10^{-5}$ nm, but this is normally broadened to 0.002–0.005 nm by two effects: *Doppler broadening* (movement of atoms in the flame) and *pressure broadening* (due to atomic collisions). If thermally stable molecular species are formed in the flame (e.g., CaOH), these can give rise to wider absorption bands (width at half height ~6 nm), reducing the effectiveness of the analysis, and interfering or masking the emission lines of other elements. This can sometimes be prevented by the use of a hotter flame to dissociate these species (see below).

The heart of a traditional atomic absorption spectrometer is the burner, of which the most usual type is called a laminar flow burner. The stability of the flame is the most important factor in AAS. Typical working temperatures are 2200–2400°C for an air-acetylene flame, up to 2600–2800°C for acetylene-nitrous oxide. The fraction of species of a particular element that exist in the excited state can be calculated at these temperatures using the Boltzmann equation:

$$\frac{N_j}{N_o} = \frac{P_j}{P_o} \exp\left(-\frac{(E_j - E_o)}{kT}\right)$$

where N_j is the number of atoms in energy level E of degeneracy P_j, and N_o the number in ground state E_o of degeneracy P_o (k is the Boltzmann constant, and T is the absolute temperature in Kelvin). Degeneracy is the number of electrons which can occupy that particular energy level, and is two for s orbitals and six for p orbitals. Thus, for the $3p$–$3s$ transition in Na, $P_j = 6$ and $P_o = 2$, and taking the ground state energy E_o to be 0, we obtain $N_j/N_o = 1.67 \times 10^{-4}$ at 2500°C. This means that, at the typical temperature of an AAS flame, only roughly 0.01% of Na atoms are in the excited $3p$ state. Conversely, at these temperatures, 99.99% of sodium atoms are in the $3s$ ground state, and are, therefore, capable of absorbing light from a sodium lamp, making absorption measurements extremely efficient for determining sodium in the flame. Calculation of the temperature dependence of this ratio also shows that a 10°C rise in temperature causes a 4% variation in the population, which is considerably more significant for the minority of atoms in the excited state. This makes atomic emission, which relies on the spontaneous decay of excited atoms, much more susceptible to variations in flame temperature than is absorption.

Instrumentation
The design of a conventional atomic absorption spectrometer is relatively simple (Fig. 3.1), consisting of a lamp, a beam chopper, a burner, a grating monochromator, and a photomultiplier detector. The design of each of these is briefly considered. The figure shows both single and double beam operation, as explained below.

Hollow cathode lamp
The light passing through the flame must be of exactly the same frequency as the absorption line, in order to stimulate the analyte atoms in the flame to absorb. Because of the narrow absorption lines of the atomic plasma in the

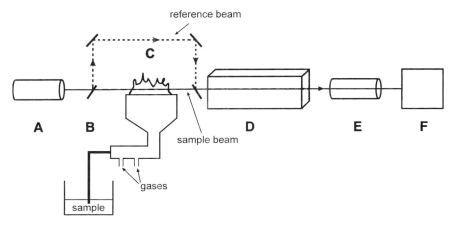

Figure 3.1 Schematic diagram of an AAS spectrometer. A is the light source (hollow cathode lamp), B is the beam chopper (see Fig. 3.2), C is the burner, D the monochromator, E the photomultiplier detector, and F the computer for data analysis. In the single beam instrument, the beam from the lamp is modulated by the beam chopper (to reduce noise) and passes directly through the flame (solid light path). In a double beam instrument the beam chopper is angled and the rear surface reflective, so that part of the beam is passed along the reference beam path (dashed line), and is then recombined with the sample beam by a half-silvered mirror.

flame, it is best to use the emission line of the same element. The most common lamp is a hollow cathode lamp, which has a tungsten anode and a cylindrical cup-shaped cathode, made of (or coated with) the element of interest. The lamp is sealed and filled with low-pressure neon or argon gas. A potential across the electrodes ionizes some of the filler gas, causing a current of 5–10 mA to flow between the electrodes. The impact at the cathode of the charged gas particles sputters off some of the cathode material, which forms an atomic cloud within the cup. Since some of these atoms will be in excited states, they will emit radiation of wavelength characteristic of the cathodic material. This passes out of the lamp and is focused and reflected towards the flame. When the lamp is switched off, the design of the cup-shaped cathode is such that the material redeposits on the cathode, lengthening the life of the lamp as much as possible. In principle, a different lamp is needed for each element, although multielement lamps are available for similar elements such as Ca/Mg, but these have poorer spectral purity and a shorter operational life.

Chopper and beam splitter
As with all other types of spectrometers operating in the UV/visible region of the spectrum, it is advantageous to modulate the primary beam using a mechanical beam chopper, and detect it at the same frequency, to reduce background noise. This is usually done with a rotating beam chopper, shaped

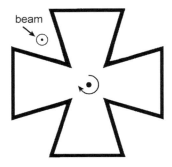

Figure 3.2 Beam chopper in AAS. In a single beam instrument it is mounted vertically off-centre, so that it "chops" the beam. In a dual-beam instrument it is angled and mirrored so that it alternately allows the sample beam through and reflects the reference beam along the secondary path.

like a Maltese cross, which interrupts the beam as the blades pass across the light path (Fig. 3.2). This modulation is primarily to eliminate emission of radiation by the flame at the frequencies being measured, since emission from the flame is continuous, but the detector can be tuned to receive only in synchronization with the rotation of the beam chopper.

As with other types of spectrometer operating in the UV/visible, instruments of the double and single beam type are available. Single beam instruments, as might be expected, operate with a single beam passing through the flame. Measurement of the reference (unabsorbed) beam intensity has to be made with a blank solution aspirated into the flame, followed by measurements on the samples, making it a relatively slow and cumbersome process. In the double beam variety, the chopper described above is positioned at an angle to the beam and is mirrored on the back, so it directs radiation alternately through the sample and around the reference beam path (Fig. 3.1). The reference beam, therefore, gives a direct measure of the intensity of the radiation emitted by the lamp at the absorption frequency, and the radiation which passes through the flame measures the absorption by the sample. The reference beam is, therefore, measured at the same time as the sample beam, thus eliminating errors that might arise from short-term power fluctuations in the lamp. The reference beam, however, does not pass through the flame and cannot, therefore, compensate for absorption or scattering in the flame.

Considering radiation from the light source being split into two by a beam splitter, we can modify Beer's law (derived in Section 12.4) in the following way. If A_S and A_R are the absorbances of the light as it passes through the sample and the reference paths respectively, then:

$$A_S = \log\frac{P'_0}{P_S} \quad \text{and} \quad A_R = \log\frac{P'_0}{P_R}$$

where P_0' is the power of the beam from the light source, and P_S and P_R are the power transmitted through the sample and via the reference beam, respectively. Subtracting:

$$A_S - A_R = \log \frac{P_0'}{P_S} - \log \frac{P_0'}{P_R}$$

$$= \log \frac{P_R}{P_S}.$$

If the only difference between the two beam paths is the absorbance in the flame, then this can be rewritten as:

$$A' = \log \frac{P_0}{P}$$

where A' is *corrected absorbance*, P_0 is power transmitted via the reference beam, and P is the power transmitted through the sample. Since P_0' does not occur in the equation, it can be seen that the effect of the reference path is to reduce the influence of any variation in the output of the lamp.

Burner

The single most important component of an AA spectrometer is the burner. Here, the fuel and oxidant gases are mixed and burned in a controlled way, to give a reproducible flame. In addition, the sample liquid is aspirated (sucked) up a capillary tube, vaporized by the flow of gases around a tip (the nebulizer) and, thus, injected into the gas stream just before combustion. The most common type is a laminar flow burner. The oxidant gas flows over the nebulizer and converts the sample solution into an aerosol, which is then mixed with fuel and passed through a series of baffles to filter out the largest droplets. Thus, most of the liquid sample drains away. The burner head is made of a heavy metal to give physical stability, and consists of a slot around 5–10 cm long, but only a few millimeters wide. The large mass of metal keeps the burner relatively cool, and because the burner is lengthways to the incoming beam, the long narrow flame creates a long path length for the beam to traverse.

The most significant advance in AAS over recent years has been the introduction of nonflame burners, since the reproducibility of flame conditions from day to day is a persistent problem (Butcher and Sneddon 1998, Jackson 1999). Nonflame (*electrothermal* or *graphite furnace* – ETAAS or GFAAS) burners consist of an electrically heated graphite or tantalum sample container (a cup or boat), in which a few microliters of liquid sample are first evaporated and then ashed at a low temperature. Then a much higher current through the heating system rapidly vaporizes the sample at high temperature (2000–3000°C), and the beam from the lamp passes through this vapor just above the sample container. This provides much greater analytical sensitivity, because all the sample is used (unlike in flame AA, where most of the sample drains away), and it also has a longer residence time in the primary beam. The sensitivity improvement is ~1000 times for some elements, but the precision is less (5–10% as compared with 1–2% for flame methods). ETAAS has been developed specifically for a range of otherwise difficult elements (including As, Bi, Cd, Cu, Ge, In, Pb, Sb, Se, Sn, Te) in biological and environmental samples (Tsalev 2000). A further development for specific elements (particularly As, Bi, Hg, Sb, and Se) is hydride generation AAS (HGAAS) or vapor generation AAS (VGAAS), and cold vapor AAS (CVAAS). In certain applications, these techniques can provide data not available with other techniques – for example, VG techniques, when coupled with chromatographic separation of the vapor, can give information on speciation, which can be critical in some environmental applications. Further details of these can be found in Dedina and Tsalev (1995).

Monochromator and detector

A monochromator is a device which disperses polychromatic radiation (UV, visible, IR) into its component wavelengths. This is usually achieved using either a prism or, more commonly, a diffraction grating. Monochromators consist of an entrance slit, a collimating mirror, which delivers a parallel beam of radiation to the diffraction grating, followed by another mirror, and an exit slit. Most diffraction gratings are of the reflection type, which consist of a metal plate with a series of parallel grooves cut into the surface. The spacing of the grooves governs the wavelength over which the grating is effective. The monochromator is tuned to the appropriate wavelength by physically rotating the diffraction grating to the correct angle with respect to the incoming beam. In addition the slit settings can be varied to allow for different line widths and sensitivities through the spectrum. Typically, slit settings give line widths of 0.2–0.5 nm at the detector.

For UV and visible radiation, the simplest detector is a *photomultiplier tube*. The cathode of the tube is coated with a photosensitive material (such as Cs_3Sb, K_2CsSb, or Na_2KSb, etc.) which ejects a photoelectron when struck by a photon. This photoelectron is then accelerated towards a series of anodes of successively greater positive potential (called *dynodes*). At each dynode, the electron impact causes secondary electron emission, which amplifies the original photoelectron by a factor of 10^6 or 10^7. The result is a pulse of electricity of duration around 5 ns, giving a current of around 1 mA. This small current is fed into the external electronics and further amplified by an operational amplifier, which produces an output voltage pulse whose height is proportional to the photomultiplier current.

Detection limits and interferences

Flame AAS can be used to measure about 70 elements, with detection limits (in solution) ranging from several ppm down to a few ppb (and these can be enhanced for some elements by using a flameless source). Both sensitivity and detection limits (as defined fully in Section 13.4) are a function of flame temperature and alignment, etc. The precision of measurements (precision meaning reproducibility between repeat measurements) is of the order of 1–2% for flame AA, although it can be reduced to <0.5% with care. The accuracy is a complicated function of flame condition, calibration procedure, matching of standards to sample, etc.

One important factor which limits the performance of flame AAS is interference, both spectral and chemical. Spectral interference occurs where emission lines from two elements in the sample overlap. Despite the huge number of possible emission lines in typical multielement samples, it is rarely a problem in AA, unless molecular species (with broad emission bands) are present in the flame (in which case, a higher temperature might decompose the interfering molecule). If spectral interference does occur (e.g., Al at 308.215 nm, V at 308.211 nm) it is easily avoided by selecting a second (but perhaps less sensitive) line for each element.

Chemical interferences are more common and more problematic. Principal reactions in the flame are: (i) formation of compounds of low volatility; (ii) dissociation; and (iii) ionization. These are considered in turn:

1   The most common low volatility compounds are anion-metal compounds, e.g., calcium with sulfate or phosphate. Others are less easy to understand, such as Al affecting Mg by forming a heat-stable Al-Mg compound (oxide). Two remedies are possible in such cases – one is to use a higher temperature, which in practice means switching from an air-acetylene flame to a nitrous oxide-acetylene flame. The second is to add an excess of a *releasing agent*, e.g., lanthanum, which replaces (for example) Mg in the Mg-Al complex, thus reducing the interference. An alternative approach to a releasing agent is to add a *protective agent*, which forms a stable (but volatile) species with the required analyte, e.g., adding ethylenediaminetetraacetic acid (EDTA) to a solution containing Ca prevents interference from Al, Si, phosphate, and sulfate species by preferentially binding with it, and allows Ca to be determined in their presence.

2   Incomplete dissociation of alkaline-earth oxides and hydroxides often causes unwanted molecular bands to be stronger than atomic lines. This can often be cured by altering flame temperatures or fuel/oxidant ratio, to shift the equilibrium in the desired direction.

3   Ionization can be a problem in high temperature flames. Clearly, once an element is ionized, it has a completely different set of electronic

energy levels, and thus the absorption/emission spectrum changes. This means that it is better to analyze alkali metals in cooler flames. Alternatively, an *ionization suppresser* (a metal with lower ionization potential, which produces excess electrons and shifts the ionization equilibrium towards the atom for the species concerned) can be used.

Atomic emission spectrometry

Essentially the same spectrometer as is used in atomic absorption spectro-scopy can also be used to record atomic emission data, simply by omitting the hollow cathode lamp as the source of the radiation. The excited atoms in the flame will then radiate, rather than absorb, and the intensity of the emission is measured via the monochromator and the photomultiplier detector. At the temperature achieved in the flame, however, very few of the atoms are in the excited state ($\sim$10% for Cs, 0.1% for Ca), so the sample atoms are not normally sufficiently excited to give adequate emission intensity, except for the alkali metals (which are often equally well determined by emission as by absorption). Nevertheless, it can be useful in cases where elements are required for which no lamp is available, although some elements exhibit virtually no emission characteristics at these temperatures.

Applications of AAS

AAS is best suited to the analysis of low concentrations of metals in aqueous solution. It is therefore ideal for environmental measurements of metals in water supplies, or metals in body fluids. It is a widely-used technique for minor and trace element measurement in solid metals, where small samples (1–10 mg) can be dissolved in mineral acids and the resulting solutions analyzed for several elements. It is also used in geological and archaeological applications for silicate analysis, where sample quantities ranging from 10 mg (archaeological) up to several grams (geological) are dissolved. Special dissolution techniques (discussed in more detail in Section 13.2) are required for silicates, since they are generally insoluble in mineral acids. Outside archaeology, AAS continues to find specialist applications, particularly in the area of clinical medicine, where electrothermal AAS and derivative techniques are the preferred methods for the measurement of Pb and other trace elements in bone (Zong *et al.* 1998), blood (Zhou *et al.* 2001), and urine (Parsons and Slavin 1999).

It is important to remember that in AAS, as in most analytical techniques where a solid sample is converted into a solution for analysis, it is the concentration of the *element* which is determined, whereas it is sometimes the concentration of the *oxide* which is often required. This is always the case for silicate samples (e.g., glass, pottery, and some minerals), but not of course for metals. This is usually easily (and often automatically) dealt with by numerical conversion of the elemental concentration to an oxide using the formula for the oxide species (e.g., multiplication by 1.4 [(40+16)/40] to convert Ca into CaO), but it is not unproblematic in cases where variable oxidation states may be present, e.g., FeO and Fe_2O_3. In these cases, it is conventionally assumed that all of the oxide is present as a single oxidation state, such as the reporting of Fe as FeO in oxide glasses.

3.3 Inductively coupled plasma atomic emission spectroscopy (ICP–AES)

As noted above, the atomic absorption spectrometer can be operated in the emission mode, but the efficiency is limited by the fact that the temperature achieved in the flame (typically 2000–3000°C) is too low to generate sufficient atoms in the excited state. There is also a problem in atomic absorption, in general, in that the temperature is not always sufficient to dissociate refractory compounds in the flame. Both of these problems are reduced, or eliminated, if higher temperatures could be achieved. During the 1980s a radically new design of flame source was developed, called a *plasma torch*, capable of supporting an argon plasma at temperatures in the region of 8000–10 000°C. A plasma is a low pressure gas which is neutral overall, but which contains unbound negative electrons and positive ions. It is the fourth state of matter, along with solids, liquids, and gases. More than 99% of matter in the universe is thought to exist as plasma. In order to sustain these high temperatures, the torch must be specially designed to prevent the plasma melting the silica tubing from which it is made (melting point c. 1700°C). It consists of three concentric silica tubes, with copper coils wound around the outside at the top (Fig. 3.3). The argon gas, which is to form the plasma, is injected vertically through the central tube, but a larger volume enters between the two outer envelopes tangentially, and spirals up between the outer casing, acting as a coolant and lifting the plasma away from the tubing by the toroidal gas flow. The heating is maintained by a high power radio frequency (RF) alternating current at 27 MHz in the water-cooled copper coils, which causes the charged particles in the plasma to flow through the gas in a circular path by induction. The "friction" caused by this rapid motion through the gas holds the temperature at several thousand degrees, and ensures that the plasma is sufficiently ionized to respond to the RF heating. Because argon at room temperature is inert, an external spark is required to "light" the torch. When passed through the argon, the spark causes some of the gas to ionize, which enables it to respond to the RF heating. Frictional heating soon raises the temperature sufficiently for the ionization to become self-sustaining.

The instrument which uses this plasma torch is called an *inductively coupled plasma atomic emission spectrometer* (ICP–AES) or an *inductively coupled plasma optical emission spectrometer* (ICP–OES). It is similar to an

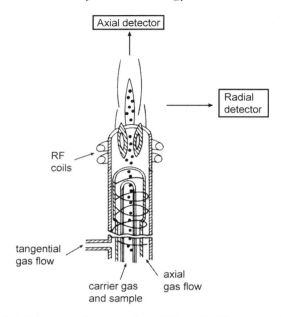

Figure 3.3 Schematic diagram of an ICP torch. The sample is carried into the torch by the carrier argon gas, and is ignited by radio-frequency heating from the RF coils. The tangential argon flow lifts the flame from the burner, preventing melting. The position of the detector in axial or radial mode is shown.

atomic absorption spectrometer operated in the emission mode, with the exception that the gas burner is replaced by the torch. The hotter flame results in more complete atomization and less spectral interference than in AAS. Ionization in the flame is also suppressed by the abundance of electrons produced by the argon stream. The relative stability of the source allows automated sequential detection to be used, rather than photographic or simultaneous recording. ICP–AES shows remarkable linearity during calibration over wide concentrating ranges, coupled with detection limits several orders of magnitude lower than with other absorption or emission methods – several elements are detectable down to 1–10 ppb (parts per billion, or 1 in 10^9) in solution. More recently, another benefit of the plasma torch has been exploited – the fact that it also produces a stream of charged particles (ions) from the sample. In ICP–AES, these are completely ignored and swept away with the exhaust gases, but if the plasma torch is connected to a mass spectrometer, it provides an alternative and extremely sensitive means of inorganic analysis known as *inductively coupled plasma mass spectrometry*, ICP–MS. This is the subject of Chapter 9.

In most applications of ICP–AES, the sample is introduced as a liquid (although solid samples can be dealt with using laser ablation, discussed in Section 9.1 in the context of ICP–MS). Usually a small pump sucks up the sample and injects it into the argon stream, which carries it into the torch. At the high temperatures in the plasma, all compounds are completely dissociated and are in an excited state, so that they strongly emit characteristic lines in the visible and ultraviolet. The optics of the spectrometer are designed to collect these emission lines, and subsequently disperse them using a diffraction grating and slit system similar to that used in atomic absorption. Detection is usually by one or more photomultiplier tubes, although, more recently, solid state *charge-coupled devices* have been used to give better spectral resolution and longer linear response ranges (Barnard *et al.* 1993: see Section 4.1). Instruments which are used for the routine analysis of a particular material, and therefore which have a restricted and fixed range of elements to detect, can be set up with a bank of photomultipliers (up to 50), each positioned at a fixed angle relative to the diffraction grating, at a wavelength corresponding to a particular element. In this manner, simultaneous measurements of up to 50 (but typically around 20) elements in a single sample can be achieved. More usually, however, the ICP–AES is fitted with a single computer-controlled detector, which automatically performs sequential analysis of as many elements as are required whilst the sample is being aspirated into the machine. The detector moves to the correct position for a particular element, measures the emission intensity for a preset time, and then moves on to the next element or a background position, according to a preset program in the instrument's computer. Although sequential in operation, this combination of software-controlled analysis and automated sampling makes the machine relatively fast and effective for a wide range of materials. Since its introduction in the 1980s, ICP–AES has almost completely replaced AAS as the industrial standard for the multielement analysis of solution samples (Thompson and Walsh 2003). It has, however, in the last five or ten years, itself been partly surpassed by a development of the same technology which uses a mass spectrometer as a detector (ICP-MS), and has, more recently still, been updated by the use of a laser to ablate a solid sample into the argon stream (LA–ICP–MS; see Chapter 9).

The biggest development within ICP–AES instrumentation occurred in the 1990s with the introduction of *axially viewed spectrometers*. Conventional spectrometers (now referred to as *radial ICP–AES*), as described above, employ a detector which is aligned radially or side-on to the plasma. Although it was realized as early as the 1970s that there were potential advantages to viewing the flame axially, or end-on to the ICP flame, it was not until the 1990s that the first axial ICP–AES instruments became available, as a result of technical developments and the increased use of charge-coupled devices as solid state detectors. There are a number of different approaches to achieving this configuration, including shear gas introduction, in which the flame is turned through almost 90° to protect the detector, or various skimmer cones similar to those used in ICP–MS (Brenner and Zander 2000). Analytical improvements stem essentially from the fact that temperature gradients exist within the plasma fireball, with the outer layers being cooler than the center. In axial ICP–AES, the intention is to eliminate emission from cooler parts of the flame. This results in improved limits of detection, by a factor of 2 to 20 depending on element, configuration, matrix, etc.

3.4   Comparison of analysis by absorption/emission spectrometries

Until recently, flame AAS has been the "workhorse" of most commercial analytical laboratories for trace element inorganic determinations. It has many advantages – large elemental coverage (more than 70 elements), good precision, cheap and reliable instrumentation, and ease of operation and maintenance. Although it is strictly sequential in operation, in practice it can be automated (automatic sampling, and even continuous flow injection systems – see Fang 1995) and therefore multielement operation is relatively straightforward. In comparison, however, with the other techniques discussed in this chapter, it has relatively poor limits of detection (typically quoted as no better than 0.1 ppm down to 1 ppb in solution). This is often inadequate for routine biological and environmental applications. It still has a role as a simple, widely available, cheap and robust technique, but as a general multielement method, it is inferior to ICP–AES and ICP–MS. Improvements in injection technology, such as electrothermal or graphite furnace sample introduction, can give significant improvements in sensitivity for a wide range of elements (two or three orders of magnitude – typically 0.1–0.001 ppb limits of detection in solution). This also makes it possible to handle material in difficult matrices such as slurries without complicated sample pretreatment. Vapor generation techniques can give unrivaled performance for certain analytically difficult, but environmentally important, elements such as As, and, when coupled with other techniques such as chromatography, can give detailed speciation information.

Since its introduction in the 1970s, ICP–AES has offered all of the advantages of AAS at similar or better levels of detection, with true multielement capability, but with increased capital and operational cost, and increased operator and maintenance complexity. The development of axial ICP–AES has given a significant improvement in detection levels (typically by an order of magnitude over radial ICP–AES). The conventional wisdom is that axial ICP–AES provides better sensitivity in applications without complex sample matrices, but that radial ICP–AES is still superior for complex sample matrices, although this is now being questioned (Silva *et al.* 2002). The recent widespread adoption of ICP–MS (discussed in Chapter 9) has given a further major improvement in sensitivity, with minimum limits of detection in solution better than parts per trillion (ppt) for a wide range

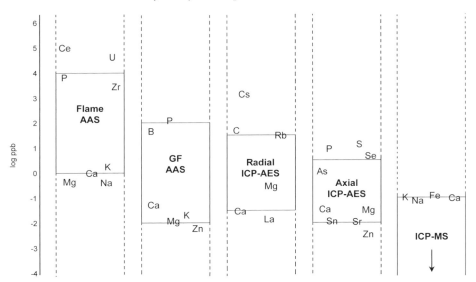

Figure 3.4 Schematic comparison of limits of detection (LoD) in solution (log ppb) for various absorption/emission spectrometries. For each technique, the solid box encompasses the majority of elements reported. A few relevant elements have been marked on specifically at the upper and lower end of the range for each technique. Note that LoD can vary for the same element depending on matrix and analytical conditions, and that not all elements are detectable by every technique. Data courtesy Thermo Electron Corporation from PDF file ("AAS, FAAS, ICP or ICP-MS? Which technique should I use") posted on TJA Solutions website in 2000.

of elements. Figure 3.4 shows a schematic comparison of the limits of detection for all these analytical techniques, based on data electronically published by TJA Solutions (2000). (At the time of writing this website no longer exists.)

These detection levels for ICP–MS are competitive with neutron activation analysis (see Chapter 6), without the disadvantages associated with this technique – storage or disposal of radioactive samples and the rapidly decreasing availability worldwide of nuclear reactors to generate the required neutron fluxes. Additionally, with improvements in mass spectrometric detection technology interfaced with ICP, plasma instruments are now available with isotopic ratio capabilities for elements such as Pb, U, and Sr, which are comparable with conventional thermal ionization mass spectrometry (Chapter 8). When all of this is combined with the ability to use laser ablation as a means of introducing material from solid samples into either ICP–AES or ICP–MS, it is little wonder that ICP spectrometry, in its many guises, has virtually become the "industry standard" for all forms of inorganic analysis in the earth, environmental, and biological sciences.

3.5   Greek pots and European bronzes – archaeological applications of emission/absorption spectrometries

One of the major applications of OES to archaeology was the large program of pottery analyses carried out in the Research Laboratory for Archaeology and the History of Art, Oxford University, and the Fitch Laboratory of the British School at Athens, from 1959–76 (RLAHA) and from 1975–82 (FL). This project focused on Greek and Cypriot pottery, but comprehensively covered the Neolithic to the end of the Bronze Age for Greece, the Aegean, Cyprus, and other sites in the eastern Mediterranean, as well as outlining ceramic types from the end of the Bronze Age to the Byzantine period. The summary publication (Jones 1986) is monumental in many ways – it publishes and analyzes the results of more than 4370 OES analyses from the region (for nine major and minor oxides – Al_2O_3, CaO, MgO, Fe_2O_3, TiO_2, Na_2O, MnO, Cr_2O_3, NiO), as well as containing comprehensive information about analytical details, interlaboratory comparisons, and intermethod comparisons. It also provides a great deal of archaeological contextual information to the analyses, and technological background to pottery manufacture in the ancient eastern Mediterranean. It remains, 30 years later, a model of how such a large-scale analytical program should be managed and published, and particularly how an analytical program should be embedded in an archaeological research scheme. It does, however, also pose a fundamental question for archaeological chemistry: to what extent can later researchers use published analytical data, from techniques which have been superseded?

The results of this comprehensive survey contained many archaeological surprises and indicators of the need for further work. For example, during the first part of the Late Bronze Age in the Aegean (conventional dates for Aegean LBA 1550–1100 BC), when Aegean and mainland Greek pottery styles were increasingly coming under the influence of Minoan Crete, chemical analysis showed further complexity in the picture. One of the most distinctive Cretan pottery styles of this period, Late Minoan 1B marine style, was found outside Crete. Chemical analysis (Mountjoy *et al.* 1978) confirmed the stylistic perception that these vessels were not imports from Crete, but no alternative production centers could be identified. Nor did analysis of marine style vessels found on Crete identify the exact production site in Crete. Distributional analysis suggested either eastern Crete or, perhaps more likely, Knossos itself. Jones (1986: 457) observed that all LM 1B pottery from Knossos is heterogeneous in composition, and concluded that, because of this lack of diagnostic sensitivity, "OES is obviously not the most appropriate technique in this case".

This massive study of prehistoric pottery in the eastern Mediterranean serves to highlight a number of issues relating to the scientific study of provenance, beyond the obvious scientific and archaeological questions of how do the analyses relate to the archaeological question (Wilson and

Pollard 2001; see also Section 1.2). These can be divided into three related areas:

1 How is analytical consistency maintained and monitored over a long period of time (in this case, 23 years, from two different laboratories)?

2 How do analyses obtained using one technique (in this case OES) relate to those collected using a different technique (principally neutron activation analysis, NAA), covering a different suite of elements?

3 How can subsequent researchers best use analytical data from obsolete scientific techniques?

Issues 1 and 2 are dealt with extensively in Jones (1986), and are addressed by adequate quality assurance procedures (Section 13.5). Naturally, question 3 can only be judged retrospectively. Appendix A of Jones (1986) describes in some detail the various calibrations used between 1960 and 1982, as well as listing the materials used as primary and secondary standards for each calibration. Internal corrections were made to compensate for differing photographic plate responses, but no attempt was made to "standardize" results from run to run or between laboratories. Question 2 was an important one at the time, because complementary databases of prehistoric eastern Mediterranean ceramics were being constructed by other laboratories (Lawrence Berkeley Laboratory, Brookhaven National Laboratory, Demokritos, Manchester University) using neutron activation analysis (NAA), which yields data on a much larger suite of (principally) minor and trace elements. Much of this data is still unpublished, although the Perlman–Asaro database of 900 Mycenaean and Minoan samples measured at Berkeley in the 1970s has now been summarized by Mommsen *et al.* (2002). Of the elements routinely measured by both OES and NAA, four are common – oxides of Fe, Na, Mn, and Cr. Several interlaboratory comparisons were run between OES and NAA (most importantly Harbottle (1970) and Bieber *et al.* (1976)). Only broad agreement was recorded, with (not unexpectedly) OES showing a broader scatter of concentrations. Clearly, NAA data could not be directly compared with OES data in any rigorous way. Comparisons between the results of the two approaches were restricted to comparing conclusions from parallel studies of similar material.

The replacement of OES by AAS in Oxford in 1976 immediately called into question the long-term compatibility of the huge analytical database amassed by OES with subsequent analytical techniques. Detailed inter-technique comparisons were carried out, both in Oxford (Hatcher *et al.* 1980) and elsewhere (White 1981). Both pointed toward the same conclusion: OES data are generally more scattered, and systematic differences of calibration occur between OES and AAS. Hatcher *et al.* contemplated the use of "correction factors" for each oxide, to allow OES data to be converted into an AAS-compatible form, but rejected this idea – "OES values cannot be made compatible with AAS results by the application of a single calibration factor for each oxide" (Hatcher *et al.* 1980: 145). They concluded that there are "serious questions about the compatibility of AAS and OES results", although recalibration of the original data over limited concentration ranges may be possible. It is hard to avoid the conclusion that the ability to add new data to this pioneering database is unlikely to be achievable, and that, beyond broad generalities, the original OES data cannot be reused in subsequent analyses of the unresolved archaeological questions. The wider implications of this somewhat unhelpful conclusion are considered below.

Similar issues surround the massive database of OES chemical analyses of European Bronze Age metalwork, begun in Britain in the 1930s, initially under the guidance of Vere Gordon Childe (1892–1957). Childe was a founding member of the Ancient Mining and Metallurgy Committee of the Royal Anthropological Society, and had a particular interest in the use of chemical analysis to trace the extent and duration of use of native copper deposits, presumably exploited as the only source of copper before the introduction of smelting. This interest naturally led into the broader question of the use of "chemical fingerprinting" to identify the source ores used to produce copper artifacts – an interest which continues today. Unfortunately, during the 1940s an alternative methodology was adopted, in response to fears that it was impossible to adequately collect and characterize all of the ore sources available in antiquity. This methodology was the wholesale analysis of as many Bronze Age European archaeological copper alloy artifacts as possible, followed by the numerical investigation of the data to search for "chemical groupings" which might be related to a single copper metal production "tradition" (which may or may not be synonymous with an ore source). This "sledgehammer" approach, which has extended beyond the original remit of chemical analysis of metalwork into isotopic studies, and into other materials, has dogged archaeological science for many years, and has been the subject of many debates (e.g., Budd *et al.* 1996, and many other references).

The pinnacle of this OES work was the large SAM program (Studien zu den Anfangen der Metallurgie), where more than 10 000 analyses have been published (Junghans *et al.* 1960, 1968–74), and recently reviewed by Krause and Pernicka (1996). SAM 1 (Junghans *et al.* 1960) published 861 OES analyses of copper alloy objects, reporting values for Sn, Pb, As, Sb, Ag, Ni, Bi, Au, Zn, Co, and Fe. Because several of these elements were recorded as "0", and tin included entries such as ">10%", only five elements (Bi, Sb, Ag, Ni, and As) were used to categorize these analyses into five major groups (A–C, E, F), further subdivided into A, B1 and B2, C1–3, E01, E00, E11 and E10, and F1–2. SAM 2 (Junghans *et al.* 1968) saw the publication of analyses

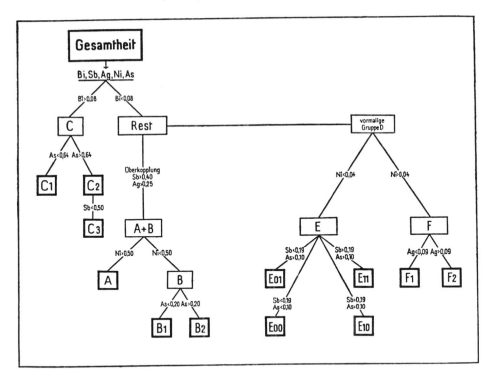

Figure 3.5 A "decision tree" for allocating European Bronze Age copper alloys to metal type (C_1, C_2, C_3, A, B_1, etc.), based on the values of Bi, Sb, Ag, Ni, and As. From Junghans *et al.* (1960: 210), Tabelle 1, reproduced with permission from Gebr. Mann Verlag, Berlin.

985 to 10 040 for the same nine elements, with a concomitant rise in the complexity of the interpretation. Based on the same five elements, the number of chemical groups had risen to 29 (E00, N, C1B, E10, E01, E01A, etc.), with a complex "decision tree" to aid classification (Fig. 3.5).

The total project considered over 12 000 analyses, and the final publications are truly monumental. The outcomes are, as noted above, cumbersome in the extreme, and are difficult to interpret archaeologically. Critically, there are significant inconsistencies between the interpretations offered from the German data, compared with similar, but smaller, data sets obtained by British researchers. For example, the SAM 2 analysis had included data published by Coghlan and Case (1957), some of which (Group 1) the original authors had classified as deriving from Irish ores. The SAM analysis attributed much of the British Isles data to sources in Central or Eastern Europe, with very little being allocated to their own "Irish" type (E11). Perhaps because of these discrepancies of interpretation, but also because of the rising recognition that ore processing, changing technology and recycling of metalwork might confuse the picture (Wilson and Pollard

2001), literature searches today reveal very little active reference to these classifications. The most substantial and comprehensive recent reworking is that of Krause and Pernicka (1996), who have taken the entire Stuttgart database of metal analyses (some 36 000 measurements in total) and checked the original groupings using cluster analysis. Despite the restricted range of elements and the relatively poor analytical sensitivity, this still shows that some of the original chemical groupings, when combined with typological and distributional data, are capable of providing useful information. Sadly, however, this type of project perhaps stands as a monument to the "heroic" years of archaeological science, when interpretations were secondary to analysis, and the concept of testing theoretical models was somewhat alien.

As with the OES data on Aegean ceramics, the most relevant question now is "to what extent can these analyses be used to test new hypotheses?". The answer is emphatically "only in the broadest generalities". Apart from the generally poor levels of sensitivity and reproducibility attributed to OES, Hughes *et al.* (1982) carried out a reanalysis by AAS and electron microprobe of some Late Bronze Age sword samples from Selbourne, Hampshire, analyzed more than 20 years earlier by Brown and Blin-Stoyle (1959) using OES. The results were poor, and the discrepancies were attributed, at least in part, to phase separation during casting (the swords were large, and with 1–15% Pb). Although this problem would occur with any analytical technique which requires microsampling, the results are sufficient to show that the OES data, particularly for the later leaded bronzes, are generally unreliable.

As a result of the growing unease with OES as a tool for chemical analysis, it was replaced in archaeological chemistry by AAS during the 1970s. Those laboratories (the main ones of which are listed above) which had preferred NAA from the 1950s onwards were, of course, unaffected by these changes, and indeed did not encounter any analytical problems until the 1990s, when the decreasing availability of neutron irradiation facilities largely enforced a change to ICP–MS. Hughes *et al.* (1976) published a comprehensive methodological guide to the application of AAS to archaeological materials, including copper, lead, silver and gold alloys, silicates (pottery and glass), flint, and iron. For a 10 mg solid sample, they quote detection limits in the parent object of better than 0.01% for a suite of 23 elements of interest. Using an electrothermal burner, this figure improves to better than 2.5 ppm in the sample, for all elements except Ti (50 ppm). Although AAS is no longer widely used for archaeological chemistry, and more recent summaries exist (e.g., Segal *et al.* (1994) for the preparation of archaeological bronzes for ICP–AES), this detailed paper contains extremely useful sample preparation methods which apply to any analytical technique requiring an aqueous sample.

Almost inevitably, during the late 1980s and 1990s, AAS itself was gradually replaced by plasma source methods – originally ICP–AES, but subsequently by ICP–MS. With this switch, the inevitable question of compatibility between AAS and ICP–AES data arose. This was studied by Hatcher *et al.* (1995), comparing data on ten major and minor oxides (Al_2O_3, TiO_2, Fe_2O_3, MnO, NiO, Cr_2O_3, CaO, MgO, Na_2O, K_2O) on 22 silicate standard reference materials and in-house pottery standards. For the 17 samples with certified values, agreement between the one sigma range of ICP and AAS determination and the certified value was reasonable – in the best case all values agree, in the worst (NiO measured by ICP) only two agreed with the nine certified values available. More importantly, significance testing (two-tail *t*-test) showed that Al, Ca, Mg, Fe, and Na are statistically indistinguishable by ICP and AAS, whereas K, Ti, Mn, Cr, and Ni are significantly different, when measured by the two techniques. This paper concludes that "for most of the major elements, ... a common data bank could be established", but notes that "if the data arising from both methods were being examined by multivariate statistical techniques, ... it is very possible that these differences would create 'subgroups' ". This is likely to be the case when data from any pair of analytical methods are compared using anything other than broad generalities.

There has been a substantial literature devoted to the elucidation of the "best" elements, and therefore the "best" analytical technique, to use, particularly when determining provenance for ceramics. In the late 1970s, this debate focused on the relative advantages of neutron activation analysis (NAA) over inductively coupled plasma emission spectrometry (ICP–AES). In ceramic provenancing, for instance, it is widely (and reasonably) argued that trace elements are more useful than major and minor elements, on the grounds that these are more variable in clay sources. Also, trace elements are less susceptible to anthropogenic control than the major and minor elements, which are more likely to influence the firing and performance characteristics of the pot. It has even been argued, incorrectly, that there exists some universal but restricted suite of elements which invariably give adequate characterization of clay sources (e.g., Mallory-Greenough and Greenough 1998). It is worth recalling that many trace elements behave predictably in the sedimentary geochemical environment, and that these elements, therefore, are more likely to be valuable in provenance studies. On the other hand, other factors such as likely firing temperature range, and a host of technological properties such as plasticity, can be estimated if the major elements in ceramics are measured.

AAS has been widely used in Europe to study archaeological ceramics and metals, ranging from Chinese celadons (Pollard and Hatcher 1986) to Roman terra sigillata (Mirti *et al.* 1990), and from Benin bronzes (Willett and Sayre 2000) and Islamic brasses (Al-Saad 2000) to Chalcolithic and Early Bronze Age copper alloys from ancient Israel (Shalev 1995). ICP–AES, using solution sampling, can potentially provide data on a wider range of elements in a shorter time, using the same sample preparation procedures. The sensitivity of the two techniques is broadly similar (Fig. 3.4). Consequently, a very similar range of archaeological applications has arisen, ranging from early studies of Romano-British pottery (Hart and Adams 1983, Hart *et al.* 1987) to more recent investigations of Chalcolithic pottery from the Tehran Plain (Fazeli *et al.* 2001), and also metals (e.g., Segal *et al.* 1994, Ponting and Segal 1998), glass (e.g., Hartmann *et al.* 1997, Mirti *et al.* 2000), and lithics (e.g., Emerson and Hughes 2000).

A particularly interesting case study is the use of multielement ICP techniques to analyze inorganic residues in soils – originally ICP–AES (Bethell and Smith 1989, Lindholm and Lundberg 1994, Middleton and Price 1996), but more recently ICP–MS (Entwistle and Abrahams 1997). The first work by Bethell and Smith (1989) was carried out at Sutton Hoo in Suffolk, England, which is famous for the Boat Burial and the rich grave goods, presumed to belong to an Anglo-Saxon king. The soil conditions are, however, not conducive to the preservation of buried bodies, and the evidence for human burials consists of dark stains in the sand, referred to as "silhouettes" or "sand-men". Analytical work was carried out by ICP–AES in an attempt to "fingerprint" the soil residue in the silhouette using a range of inorganic elements. This approach was subsequently extended to the analysis of soil samples for a whole suite of trace elements, with the intention of identifying anthropogenic input into the soil in general, and using this to distinguish between different areas of activity on an archaeological site. In effect, it is a multielement extension of the well-established geochemical prospection technique using phosphorus (Heron 2001; see Section 4.4). Middleton and Price (1996) studied the chemistry of sediment samples from the floors of one modern and two archaeological house compounds from British Columbia, Canada, and Oaxaca, Mexico. They concluded, using data from a modern structure as a control, that analysis of Al, Ba, Ca, Fe, K, Mg, Mn, Na, P, Sr, Ti, and Zn in soils by ICP–AES could readily delineate different activity areas in the modern compound, and that archaeological features were chemically distinct from natural soils, and distinct from each other, suggesting that this method could, following "calibration" against ethnographic data, be used to determine activity patterns in archaeological settlements. This potential was further developed by Entwistle and Abrahams (1997), using the speed and multielement sensitivity of ICP–MS to provide a "rapid screening" of sediment samples, in advance of excavation, in order to direct the excavation strategy.

This case study illustrates an interesting aspect of the use of analytical chemistry in archaeology. It has long been established that soil becomes enriched in phosphorus as a result of human and animal activity (largely as a result of manuring), and thus enhanced phosphorus levels are an indicator of areas of more intense human activity. It is reasonable to suppose that other inorganic elements will also be enhanced by human activity, and also that some elements might provide evidence of different sorts of human activity. Empirically, therefore, there is good reason to carry out such analyses, and it might seem logical to use the most sensitive technique available to determine as many elements as possible. What is missing, however (even for phosphorus in the archaeological literature), is any discussion of the way in which soil processes might control the speciation, mobility, and accumulation rates of the various elements, even though some of this information is available in the soil science literature. Undoubtedly, in the published examples, the authors have gained useful insights into the specific activities at their particular sites. Is this sufficient justification for the expense of a soil chemistry survey? It is hard to avoid the conclusion that, with a more fundamental understanding of soil chemical processes, better-formed questions could be asked of such data, and more reliable and universally applicable interpretations might thus be obtained.

4

MOLECULAR ANALYSIS BY ABSORPTION
AND RAMAN SPECTROSCOPY

This chapter discusses those spectroscopic techniques which use the ultraviolet, visible, and infrared part of the electromagnetic spectrum to give information about molecules and compounds, rather than about elements as discussed in Chapter 3. Three techniques are presented, each of which uses that relatively narrow part of the electromagnetic spectrum in or close to the visible region. Colorimetry is the use of the absorption of visible or UV radiation by solutions to quantitatively measure the concentration of the absorbing species. An important archaeological example is the determination of soil phosphorus by the "molybdenum blue" method. Infrared radiation (heat) is emitted and absorbed by the rotation, stretching, or vibration of molecular bonds, and thus gives details of the molecular species present. It is an important tool for the analysis of the bonds present in organic samples, although it rarely gives a unique identification. An important development for IR analysis is the use of Fourier transform (FT) techniques to increase the rate of collection of the data, which in turn has allowed the development of the infrared microscope. A related technique is Raman spectroscopy, which also employs FT techniques, and can be used in a microscope. The value of Raman spectroscopy is that those bonds which are infrared inactive (because of the lack of a change in dipole during the vibration) are Raman active, making the two techniques extremely complementary. These last two techniques are often referred to as vibrational spectroscopies, since they measure the frequency of vibration of molecular bonds.

4.1 Optical and UV spectrophotometry

The absorption and emission of radiation in the near ultraviolet (UV) and visible region of the spectrum (wavelength range 200–900 nm) are the result of valence electron transitions (explained in more detail in Chapter 12). In atomic spectra, this can give rise to absorption or emission lines which are characteristic of the element, and thus form the basis of a range of elemental analysis techniques, as described in Chapter 3. In molecules, however, the outer energy levels are much more numerous, because the bonds have vibrational, rotational, and stretching energy states associated with them, the energy levels of which are also quantized and can be shown as multiple lines on energy level diagrams. The absorption spectra of molecular species therefore consist of broad bands rather than sharp lines, as is the case with

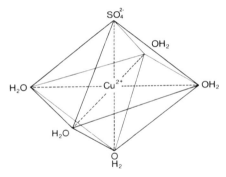

Figure 4.1 Copper sulfate pentaquo complex. In solution, $CuSO_4$ exists as a Cu^{2+} ion in octahedral co-ordination surrounded by the SO_4^{2-} ion and five water molecules orientated so that the oxygen atom points towards the copper ion. It is the effect of this hydration sphere on the electronic orbital structure of the copper which gives rise to d–d band transitions, and hence the blue color of the solution.

atomic spectra. Nevertheless, the frequency or wavelength of these bands gives important and quantifiable information about the bonds present in the sample. The UV/visible absorption spectrum of a material can, therefore, be used to identify the functional groups present in the material – mainly organic, and also nitrates (NO_3^-), carbonates (CO_3^{2-}), phosphates (PO_4^{3-}), etc.

The absorption of radiation as it passes through a complex sample, containing molecular species, can be quantified using Beer's law to give an estimate of the concentration of the absorbing species in the medium, as described in Section 12.4. If the radiation is in the visible or near UV part of the spectrum, the technique is known as *colorimetry*. A colored solution absorbs visible light strongly in its complementary color, e.g., the concentration of copper in a blue sulfate solution may be determined by measuring the absorbance of the solution in the yellow region of the visible spectrum. According to Beer's Law, the "depth of color" (i.e., the intensity of the absorption band) is proportional to the concentration of the chromophore species (in this case the copper ion) in the solution.

Although this example, at face value, looks to be a case of the use of the absorption of UV/visible radiation to determine the concentration of a single ionic species (the Cu^{2+} ion) in solution, and, therefore, the province of the previous chapter, it is, in fact, the quantification of a molecular absorption band. In a sulfate solution, the copper ion actually exists, not as a bare ion, but as the pentaquo species, in which the central copper ion is surrounded by five water molecules and a sulfate ion in an octahedral structure (Fig. 4.1). The color of the transition metal ions arises directly from the interaction between the outer d orbital electrons of the transition metal and the electric field created by the presence of these co-ordinating molecules (called *ligands*). Without the aquation sphere of the surrounding molecules, the Cu^{2+} ion would be colorless (Pollard and Heron 1996, 165), and, therefore, the application of colorimetry as a means of quantifying metal ions in solution is effectively the result of molecular interaction, rather than a property of the ion itself.

Of course, not all dissolved ions produce colored solutions, and therefore not all ions in solution can be quantified by colorimetry. Noncolored solutions can sometimes, however, be converted to colored solutions by introducing chromophore species which complex with (i.e., attach themselves to) the target ion to produce a colored solution, which may then be measured by UV/visible colorimetry. An important archaeological example of this is the determination of phosphorus in solution (which is colorless) by complexation with a molybdenum compound, which gives a blue solution (see below). The term *colorimetry* applies strictly only to analytical techniques which use the visible region of the spectrum, whereas *spectrophotometry* may be applied over a wider range of the electromagnetic spectrum.

Instrumentation
A UV/visible spectrophotometer consists of a radiation source, a mono-chrometer and a detector, and may be a single or double beam instrument (the latter containing a sample and a reference cell). The typical wavelength range for a UV/visible spectrophotometer is from 150–200 nm up to 600–1000 nm. The sample is usually presented to the spectrometer as a solution in a small vessel (usually of square cross-section, with sides of dimension 1 cm) known as a cuvette. The material from which the cuvette is made depends on the wavelength range being used. For absorption in the near UV (below 350 nm) a quartz or fused silica vessel is necessary. These materials can also be used in the visible and the infrared, but for the visible to the near infrared (350–2000 nm) ordinary silicate glass can provide a cheaper alternative. Plastic can also be used in some situations, depending on what solvent has been used to dissolve the sample. Certain organic solvents can have a disastrous effect on some plastics. The quality of the analysis depends critically on the quality of the cuvettes used, particularly when a dual beam spectrometer is used, in which case the two cuvettes must be an optically matched pair.

UV/visible radiation sources
Continuous ("white") radiation can be satisfactorily produced in the infrared and visible (but not easily in the UV) by incandescent (black body) radiation, such as is produced by heating the metal filament in a light bulb. High pressure gas discharges also produce continuous radiation. Although at low pressure passing an electric current through a gas produces a line emission spectrum, at a sufficiently high pressure the discharge becomes continuous. This is the basis of domestic fluorescent lighting. The wavelength range produced depends on the filler gas and the pressure. Lasers can

provide highly monochromatic (bandwidth typically less than 0.01 nm) and coherent (i.e., completely in phase) radiation, principally in the IR and visible region of the spectrum. Because the laser beam is coherent, it does not tend to diverge as it travels, and so it can provide intense power in a beam of very small cross-section. This intensity can be used to vaporize solid samples, such as when a laser is used as an ablation source for mass spectrometry (Section 9.1). Lasers can provide either very short pulses suitable for studying processes with timescales of 10^{-9} of a second or less, or continuous high intensity radiation.

The original lasers consist of a short rod made from a single crystal of ruby, which is composed primarily of Al_2O_3 with traces of Cr_2O_3, giving the characteristic red color. The ends of the rod are mirrored to reflect light internally up and down the rod, but one end is only partially mirrored, so some of the light can escape. Light from an external Xe gas discharge tube excites some of the Cr atoms in the rod (termed pumping), promoting orbital electrons to higher energy levels, all of which have a number of vibrational states. These will relax almost instantaneously to the lowest vibrational state of each of the higher energy levels. Some of these excited states will then decay spontaneously back to the ground state, as described in Section 10.4, emitting a characteristic photon. In a ruby laser, the dominant wavelength emitted by the Cr atom is 694.3 nm. This light can then be absorbed by other Cr atoms in the ground state, as described previously, but, under certain conditions, it can also cause another process – that of *stimulated emission*. If it encounters another atom in the correct excited state, the light can cause this atom to de-excite and emit a second photon of exactly the same frequency (and also of exactly the same phase – hence the coherence of laser light). Stimulated emission effectively provides an amplification process, as light of the characteristic wavelength travels repeatedly up and down the rod. Laser amplification will occur if stimulated emission exceeds absorption, which requires more atoms to be in the excited state than in the ground state (called a *population inversion*). The purpose of the initial pumping is to create just such conditions. The net result is that the multiple internal reflections provide huge light amplification, and a small amount of light escapes from the partially mirrored end of the rod at each reflection, providing a highly collimated, coherent, and virtually monochromatic beam of high intensity radiation.

Laser technology has now developed so that the lasing medium, originally a ruby rod, can now be other crystals (e.g., yttrium aluminium garnet – YAG), glass doped with neodymium (Nd) or other lanthanides, semiconductors, a liquid containing an organic dye, or a gas (e.g., He/Ne, Ar, N, or CO_2). Dye lasers, in which a solution containing fluorescent organic compounds can be made to emit over a wide range of wavelengths, are particularly useful, because the emitted light can be tuned to a particular wavelength.

Monochromators

If a laser is not used as the light source, it is necessary to monochromate (i.e., isolate a selected narrow band of wavelengths) the radiation before passing it through the sample cell. A monochrometer is something which will disperse polychromatic radiation and then allow the selection of a restricted wavelength region. Usually this is either a prism or a diffraction grating. All monochromators contain an entrance slit, a collimating lens or mirror which provides a parallel beam of radiation at the prism or grating, followed by a second collimating lens or mirror and an exit slit. As with the sample cuvette, the materials from which the components are made depend on the type of radiation being considered. Ideal construction materials for lenses and windows should show little change of refractive index (RI) with frequency to reduce chromatic aberration, and have high transmission at the selected wavelength. In practice, silica (fused quartz) and alumina are suitable for UV, but in the visible region quartz is inferior to optical glass. In the infrared, suitable materials include crystals of NaCl, KBr, or CsBr.

The *angular dispersion* of a prism is the rate of change of θ, the refraction angle, with λ, the wavelength of the radiation, i.e., $d\theta/d\lambda$. Now:

$$\frac{d\theta}{d\lambda} = \frac{d\theta}{dn} \times \frac{dn}{d\lambda}$$

where n is the refractive index of the material and $dn/d\lambda$ is the dispersion of the material. Ideally, we need material with high $dn/d\lambda$ to give good separation of wavelengths. The *resolving power* R of a monochromator is the limit to its ability to separate adjacent ranges of slightly different wavelengths, i.e.:

$$R = \frac{\lambda}{\Delta\lambda}$$

where λ is the average wavelength of the two lines to be resolved, and $\Delta\lambda$ is the difference between them. R increases with the physical size of the prism and value for the optical dispersion ($dn/d\lambda$) of the material. The best resolving power therefore comes from large prisms made from a material with good optical dispersion at the appropriate wavelength.

Diffraction gratings can be of either the *transmission* or the *reflection* type. The most common type of grating is the echellette reflection grating (see, for example, Skoog *et al.* (1998), 160, Figs. 7–19). This consists of a sheet of material, the top surface of which has engraved onto it a series of asymmetric but parallel grooves. Originally, these grooves were mechanically engraved on the surface of a material such as glass, but nowadays the grating is produced using a holographic process. If a parallel beam of monochromatic radiation strikes the surface of the diffraction grating at an angle *i* to the grating normal (i.e., the plane of the grating, not the angle at the grooved surface), then the criterion for constructive interference is that the path difference CD − AB should equal $n\lambda$. If d is the spacing between lines on the grating, then:

$$CD = d \sin i \quad \text{and} \quad AB = -d \sin r$$

(taken as negative because of reflection). Therefore:

$$n\lambda = d(\sin i + \sin r).$$

For a given r, a number of combinations of n and λ can satisfy this equation (e.g., 1×800 nm, 2×400 nm, 3×266.7 nm, etc.). The value of n is the order of the diffraction. It is usual to design echellette blazings such that nearly all the power is concentrated in the first order.

The ability of a diffraction grating to separate different adjacent wavelengths is known as its *dispersion*. The angular dispersion of a grating ($dr/d\lambda$) is given by differentiation of the above equation at constant i and inversion:

$$\frac{dr}{d\lambda} = \frac{n}{d \cos r}$$

Thus, dispersion of the grating increases as d decreases (i.e., as the grating contains more lines per cm). Also, dispersion is not a function of λ, and the linear dispersion is therefore a constant, unlike in the case of a prism. The resolving power of a diffraction grating is proportional to the size of the grating and the order of the diffraction used.

Detectors

For UV and visible radiation, the simplest detector is a photomultiplier tube, as described in Section 3.2. Photomultiplier detectors for visible radiation have, however, been largely superseded in the past 20 years by the advent of charge-coupled devices (CCDs). These have revolutionized the detection and recording of visible radiation, to the extent that they are now ubiquitous for image capture in digital cameras and even mobile phones, and can also be used in other regions of the electromagnetic spectrum. CCDs are semi-conductors based on metal-oxide semiconductor (MOS) devices, which, at their simplest, consist of a p-type silicon chip with a surface layer (c. 0.1 μm) of silicon dioxide, to which is attached a series of metal electrodes (Fig. 4.2: Beynon and Lamb 1980). When a positive voltage is applied to any one of the electrodes, a depletion layer is created in the semiconductor beneath the electrode, because the negative charges (holes) are repelled. This creates a "potential well" below the electrode, which will trap any charge which is deposited in the semiconductor. The device is acting as a localized capacitor, and the amount of stored charge can, therefore, be measured by "running down" the capacitor. When the device is used as an optical detector, light

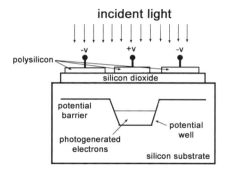

Figure 4.2 Schematic diagram of a charge-coupled device (CCD) imaging sensor. It consists of a semiconducting substrate (silicon), topped by a conducting material (doped polysilicon), separated by an insulating layer of silicon dioxide. By applying charge to the polysilicon electrodes, a localized potential well is formed, which traps the charge created by the incident light as it enters the silicon substrate.

passes through the thin surface electrode and the oxide layer into the semiconductor, and creates photoelectrons in the silicon as a result of the photoelectric effect (Section 12.2). The number of photoelectrons, and hence the charge stored, is proportional to the photon energy, and thus the detector is capable of measuring the number and energy of incident photons. The "clock" on the detector dictates the rate at which the potential wells are emptied and measured, and, thus, the integration period of the detector. When a CCD device is used as an imaging device, the surface is covered by a number of discrete electrodes, the number and distribution of which govern the image resolution (referred to as pixel size) of the device. A beam of light striking the surface of the detector is spatially recorded, because the resultant trapped charge is localized beneath the electrodes, and thus a two-dimensional image can be recorded. Again, the clock timing determines the refresh rate of the image. Since Bell Systems in the USA developed the charge-coupled semiconductor device as the image capture component in a solid state camera in the early 1970s, digital image capture technology has now replaced film in most applications – not only in the visible (digital cameras, etc.), but also in medical and dental X-rays, for example, and also as the detector of choice for a wide range of spectroscopic techniques.

Dual-beam spectrometers

Like much instrumentation working in the IR/visible/UV region of the spectrum, most modern UV/visible spectrometers are of the dual-beam type, since this eliminates fluctuations in the radiation source. The principle of this has been described in detail in Section 3.2. Radiation from the source is split into two by a beam splitter, and one beam is passed through the sample cell (as in a single beam instrument). The other beam passes through a reference cell, which is identical to the sample cell, but contains none of the analyte (i.e., if the sample is a solid dissolved in water, then the reference cell is physically identical to the sample cell [a matched pair] but contains only water). As shown in Section 3.2, we can modify Beer's law to give the following expression:

$$A' = \log \frac{P_0}{P}$$

where A' is the *corrected absorbance*, P_0 is the power transmitted by the reference cell, and P is the power transmitted by the sample cell. The advantage of this is that the corrected absorbance, as defined, compensates for reasonable variations in output intensity from the radiation source.

For the highest spectral resolution, the light source (usually a H_2 or W vapor discharge lamp) is followed by a dual monochromator system – a prism, followed by a diffraction grating. This gives better discrimination against stray light, which can limit the sensitivity of a single monochromator. As in the dual beam AAS spectrometer (Fig. 3.1 in Section 3.2), a chopper also acts as a beam splitter and therefore performs two functions. Primarily, the purpose is to divide the beam into a reference and sample signal, sending alternative pulses of radiation down either the reference or sample cell paths at a frequency of 30 Hz. By tuning the detector to respond at 30 Hz, the two absorbances can be separated, and thus be used in the modified Beer's law equation. It also, however, has the added advantage of reducing noise, since noise at 30 Hz is considerably less than noise at 0 Hz. This is the principle of the *phase-sensitive detector* (PSD).

4.2   Infrared absorption spectroscopy

Infrared radiation is longer in wavelength than the optical region (400–750 nm) of the electromagnetic spectrum, and is conventionally split into three subregions – the *near infrared* (i.e., closest to the visible, covering the wavelength region 750–2500 nm, or 0.75–2.5 μm), the *mid-infrared* (2.5–50 μm), and the *far infrared* (50–1000 μm). Infrared radiation is basically heat, and arises from relatively low-energy transitions between molecular vibrational and rotational energy states. Infrared radiation is usually referred to in units known as wave number, rather than wavelength. Wave number $(\bar{\nu})$ is the number of waves per cm, and is the reciprocal wavelength:

$$\bar{\nu} = \frac{1}{\lambda}.$$

Thus, a wavelength of 2.5 μm is expressed as

$$\bar{\nu} = \frac{1}{2.5 \times 10^{-6}} \times 10^{-2} = 4000 \text{ cm}^{-1}(\text{spoken as ``4000 per centimeter''}).$$

The most analytically useful region of the IR spectrum is 2.5–15 μm (wave numbers 4000–650 cm^{-1}). In this region, most organic compounds produce a

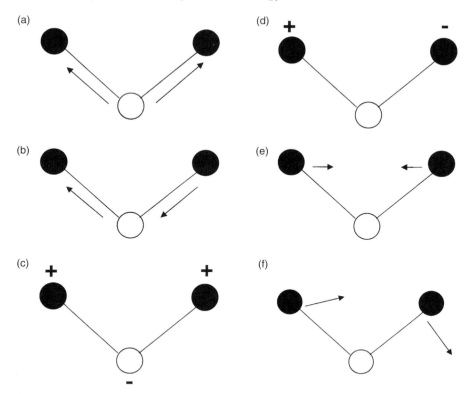

Figure 4.3 Vibrational modes of a nonlinear triatomic molecule such as H_2O. Arrows indicate motion in the plane of the paper, + is towards and – away from the observer. (a) symmetric stretching, (b) asymmetric stretching, (c) out-of-plane wagging, (d) out-of-plane twisting, (e) in-plane scissoring, (f) in-plane rocking.

unique absorption spectrum, and hence it is called the "fingerprint region". This part of the electromagnetic spectrum corresponds to the energy associated with molecular vibrations, and the absorption of infrared radiation is the result of the exact matching of the frequency of the radiation with the energy associated with a particular mode of vibration of a molecular group. At any temperature above absolute zero, all molecules are constantly vibrating. Even a simple diatomic (e.g., O_2) or triatomic (e.g., H_2O) molecule has a large number of possible vibrational modes, corresponding to the *stretching* and *bending* of the various bonds. Stretching of a bond implies that the distance between the two bonded atoms is continuously varying. Bending vibrations imply a change of bond angle between two bonds, and can involve *scissoring*, *rocking*, *wagging*, and *twisting* (Fig. 4.3). Thus, peaks in the IR spectra are labeled "C–H stretch", "C–H bend", etc., and give details of the types of chemical bonds present in a sample. IR should, therefore, be regarded as a "chemical fingerprinting" technique: it does not provide precise chemical characterization of a sample, and quite different

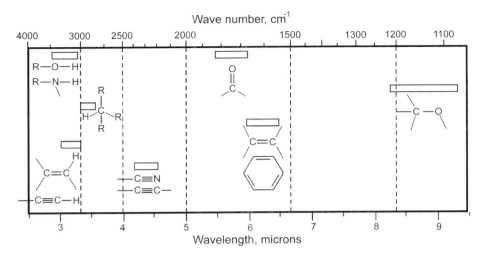

Figure 4.4 Infrared correlation chart, showing approximate wavenumber ranges of common bond vibrations in organic molecules. More detailed information can be found in, for example, Ewing (1985: 95).

compounds may have very similar IR spectra. In addition, coupling can also occur between the vibrational modes around a central atom, and small isotopic shifts can occur in the frequencies (i.e., the frequency of the vibrations of the $^{18}O-^{1}H$ bond are different from those of the $^{16}O-^{1}H$ bond, etc.). Thus the infrared absorption spectrum of even simple compounds is complex, and the complexity obviously increases with the size of the molecule. For this reason, infrared spectra are usually interpreted using a correlation chart (Fig. 4.4), or a computerized database derived from such a chart. Although useful for identifying functional groups in simple molecules, for more complex molecules and mixtures, or degraded organic material, as are often found in archaeological contexts, IR is sometimes of limited use and is often simply the starting point for a more detailed analysis, such as gas chromatography (Section 7.4).

IR spectrometers have the same components as UV/visible, except the materials need to be specially selected for their transmission properties in the IR (e.g., NaCl prisms for the monochromators). The radiation source is simply an inert substance heated to about 1500 °C (e.g., the Nernst glower, which uses a cylinder composed of rare earth oxides). Detection is usually by a thermal detector, such as a simple thermocouple, or some similar device. Two-beam system instruments often work on the null principle, in which the power of the reference beam is mechanically attenuated by the gradual insertion of a wedge-shaped absorber inserted into the beam, until it matches the power in the sample beam. In a simple ("flatbed") system with a chart recorder, the movement of the mechanical attenuator is directly linked to the chart recorder. The output spectrum is essentially a record of the degree of movement of the attenuator necessary to match the attenuation caused by the sample, as a function of wavelength. The attenuator is frequently a fine-toothed comb with tapered teeth, so that attenuation increases linearly as the device is moved into the beam. Also in IR, the sample is often put between the source and monochrometer, to reduce noise, since all components of the instrument will radiate in the infrared region of the spectrum.

Samples are usually measured in transmission, and, therefore, need to be in a physical form which allows the transmission of infrared. Samples which are gaseous at moderate temperatures can be passed directly through a gas cell, which needs to be made of an IR-transparent material such as plates of NaCl crystals. This approach is often used for monitoring changes in gas emission as a sample is heated (e.g., in thermal analysis), or as a reaction proceeds. Liquids can be handled in the same way, but the approach is severely limited by the fact that no good IR-transparent solvents exist. A standard sample preparation method for a solid is to mix a few milligrams of the material with a few drops of a heavy oil (Nujol) and to sandwich the paste between two plates made of an IR-transparent material (usually NaCl crystal plates). Alternatively, a mull can be made by mixing the solid with an excess (typically 100 to 1 by weight) of dry (desiccated) potassium bromide (KBr) powder and by pressing it in a special die to great pressures. This produces a thin transparent disk which can be mounted into the machine. If a twin beam machine is used, it is usual to make an identical blank mull (i.e., without the sample material) to put in the reference beam.

Fourier transform infrared spectroscopy (FTIR)

Although the "conventional" (direct reading) form of IR spectrometer described above is widely available (and familiar, from teaching laboratories, to undergraduate chemistry students), the most common form of infrared machine in a research laboratory is the Fourier transform infrared (FTIR) spectrometer, based on the Michelson interferometer. In this device, a single beam of IR radiation is split into two, and recombined in such a way that the relative intensities of the two beams can be recorded as a function of the path difference between them (an "interferogram"). Light from an IR source (as described above, or from an IR laser) is split by a half-mirror into a transmitted and a reflected beam (Fig. 4.5). Both beams are then reflected by two mirrors, one fixed and one moveable, and both beams pass through the sample. The moveable mirror is moved in and out (relative to the sample) by fractions of a wavelength along the path of the beams. The two beams are recombined by the beam splitter, and focused onto a thermal detector. If the path difference between the two beams is zero, then both beams are in phase and constructive interference occurs. As the mirror is moved, and a path difference of $\lambda/2$ is introduced into the relative path lengths, destructive interference occurs and the intensity at the detector falls to zero. The difference

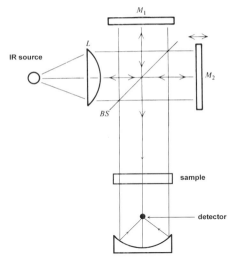

Figure 4.5 Schematic diagram of a Fourier transform infrared (FTIR) spectrometer. Infrared radiation enters from the left and strikes a beam-splitting mirror (BS) angled such that half of the beam is directed towards a fixed mirror (M_1) and half towards a moveable mirror (M_2). On reflection the beam is recombined and directed through the sample towards the detector. M_2 is moved in and out by fractions of a wavelength creating a phase difference between the two beam paths. This type of device is called a Michelson interferometer.

in path length between the two beams is termed the *retardation*, and a plot of the relative intensity of the two beams as a function of retardation is an *interferogram*. For a monochromatic source with no sample in place, the interferogram will be a pure cosine wave. Once a sample is inserted, the interferogram becomes modulated by the IR absorbance of the sample.

In mathematical terms, the relationship between the interferogram in FTIR and the absorbance spectrum obtained by conventional IR is that the interferogram is the Fourier transform of the absorbance spectrum – hence the term FTIR. Application of an inverse Fourier transform to the interferogram, therefore, converts the output of the FTIR into a conventional display.

It can be shown that the mathematical form of a pure cosine interferogram ($P(\delta)$, where δ is the phase difference between the two beams) can be expressed as:

$$P(\delta) = \frac{1}{2}P(\sigma)\cos 2\pi ft$$

where $P(\sigma)$ is the radiant power of the incident beam and f is the frequency of the interferogram (the factor of a half assumes that the beam splitter perfectly divides the beam into two). The frequency of the interferogram is directly proportional to v_M the velocity of the moving mirror (assumed to be constant), given by:

$$f = 2v_M\sigma$$

where σ is the wavenumber of the incident radiation. The mirror velocity can be related to the retardation using:

$$v_M = \frac{\delta}{2t}.$$

Combining these gives:

$$P(\delta) = \frac{1}{2}P(\sigma)\cos 2\pi\delta\sigma.$$

We can consider a real interferogram to be the summation of an infinite number of cosine terms, or:

$$P(\delta) = \int_{n=-\infty}^{n=+\infty} \frac{1}{2}P(\sigma)\cos 2\pi\sigma\delta_n \cdot d\sigma.$$

The Fourier transform of this is:

$$P(\sigma) = \int_{n=-\infty}^{n=+\infty} \frac{1}{2}P(\delta)\cos 2\pi\sigma\delta_n d\sigma.$$

Since the interferogram is a record of $P(\delta)$ as a function of δ, this equation can be mathematically integrated using the computer which runs the instrument, resulting in an output which is equivalent to the absorbance spectrum produced by a conventional spectrum. A conventional infrared spectrometer might, however, cover the wavenumber region $500–5000\,cm^{-1}$, which it does at a typical resolution of around $3\,cm^{-1}$. Thus, the spectrum actually consists of roughly 1500 sequential absorbance measurements, each of which might take half a second to collect, meaning that the spectrum accumulates over 12.5 minutes. Improving the resolution to less than $3\,cm^{-1}$ gives a better spectrum, but loses signal intensity and takes longer to collect. A Fourier transform instrument collects information from all wavenumbers simultaneously in roughly the time it takes to collect a single absorbance measurement in a conventional spectrometer. This huge increase in data acquisition speed is used to collect a large number of replicate spectra for the sample, which are then averaged to give a much cleaner spectrum, with vastly improved signal-to-noise ratio compared to a conventional spectrum.

The value of infrared spectroscopy in archaeology and materials conservation has been greatly enhanced in the last ten years or so by the development of infrared microscopes (Kempfert *et al.* 2001). Especially when using laser illumination and Fourier transform detection, these microscopes are capable of recording the IR spectrum of, for example, minute patches of mineralized textile preserved in metal corrosion layers (Gillard *et al.* 1994), or analysing the ink in handwriting (Wang *et al.* 1999). Fourier transform infrared microscopy offers a versatile analytical tool, which is fast and easy to use, and in which sample preparation is minimal or unnecessary, for characterizing micro- and macro-samples.

4.3 Raman spectroscopy

The previous discussion relates to the measurement of the absorption spectrum of infrared radiation as it passes through matter. The absorption bands are characteristic of the bonds present in the sample, and, thus, the structure (and sometimes the identity) of some of the sample constituents can be inferred. Absorption, however, is not the only mechanism by which electromagnetic radiation can interact with matter. As radiation passes through a transparent medium, a small proportion of the incident beam is scattered in all directions. Unless the medium contains particles whose size is comparable to the wavelength of the incident radiation, most of the incident radiation is scattered at exactly the same wavelength as the incident radiation, which is known as *Rayleigh* or *elastic* scattering. In 1928, however, the physicist Chandrasekhara Venkata Raman (1888–1970) noticed that a small amount of radiation was scattered at wavelengths different from those of the incident radiation, and, moreover, that the *difference* in wavelength between the incident and scattered radiation is characteristic of the material responsible for the scattering. The effect is very weak, with only one photon in a million scattering at a wavelength shifted from the original wavelength. The process was later named after Raman, and the shifting of frequency is known as the Raman effect. Sir Venkata Raman was awarded the 1930 Nobel Prize in Physics for his discovery.

This scattering is due to interactions between the incident radiation and the vibrational frequencies of the target material. Because these vibrations, as described above, are quantized, the energy of the incident radiation is reduced (or increased) by a whole number of multiples of the vibrational energy of the bond. If the Raman spectrum is displayed in the conventional manner, then the Rayleigh (elastic) scattering peak is dominant, with a wavenumber shift of zero, and symmetrically above and below this is a series of much smaller peaks which are the result of inelastic scattering. Those below the Rayleigh peak in wavenumber terms represent energy lost by the incident radiation, and are termed *Stokes lines*. Those above represent quanta of energy gained by the incident radiation, and are called *anti-Stokes lines*. In general, anti-Stokes lines are less intense, and it is normal to consider only Stokes lines in Raman spectroscopy.

The discussion above relating to the vibrational frequencies of molecules implied that all vibrational modes are capable of absorbing infrared radiation. This is not the case. Infrared absorption can occur only if the vibrational mode produces a change in the dipole moment of the molecule. Dipole moment, as discussed in Section 11.3, arises because the charge distribution associated with the valency electrons in heteronuclear species (molecules containing more than one type of atom) is not uniform. For example, in the simple water molecule H_2O, which may be regarded as a covalent molecule with an H–O–H bond angle of about 104°, the bonding electrons do not spend equal amounts of time around the hydrogen and oxygen atoms. The greater electronegativity of oxygen compared to hydrogen (see Fig. 11.2 in Chapter 11) means that bonding electrons spend more of their time around the oxygen centre, and less time around the two hydrogens. The positive nucleus of each of the hydrogen centers is thus deficient in negative orbital electron charge, which results in each of the hydrogen termini of the molecule developing a small positive charge (δ^+) and the oxygen centre developing a balancing negative charge ($2\delta^-$) on the side away from the hydrogen centers (see Fig. 11.7 in Chapter 11). The overall charge on the molecule is still neutral, but the charge distribution is such that one part is more negative, whilst another is more positive. This imbalance is measured as the permanent dipole moment of the molecule. A domestic analogy would be two people in bed, and because of inequalities of size and strength of grip, almost inevitably, the duvet is unevenly distributed, resulting in parts of the anatomy of one person being more exposed to the cold!

Because of this, some molecular vibrations are incapable of absorbing infrared radiation, and do not, therefore, appear in the infrared absorption spectrum. In the case of water, because it is not a linear molecule, the vibrational modes for polyatomic molecules (as shown in Fig. 4.3) will all give rise to changes in the dipole moment. Thus, all these vibrational modes are infrared active, and, consequently, give rise to absorption bands in the infrared spectra. Water is, therefore, a very strong absorber of infrared radiation. In contrast, in the triatomic molecule CO_2, which is linear, the symmetric stretching mode does not give rise to a change in dipole moment, and consequently it is infrared inactive, but the asymmetric stretching mode (Fig. 4.3) does, and this vibration is, therefore, infrared active. These systematic differences between IR and Raman spectroscopy can be used, therefore, to give clues about the shapes of molecules.

Instrumentation for Raman spectroscopy consists of an intense light source (often a helium/neon laser), a sample illumination system, and a spectrophotometer. The illumination system can simply be a means of getting the laser light to shine on the sample, and a means of observing the scattered radiation at an angle of 90° to the incident beam. Because the incident and scattered radiation is in the visible region of the electromagnetic spectrum (depending on the light source used), optical components can be made from glass, and the Raman system can be operated through a microscope to allow chemical investigation of extremely small samples. A standard Raman instrument has a spectrometer which contains a wavelength dispersive device (a diffraction grating or prism) and a photomultiplier to record peak intensity as a function of wavenumber difference from the Rayleigh peak. In practice, most Raman spectrometers now operate on the Fourier transform principle described above, using an interferometer as the spectrometer, and giving the same signal-to-noise advantages as discussed above.

It is important to appreciate that Raman shifts are, in theory, independent of the wavelength of the incident beam, and only depend on the nature of the sample, although other factors (such as the absorbance of the sample) might make some frequencies more useful than others in certain circumstances. For many materials, the Raman and infrared spectra can often contain the same information, but there are a significant number of cases, in which infrared inactive vibrational modes are important, where the Raman spectrum contains complementary information. One big advantage of Raman spectroscopy is that water is not Raman active, and is, therefore, transparent in Raman spectra (unlike in infrared spectroscopy, where water absorption often dominates the spectrum). This means that aqueous samples can be investigated by Raman spectroscopy.

4.4   Soils, bone, and the "Baltic shoulder" – archaeological applications of vibrational spectroscopy

UV/visible spectrophotometry

Soil phosphorus analysis has emerged, since the 1920s, as the most widely used form of geochemical prospection to locate archaeological sites and to identify different types of activity taking place within sites (Heron 2001). Phosphate enhancement in soils occurs as a result of human and animal activity by the incorporation of organic waste, refuse, and ash into occupation sites, or associated with burials due to the presence of calcium phosphate in bone and organic phosphorus in soft tissue, or as a result of intensive land use practices such as manuring. Most inorganic phosphorus compounds are insoluble, but soil processes act to solubilize such compounds to render them suitable for uptake into plants.

The determination of phosphates in soil was originally carried out by classical chemical spot tests, but, more recently, soil chemistry fractionation techniques have been applied to differentiate between different forms of phosphate in the soil (total, organic, inorganic, and various bound forms with Al and Fe minerals) based on the pioneering soil chemistry work of Chang and Jackson (1957). Although this is a scientifically rigorous approach, it has been observed that the archaeological value of this approach remains difficult to justify (Bethell and Máté 1989). Whatever the degree of fractionation employed, however, the most common method of

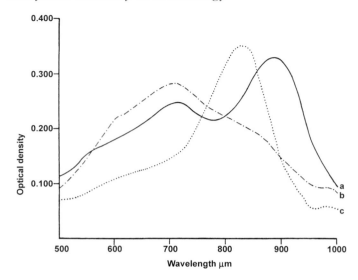

Figure 4.6 Infrared absorption spectrum of phosphomolybdenum blue solution (a) reduced with ascorbic acid and antimony (giving maximum absorbance at 882 μm), (b) reduced with tin(II) chloride, (c) reduced with ascorbic acid. Reprinted from *Analytica Chimica Acta* 27, Murphy, J. and Riley, J. P., "A modified single solution method for the determination of phosphate in natural waters", pp. 31–6, copyright 1962, with permission from Elsevier.

quantification of the phosphate extracted from archaeological soil samples is colorimetric, as described above. Full details of the various methods of quantification of phosphorus compounds in solution can be found in Corbridge (1995: 1127–61).

The simple colorimetric method is based on that originally published by Murphy and Riley (1962). Phosphates are colorless or pale in solution, so the phosphorus in the test solution is quantitatively converted to a colored compound, firstly using an acidic molybdate solution (ammonium molybdate in nitric acid):

$$H_3PO_4 + 12(NH_4)_2MoO_4 + 21HNO_3 \longrightarrow$$
$$(NH_4)_3PMo_{12}O_{40} + 21NH_4NO_3 + 12H_2O.$$

This ammonium phosphomolybdate complex is yellow, but if mildly reduced by ascorbic acid in the presence of potassium antimonyl tartrate a solution of stable bluish-purple color ("molybdenum blue") develops after about ten minutes, which has its strongest absorption at 882 μm (Fig. 4.6). Other mild reducing agents have also been used, including tin(II) chloride, or hydrazine sulfate, which give maximum absorbances at slightly different wavelengths. The intensity of the color which develops is linearly proportional to the concentration of phosphate in the test solution. It is measured with a simple UV/visible spectrophotometer, and can be quantified simply by a series of calibration solutions of different strengths. The advance proposed by Murphy and Riley (1962) was to prepare the complexation and reduction reagent as a single solution, which must, however, be freshly prepared before use.

Although it has not yet been widely used, if at all, in archaeology, one more recent development in colorimetry is the use of continuous flow techniques, in which the sample and reagent are injected into a continuous stream of liquid passing through a flow cell in a UV/visible spectrometer. By linking the timing of the detection process to the injection sequence and flow rate through the cell, it is possible to measure continuously a large number of samples (Zhang and Chi 2002). This, together with recently published methods for continuous sequential extraction procedures for phosphates from soil (Tiyapongpattana *et al.* 2004) offers the prospect for the development of very rapid quantitative techniques for soil phosphate surveys.

The value of soil phosphorus analysis to archaeological interpretation has been questioned in the literature (Bethell and Máté 1989: 17). There are numerous case studies of particular applications in the archaeological literature, but the key question of how an anthropogenic signal can be detected within the dynamic soil chemical processes remains (Crowther 1997), as well as the inherent complexity of phosphorus chemistry in the soil environment (Corbridge 1995: 512). One possible solution is to combine phosphate analysis with other forms of soil analysis (e.g., loss on ignition, organic carbon content, particle size distribution, micromorphology, other elemental distributions), but this seems to avoid the fundamental question, and ultimately, therefore, to be potentially weak science. There are always dangers if "black box" techniques are applied in the absence of an understanding of the underlying principles. Conversely, of course, it could be argued that if a method answers a particular archaeological question – e.g., "where is the focus of occupation in a large survey area?" – then why should it not be used? There may well be a value in using soil phosphorus as a rapid onsite screening test, possibly using very simple and rapid quantification techniques such as test papers (e.g., Terry *et al.* 2000). There does, however, appear to be an opportunity for some more fundamental research into soil processes occurring in anthropogenic deposits, leading to the recommendation of standardized methods of extraction and quantification.

Infrared spectroscopy
In chemistry, infrared spectroscopy is usually the first method of choice for the identification of organic functional groups and inorganic species such as CO_3^{2-} in a wide range of materials. Because it can easily identify the OH^- group in many materials (a broad absorption band at 3700–2700 cm^{-1}), it has proved useful for the study of corroded glass and weathered obsidian, where the corrosion

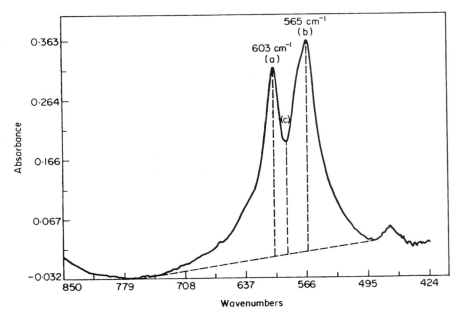

Figure 4.7 Measurement of crystallinity index from IR spectrum of bone apatite. Reprinted from *Journal of Archaeological Science* **17**, Weiner, S. and Bar-Yosef, O., "States of preservation of bones from prehistoric sites in the Near East: a survey", pp. 187–96, copyright 1990, with permission from Elsevier.

manifests itself as a hydrated layer penetrating into the material from the surface. Many IR spectrometers can be modified with an attachment which allows multiple reflections to be collected from the surface of a solid sample, converting it into an *infrared reflectance spectrometer*. This is particularly suitable for measuring the water content in glass surfaces (Behrens and Stuke 2003), which makes it convenient for studying obsidian hydration, used as a dating technique (Stevenson *et al.* 2001).

Infrared spectroscopy has been used in archaeological bone studies to quantify the degree of degradation of the biological hydroxyapatite mineral (Weiner and Price 1986, Weiner and Bar-Yosef 1990, Stiner *et al.* 1995, Wright and Schwarcz 1996). In vivo, human bone is characterized by a very small crystal size distribution (plate-like, with typical dimensions $2-5 \times 40-50 \times 20-25$ nm). This gives bone mineral a massive surface area upon which physiological processes can occur (about 85 to 170 m^2 g^{-1} of deproteinated bone: Lowenstam and Weiner 1989). During post-mortem diagenesis, the bioapatite dissolves and recrystallizes into bigger and thermodynamically more stable crystals (*Ostwald ripening*). This is usually referred to as increasing the *crystallinity* of the bone mineral. In fact, crystallinity is related not only to crystal size, but also to the frequency of structural defects and the presence of strain in the structure. In practice, these parameters tend to be inversely correlated to some extent. Archaeological bone usually has higher crystallinity than modern bone, as a result of the diagenesis of the inorganic fraction of bone (Weiner and Price 1986).

The estimation of the "crystallinity index" (CI) of bone is based on one of the four vibrational modes associated with the apatite phosphate group. In amorphous calcium phosphate, the absorption band at 550–600 cm^{-1} appears as a single broad peak, whilst in hydroxyapatite it is split into bands of unequal intensity by the apatite crystal field (Sillen and Parkington 1996). Based on the splitting factor introduced by Termine and Posner (1966), Weiner and Bar-Yosef (1990) proposed the use of a crystallinity index to measure the crystallinity of bone mineral. As illustrated in Fig. 4.7, the CI is estimated by drawing a base line from 750 to 495 cm^{-1} and measuring the heights of the absorption peaks at 603 cm^{-1} (measurement *a*), 565 cm^{-1} (measurement *b*) and the distance from the base line to the lowest point between the two peaks (*c*). CI is calculated from the formula:

$$CI = \frac{(a + b)}{c}$$

The CI reported by Weiner and Bar-Yosef (1990) is 2.8 for modern fresh bone, and can be as high as 7 for archaeological bone, with an error of ± 0.1. However, most of the bones they studied have values between 3 and 4. In a large study of archaeological human femurs from a variety of contexts, de la Cruz Baltazar (2001) measured the CI of the archaeological bone as being between 2.8 and 4. CI is frequently used along with other measures of degradation (C/N ratio of the collagen fraction [DeNiro 1985], Oxford histology index [Hedges *et al.* 1995], bone porosity [Robinson *et al.* 2003]) as a screening technique for identifying those bones which have been least altered by post-mortem processes. It is expected that these least altered bones are most likely to provide reliable palaeodietary and other information from bone chemistry.

Infrared spectroscopy has also been used to characterize the sources of European amber (Beck 1986, 1995, Beck and Shennan 1991), using a diagnostic feature in the absorption spectrum of amber, subsequently known as the "Baltic shoulder" (Beck *et al.* 1964). Amber is a fossil tree resin, the richest sources of which are around the eastern Baltic coast and the west Jutland peninsula, but it is widely dispersed over large areas of northern Europe. Although it was originally thought that all European prehistoric amber artifacts originated from the Baltic region, it was subsequently pointed out that there were many other European sources of similar fossil tree resins, and this triggered, in 1874, one of the first controversies in archaeological science (Beck 1995). Early attempts to distinguish chemically between the various geographical sources focused on the determination of succinic acid, which is liberated in quantities up to 8% from the resin by burning or dissolving in water. Unfortunately, other fossil resins contain very similar

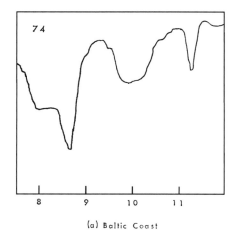

(a) Baltic Coast

Figure 4.8 Infrared absorption spectrum of amber from the Baltic coast, showing the characteristic "Baltic shoulder" at 8.7 μm ($1150\,cm^{-1}$). From Beck *et al.* (1965: 104) with permission from the University of Oxford.

amounts of succinic acid to Baltic amber, and Otto Helm, who was determined to show that some of the most famous jewels of all antiquity – the amber beads from Grave Circle A at Mycenae – came from the Baltic, ultimately failed in his quest. The problem was not returned to for nearly a century, when Beck and co-workers showed that Baltic amber had a unique infrared absorption spectrum, characterized by a single absorption band between 1100 and $1300\,cm^{-1}$, preceded by a broad shoulder (the "Baltic shoulder": Figure 4.8). It was shown by exhaustive sampling of over 2000 fossil resins that this feature was unique to Baltic amber. Thus, using a technique which requires only 1–2 mg of sample, and a routine piece of chemistry lab equipment, one of the great controversies of nineteenth century archaeology was quietly settled. After extensive analysis of Bronze Age amber artifacts from the Mediterranean, including Schliemann's finds from Greece, almost all proved to be made from Baltic amber.

Raman spectroscopy
Raman spectroscopy, because of its versatility and wide applicability, has been used for a wide range of art historical and conservation science (Edwards 2000) and archaeological applications (Smith and Clark 2004). Fourier transform Raman spectroscopy (FTRS) in particular has the advantage of being a reflective method which allows direct, nondestructive analysis. It can also be used through a microscope to allow the characterization of small samples.

FTRS was not originally used on calcified tissue because of problems with sample fluorescence and low signal-to-noise ratio. However, the introduction of near infrared lasers and improvements in the technique have allowed these

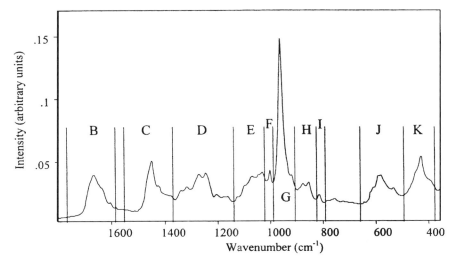

Figure 4.9 FTRS spectrum of mammalian ivory. Letters show regions of the spectrum which were quantified to discriminate between ivory from different species. Reprinted from *Analytica Chimica Acta* 427, Brody, R. H., Edwards, H. G. M., and Pollard, A. M., "Chemometric methods applied to the differentiation of Fourier-transform Raman spectra of ivories", pp. 223–32, copyright 2001, with permission from Elsevier.

problems to be overcome and good spectra of biominerals have now been obtained. Raman spectroscopy has been used in studies of synthetic hydroxyapatites (Rehman *et al.* 1995) and on biological samples of bone (Walters *et al.* 1990), teeth (Walters *et al.* 1990, Kirchner *et al.* 1997) and for the identification of ivory (Edwards *et al.* 1997).

In a subsequent publication (Brody *et al.* 2001), the use of FTRS was investigated as a rapid means of screening ivory from various mammalian species, with a view to its potential use by customs officers to identify material from controlled species (particularly Asian and African elephants) being imported. Initial results showed that there were spectral differences between different species, and a "decision tree" was proposed for rapid identification (Edwards *et al.* 1997). Subsequent, more detailed work, with a larger number of control samples and a more thorough chemometric protocol (Brody 2000) suggested that this discrimination was not as certain as had originally been thought. Multiple samples of tusk and tooth ivory from six species (African elephant, Asian elephant, hippopotamus, walrus, sperm whale, and mammoth, plus modern bone from cattle, pig, and sheep) were analyzed by FTRS (Fig. 4.9), and the spectra quantified at 22 points. Analysis of these data showed that there was no visual difference between the spectra from the dentine of each species, although those of the marine mammals were distinguishable from the terrestrial species. Principal components analysis and discriminant analysis of the quantified measurements, however, demonstrated that the spectra differed between each species, in terms of the ratio of organic to inorganic components. It was shown that dentine samples of unknown origin could be allocated to species from their Raman spectra with a 90% success rate, making it of interest to customs officers. It was also found, however, that spectra taken from small osseous archaeological samples from a range of burial environments were so altered that they could not even be classified as bone or dentine, let alone to species. Again, archaeological applications turn out to be more complex than might originally have been thought from a knowledge of the behavior of modern samples.

5

X-RAY TECHNIQUES AND ELECTRON BEAM MICROANALYSIS

This chapter discusses the range of analytical methods which use the properties of X-rays to identify composition. The methods fall into two distinct groups: those which study X-rays produced by the atoms to chemically identify the elements present, and X-ray diffraction (XRD), which uses X-rays of known wavelengths to determine the spacing in crystalline structures and therefore identify chemical compounds. The first group includes a variety of methods to identify the elements present, all of which examine the X-rays produced when vacancies in the inner electron shells are filled. These methods vary in how the primary vacancies in the inner electron shell are created. X-ray fluorescence (XRF) uses an X-ray beam to create inner shell vacancies; analytical electron microscopy uses electrons, and particle (or proton) induced X-ray emission (PIXE) uses a proton beam. More detailed information on the techniques described here can be found in Ewing (1985, 1997) and Fifield and Kealey (2000).

5.1 Introduction to X-rays

X-rays are electromagnetic radiation (see Chapter 12) of very short wavelengths, in the range 10^{-8}–10^{-12} m. X-rays have the same numerical relationship between frequency, wavelength, and energy as all regions of the electromagnetic spectrum. As they have short wavelengths, X-rays are characterized by high energies. The corresponding photon energy can be calculated:

$$E = h\nu = \frac{hc}{\lambda}$$

where c is the speed of electromagnetic radiation through a vacuum, ν is the frequency of the radiation, λ its wavelength and h is Planck's constant (see Section 12.2). Historically, and for convenience, X-ray spectroscopists use a non-SI unit, the ångström, for wavelength, where 1 ångström (Å) is 10^{-10} m. More simply therefore, inserting the values of the constants:

$$E \text{ in keV} = \frac{12.4}{\lambda \text{ in ångströms}}$$

Using these units, the wavelengths of X-rays used in analytical work are in the range 1–10 Å.

As electromagnetic radiation, X-rays have many properties in common with other parts of the electromagnetic spectrum, such as light. They travel in straight lines, cannot be deflected by electric or magnetic fields, but can be reflected, diffracted, refracted, and absorbed. Techniques of X-ray analysis have close parallels with other spectroscopic methods using light (Chapters 3 and 4). The key distinction is that they have higher photon energies than radiation from lower energy, higher wavelength, regions of the spectrum, and this influences the way in which they interact with matter.

Principles of X-ray production
X-rays are produced by transitions between energy levels deep within the orbital electron structure of the heavier elements. When electrons move in or out of these innermost electron shells, the energy differences are so high that transitions give rise to quanta whose energy lies in the X-ray region of the spectrum. As they are associated with the inner electrons their energies are characteristic of the element producing them, rather than their chemical state, and that is the key to their application in archaeological analysis. The most common method of producing X-rays is by the interaction of high energy electrons with solid targets. Two distinct phenomena occur, the production of X-rays characteristic of the target element and the production of a continuum of X-rays.

Characteristic X-rays
For historical reasons (probably because the origins of X-ray spectroscopy are in physics rather than chemistry), X-ray spectroscopic notation for atomic energy levels is fundamentally different from chemical notation (explained in Section 10.4). The innermost orbitals are designated K, L, M, N etc., corresponding to the principal energy levels $n = 1, 2, 3, 4$, etc., and X-ray spectroscopists use a different notation for defining the subshells of each energy level (i.e., not l, m_l, and s, as described in Chapter 10). Thus, $2s$ is designated L_I, but the $2p$ orbital is split into two rather than three levels, labeled L_{II} and L_{III}. The correspondence between these different systems is set out in most books on X-ray spectroscopy, such as Jenkins (1988; see Chapter 10). A transition is labeled according to the shell in which the primary vacancy occurs (K = 1, L = 2, M = 3, N = 4, etc.) and the level from which the electron falls to fill the vacancy is denoted by a Greek suffix, in an order which is difficult to predict from the "normal" chemical nomenclature.

If an electron is removed from an inner energy level of one of the heavier elements (in practice, with an atomic number greater than sodium), a *vacancy* or *hole* is produced in the electronic structure. This is an unstable arrangement, and two competing processes act to rectify this:

- the X-ray process, resulting in emission of an X-ray
- the Auger process, resulting in emission of an electron.

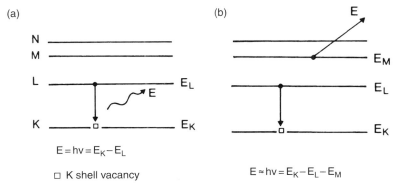

(a)   (b)

Figure 5.1 The X-ray emission and Auger processes (Pollard and Heron 1996: 37). An inner shell vacancy is created in the K shell by the photoelectric process (emitted photoelectron not shown). (a) shows the X-ray emission process, where an L shell electron drops down to fill the vacancy, and the excess energy ($E_K - E_L$) is carried away as an X-ray photon. In (b), an L shell electron drops down, but the excess energy is carried away by an Auger electron emitted from the M shell, with kinetic energy approximately equal to $E_K - E_L - E_M$. Reproduced by permission of the Royal Society of Chemistry.

In the *X-ray process* there is an internal rearrangement of the outer electrons with an electron from a higher energy level dropping down to fill the vacancy. The energy difference between the two levels is emitted as an X-ray of energy E. For example, if the vacancy is created in the innermost K shell with an L electron dropping down, then:

$$E = E_K - E_L = \frac{hc}{\lambda}.$$

In the *Auger process* an outer electron drops down to fill the vacancy as before but, instead of emitting an X-ray photon, a third electron is ejected, the kinetic energy of which is approximately given by the difference between the energy levels involved. For example, if the vacancy is created in the innermost K shell with an L electron dropping down and an M electron being emitted as an Auger electron, then the kinetic energy of the emitted electron (KE) is given by:

$$KE \approx E_K - E_L - E_M.$$

This is termed a radiationless transition, and the emitted electron is called an *Auger electron*. Figure 5.1 shows a schematic diagram of the X-ray emission and Auger processes.

The probability that the inner shell vacancy will de-excite by one or other of these processes depends on the energy level of the initial vacancy and the atomic weight of the atom. The *fluorescent yield*, ω, is defined as the number of X-ray photons emitted per unit vacancy, and is a measure of the probability (value between 0 and 1) of a particular vacancy resulting in an emitted X-ray. Fluorescent yields are defined for each energy level (ω_K, ω_L, etc.) of every element, but in practice, ω is only low for very light elements and for vacancies not in the K shell. Hence, Auger processes are only really significant for vacancies in the L and higher level shells and the K shell of lighter elements. All other circumstances give rise to X-ray photons.

As with optical emission lines (Section 12.3), selection rules apply to X-ray production, defining the allowed transitions. Details are available in standard texts (e.g., Jenkins 1988), but the net result for most elements is that vacancies created in the K shell give rise to two spectroscopically distinct emission lines, termed the K_α and K_β lines. K_α is the stronger of the two, resulting from $2p–1s$ transitions, whereas K_β is a weaker line arising from $3p–1s$, $4p–1s$, $3d–1s$, and $4d–1s$, transitions. Although several transitions may contribute to these α and β lines, the resolution of most detection systems is insufficient to separate the fine detail, and spectroscopic tables list only the average values. The energy separation between K_α and K_β lines varies from element to element, increasing with atomic weight, and the intensity of the K_β line is typically only 10% of the K_α. As an example, Fig. 5.2 shows the electronic transitions giving rise to the K spectrum of tin.

L spectra originate with a vacancy created in the second ($n = 2$, or L) shell and are considerably more complicated, but are usually only resolved into three lines, termed L_α, L_β, and L_γ. The L_α line is the strongest, resulting from some $3d–2p$ transitions. The L_β line, principally due to another $3d–2p$ transition, but including many others, is normally only slightly weaker in intensity (perhaps 70% or more of the L_α). The L_γ is considerably weaker (typically 10% of L_α) and largely due to a $4d–2p$ transition. The precise details of the relative intensities of each transition in X-ray emission depend on the quantum mechanical transition probabilities. Some are theoretically forbidden by transition rules but can occur and appear as very weak lines. Other lines can appear in the emission spectrum, such as *satellite lines*, which result from transitions in doubly ionized atoms (for example the Auger process leaves an atom in such a state), but these are usually very weak and not normally used for bulk chemical analysis. Transitions occur from higher electron shells as well, but the intensity of these is so low that they are rarely used in analytical measurements.

The characteristic X-ray wavelengths are tabulated in all standard texts on X-ray spectrometry, but can also be calculated from the atomic number of the element by Moseley's law:

$$\frac{1}{\lambda} = k(Z - s)^2$$

where λ is the wavelength, k is the constant for a particular series, Z is the atomic number of the element, and s is a screening constant which accounts

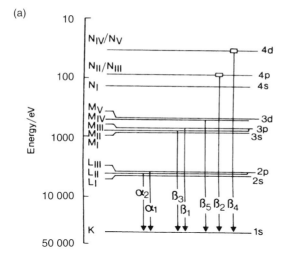

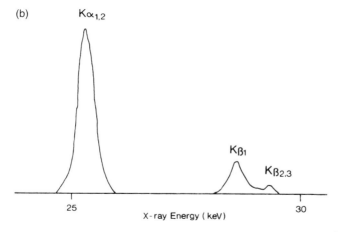

Figure 5.2 Electronic transitions giving rise to the K X-ray emission spectrum of tin. (a) shows the energy levels and the allowed transitions in X-ray notation. (b) shows the resulting spectrum, in which, at normal resolution, the two α lines are unresolved, and the $\beta\beta_2$, $\beta\beta_3$, and higher order transitions are only partially resolved from the $\beta\beta_1$, giving the characteristic twin-peak profile of the K spectra of the elements. From *An Introduction to X-Ray Spectrometry* (Jenkins 1974), Figs. 2–4. Copyright John Wiley and Sons Ltd. Reproduced with permission.

for the repulsion of other electrons in the atom. In the case of the important K_α and L_α radiations, the wavelengths (in microns) are given by:

$$\lambda_K = \frac{0.12}{(Z-1)^2} \quad \text{and} \quad \lambda_L = \frac{0.65}{(Z-7.4)^2}$$

Elements readily absorb X-radiation with a wavelength of less than the peak wavelength of their emission lines. More obviously, in energy terms, elements

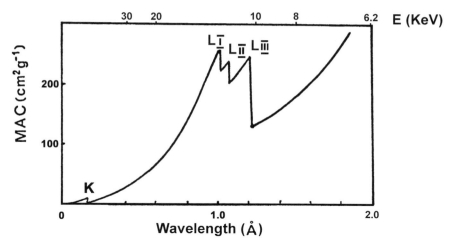

Figure 5.3 K and L absorption edges of tungsten. The absorption of the solid decreases as the energy of the X-rays increases (i.e., as the wavelength decreases), but when the energy exceeds the threshold for a particular excitation process to occur (e.g., the eviction of an L_{III} electron at 10.2 KeV), the absorption jumps substantially.

absorb X-radiation with an energy above the energy of their major emission lines. This wavelength (or energy) is called the *critical absorption edge* of the element. Figure 5.3 shows the K and L absorption edges for tungsten. Detailed study of the structure of these absorption edges of solid materials can give a great deal of chemical information, particularly if a synchrotron X-ray source is used (Section 12.6), but that technique (known as EXAFS – *extended X-ray absorption fine structure*) is beyond the discussion here.

In circumstances where the Auger process takes place, the precise energy of the Auger electron is particularly sensitive to the chemical state of the atom from which it is ejected, because the Auger electron itself originates from outer orbitals which are often involved in chemical bonding. Therefore Auger electron spectroscopy (AES) is valuable for looking at the chemical state of the surfaces of solids (Turner 1997). The extreme surface sensitivity of the method arises because Auger electrons have very low kinetic energies (typically less than 1500 eV) and so only emerge with interpretable information from the top 25 Å of the solid (i.e., the top two or three atomic layers). Hence, a study of Auger electrons has applications in the investigation of the surface of materials. In contrast, X-rays emitted from the competing de-excitation process are not, in general, influenced by the chemical bonding or physical state because they arise from inner shell transitions. Therefore X-ray emission spectra uniquely and quantitatively characterize the parent atom, making techniques which use such X-rays very powerful for bulk chemical analysis.

Continuum X-rays

In addition to the line spectra, a solid is capable of emitting a continuous X-ray spectrum when bombarded with electrons. This happens because the high energy electrons impacting the target material can repeatedly excite the atoms in the target without creating holes (ions) in the electronic structure, which then de-excite immediately and release a photon of the same energy. These energies can vary from the infrared region of the spectrum for outer electron excitation, up to the X-ray region for inner shell excitations. The impacting electrons will give up their energy in multiple such interactions, thus undergoing stepwise deceleration. The result is a broad spectrum of continuous radiation, including the X-ray wavelengths, termed *bremsstrahlung* ("braking radiation"), upon which is superimposed the characteristic emission lines of the target material. This mixture of bremsstrahlung and characteristic emission lines is important because it is the basis of the output of X-ray tubes, which are used as sources of X-rays in a wide range of analytical and radiographic applications (see below). The intensity distribution $I(\lambda)$ of the bremsstrahlung from such a source is given by Kramer's formula:

$$I(\lambda) = KiZ\left(\frac{\lambda}{\lambda_{min}} - 1\right)\frac{1}{\lambda^2}$$

where i is X-ray tube current and Z is the atomic number of the target. The continuum distribution shows a sharp minimum wavelength λ_{min} which corresponds to the situation in which all the kinetic energy of the electron is given up in a single excitation event. The value of λ_{min} (in Å) is given by:

$$\lambda_{min} = \frac{12.4}{V}$$

where V is the X-ray tube operating voltage (in kV).

X-ray sources

For many of the analytical techniques discussed below, it is necessary to have a source of X-rays. There are three ways in which X-rays can be produced – in an X-ray tube, by using a radioactive source, or by the use of synchrotron radiation (see Section 12.6). Radioactive sources consist of a radioactive element or compound which spontaneously produces X-rays of fixed energy, depending on the decay process characteristic of the radioactive material (see Section 10.3). Nuclear processes such as electron capture can result in X-ray (or γ ray) emission. Thus many radioactive isotopes produce electromagnetic radiation in the X-ray region of the spectrum, for example ^{3}He, ^{241}Am, and ^{57}Co. These sources tend to produce "pure" X-ray spectra (without the continuous radiation), but are of low intensity. They can be used as a source in portable X-ray devices, but can be hazardous to handle because they cannot be switched off. In contrast, synchrotron radiation provides an

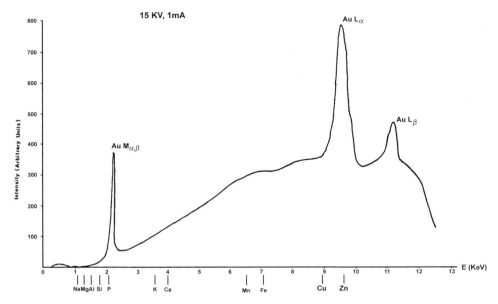

Figure 5.4 X-ray tube output spectrum, showing continuous emission and line spectra of the target material (in this case gold). The K absorption edges for major elements in silicate glasses are shown below the diagram, indicating that the gold M lines are particularly effective for the analysis of the light elements Na to P.

extremely intense and highly collimated beam of X-rays, but it requires a large machine to produce the radiation, and the objects therefore have to be taken to the source.

The majority of laboratory analytical equipment uses an X-ray tube, which consists of a sealed vacuum tube with a heated filament as an electron source, a cooled anode, and a beryllium exit window which is essentially transparent to X-rays. Electrons from the heated filament cathode are accelerated by a high positive potential towards the target anode which is made from a suitable metal (often rhodium, tungsten, or molybdenum) which emits X-rays efficiently when bombarded with electrons. Thus, a tungsten anode will emit the characteristic X-ray lines of tungsten by the processes outlined above. The output of an X-ray tube (Fig. 5.4) therefore consists of a continuum of X-rays up to a maximum energy defined by the operating voltage of the tube, superimposed upon which is the line spectrum of the target material. It is important to know what the target material is when using an X-ray tube, because its characteristic lines will almost certainly be detected in the secondary X-ray spectrum of the sample, and must be discounted (otherwise a spurious element will be measured).

In practice, the continuum ("white") radiation causes difficulties when X-ray tubes are used as sources in chemical analysis because continuous radiation, unlike sharply defined characteristic radiation, is difficult to model accurately for analytical interpretation because of self-absorption and backscattering effects. It tends to show up as a high background in the analytical spectrum, making it more difficult to measure the intensity of the characteristic X-ray peaks from the elements in the sample. For high precision work it is sometimes possible to use a secondary anode to give less background in the primary X-ray spectrum.

5.2. X-ray fluorescence (XRF) spectrometry

XRF spectrometry is based on the principle that *primary* X-rays (from an X-ray tube or radioactive source) are incident upon a sample and create inner shell (K, L, M) vacancies in the atoms of the surface layers. These vacancies de-excite by the production of a *secondary* (*fluorescent*) X-ray whose energy is characteristic of the elements present in the sample. Some of these characteristic X-rays escape from the sample and are counted and their energies measured. Comparison of these energies with known values for each element (e.g., Van Grieken and Markowicz 1993, Parsons 1997) allow the elements present in the sample to be identified and quantified.

When primary X-rays strike the sample two processes take place – scattering and absorption – of which absorption is usually the dominant process. *Scattering* may be elastic (coherent or Rayleigh scattering), in which case the scattered ray has the same wavelength (energy) as the primary beam, or inelastic (incoherent or Compton scattering), which results in longer wavelength (lower energy) X-rays. Coherent scattering results in the primary spectrum of the X-ray tube being "reflected" into the detector, which is why the lines characteristic of the X-ray tube target material appear in the resulting spectrum. Incoherent scattering sometimes gives rise to a broadened inelastic peak on the lower energy side of the coherently scattered characteristic tube lines, as well as contributing to the general background. When X-rays are *absorbed* by matter, part of their energy is transferred to the material, resulting in the ejection of an orbital electron and vacancies in the atoms of the sample. When an electron is ejected from an atom as the result of the impact of an X-ray photon, *photoelectric absorption* is said to have occurred, and the ejected electron is termed a photoelectron (referred to in Fig. 5.1). Study of these photoelectrons is the basis of another surface sensitive chemical analytical technique called X-ray photoelectron spectroscopy (XPS; see below).

Thus, on passage through matter, both the primary and the secondary X-ray beams will be attenuated as a result of these processes. Absorption follows Beer's law (Section 12.4), in which the intensity of the beam, $I(\lambda)$, after traveling a distance x through a solid, is given by:

$$I(\lambda) = I_0 \exp(-\mu \rho x)$$

where μ is the *mass absorption coefficient* of the material of density ρ, and I_0 is the intensity of the primary beam. The mass absorption coefficient (MAC) μ is a function of wavelength (or energy) and atomic number of the absorber only, and so is independent of physical or chemical state and is an additive property of a multicomponent material. The amount of attenuation experienced by the X-ray beam can therefore be calculated at any wavelength for a complex material by summing the mass absorption coefficients of all the elements present, weighted by their fractional abundance. Several tabulations of mass absorption coefficients are available over the normal range of X-ray wavelengths (e.g., Jenkins 1988). If XRF is to produce fully quantitative analytical data, then the absorption of the primary and secondary X-rays needs to be calculated for the sample concerned. This is now normally done automatically using software to process the output of the detector. If attenuation is very severe, secondary X-rays generated at or below a particular depth in the sample (known as the *escape depth*) cannot escape from the solid. "Escape depth" is defined as the depth within the sample from which 99% of all fluorescent photons are absorbed before leaving the sample, and varies with atomic number and matrix, but is typically a few microns for light elements (e.g., Na) up to several hundred microns for heavier elements (e.g., Pb, W), effectively limiting X-ray fluorescence analysis to less than the top millimeter.

The secondary X-radiation which emerges from the irradiated sample has a number of components:

- the characteristic line spectra of the elements contained in the sample (which is the analytical information of interest)
- elastic and inelastic scattered versions of the primary radiation from the X-ray tube including the characteristic lines of the tube target material and the continuous background, and
- spurious peaks, including *sum peaks* where the detector is unable to separate two photons arriving close together in time and registers a single photon of twice the energy.

An X-ray fluorescence spectrometer needs to resolve the different peaks, identify them and measure their area to quantify the data. There are two forms of X-ray spectrometers (Fig. 5.5), which differ in the way in which they characterize the secondary radiation – *wavelength dispersive* (WD), which measures the wavelength, and *energy dispersive* (ED), which measures the energy of the fluorescent X-ray (an illustration of the particle–wave duality nature of electromagnetic radiation, described in Section 12.2).

Energy dispersive XRF (EDXRF)

In EDXRF the secondary X-ray emitted by the excited atom is considered to be a particle (an X-ray photon) whose energy is characteristic of the atom whence it came. The major development which has facilitated this technique is the solid state semiconductor diode detector. An EDXRF system consists of a solid state device which provides an electronic output that is

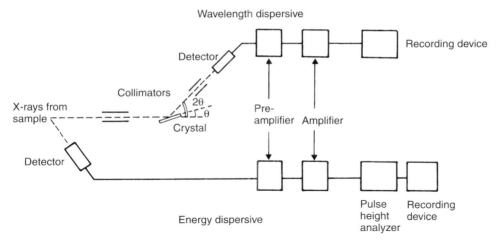

Figure 5.5 Comparison of EDXRF and WDXRF detection systems. Fluorescent X-rays are emitted by the sample on the left. The upper line shows a wavelength dispersive XRF system; the lower shows an energy dispersive system.
(Reproduced from Pollard and Heron 1996: 44, by permission of the Royal Society of Chemistry.)

proportional to the energy spectrum of the X-rays emitted by the unknown sample, simultaneously measuring the energy of the incident photon and counting the number of photons with known energies. There are two major types of energy dispersive detectors: a single crystal of silicon or germanium, doped with lithium to reduce conductivity from impurities, or a high-purity germanium detector. In the former type, the crystal is kept at liquid nitrogen temperatures to prevent the lithium drifting out and to reduce electronic noise in the device. An incident X-ray photon strikes the crystal and releases all of its energy by creating a large number of electron–hole pairs in the semiconductor. For a Si(Li) detector, each electron–hole pair requires 3.8 eV to form, and therefore the number of pairs created is equal to the energy of the incident photon divided by 3.8. A voltage is applied across the crystal, usually via gold surface contacts, and the electrons created in the crystal move towards the positive terminal, forming an electric current, the magnitude of which depends upon the energy of the incident photon. The current is amplified and measured and a count of one added to the relevant channel of a multichannel analyzer, which records the arrival of the photons as a histogram with a "bin width" of a specific energy band (usually 20 eV). The histogram, or energy spectrum, is typically recorded over a range of either 0–20 keV or 0–40 keV, which includes the K and L emission lines of most of the elements of interest.

This solid state detector is therefore capable of detecting information from all elements simultaneously. Software allows peaks to be identified and quantified, and usually includes calibration programs which perform absorption corrections, as outlined above. The detector must be maintained under vacuum to ensure cleanliness and is usually separated from the rest of the spectrometer by a thin beryllium window, which limits the performance of the system at the light element end of the periodic table, as X-rays from these elements are of low energy and will be absorbed by the window. In a fully evacuated ("windowless") system, in which the sample chamber is evacuated to the same pressure as the spectrometer, following which the window can be removed, it is possible to detect elements as light as sodium, but the sensitivity is usually still quite poor. Performance at the heavier end of the periodic table is limited by the fact that more energetic X-rays from heavy elements may pass straight through the thin detector crystal without being absorbed and therefore reducing analytical sensitivity. The main disadvantages of EDXRF are poorer resolution and sensitivity than WDXRF, typically not being able to detect below 0.1% of any particular element, and the necessity to keep the detector at liquid nitrogen temperatures, although detectors which operate at ambient temperatures (high purity germanium detectors, which do not require doping with lithium) are becoming more common. Its main advantage is that all elements can be measured simultaneously, enabling a useable spectrum to be obtained in less than 100 s, making the analysis quicker than WDXRF. As there is no dispersion, unlike WDXRF, a higher proportion of X-rays emitted by the source reach the detector and therefore a weaker X-ray source can be used initially, allowing the use of radioactive sources (e.g., ^{3}H, ^{241}Am, ^{57}Co) rather than a high voltage X-ray tube. The instrument can be constructed so that a small area of the surface of the sample can be analyzed (c. 1 mm in diameter), allowing a degree of spatial resolution in the analysis.

Wavelength dispersive XRF (WDXRF)

In WDXRF the detection and energy measurement processes are separated. The secondary X-rays are regarded as electromagnetic waves, whose wavelength is characteristic of the atom from which they came, and a wavelength dispersive X-ray spectrometer is very similar in concept to an optical emission spectrometer (Section 3.1). X-rays from a radiation source (an X-ray tube, as described above) are passed through a filter to remove unwanted radiation, onto a primary collimator consisting of parallel metal tubes or slits and then through a mask to restrict the radiation to the desired area of the sample. The atoms of the sample emit their characteristic X-rays, which are directed onto a dispersion device. The dispersion device separates the secondary radiation into its component wavelengths and a detector records the intensity of radiation as a function of wavelength. As X-rays have a short wavelength (typically 1–10 Å) a conventional prism or diffraction grating would not be suitable, as the spacings on the diffraction grating need to be commensurate with the wavelength to be diffracted. Hence a crystal is used as a dispersion device because the atomic spacings in crystalline material are similar to the wavelength of X-rays. Early applications used calcite or rock salt crystals to disperse the beam, but modern spectrometers use LiF for general work and specialist crystals for other applications (Jenkins 1974: 88, Parsons 1997). Clearly no crystal covers the entire wavelength range satisfactorily and therefore interchangeable crystals can be used.

Detectors for WDXRF systems are essentially photon counters: they produce a pulse of electricity when the photon is absorbed by some medium, and the number of pulses per unit time gives the intensity of the beam. There are a number of different types of gas-filled photon counters (Geiger counters, proportional counters, and ionization chambers), which all differ principally in the applied potential between two electrodes. They all have similar construction, being inert gas filled devices through which X-rays can pass. The X-rays ionize the gas, and the charged particles are swept to the anode and cathode. Amplification occurs by collisions during passage of the initial ion–electron pair to the electrodes; the amplification depends on the applied potential. Geiger tubes have amplification of 10^9, and produce easily measured pulses, but they have a high dead time (i.e., the time required by the detector between measuring pulses) of 50–200 µs, and are therefore not used in X-ray spectrometers. A proportional detector has less amplification (10^3–10^4), but lower dead time ($\sim$1 µs) and is commonly used, with additional amplification. Scintillation counters, which comprise a phosphor screen (e.g., ZnS) that produces a flash of light when struck by a photon, were an early form of detector. These can be amplified with a photomultiplier tube, and have a short dead time (0.25 µs), and for this reason scintillation counters with improved electronics are now being used again. With all detectors, the angle at which the peak comes off from the dispersion device gives the wavelength of the secondary X-rays, and therefore identifies the element; the peak height gives the intensity of the X-rays, which relates to the concentration of the detected element.

The typical sensitivity for most elements is 0.01%, which is an order of magnitude better than EDXRF, but the analysis is usually slower, and the instruments more expensive. A WDXRF system can be operated in two modes:

- *simultaneously*, where a bank of X-ray detectors are aligned with the dispersive crystal, each making a specific angle with the crystal and therefore detecting the characteristic wavelength of a predetermined element. Up to 20 detectors can be used to provide information on up to 20 elements. This mode of operation is ideal if the requirement is to analyze a large number of virtually identical samples quickly, for example in industrial quality control.
- *sequential* mode, with a moving single detector linked to the crystal via a goniometer with X-ray intensity being recorded as the diffraction angle changes. The output of a WDXRF system is therefore a plot of intensity I (proportional to number of pulses per second) vs. 2θ angle (proportional to wavelength using the Bragg equation described below). In a modern system the detector is computer

controlled and can be programmed to record as many elements as required by moving to the position corresponding to the diffraction angle of the characteristic wavelength of the element of interest, counting, and then moving onto the next.

Practicalities of XRF analysis

Both ED and WD systems usually use an X-ray tube, typically 40 kV, as a source of continuous X-rays for the primary X-rays. The system is shielded to protect the user. The choice of anode material is vital and varies according to use; it must be able to generate X-rays of appropriate energy, but not produce characteristic lines which may be confused with those of the material being analyzed. For example, in most archaeological applications gold or copper anodes are not appropriate, since these may be elements to be analyzed, and therefore rhodium or molybdenum are more commonly used. In silicate analysis, however, gold is good because its characteristic lines (at around 2.3 keV) excite the light elements (Mg to Si, energies 1.1–1.7 keV) more effectively than other target materials. Some X-ray tubes have interchangeable anodes, but this is very expensive. The primary radiation can be filtered to remove less intense lines and background if required, so as to approximate a monochromatic source. The filter consists of a thin layer of metal that has an absorption edge falling between the K_α and the K_β emissions from the target. For example, in copper the Cu K_α line has an energy of 8 keV, and K_β has an energy of 8.4 keV, and a nickel filter will absorb at approximately 8.2 keV, therefore a nickel filter will substantially reduce the intensity of Cu K_β line from a Cu target, making the subsequent calculations simpler. Commercial instruments commonly have a variety of filter options. (See Parsons [1997: 572] for a table of filter characteristics.) An alternative is to use an isotope source (see above). This gives much lower primary intensity, but is often monochromatic or shows only a few lines. It is useful for portable instruments, e.g., for pollution control measurements.

X-rays are absorbed in air, with an absorption that increases with decreasing energy (and therefore increasing wavelength) and so the secondary X-rays from elements with low atomic numbers are most strongly absorbed. In practice, X-rays from elements with atomic numbers <22 (Ti) are completely absorbed by a few centimeters of air. If it is intended to analyze light elements, a vacuum is required and even then elements <12 (Mg) frequently cannot be detected or can only be detected at lower sensitivity. The primary and secondary beams are attenuated by the sample itself, as discussed above. The amount of attenuation experienced by the secondary X-ray beam depends on atomic number and matrix of the material being analyzed, but is typically a few microns for light elements (e.g., Na) up to several hundred microns for heavier elements (e.g., Pb). This means that the depth from which analytical data is obtained is different for different elements in the same sample (and different from sample to sample for the same element if the matrix is substantially different). This effectively limits analysis to less than the top millimeter, making XRF essentially a surface analytical technique, although not as surface sensitive as AES or XPS.

XRF spectrometers are generally designed for the analysis of solid samples, preferably of a standard shape (usually a disk) and mounted flat in a sample holder. Metal samples for commercial analysis are simply cut into shape and polished. Geological materials can be either sectioned, cut, mounted, and polished; or powdered and pressed into a disk with a suitable binding medium; or converted to a glass bead by fluxing with excess lithium metaborate. The latter two methods are time-consuming and care is needed in the selection of binding medium and flux. An alternative approach is to support grains of the material on a plastic film, e.g., Mylar, which is not detectable by XRF. Samples can be small (100 mg–2 g), but if it is not easy or acceptable to take samples, then the spectrometer can be modified to accommodate large, irregularly shaped objects, either in a specially designed sample chamber or by simply holding the sample in some fixed geometry in front of the spectrometer in air. If the sample chamber cannot be evacuated, information on the lighter elements (<19, K) is lost due to air absorption of the characteristic X-rays. The advantages are that it gives a machine which allows quantitative analysis of some museum objects without sampling (Hall *et al.* 1973), possibly even a portable instrument (Bronk *et al.* 2001). However, these results are less reliable than for uniformly flat prepared specimens, partly due to the more complex geometry, but also due to the likelihood of the surface composition not being representative of the whole.

One of the principal problems with XRF investigation of solid samples (either prepared "beads" or natural-state solids) arises because XRF is a (relatively) surface sensitive technique. Inhomogeneous samples can present serious problems, for example surface inhomogeneity caused by manufacturing problems (e.g., migration of volatile species to the surface) or corrosion (resulting in the removal of certain species). This means that, for example, surface analysis of a metal artifact might give information on the metal corrosion or any surface gilding, but not necessarily on the metal itself. Unless it is the surface that is specifically of interest, these effects must be minimized by appropriate sample preparation, such as preparing a clean surface or drilling a sample from the interior.

Quantitative concentration data are often required from XRF analyses. In principle (for both WD and ED) the intensity of the fluorescent X-ray peak is proportional to the amount of the element present. This is complicated, however, by absorption and enhancement processes. Absorption can cause both attenuation of the input (primary) radiation and the fluorescent (secondary) radiation, as discussed above. Enhancement is the result of the observed element absorbing secondary radiation from other elements present in the sample, thus giving more fluorescent radiation than would otherwise be present (*secondary fluorescence*). Mathematical treatment of these factors is possible and most large XRF machines now come with computational software to allow these "matrix effects", known as "ZAF", to be calculated. Normally the problem is approached using standards, either internal standards calibrated against a single element standard or a multielement standard of composition close to the unknown. For good analytical results it is essential to have calibration samples and standards identical in all respects. In most circumstances concentrations of 10 ppm to 100% can be measured. Precision depends on many factors, and can be as good as 2%, although 5–10% is more typical. One limiting factor is the presence of surface irregularities on poorly prepared samples, which make it hard to obtain a good match with the surfaces of the calibration standards, resulting in poor quality data. Using commercially available systems it is generally assumed that WDXRF has lower limits of detection than does EDXRF, and is capable of higher precision. However, detailed comparisons of the trace element analysis of geological materials has shown that this is not necessarily the case (e.g., Potts *et al.* 1985), concluding that the limit on the accuracy of data produced was not the analytical technique employed but the quality of the standards used for calibration.

The measurement of a given element in a complex material may be affected by the presence of other elements, due to spectral overlap. A common example which occurs in archaeological metal analysis is lead and arsenic – the Pb L_α line occurs at 10.55 keV, and the As K_α at 10.54 keV. Lead can, however, easily be distinguished from arsenic by the fact that it has an L_β line (of similar intensity to the L_α line) at 12.61 keV, which allows lead to be quantified in the presence of arsenic using this line with no loss of sensitivity. Measuring arsenic in the presence of lead is more difficult, because although the K_β line of arsenic at 11.73 keV is clear of lead interference, it is much weaker than the K_α line (about 10% relative intensity), and the determination using this alternative line is therefore much less sensitive. Careful investigation of tables of X-ray emission lines will reveal any such problems for any particular pair of elements, and will usually suggest a solution, but possibly not an entirely satisfactory one.

XRF is widely used in industrial applications where a large number of elements need to be determined quantitatively. It is used for continuous quality control in the steel industry (e.g., the determination of Mn, Cr, Ni, Co, etc., in the production of stainless steels), and also for casting quality of coins in the Royal Mint (where Cu, Ni, and Zn are continuously monitored). Geological applications include whole rock analyses and clay identification. The power industry uses it as pollution control management, measuring sulfur and heavy metal concentrations in fuels (coal, oil) and ash.

In summary, the key factors to be borne in mind when using XRF are:

- the possibility of analysis without sample removal or extensive preparation
- the surface nature of the analysis

- the speed of the analysis
- its applicability to detection of elements above Na in the periodic table in vacuum and above K in air, and
- possible problems arising from overlapping peaks derived from the elements of interest.

5.3   Electron microscopy as an analytical tool

Analytical electron microscopy combines the high image resolution of the electron microscope with analysis of the characteristic X-rays produced when the sample is bombarded with electrons. This combination produces a very powerful method of chemical analysis, particularly suitable for analysis of small regions of a solid, and for the detection of spatial variation in composition. The underlying principles are very similar to those of XRF; the major difference is that electrons, not X-rays, are used to produce the initial vacancies in the inner electron shells. The image resolution of an optical microscope is limited by the wavelength of light (5000–7000 Å). In order to image smaller objects, it is necessary to use radiation of shorter wavelength. Using a beam of high energy electrons, radiation of wavelengths of the order of a few ångströms can be produced (again, by considering the beam of electrons as a wave using particle–wave duality) and therefore in theory individual molecules can be imaged. Many standard texts describe the use of electron microscopy in a wide variety of applications within archaeology and in a broader context (e.g., Olsen 1988, Reed 1993).

In a simple electron microscope, a primary beam of electrons is produced using a conventional electron gun, where a heated cathode, maintained at ground potential, emits electrons which are drawn out by a positive potential (typically 30 kV) to form a high energy electron beam. This beam is easily electrostatically and/or magnetically focused (since electrons are charged particles) to a few microns across, and can be directed to any point on the sample by a series of magnetic lenses. The system must be evacuated to reduce attenuation and scatter of the electron beam. When an electron beam strikes the sample, a number of processes take place (Fig. 5.6; Pollard and Heron 1996: 51).

- *Secondary electrons* are very low energy electrons (less than 50 eV) knocked out of the loosely bound outer electronic orbitals of surface atoms. Because of their low energy, they can only escape from atoms in the top few atomic layers and are very sensitive to surface topography – protruding surface features are more likely to produce secondary electrons which can escape and be detected than are depressed features. The intensity of secondary electrons across the sample surface therefore accurately reflects the topography and is the basis of the image formation process in electron microscopy.
- *Backscattered electrons* are of higher energy and result from interactions of the incident beam with the nucleus of the atoms. Their higher energy means that they can escape from deeper within the sample than secondary electrons, so they do not reflect the surface topography. Their intensity is, however, proportional to the atomic weight (and therefore atomic number) of the interacting nucleus, and the

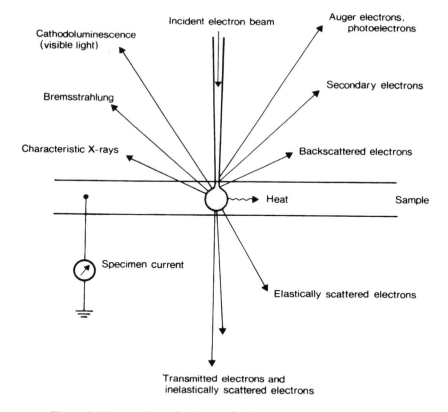

Figure 5.6 Interaction of a beam of primary electrons with a thin solid sample, showing the various processes which can take place (Pollard and Heron 1996: 51). Various types of electron can be scattered or ejected back towards the source, or transmitted through the sample. Characteristic X-rays and bremsstrahlung can be produced, and also cathodoluminescence. These products form the basis of analytical and imaging electron microscopy, and of a range of other techniques. (After Woldseth 1973; Fig. 4.1 – reproduced by permission of the Royal Society of Chemistry.)

intensity variation across a surface is therefore proportional to the average atomic number of the surface. This gives what is known as a *backscattered electron (bse) image*, which contains useful chemical information.

- Some incident electrons will create inner shell vacancies as described above. The electrons ejected by the primary beam (*photoelectrons*) can be used analytically (in XPS) but are generally ignored in electron microscopy. The inner shell vacancy can de-excite via the Auger process (Auger electrons are also generally neglected in this application) or via the emission of characteristic X-rays, which are detected and which form the basis of the analytical operation of the electron microscope.

- If the sample is thin enough, for example a specially prepared thin section, electrons may go straight through and be detected, as well as elastically and inelastically scattered electrons which are scattered in a forward direction. These form the basis of *transmission electron microscopy* (TEM).

For analytical purposes the electron microscope, sometimes referred to as a microprobe, is fitted with an X-ray analyzer, with either one or more wavelength dispersive X-ray detectors or an energy dispersive detector, or both, each with the attendant advantages and disadvantages as outlined above. Simultaneous multielement analysis is therefore available with an ED detector, or sequentially with a WD detector. Quantitative results are obtained either by using suitable calibration standards or, if necessary, by calculation from first principles. Both processes are simpler than the equivalent calculations for XRF, since the interaction of a monoenergetic electron beam with a solid sample is simpler to deal with mathematically than is the case with a broad spectrum of X-rays. In older machines the geometry is such that they are designed either for imaging or analysis, but not both. More recent instruments combine the two functions to produce an analytical scanning electron micrograph (SEM) with high quality images and fully quantitative analytical capabilities.

Practicalities of electron beam microanalysis

Most routine analyses are carried out on prepared samples of thin polished sections or perfectly flat surfaces, cut and mounted to fit standard sample holders, typically several millimeters across. Samples larger than $1\,cm^3$ often need little preparation other than cleaning; smaller samples are embedded in resin or a mounting compound. Some modern instruments have larger sample chambers to allow the analysis of large, unprepared samples, and some also allow the analysis and imaging to be carried out under low (as opposed to the more usual high) vacuum, which is useful for wet samples and biological tissue (*environmental chambers* – see Thiel 2004). One problem with electron microscopy is that the incident beam is electrically charged, and therefore, if the sample is electrically insulating, it will collect charge and eventually deflect the incident electron beam. This presents no problems with the analysis of metals, but for electrical insulators, such as glass or ceramics, it has to be overcome by depositing a thin conducting layer (usually of gold for imaging, or graphite for analysis) onto the surface of the sample prior to loading it into the microscope.

Comparative studies of WD and ED detectors in electron microanalysis have shown that the accuracy and precision of both techniques are comparable over typical ranges for geological and archaeological materials, but ED has considerably poorer limits of detection for all elements, typically by one or two orders of magnitude. The exact figures depend upon the matrix and the counting time, but representative figures for the limit of detection using ED are 0.05–0.26 wt% of the element. These figures are comparable to, or slightly poorer than, the equivalent XRF instruments but there are a number of advantages of using electrons to create the inner shell vacancy, rather than a primary beam of X-rays. Firstly, electrons are charged particles and can therefore be focused and steered by electrostatic lenses (X-rays are electromagnetic radiation and cannot be focused other than by using curved crystals). An electron beam can be focused down to a spot of diameter 1 μm or less, allowing the analysis of very small areas of solid samples, e.g., individual mineral inclusions in a ceramic matrix, carcinogenic inclusions in tissue matrix, or different phases in the microstructure of metals. The beam can also be scanned across the sample surface giving spatially resolved analyses, for example analyzing changes in composition across an interface. An element can be selected (by choosing its appropriate fluorescent X-ray energy) and a distribution map produced of that element over the sample surface (*elemental mapping*). False color images allow a number of elements to be displayed in this way. This is particularly useful when studying grain boundary phenomena such as segregation in metals or samples which are inhomogeneous or corroded. Secondly, the optical imaging capability of a microscope using an electron beam can be combined with the analytical facility allowing the operator to observe the components of the sample being analyzed. Thirdly, using electrons rather than primary X-rays to stimulate the characteristic X-rays reduces the X-ray background in the detector. This means that there is no scattered version of the primary X-ray spectrum in the background signal and therefore improves the analytical detection levels. Finally, the various phenomena associated with electron scattering from solid surfaces can be used to estimate average atomic weight of different regions of the sample, helping to characterize the phase structure of the sample, e.g., the stoichiometry of iron oxide particles.

The main disadvantage is the constraint placed on the size and shape of the sample. The requirement for integral optical, electron, and X-ray optics means that the samples must be presented in a uniform manner. Care is therefore required in producing flat, homogeneous samples (this is particularly restrictive in the case of archaeological material). The charged nature of the incident beam also produces problems. In addition to requiring the sample to be conductive, the analysis of highly mobile species (e.g., Na^+ in glasses or minerals) means that the ions may migrate away from the negative charge during the analysis. The mechanism of this *beam stimulated migration* is not well understood, but it is probably the result of a combination of heating effects and charge build-up. The result is that in nonconducting samples (e.g., glass and ceramics), mobile species may cause analytical inaccuracies. The necessity for the sample to be under high vacuum can also cause problems with porous samples such as bone, with difficulties encountered in achieving adequate vacuum for analysis, or the vacuum having a damaging effect on the sample. Low vacuum SEMs, mentioned above, have been developed for the investigation of organic materials, but the problem of attenuation of the electron beam and the resultant X-ray remains, giving generally poorer analytical data. Prolonged exposure to the electron beam itself can also cause damage to sensitive materials, e.g., inducing opacity in some glasses.

As with XRF, electron microscope-based microanalysis is relatively-insensitive to light elements (below Na in the periodic table), although this can be improved upon with developments in thin-window or windowless detectors which allow analysis down to C. It is better than XRF because of the high vacuum used ($\sim 10^{-8}$ torr), but a fundamental limitation is the low fluorescent yield of the light elements. As with XRF analysis it is surface sensitive, since the maximum depth of information obtained is limited not by the penetration of the electron beam but by the escape depth of the fluorescent X-rays, which is only a few microns for light elements. In quantitative analysis concentrations may not add up to 100% because, if the surface is not smooth, some X-rays from the sample may be deflected away from the detector. It may be possible in such cases to normalize the concentration data to 100% if the analyst is certain that all significant elements have been measured, but it is probably better to repeat the analysis on a reprepared sample.

In summary, the advantages offered by analytical SEM are primarily:

- simpler calculation of quantitative results
- small analytical spot size whose location can be controlled
- combination of imaging and analysis, and
- improved detection levels over XRF.

5.4   X-ray diffraction

X-ray diffraction uses X-rays of known wavelengths to determine the lattice spacing in crystalline structures and therefore directly identify chemical compounds. This is in contrast to the other X-ray methods discussed in this chapter (XRF, electron microprobe analysis, PIXE) which determine concentrations of constituent elements in artifacts. Powder XRD, the simplest of the range of XRD methods, is the most widely applied method for structural identification of inorganic materials, and, in some cases, can also provide information about mechanical and thermal treatments during artifact manufacture. Cullity (1978) provides a detailed account of the method.

In powder X-ray diffraction measurements the solid sample is irradiated by a collimated beam of monochromatic X-rays of known wavelength. A proportion of these are diffracted at angles which depend on the crystal structure of the specimen. The wavelength of the incident radiation must be of the same magnitude as the distance between the scattering points and a typical choice of X-ray wavelength is 1.54059 Å, the K_α transition for copper, using a Ni filter to remove the K_β wavelength as described above. The X-rays are reflected in a manner which appears similar to the reflection of light from a mirror (i.e., angle of incidence = angle of reflection). In reality the X-rays penetrate below the surface of the crystal and are "reflected" from the

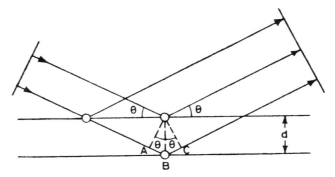

Figure 5.7 Derivation of Bragg's law of X-ray diffraction. Parallel X-rays strike the surface at an angle θ, and are reflected from successive planes of crystals of interplanar spacing d. The path difference between reflections from successive planes is given by AB + BC, which, by geometry, is equal to 2dsinθ. For constructive interference, this must be equal to a whole number of wavelengths of the incoming radiation.

successive atomic layers in the crystal lattice creating constructive and destructive interference (see Section 12.1) from successive layers (Fig. 5.7). The path difference (i.e., the difference in distance traveled) between "reflections" at an angle of θ from successive layers of atoms separated by a spacing of d is equal to 2dsinθ. A maximum in the reflected X-ray intensity therefore occurs at this angle if the contributions from successive planes are in phase, the condition for which is given by the Bragg relationship:

$$n\lambda = 2d\sin\theta$$

where n is an integer (the order of the diffraction) and λ is the wavelength of the incident X-rays.

Therefore, a crystalline specimen will produce a series of reflected X-ray intensity maxima (a diffraction pattern) at angles determined by the spacings between crystal planes of its constituent minerals. The diffraction pattern is characteristic of the minerals present, and can be used to identify them. The power of the diffracted beam is dependent on the quantity of the corresponding crystalline material in the sample and therefore relative amounts of different minerals can also be determined. The processes in XRD are identical to those of wavelength dispersive detection in XRF, except that in XRD the wavelength of the X-rays is known and the lattice spacings are to be determined, whereas in WDXRF the lattice spacing is known and the wavelengths of the secondary X-rays are to be determined.

Practicalities of XRD analysis
The simplest method of XRD analysis, used in early studies and described by Tite (1972: 286), is the powder diffraction method. A small sample, typically 5–10 mg, is removed from the artifact, either by scraping the surface, cutting

or drilling. It is ground to a fine powder and formed into a thin rod, either by mixing with a suitable adhesive or by inserting into a thin-walled capillary vitreous silica tube. Sample preparation is often the most difficult and time-consuming part of the process. The rod is then mounted on the vertical axis of a cylindrical X-ray camera (a Debye–Scherrer powder camera) around the inside of which is wrapped a photographic film, and is mechanically rotated slowly about its vertical axis to ensure all possible crystal reflections are activated. Monochromatic, collimated and filtered X-rays are directed onto the sample rod. The exposure takes several hours, following which the film is removed and photographically developed. Crystal planes with a specific spacing (d) will give reflections along the surface of a cone with semiangle 2θ (from Bragg's law; see above) since, in a finely powdered rotating sample lattice planes exist in all orientations with respect to the incident X-ray beam. This cone of X-rays appears on the film as a pair of arcs. Other lattice spacings will produce further pairs of arcs and therefore the diffraction pattern appears as a series of dark arcs on the film (Fig. 5.8). From the distances between the pairs of arcs, the associated crystal lattice spacings can be calculated and the mineral identified by comparison with tables of known lattice spacing (Jenkins 2002: 671). The degree of blackening of the arcs indicates the intensity of the diffracted X-rays and so gives an indication of the relative concentration of the associated mineral. In practice, every mineral has a large range of d values, corresponding to the different possible crystal planes in the structure, and the intensity of reflection from each plane is slightly different because of different packing densities, and the fact that different elements tend to reflect X-rays with differing efficiency.

More modern systems (diffractometers) follow the same principles but the diffracted X-rays are detected with a solid state detector, as described earlier. Typically, the X-ray source is static and the sample and detector are rotated, with the detector moving at twice the angular velocity of the sample to maintain the equivalent angle. Such instruments typically make use of relatively large samples compressed into the window of a 35 mm sample holder. However, where the sample size is restricted, as is common with archaeological applications, a smaller sample (a few mg) can be attached to a silica wafer. In all cases the sample needs to be finely ground to ensure a uniform diffracted beam.

Computer software packages assist in matching the unknown diffraction patterns with a stored database. Problems arise if the sample contains more than one mineral species, since the pattern for each species gives rise to a complex overlapping pattern that cannot be easily interpreted. If one species can be easily identified and its reflections subtracted from the pattern, it may then be possible to identify a second species. Three species becomes even more complicated. In such circumstances it is advisable if possible to physically sort ("pick") the sample into different minerals under the microscope before

(a)

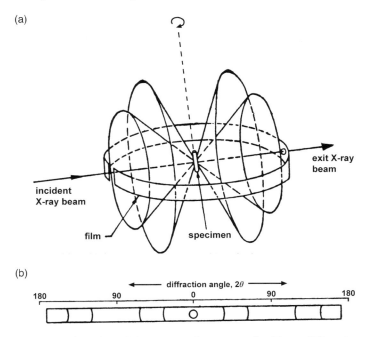

exit X-ray
beam

incident
X-ray beam

film

specimen

(b)

diffraction angle, 2θ

180   90   0   90   180

Figure 5.8 A Debye–Scherrer powder camera for X-ray diffraction. The camera (a) consists of a long strip of photographic film fitted inside a disk. The sample (usually contained within a quartz capillary tube) is mounted vertically at the center of the camera and rotated slowly around its vertical axis. X-rays enter from the left, are scattered by the sample, and the undeflected part of the beam exits at the right. After about 24 hours the film is removed (b), and, following development, shows the diffraction pattern as a series of pairs of dark lines, symmetric about the exit slit. The diffraction angle (2θ) is measured from the film, and used to calculate the d spacings of the crystal from Bragg's law.

analysis. The sensitivity of the powder X-ray diffraction method depends on the mineral concerned: a well-crystallized mineral for which a particular reflection happens to be strong can be detected at the 1% level, whereas for a poorly crystallized mineral, concentrations in excess of 10% may be necessary. A diffractometer can detect species if present in amounts greater than 5%; amounts of 0.1% are detectable using a powder camera.

5.5 Other X-ray related techniques

Proton induced X-ray emission (PIXE)

Protons can also be used instead of X-rays or electrons to create the initial vacancies in the inner electron shells, giving rise to a method known as proton induced X-ray emission (PIXE). In these instruments a high intensity, highly focused beam of protons is produced by a van de Graaff accelerator, which can be focused and steered just like an electron beam (Mando 1994). A beam diameter of the order of microns is possible (Johansson and Campbell 1988), giving spatial resolution similar to that obtainable by electron beam microanalysis. The proton beam strikes the sample, producing inner shell vacancies, which, as before, may de-excite via emission of characteristic X-rays, which are detected using an energy dispersive detector.

The major advantage of this instrument over the electron microprobe is that protons, being heavier and accelerated to a higher energy than electrons, tend to suffer less energy loss on their passage through the sample, giving rise to less bremsstrahlung and therefore producing a lower X-ray background (see above). Detection levels in conventional PIXE may be as low as 0.5–5 ppm for a wide range of elements. For archaeological applications the other main advantage is that the proton beam can be focused onto a sample outside the accelerator (i.e., not in a vacuum chamber) which removes the need for sampling. Of course, in this case, the passage of the primary beam and (more importantly) the characteristic X-rays through air limits the sensitivity of the method, particularly for the lighter elements, as discussed above. Even so, limits of detection of better than 100 ppm have been reported for elements above calcium in the periodic table. Therefore, PIXE may be more appropriate than electron microscope based microanalysis for small areas of light materials (Perezarantegui *et al.* 1994).

Particle induced gamma ray emission (PIGME or PIGE)

This method does not involve X-rays, but follows similar principles to the methods discussed above, and is therefore included here. In PIGE the nucleus, as opposed to the orbital electrons, is excited with charged particles, typically protons. Gamma rays are emitted as the nucleus returns to the ground state – for historical reasons electromagnetic radiations emitted from the nucleus are called gamma rays rather than X-rays, even though the wavelength ranges of these two radiations overlap. The gamma rays are usually detected by solid sate germanium detectors and their energy is characteristic of the element, and therefore their measurement can give elemental composition and their yield can quantify concentration. This method is mainly appropriate for lighter elements (such as Li, F, Na, Mg, and Al) and is typically used in conjunction with PIXE. Detection limits vary from element to element but are typically 10–100 ppm (Ewing 1985: 219).

X-ray photoelectron spectroscopy (XPS)

This technique is also known as *electron spectroscopy for chemical analysis* (ESCA). Although it is concerned with the detection of electrons, it is discussed here because the way in which the photoelectrons are produced is fundamental to the XRF process. As described above, an incident X-ray photon produces an excited ion by ejecting an inner shell electron. The excited ion will then relax by either the Auger or the X-ray fluorescence process. The ejected inner shell electron, however, has a kinetic energy E_k which is given by:

$$E_k = h\nu_i - E_b$$

where $h\nu_i$ is the energy of the incident photon and E_b is the binding energy of the ejected electron. E_b is characteristic of the electronic structure of the parent atom, and therefore of the elemental species. If E_k is measured, the electron energy spectrum can be used to determine binding energy using the above relationship. Since binding energies are affected by bonding, XPS provides information on the chemical environment of the species, unlike XRF, which is largely unaffected by chemical bonding. Energy differences of 10 eV are observed between different bonding states of the same element. It, therefore, can provide structural information compatible with that obtained by nuclear magnetic resonance and infrared spectroscopy. In chemical analysis terms, its usefulness lies in its ability to measure very light elements (e.g., carbon), but it is limited to surfaces, since photoelectrons have low kinetic energies ($\sim$ 1 keV) and are absorbed if they originate from deeper than 20–50 Å within the solid. A review of the method is given by Turner (1997).

5.6   A cornucopia of delights – archaeological applications of X-ray analysis
XRF and electron microprobe analysis have become routine techniques in the investigation of elemental composition for a wide variety of archaeological materials and numerous examples can be found in the relevant literature, such as the journals *Archaeometry*, *Journal of Archaeological Science*, *X-ray Spectrometry*, *Nuclear Instruments and Methods in Physics*, and specialist reports including British Archaeological Reports and English Heritage Ancient Monuments Laboratory Reports. XRD has a somewhat more limited scope but for specific archaeological questions it provides information that cannot be obtained with other methods. Newer methods, such as PIXE, PIGE, XPS, and synchrotron X-ray techniques, are gradually gaining popularity for specific applications.

Applications of XRF and analytical electron microscopy
In archaeology, the main application of EDXRF is for rapid identification and semiquantitative analysis of a wide range of materials including metals and their alloys, ceramics, glass, jet, faience, pigments, glazes, gemstones, and industrial debris. This makes the method ideal as a preliminary analytical survey method, for example prior to XRD to narrow the scope of analysis, or for rapid identification of composition for conservation purposes. WDXRF has found more restricted application except in the study of ceramics and vitreous tephra (volcanic glass), where the material can be treated effectively as geological samples. A major advantage of EDXRF is its use as a "nondestructive" technique on full-sized museum objects. However, as only the surface layer

(a millimeter at most) is analyzed, problems of surface inhomogeneity can be very serious. Interpretation of such data must take this into account in some cases, e.g., surface enrichment of coins, corrosion products on metals, de-alkalization of glasses. Careful sample preparation is required if the intention is to determine the original underlying composition of the object. Often, realistically, the data can only be qualitative, identifying presence/absence, or semiquantitative, giving an approximate indication of concentration.

Electron microprobe analysis is virtually the only readily available method of analyzing small regions such as those produced in multiphase ceramics and metals. It is also vital for the study of small particles in biological tissues. It is widely used for grain boundary studies, and also for studying corrosion and diffusion phenomena in the solid state. The small spot size means that different layers within the same sample can be analyzed, for example the glaze, underglaze, and fabric of a pot can be analyzed separately, or even multiple paint layers from a painting.

There are a large number of examples of the use of XRF in distinguishing pottery shards from different regions, usually in combination with other methods. Pollard and Heron (1996: 134–43) provide a detailed account of the use of XRF and AAS in investigating the relationship between Roman "Rhenish" wares and *terra sigillata*. Druc *et al.* (2001) describe the use of SEM–EDX to establish patterns of ceramic exchange in Peru, and Leung *et al.* (1998) conducted a similar study on Chinese porcelain. The surface sensitive nature of XRF can be used to advantage in addressing specific questions. For example, Al-Saad (2002) and Duffy *et al.* (2002) investigated the development of techniques of glazing ceramics in Jordon and eighteenth-century North America respectively. An XRF study of native Brazilian pottery not only looked at the body of the ceramic but also the surface decoration, identifying differences in the sources of raw materials for each (Appoloni *et al.* 2001). The development of portable XRF systems has allowed the analysis of materials that cannot be transported or sampled, such as the bluestones at Stonehenge (Williams-Thorpe and Thorpe 1992), British stone axes (Williams-Thorpe *et al.* 1999), and museum artifacts (Fiorini and Longoni 1998, Janssens *et al.* 2000).

One of the strengths of XRF lies in its applicability to a wide variety of materials. There has been considerable interest in the use of XRF and spatial analysis to look at the trade and exchange of obsidian in both Russia (Kuzmin *et al.* 2002) and the US (Giauque *et al.* 1993, Bayman 1995). Other artificial glasses, such as Italian medieval glass (Bertoncello *et al.* 2002), Chinese glass beads (Miksic *et al.* 1994) and fifteenth- to seventeenth-century glass vessels excavated in Antwerp (Janssens *et al.* 1998a) have been successfully grouped by composition, although identifying a specific source for raw materials using only major and minor elements is difficult (Wilson and Pollard 2001). Applications to lithic materials have included the investigation of jasper artifacts (Warashina 1992, King *et al.* 1997) and stone axe production in Ireland (Mandal *et al.* 1997). A number of studies have also applied the method to distinguishing jet from other black lithic materials (Hunter *et al.* 1993). Recently, the method has been used to characterize suitable soils for use in reburial of archaeological sites (Canti and Davis 1999). A wide variety of applications to metal studies include mechanisms of corrosion of silver coins (Linke and Schreiner 2000) and copper artifacts (Spoto *et al.* 2000, Giumlia-Mair *et al.* 2002); the study of early scientific instruments (Mortimer 1989); patinas on metals (Wadsak *et al.* 2000); and tin processing (Yener and Vandiver 1993).

Applications of XRD
The key characteristic of XRD is its ability to identify crystalline minerals. The primary use of the powder XRD method has been the identification of clay minerals in pottery in order to characterize pottery types and to investigate sources for raw materials. Recent examples of such applications include Hispanic pottery from Teotihuacán, Mexico (Ruvalcaba-Sil *et al.* 1999), Late Bronze Age pottery from Crete (Buxeda i Garrigos *et al.* 2001), ceramics from Syria (Eiland and Williams 2001) and Iberian amphora (Petit-Dominguez *et al.* 2003). XRD also allows the examination of firing temperatures, as different minerals are destroyed or begin to form at different temperatures, for example in the study of daub by Parr and Boyd (2002). XRD (in combination with some NAA) was used to demonstrate that Rouletted Ware from the Indonesian Island of Bali came from the same geological source as examples of similar pottery from Sri Lanka and south India, suggesting trade networks linking the areas in the first century BC (Ardika and Bellwood 1991). Other applications include the identification of pigments such as those on Roman pottery in Italy (De Benedetto *et al.* 1998, Sabbattini *et al.* 2000), in glazed pottery (Clark *et al.* 1997), and Mexican wall paintings (Rodriguez-Lugo *et al.* 1999). XRD is also commonly used in the study of corrosion products formed on the surface of metals, including iron (Dillman *et al.* 2002) and copper alloys (Spoto *et al.* 2000; Giumlia-Mair *et al.* 2002). Other degradation mechanisms have also been studied by XRD, including the weathering of ancient marble (Moropoulou *et al.* 2001) and ivory (Godfrey *et al.* 2002).

One area in which XRD has proved particularly valuable has been in the study of diagenetic changes in bone, enamel, and dentine (Weiner and Bar-Yosef 1990, Hedges *et al.* 1995, Shimosaka 1999). Some studies have focused on chemical and structural changes that occur during fossilization and the consequent implications for dating of such materials (Person *et al.* 1995, Michel *et al.* 1996, Wess *et al.* 2001, Blau *et al.* 2002) and others on using XRD to distinguish heat induced recrystallization, and therefore cooking, from diagenetic processes (Reiche *et al.* 1999, 2002a).

Applications of other X-ray methods

The strengths of PIXE lie primarily in the method's ability to detect low concentrations of elements without needing to subsample. Johansson and Campbell (1988) and Swann (1997) provide detailed reviews of applications. Studies have predominantly concentrated on characterizing pottery and metals based on their minor element composition and attempting to match these to source materials. These have covered Chinese (Fleming and Swann 1992) and American ceramics (Gosser *et al.* 1998, Salamanca *et al.* 2000, Kuhn and Sempowski 2001), copper (Fleming and Swann 1993, Gersch *et al.* 1998), and glass (Swann *et al.* 1993). Insights into technological processes have been provided by PIXE analysis of Roman onyx glass and recipes for its colorants (Fleming and Swann 1994) and lead in Roman mosaic glass (Fleming and Swann 1999). A number of studies have used the surface sensitivity of the analysis and the ability to investigate small areas to study corrosion processes in metals (Swann *et al.* 1992, Abraham *et al.* 2001), glazes (Duffy *et al.* 2002), composition of ink on documents (Cahill *et al.* 1984), pigment source (Erlansdson *et al.* 1999, Ferrence *et al.* 2002, Zoppi *et al.* 2002), and useware on flints (Christensen *et al.* 1998). The nondestructive nature of analysis has led to applications in identifying sources for garnets in Merovingian jewellery (Calligaro *et al.* 2002), geographical differences in workmanship of goldsmiths (Demortier *et al.* 1999), and the classification of coins from first century BC Romania (Constantinescu and Bugoi 2000). Novel applications have included identifying the therapeutic use of dental repairs using healthy tooth tissue in a pre-Colombian human skeleton (Andrade *et al.* 1998), the distribution of elements in archaeological teeth and dentine (Buoso *et al.* 1992, Mansilla *et al.* 2003), and in soil micromorphology (Davidson and Simpson 2001).

As discussed above PIGE is generally used in conjunction with PIXE, its main advantage being the ability to detect lighter elements. Climent-Font *et al.* (1998) applied a variety of ion beam analytical techniques including PIXE and PIGE, along with Auger electron spectroscopy, to characterize bronzes from pre-Roman sites in Spain. A comprehensive investigation of gold jewellery from a variety of regions (Mesopotamia, Greece, Italy, and Mesoamerica) using PIGE, in conjunction with PIXE, allowed distinctions to be made between ancient samples and modern or repaired items (Demortier 1997). A study by Elekes *et al.* (2000) of obsidian sources allowed grouping of samples based on their light element concentration data and allowed comparison of PIGE with LA–ICP–MS on heavier elements in the same samples. Novel research by Reiche *et al.* (1999), combining PIXE and PIGE analyses on archaeological bone, allowed quantification of post-mortem alteration by examining the concentration profile of trace elements in bone sections. A similar approach to the study of fluorine in archaeological bone and dentine demonstrated that fluorine content could not be correlated with the age of the specimens (Reiche *et al.* 2002b).

Transmission electron microscopy has had relatively limited application as an analytical method in archaeology, with a few notable exceptions. Barber and Freestone (1990) used TEM to identify the cause of the dichromatic effect in the Roman glass Lycurgus cup. There have also been a number of applications to the study of pigments in prehistoric paintings (Baffier *et al.* 1999, Pomies *et al.* 1999a, 1999b) and in murals in Mesoamerica (Polette *et al.* 2002) with the aim of identifying pigment source. TEM has also been used to identify weathering mechanisms on ancient marbles and granites in Delos (Chabas and Lefevre 2000) and the causes of degradation of archaeological wood (Kim and Singh 1999). TEM has also been used in conjunction with FTIR to study bone diagenesis (Reiche *et al.* 2002b) and tooth diagenesis (Restelli *et al.* 1999).

6

NEUTRON ACTIVATION ANALYSIS

Neutron activation analysis (NAA) is an analytical method which allows the determination of the concentration of a large number of inorganic elements in a wide range of archaeological materials. Because it offers bulk analyses of solid samples and is sensitive down to the ppm level (and often below) for a wide range of elements, NAA has been one of the standard methods for multielement analysis since the 1950s. Although it was quickly adopted by geologists for lithic analysis, the technique was pioneered by the archaeological chemistry community – a rare example of the earth sciences adopting a technique from archaeology. It was the standard technique for the determination of trace elements in solid samples across a wide range of sciences until the development of ICP and PIXE in the 1980s. Although it is becoming less common now, as a result of the decreased availability of neutron irradiation, a vast amount of chemical data on a wide variety of archaeological materials has been obtained by this method, and if these results are to be used in future, it is important to understand how they were obtained and how they relate to those from other methods. Detailed accounts of the method can be found in Neff (2000) and Herz and Garrison (1998).

6.1 Introduction to nuclear structure and the principles of neutron activation analysis

In essence, NAA involves converting some atoms of the elements within a sample into artificial radioactive isotopes by irradiation with neutrons. The radioactive isotopes so formed then decay to form stable isotopes at a rate which depends on their half-life. Measurement of the decay allows the identification of the nature and concentration of the original elements in the sample. If analysis is to be quantitative, a series of standard specimens which resemble the composition of the archaeological artifact as closely as possible are required. NAA differs from other spectroscopic methods considered in earlier chapters because it involves reorganization of the nucleus, and subsequent changes between energy levels within the nucleus, rather than between the electronic energy levels.

As explained in Chapter 10, the number of protons in the nucleus is called the atomic number (Z) and governs the chemical identity of the atom. The number of neutrons in the nucleus (N) plus the number of protons is given the symbol A, the atomic mass number, i.e.:

$$A = N + Z.$$

The number of protons is unique to the element but most elements can exist with two or more different numbers of neutrons in their nucleus, giving rise to different isotopes of the same element. Some isotopes are stable, but some (numerically the majority) have nuclei which change spontaneously – that is, they are radioactive. Following the discovery of naturally radioactive isotopes around 1900 (see Section 10.3) it was soon found that many elements could be artificially induced to become radioactive by irradiating with neutrons (activation analysis). This observation led to the development of a precise and sensitive method for chemical analysis.

Artificial radioactivity is normally induced by irradiating the sample with low energy (*thermal*) neutrons (with kinetic energies of less than 0.2 eV) within a nuclear reactor. Since neutrons are neutral, they penetrate atoms without having to overcome an electrical energy barrier. A number of nuclear reactions are possible between the incoming neutrons and the constituents of the nucleus. They are conventionally labeled as (*n*, X) reactions, signifying that the incoming particle is a neutron, and that the ejected particle is X, where X might be a proton, an α particle (the helium nucleus, or $^4_2$He), or something else. Perlman and Asaro (1969) have summarized the common reactions as follows:

(n, α) reactions

$$^A_Z X + {}^1 n = {}^{A-3}_{Z-2} Y + {}^4_2 He$$

an example of which is $^{27}_{13}Al(n, \alpha)^{24}_{11}Na$. In this notation, the target element is Al, which undergoes an (*n*, α) reaction, and transmutes to Na.

(n, p) reactions

$$^A_Z X + {}^1 n = {}^A_{Z-1} Y + {}^1_1 H$$

e.g., $^{27}_{13}Al(n, p)^{27}_{12}Mg$, where the target aluminium nucleus is transmuted to magnesium. One particular (*n*, *p*) reaction occurs naturally in the atmosphere when thermal neutrons (produced as a result of cosmic rays interacting with the atmosphere) transmute nitrogen into radioactive carbon – $^{14}_7N(n, p)^{14}_6C$. This is of great interest archaeologically speaking, since it is, of course, the basis of radiocarbon dating.

(n, γ) reactions

$$^A_Z X + {}^1 n = {}^{A+1}_Z X + \gamma$$

e.g., $^{27}_{13}Al(n, \gamma)^{28}_{13}Al$. In this reaction the target nucleus is unchanged chemically, but becomes a heavier isotope by capturing the neutron.

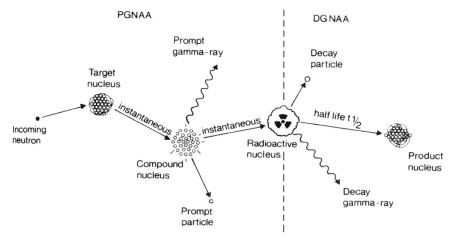

Figure 6.1 Schematic diagram of the nuclear processes involved in NAA. Thermal neutrons strike the target nucleus in the reactor producing a compound nucleus which decays instantaneously, emitting a prompt gamma (measured in PGNAA) and (usually) producing a radioactive daughter. The dotted line shows symbolically the removal of the sample from the reactor, and the subsequent measurement of the decay of the radioactive daughter nucleus (DGNAA). After Glascock (1994) Fig. 1. Copyright John Wiley and Sons Ltd. Reproduced with permission.

The lighter elements in the periodic table undergo chiefly (n, α) and (n, p) reactions, whilst (n, γ) occurs mainly amongst the heavier elements. The most relevant nuclear processes in NAA are (n, p) or, more commonly, (n, γ) reactions. Figure 6.1 shows a schematic diagram of the nuclear processes involved in NAA. As shown above, in an (n, γ) reaction some of the target nuclei capture a neutron to give a new nucleus (known as a *compound nucleus*) of the same element but with a mass greater by one unit – a different isotope of the original species. This compound nucleus is initially formed in an excited nuclear energy state, and it de-excites by emission of a γ particle of fixed energy from the nucleus, and possibly other particles. This γ particle is emitted virtually instantaneously on capture of the neutron, and is known as a *prompt γ*. It can be used analytically (see below) but is usually lost within the nuclear reactor. The new isotope formed by this process may be radioactively unstable and will then decay with a characteristic half-life to form the final product nucleus. It is this secondary decay process which is used in ordinary (*delayed*) NAA. If the daughter nucleus is stable after emitting the prompt γ, then the reaction will not be detected in delayed NAA. For example, when ^{23}Na captures a neutron, it becomes the radioactive nucleus ^{24}Na. A prompt γ particle is emitted virtually instantaneously. The radioactive isotope ^{24}Na decays by beta emission to magnesium with a half-life of approximately 0.623 days. During this decay process another γ particle with a characteristic energy of 1369 keV is also produced, because the emission of the β particle leaves the magnesium nucleus in an excited state, which virtually instantaneously relaxes to the ground state by the emission of a γ particle (nuclear energy levels, like orbital energy levels, are quantized, but the energy differences are so large that transitions between them result in the emission of γ particles). Hence the decay process of the ^{24}Na nucleus can be monitored by measuring the energy of either the β particle or the second γ particle.

The (n, p) reaction, known as transmutation, is also used in the analysis of archaeological material, but is more complex. Here the nucleus captures the neutron, but internal rearrangements occur and a proton is immediately ejected from the nucleus (the "prompt particle") changing the atomic number and therefore the chemical identity of the element. For example, neutron irradiation of titanium does not produce any isotopes of titanium by (n, γ) reactions with half-lives suitable for measurement, but transmutation by the (n, p) reaction produces the radioactive isotope ^{47}Sc, which decays with a half-life of 3.43 days by beta emission, also producing a γ particle with an energy of 159 keV as a result of nuclear relaxation. Other types of nuclear reactions are possible in the reactor as a result of the high neutron fluxes, but (n, γ) and (n, p) are the most important in analysis.

Delayed neutron activation analysis
As a result of slow (thermal) neutron irradiation, a sample composed of stable atoms of a variety of elements will produce several radioactive isotopes of these "activated" elements. For a nuclear reaction to be useful analytically in the delayed NAA mode the element of interest must be capable of undergoing a nuclear reaction of some sort, the product of which must be radioactively unstable. The daughter nucleus must have a half-life of the order of days or months (so that it can be conveniently measured), and it should emit a particle which has a characteristic energy and is free from interference from other particles which may be produced by other elements within the sample. The induced radioactivity is complex as it comprises a summation of all the active species present. Individual species are identified by computer-aided de-convolution of the data. Parry (1991: 42–9) and Glascock (1998) summarize the relevant decay schemes, and Alfassi (1990: 3) and Glascock (1991: Table 3) list γ ray energy spectra and percentage abundances for a number of isotopes useful in NAA.

The sensitivity of the method depends upon the neutron flux, the ability of an element to capture neutrons (the *neutron capture cross-section*) and the half-life of the induced activity (Ewing 1985: 458). This can be expressed as:

$$A = N\sigma\phi\left[1 - \exp\left(\frac{-0.693t}{T_{1/2}}\right)\right]$$

where A is the induced activity at the end of irradiation, N is the number of atoms of the isotope present in the sample, σ is the neutron capture cross-section, ϕ is the neutron flux, t is the time of irradiation, and $T_{1/2}$ is the half-life of the product. In principle, quantitative results can be obtained using this equation, but there are rarely sufficient reliable data to do so and neutron flux in the reactor is often nonhomogenous and varies with time. In practice, quantitative data are obtained using reference samples, as discussed below, and described in detail by Glascock and Neff (2003). Neutron capture cross-sections are energy dependent, but are normally higher at lower neutron energies, which is why neutrons are usually slowed using a moderator to give low energy (thermal) neutrons.

Measuring radioactive emissions from the irradiated samples almost always involves the detection of γ radiation, as this radiation is least influenced by the structure of the material, and since γ rays from radioactive decay are either a single mono-energetic emission or a fixed pattern of mono-energetic emissions, the pattern of γ energies can be used to determine the isotope which has emitted them. The half-life of the radioactive isotope as deduced from the time-dependent intensity profile of the emitted γ rays serves as an additional check on the identity of the isotope created by neutron bombardment (Herz and Garrison 1998). The instrumentation used for detecting γ rays is essentially identical to the instruments used in energy dispersive X-ray fluorescence (Section 5.2), with the exception that the solid state detector is usually a single crystal of germanium rather than silicon. This is because γ rays have energies which are typically 100 times greater than those of X-rays, and germanium is more efficient at measuring energies in this region. The spectra produced generally have relatively sharp peaks corresponding to the γ rays, superimposed on and/or interspersed with relatively broad peaks, arising from the Compton (or inelastic) scattering of γ rays (as discussed in Section 5.2 for X-rays). The height of the sharp peak is proportional to the intensity of the radioactivity of the isotope that produces the peak, unless it is superimposed on a Compton peak.

Because the artificially produced radioisotopes of interest can have a wide range of half-lives in a mixed sample such as a rock or a fragment of pottery, the measuring strategy has a series of distinct steps. Some half-lives are so short (minutes or even seconds) that they have to be measured onsite immediately after removal of the sample from the irradiation source. Other half-lives (of the order of hours) need to be measured within a few days, but those with relatively long half-lives (days to months or even years) are better measured after the short lived isotopes have decayed away, reducing the background radiation. The timing of the measurements needs to be carefully chosen to maximize the chances of detecting the isotopes of interest.

Prompt gamma neutron activation analysis (PGNAA)

PGNAA involves the measurement of the prompt γ rays emitted when the nuclei first absorb the neutrons. By energy and intensity analysis of the prompt γ spectrum it is possible to reveal the elements present and determine their concentrations. Because the analysis is carried out during the irradiation, the method is quicker than delayed NAA, but it needs special equipment on site at the reactor to record the γ spectrum whilst the sample is being irradiated (Glascock *et al.* 1984, Glascock 1994). It can, however, measure some elements more efficiently than delayed NAA (e.g., Pb), since it does not require the daughter nucleus to be radioactively unstable.

6.2 Neutron activation analysis in practice

One of the main advantages of NAA for archaeological materials is that solid samples can be analyzed, and the results represent the analysis of the whole sample as irradiated. This is because neither the incoming neutrons nor the emitted γ particles are subject to significant attenuation in the sample material. If the object is small, e.g., a coin or glass bead, it can usually be analyzed without sampling. Otherwise a small sample (typically 100 mg of powder for rocks, archaeological ceramics, etc.) must be removed from the object to be analyzed. For pottery, the sample is drilled from the interior of the fabric, either using an existing cross-section or by drilling from the surface and discarding the (possibly contaminated) surface layers. Alternatively, a fragment is broken off and pulverized in a mortar. Great care must be taken to avoid contamination during the sampling process, e.g., from drill bits or the mortar. NAA is usually described as "nondestructive", meaning that the irradiated sample is not destroyed. However, apart from the smallest objects which are analyzed whole, a sample has to be removed from the object, and the method should be regarded as "semidestructive", at least for museum display purposes. Even if an entire object can be irradiated, the method is only nondestructive in the sense that the physical appearance is unchanged: there will be a change in the trace element composition, and the sample itself will remain radioactive for several years, depending on the half-life of the isotopes formed. This places a restriction on the rapidity with which an irradiated sample can be returned to the museum whence it might have come. After irradiation the sample cannot be used reliably for dating methods such as thermoluminescence, radiocarbon, or electron spin resonance spectrometry.

Typically, the sample or object to be activated is placed in a container for irradiation. This may be aluminium foil (as aluminium cannot easily be measured by this technique) or silica glass tubes. Several samples and standards are placed in the same container for irradiation, to ensure the same conditions for samples and standards. For example, in the case of ceramics measured at the British Museum laboratories (Hughes *et al.* 1991), powdered samples of 40–80 mg were removed by drilling or abrasion. These were sealed in silica glass tubes (2 mm internal diameter, 33 mm length). Bundles of tubes were wrapped in aluminium foil and several bundles packed into an aluminium irradiation canister. Three possible neutron sources are available: nuclear reactors, which provide the highest neutron flux, large particle accelerators, and radioactive sources. A high flux neutron source means that more isotopes reach detectable levels of radioactivity, making the analysis more sensitive. For this reason, most irradiations are carried out using a nuclear reactor. Here neutrons are produced by the fission of ^{235}U and are emitted with high velocities ("fast" neutrons). For a controlled reaction, the fast neutrons are slowed down using a moderator, e.g., water or graphite, with which fast neutrons can collide without being absorbed. In a typical reactor, the neutron flux is 10^{12}–10^{13} neutrons $cm^{-2}s^{-1}$ and irradiation times vary from a few minutes to several hours. Higher energy neutrons can be used in FNAA (fast NAA) (e.g., Hult and Fessler 1998, Constantinescu and Bugoi 2000) but for most elements slow neutrons are the most effective at causing nuclear transformations.

The γ rays produced are usually measured some time after bombardment of the sample, and the counting strategy depends on the elements of interest, since the half-lives of the radioactive species vary from fractions of a second (making the element very difficult to determine) to thousands of years (which is equally problematic). If the detector is close to the reactor, it is possible to measure the irradiated sample several times – once after a few hours have elapsed (to measure the short-lived species), once after a few days, and then again after a few weeks, when the rapid decay of the short-lived species makes it easier to detect the longer-lived isotopes. Hence, a laboratory with an onsite reactor has an advantage. When this is not possible, measurements are made as soon as samples arrive at the laboratory after irradiation. For example, the British Museum protocol involved measuring ceramic samples in a gamma detector for 3000 seconds on receipt of samples (which was four days after irradiation) and then again for 6000 seconds 18 days after irradiation (Hughes *et al.* 1991). The measurement of successive spectra can also be used to provide a check on isotope identification, as described in Herz and Garrison (1998). For example, if a single nucleus emits three γ rays of different and measurable energies, then these will all be seen to diminish with the same half-life in successive spectra.

As discussed above, the measurement of characteristic γ rays is very similar to the methods used in EDXRF. Early studies used a scintillation counter, typically a crystal of sodium iodide containing a small amount of thallium (Tite 1972). γ ray absorption by these counters produces visible light, which is converted into an electrical pulse using a photosensitive detector. More recently semiconductor detectors have been used, either a lithium drifted germanium crystal, or, more typically, a pure ("intrinsic")

Ge detector. Ionization into electron–hole pairs occurs when γ rays are absorbed by the crystal and an electrical pulse is associated with each absorbed γ ray photon, the amplitude of which is proportional to the energy of the photon analyzed as discussed in Section 5.2 for X-ray detectors. The detection crystal is maintained at liquid nitrogen temperatures to reduce electronic noise. The advantage of a semiconductor counter over a scintillation counter is that the former gives much higher energy resolution and the peaks corresponding to γ rays of a particular energy are much sharper and better resolved. Therefore the difficulty of overlapping peaks, which occurs when a large number of elements are present in the spectrum, is reduced (Tite 1972: 276). In addition, lower concentrations can be measured because the peaks are more easily distinguished from background γ ray counts associated with Compton scattering.

Although quantification of the elements present in the γ spectrum can in theory be achieved from first principles using the equation given above, in practice uncertainties in the neutron capture cross-section and variations in the neutron flux within the reactor mean that it is better to use standards. These standards must be included in each batch of samples irradiated in order to account for variations in neutron flux inside the reactor. For analysis of minor and trace elements calibration is easier than with other analytical methods provided that the major element composition remains reasonably constant, as the γ ray intensity is proportional to concentration over a very wide range of concentrations. However, for analysis of major elements, e.g., silver in silver coins, the relationship between intensity and concentration is more complex, due to progressive absorption of neutrons as they pass through the specimen. In such cases γ ray intensity will also depend on the thickness of the sample and therefore specialized calibration methods are required (Tite 1972: 277).

Detection levels can be as low as 1.5×10^{-5} ppb for very sensitive elements in a suitable matrix (Glascock 1994), but are more typically 10 ppb to 10 ppm. Not all elements can be analyzed by "normal" (i.e., delayed) NAA, because either they do not produce suitable radioactive nuclei, or the resulting spectrum suffers from severe spectral interference. Such problems occur with the analysis of lead and silicon, which precludes total analyses of some metals, ceramics, and glasses. In practice it is hard to separate peaks in γ spectra differing in energy by less than 5%, e.g., a 0.83 MeV γ from nickel would overlap with a 0.84 MeV γ from manganese, but overlapping peaks can frequently be separated by observing the half-lives since the isotope with the shorter half-life will diminish more rapidly, leaving a measurable peak from the isotope with a longer half-life.

6.3   Practical alchemy – archaeological applications of NAA

Archaeometry (using this term to denote the applications of the physical sciences in archaeology) is often accused of being a discipline which has borrowed freely of techniques developed elsewhere (sometimes, perhaps, without being fully aware of the limitations of the method). NAA is one of the few cases in which the archaeological application can undoubtedly claim to have come first. The idea that nuclear reactions might be used for quantitative chemical analysis was first formulated by radiochemists in the 1930s (Glascock and Neff 2003), but it was limited as a viable technique because the only sources of neutrons available at the time were naturally radioactive neutron emitters. As a result of the Manhattan Project to develop the nuclear bomb (1942–5), however, the 1950s saw the construction in the USA of a number of nuclear reactors with sufficient neutron flux to allow the development of NAA as an analytical tool. At this time many of the fundamental nuclear reactions were studied and the necessary measurements of nuclear parameters were made. The "father" of the nuclear bomb, J. Robert Oppenheimer (1904–67), was the first to recognize the potential of NAA as a tool to distinguish the provenance of archaeological ceramics. In 1954, he suggested such an approach to Ed Sayre and R. W. Dodson at the Brookhaven National Laboratory, USA, and the resulting study (on the analysis of Mediterranean pottery) was reported to archaeologists and chemists at Princeton University in 1956 (Sayre and Dodson 1957). Very shortly after this, a group at the Research Laboratory for Archaeology and the History of Art, University of Oxford, began using NAA to study the provenance of coins (Emeleus 1958) and Roman pottery (Emeleus and Simpson 1960). These early studies were carried out using a low resolution sodium iodide crystal detector to detect the γ emissions. The first reported use of the higher resolution lithium-drifted germanium solid state detector was also by Ed Sayre, in his archaeometric study of ancient glass (Sayre 1965). Thus, the first application of NAA was in the field of archaeometry (Harbottle pers. comm.), and only subsequently did geology adopt the method.

Because of the quantity of data produced by NAA, archaeometrists were also amongst the first to develop the applications of what is now called "pattern recognition", with the use of chemical profiles in provenance. By the early 1970s provenance research was carried out by plotting, first by hand and then by computer line-printer, the log of elemental concentration vs. the elements analyzed, and then holding them up to the light to see the similarities (Harbottle pers. comm.). Shortly after this, with increasing computer power, multivariate distance metrics were employed (borrowing here from methods of numerical taxonomy in biostatistics), and the compositional dendrogram was unleashed on the archaeological world. Harbottle (1976, 1986, 1990), Glascock (2000), and Glascock and Neff (2003) have provided reviews of the subsequent applications of NAA in archaeology.

Until ICP and PIXE were developed in the 1980s NAA was the standard analytical method for producing multielement analyses, with detection levels in the ppm or ppb range. Between 1990 and 1992, 50% of the trace element data reported in the major geochemical journals were obtained by NAA (Pollard and Heron 1996: 54). The strengths of NAA lie in its ability to measure both very low and very high concentrations of a wide range of elements with high precision, using small samples. The method is capable of producing data on 40–50 elements per sample, with a rapid rate of sample throughput. The challenge, therefore, principally arises in interpreting the large volume of analytical data rather than obtaining it. The main archaeological application of NAA studies is in the chemical characterization and provenancing of archaeological materials. Such approaches have been applied to obsidian, flint, coins, faience beads, pottery, glass, and jade (Glascock and Neff 2003). The wide use of NAA over a long period of time, particularly in ceramics studies, has led to the creation of large databases of analytical results and several interlaboratory standardizations of methods and calibrations (e.g., Hein *et al.* 2002). It has also led to the development of automated means of interrogating such databases to detect similarity between the contents of the database and analyses of unknown material (Mommsen 1981). The assumptions made in the interpretation of NAA data (and other chemical analytical data) for provenancing have been explored by a number of authors, notably Evans (1989), Neff (2000), Wilson and Pollard (2001), and Glascock and Neff (2003).

NAA as a tool for determining archaeological provenance
The provenancing of ceramics is particularly challenging because of the variability of source material and anthropogenic influences on the product (Evans 1989, Bishop and Blackman 2002, Buxeda i Garrigos *et al.* 2001). NAA provides one of the most versatile provenancing methods for ceramics because it allows the detection of a large number of trace elements which are unlikely to have been deliberately controlled by the potter, and therefore gives the best chance of sourcing the clay. The method works best if used in conjunction with fabric analyses and when applied to a particular form or fabric type for which there are known kilns (Evans 1989). There have been widespread applications of NAA to the provenancing of ceramics through-out the world: examples include Mesoamerica (Neff 2000), Syria (Bakraji *et al.* 2002), Micronesia (Descantes *et al.* 2001), Cyprus (Gomez *et al.* 2002), Egypt (Hancock *et al.* 1986), and China (Xu *et al.* 2001).

The most intense NAA study of archaeological ceramics has been focused on the Bronze Age Mycenaean and Minoan pottery of Greece and Crete, and related areas around the eastern Mediterranean (Mommsen *et al.* 2002). This work began in Berkeley, California, in the 1960s with the work of Perlman and Asaro (1969), who went on to analyze 878 shards of pottery. The results were never fully published: according to Asaro and Perlman (1973, 213), "the question of provenience of the vast quantities of Mycenaean wares has proved perplexing". In 1985 Perlman gave this dataset (handwritten!) to the Manchester radiochemistry group led by V. J. Robinson and G. W. A. Newton, whose own archaeometrical research had largely focused on the NAA of Roman wares from the Mediterranean (Wolff *et al.* 1986). The Manchester group converted these notes into a computer database, and subsequently made this available to the Bonn group in 1990. The Bonn NAA group, led by Hans Mommsen, were already active in the field of Late Helladic (c. 1550–1050 BC) Mycenaean ceramics, and by 1999 their own database of this material consisted of measurements of 30 elements from around 2000 shards (Hein *et al.* 1999). Fortuitously (or, more realistically, because of considerable foresight and the adherence to good scientific practice), the Bonn NAA protocol had been based on that used in Berkeley, including the whole of the NAA measurement procedure and data evaluation method, even to the extent that the Bonn pottery standard was prepared from the same raw clay that was used for the Berkeley standard (Perlman and Asaro 1969), which has actually been widely used as an international calibration standard for archaeological ceramic studies, not just using NAA. This, combined with the observed long-term stability of NAA measurements on the standard, means that the Bonn and Berkeley databases are fully compatible, and can be combined into a single database of over 3000 analyses without difficulty (Mommsen *et al.* 2002).

The problems of intercompatability of this (and other) NAA databases with the contemporary (and equally large) database of analyses of Greek and Cypriot ceramics compiled by OES and AAS in Oxford and Athens have been discussed in Section 3.5. A systematic comparison of 40 shards from Knossos and Mycenae analyzed by both NAA and OES was published by Harbottle (1970). Basically, only "broad agreement" was possible between OES and NAA data, with the OES data showing much greater analytical spread. Consequently, far greater discrimination between chemically similar groupings has been possible with NAA than with either OES or AAS. With hindsight, it might well be suggested that the choice of NAA as an analytical tool for such work has been amply vindicated. Crudely speaking, all of the OES data (and probably, at least as far as provenance goes, all the AAS data as well) are unlikely to be used again – certainly not as a resource against which to compare new data. The AAS data may well have value in studying the technology of pottery production in the Greek and Cypriot world, since it gives a reasonably accurate measure of the major element composition of the vessels, but the NAA database stands as a valuable tool for studying the provenance of such ceramics. This database is a remarkable resource, allowing (in principle, at least), the attribution of likely provenance to "unknown" ceramic material from a large part of the Classical world. And yet the future of this resource is in doubt, partly because of the doubts over the long-term future of NAA as a technique (see below), but more immediately because the impending closure of the Bonn NAA facility calls into question the long-term maintenance of the data. It is to be hoped that this, of all of the constructs of the "golden age" of archaeometry, can be salvaged and maintained for future researchers.

The possibility of analyzing entire small objects and the ability to analyze bulk rather than surface composition has led to much interest in the analysis of coins (Das and Zonderhuis 1964, Gordus 1967) and glass or faience beads. In early studies, Bronze Age faience beads from England, Czechoslovakia, and Scotland were shown to have different compositions from each other and from Egyptian beads, suggesting local manufacture (Aspinall *et al.* 1972). This was an important observation, since faience beads, in the eyes of the diffusionists (see Section 1.2), were thought of as being indicators of the transport of superior ideas and technology from the Near East. The demonstration that they were not, and were locally manufactured, was a major blow to this model. Similar methods have been applied to more recent studies of beads used as trade items in the New World (Hancock *et al.* 1996, 1999b). NAA has also been applied to metal objects other than coins and their geological sources, including copper, lead, and gold in the Old World (Kuleff and Pernicka 1995, Kuleff *et al.* 1995, Olariu *et al.* 1999) and the New (Mauk and Hancock 1998, Moreau and Hancock 1996).

The study of obsidian by NAA has proved to be particularly fruitful because of the relatively limited number of sources and the extent to which it was traded (Beardsley *et al.* 1996, Cook 1995, Darling and Hayashida 1995, Kuzmin *et al.* 2002, Leach 1996). Studies have also extended to include other volcanic materials such as pumice (Bichler *et al.* 1997, Peltz *et al.* 1999). NAA has also been used for the analysis of flint as OES is insensitive and not reproducible due to the effect of the high silica content, and AAS requires significant sample preparation (Aspinall and Feather 1972). The wide range of appropriate materials extends to organic materials such as human bone (Farnum *et al.* 1995), and its exceptional sensitivity to trace elements has led to its wide use in geochemistry (for example in determining trace [ppb] contaminants in waters) and more recently in forensic chemistry.

Compatibility with other techniques
Because of the gradual loss of neutron irradiation facilities (and the general public unpopularity of nuclear sciences), NAA is being slowly replaced by other techniques, chiefly ICP–OES, and more recently ICP–MS, which has comparable sensitivity. It has, consequently, become necessary to carry out research comparing these techniques since there is a need to know how compatible ICP data are with the vast databanks (such as the Aegean databank discussed above) of NAA. This has included comparison of NAA with ICP–OES on bone (Akesson *et al.* 1994); XRF and NAA on ceramics (Garcia-Heras *et al.* 2001); NAA, XRF, ICP–OES, and ICP–MS on ceramics

(Hein *et al.* 2002), and NAA, ICP–OES, ICP–MS, and XRF on ceramics (Tsolakidou and Kilikoglou 2002). As with previous problems created by moving from one analytical method to another (see Section 3.5), the outcome in general is slightly disappointing – the results cannot be compared directly, or not as easily as if they had been obtained by the same techniques. In particular, Hein *et al.* (2002) concluded that the differences between techniques was largely due to differences in the primary calibration standards used, and that "correction factors" could be derived to improve consistency based on average ratios between median values.

The key comparison, however, is between NAA and all the ICP-based methodologies; initially with ICP–OES (Section 3.3), but more critically with ICP–MS in solution mode and particularly in laser ablation mode (Chapter 9). This is crucial, because it is certain that these technologies will become (indeed, already are) the "industry standards" for the analysis of inorganic materials at the sub-ppm level, and if it turns out that the results are compatible with NAA data, then these data can continue to be used. Intercomparisons can be approached in two ways – either by analyzing the same samples by two or more methods (not necessarily for the same suite of elements) to see if the same chemical groupings are generated, or, more rigorously, by analyzing the same material (preferably a set of international standards with certificated values) for the same set of elements (as far as possible) and comparing the data element by element. Initial comparisons between NAA and ICP–OES tended to adopt the first approach – for example, Kilikoglou *et al.* (1997) measured 19 elements by NAA and 24 elements by two ICP–OES procedures on a sample of European obsidians (of which 13 elements – Na, Sc, Fe, Cs, Ba, La, Ce, Sm, Eu, Tb, Yb, Lu, and Hf – were common). They concluded that all three techniques worked successfully for discriminating the various Aegean and Carpathian sources represented, but that NAA was more efficient in the chemical discrimination of neighboring sources – presumably because of greater overall precision of measurement.

Laser ablation ICP–MS (LA–ICP–MS) was established in the early 1990s as a potential routine tool for the measurement of trace and ultra-trace elements in silicate systems for geology. Early studies (Perkins *et al.* 1993) used sample preparation techniques identical to that used to prepare rock samples for WDXRF, i.e., either a pressed powder disk or a glass bead fusion method (see Appendix VIII). Such studies concluded that LA–ICP–MS had "the potential to surpass XRF in terms of the limits of detection achieved and INAA in terms of the speed of analysis" (Perkins *et al.* 1993: 481). It has long been recognized that the main limit on the quantitative performance of LA–ICP–MS is the homogeneity at the trace and ultra-trace level of the solid calibration standards available. Subsequent work (e.g., Hollecher and Ruiz 1995, Norman *et al.* 1996) has demonstrated that some of the international analytical standards provided by NIST (http://www.nist.gov/) in the USA (especially the glass standards NIST 610, 611, 612, and 614) are sufficiently homogeneous to serve as calibration standards for trace element analysis of geological material by laser microprobe. More recent work on archaeological material by Gratuze *et al.* (2001) and James *et al.* (2005) have clearly demonstrated the usefulness of LA–ICP–MS as a tool for the compositional analysis of a wide range of archaeological materials, including obsidian, glass, glazes, and flint. In particular, James *et al.* (2005: 697) conclude that "while absolute accuracy and precision for the ICP data are inferior to INAA, multivariate statistical analysis of data resulting from the two methods demonstrates a high degree of compatibility". Although these conclusions fall somewhat short of demonstrating complete compatibility between NAA and ICP–MS data, it does suggest that, with good QA procedures, the comparability is likely to be reasonable, suggesting that the large banks of NAA data are not obsolete, and therefore are worth saving.

7

CHROMATOGRAPHY

The extraction of samples for organic residue analysis is discussed in Section 13.2. However, in almost all cases, this is not sufficient to enable identification of the sample. Archaeological residues are often a complex mixture of original molecules, degradation products, contamination from the burial matrix and finds processing, storage, etc. Further separation of the mixture, combined with identification of the components, is required. Chromatography is used to separate mixtures into their molecular components. Although chromatography may be used for the separation of inorganic compounds and their different species, this chapter focuses on chromatographic techniques associated with organic molecules. We start with the "classical" techniques of column chromatography and thin layer chromatography (TLC) – now not primarily used as analytical tools in their own right, but often as preparative methods for more detailed analysis. We then discuss the principles of gas chromatography (GC) and high performance liquid chromatography (HPLC). Because of the long history of these techniques, they are well described in general analytical textbooks (e.g., Ewing 1985, Skoog *et al.* 1998), as well as more specialist volumes on chromatographic analysis (e.g., Ahuja 2003, Poole 2003). The technique of GC is described in detail by Baugh (1993). We defer a discussion of mass spectrometric techniques coupled to chromatography until Chapter 8.

7.1 Principles of chromatography

Chromatography separates molecules by their physical behavior, and not by their chemical reactions. Therefore, the determining factors in chromatographic separation are molecular weight, functional group types, and molecular shape. All these factors determine the types and strengths of intermolecular bonding present (see Section 11.3), and it is the exploitation of this which causes separation of complex mixtures. The separation of different molecules is determined by the way they interact with two different phases within the chromatographic system. One of these phases is *stationary* and the other is *mobile*. As shown in Table 7.1, there are four main chromatographic techniques, each using different combinations of mobile and stationary phases.

In all chromatographic techniques, the sample to be separated passes through the system carried by a solvent (the mobile phase). The rate at which

Table 7.1. *Definition of the four main chromatographic techniques with a description of the associated stationary and mobile phases.*

Technique	Stationary phase	Mobile phase
Thin layer chromatography (TLC)	Solid (silica gel)	Liquid (solvent, often a mixture). Also called developer.
Classical column chromatography	Solid (silica gel)	Liquid (solvent, often a mixture). Also called eluent.
Gas chromatography (GC)	Bound liquid in matrix	Gas (H_2 or He).
High performance liquid chromatography (HPLC)	Bound liquid in matrix	Liquid (solvent, often a mixture).

it moves through is determined by the degree to which it "sticks" to the stationary phase. If it has a low affinity (i.e., does not "stick" very well), it will pass through quickly; if it has a high affinity, it will pass through slowly. Thus a mixture of compounds is separated according to how strongly each component "sticks" to the stationary phase. The first compound to elute (pass through) the system is that which "sticks" least, and the last is that which "sticks" most. In fact, in all chromatographic techniques, the components to be separated are partitioned between the stationary and mobile phases. This is a dynamic equilibrium, where the components compete with molecules of the mobile phase to interact with the active sites of the stationary phase. The amount of interaction determines to what extent the components will "stick", and therefore be separated. It is vital, therefore, that the stationary phase is selective for the components to be separated. If this is too great, however, the components will be strongly bound and not released at all; if too weak, there will be no chromatographic separation. It is also important that the components be soluble in the mobile phase, as it is movement in the mobile phase which causes the separation. It is therefore not surprising that, due to the large variety of organic molecules, different chromatographic systems are used for their separation and that optimization of the conditions is often required.

Resolution (R) is the measure of the chromatographic separation of two components. Ideally, mixtures should be completely separated, but in many instances spots or peaks will overlap (*co-elute*). For gas chromatography, where the components are isolated as Gaussian peaks, the resolution is given by:

$$R = \frac{(\text{Retention time of peak 2} - \text{Retention time of peak 1})}{0.5 \times (\text{Width of the base of peak 1} + \text{Width of the base of peak 2})}$$

where retention time is the time taken for a particular component to elute from the system, measured from the time the mixture is injected.

An improvement in resolution is often achieved by slight alteration of the chromatographic system (e.g., changing solvents in TLC, or decreasing the rate of heating in GC), but occasionally this is not sufficient. The resolution is clearly dependent on the widths of the peaks, and these will broaden as the components pass to the end of the stationary phase. One way to diminish this effect is to increase the number of theoretical plates (N). This is a theoretical number of partitions between the stationary and mobile phases, and each one can be thought of as a single receptor, or "sticky patch". Therefore, a chromatographic system with the greater number of plates will have the best resolution. A GC capillary column will typically have 5000 plates per meter of column, reducing to $1000 \, m^{-1}$ for a packed column, and from 30 to 30 000 for a TLC plate. However, in practice, a large number of plates requires a large amount of stationary phase, and therefore requires high pressures of mobile phases to drive the sample through the system. This will result in long retention times, which are impracticable.

7.2   Classical liquid column chromatography

Liquid column chromatography uses a glass column (typically 100 cm length by 1 cm diameter) packed with a stationary phase, usually silica gel (Fig. 7.1). The liquid mobile phase (*eluent*) is an organic solvent added to the top of the column and slowly drained from the base under gravity. Commonly, the solvents of the mobile phase are changed during the procedure to provide increasing polarity during the separation (e.g., starting with diethyl ether and moving to dichloromethane and then to methanol). The mobile phase is collected in measured aliquots (fractions) from the base of the column and contains the separated components. The solvent is then removed using a rotary evaporator, and therefore the technique is nondestructive (in the sense that all of the original sample is in theory recoverable). This technique allows the separation of larger amounts of sample (0.1 to 1 g) than the other techniques described here, but due to peak broadening (caused by the many possible migration pathways of the components through the wide diameter of the column), the resolution is not as good. More recently, the main use of liquid column chromatography is as a preseparation of a larger sample size into aliphatic, aromatic, and polar fractions (see Section 11.5) before further analysis by gas chromatography.

7.3   Thin layer chromatography (TLC)

Thin layer chromatography is reproducible, relatively easy to perform, quick, and inexpensive. The resolution of TLC is greater than classical liquid column chromatography, although usually it is still not possible to resolve individual components from a complex mixture. It is, however, able to separate compound classes (e.g., aliphatic from aromatic) and its main use is,

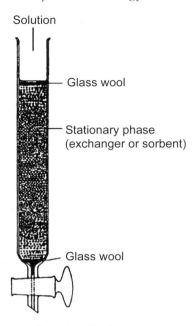

Solution

Glass wool

Stationary phase
(exchanger or sorbent)

Glass wool

Figure 7.1 Diagram of classical liquid column chromatography. The sample is introduced at the top of the column, and the different components travel downwards and are separated. They can be collected in sequence from the tap at the bottom.

therefore, as a preparative technique for unknown samples. One advantage of TLC over classical liquid column chromatography is that it is possible to run known standards alongside unknown samples, thereby providing a tentative identification. As the separated components can be removed from the stationary phase after separation, the technique is nondestructive of the organic sample. These fractions can then be rerun using different mobile phases or by other chromatographic techniques to obtain better resolution.

Thin layer chromatography uses a solid stationary phase applied in a thin layer (c. 1 mm thick) to an inert (glass or aluminium) flat plate. The particle size must be uniform and small, since chromatographic resolution increases as particle size is reduced. The thickness of the layer determines the number of available active sites in the stationary phase, and, therefore, the amount of sample it is possible to put onto the plate, although thinner layers have greater resolution. TLC plates may be bought preprepared or can be made. There are different types of stationary phase, but the most commonly used is silica gel; often this will include 5% gypsum to bind the silica particles to the plate. Another common addition is a fluorescent binder to reveal the presence of compounds when viewed under a UV light. Before use, TLC plates may need to be activated by heating to 100–110°C; this removes water and any volatile components from the stationary phase. It may also be necessary to pre-elute the TLC plate with a polar solvent, such as ethyl acetate, to remove any prior organic contamination. The contaminated stationary phase from the top of the plate should then be removed and the plate reactivated after this procedure.

Samples (~20 mg) are dissolved in a small volume (~1 ml) of volatile solvent (e.g., dichloromethane, DCM). The solution is then taken up in a small capillary tube and added as spots or lines on the origin (~1 cm above the base of the plate) avoiding damage to the stationary phase. Known standards can also be added to the plate at this stage. Once the solvent has evaporated, the plate is stood vertically in a developing tank, which contains the mobile phase to a depth of 0.5 cm below the origin. The air in the developing tank should be saturated with the mobile phase; this is achieved by including a sheet of filter paper in the tank and by keeping the tank sealed. The mobile phase is often made from a mixture of volatile organic solvents, which are sufficiently polar to carry the sample components up the plate, but not too polar so that all the sample is carried in the solvent front. To avoid contamination, the highest purity grade of solvent should be used. Once the mobile phase has migrated to near the top of the plate, the plate is removed from the tank. The position of the solvent front should be noted, and the mobile phase left to evaporate from the plate.

Figure 7.2 shows a typical TLC plate. Some components are visible to the naked eye, but others may need to be visualized. Commonly this can be achieved under a UV light if the compounds themselves fluoresce, or if they alter the behavior of the fluorescent binder. It is also possible to spray the plate with dye or oxidize the compounds with sulfuric acid to make them visible, although the last method will result in the destruction of the sample. Once identified, areas of the stationary phase can be scraped from the inert plate and solvent extracted to yield the separated components for further analysis, if needed.

The distance that the spots or bands move up the plate is measured relative to the distance the solvent front has moved from its point of origin. Thus the retention factor (Rf) is:

$$Rf = \frac{\text{Distance of solute from origin}}{\text{Distance of solvent front from origin}}.$$

The factors affecting Rf include the quality of the stationary and mobile phases, the thickness and activity of the layer, and the amount of sample. Although standards may have the same Rf value as the sample, this does not uniquely identify the compound. For archaeological samples, the best identification achievable is only at a general class level (e.g., triacylglycerols, fatty acids, aromatic, or aliphatic) and not to individual molecular components.

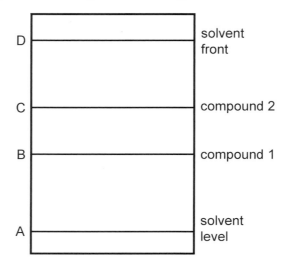

Figure 7.2 Diagram of a TLC plate. The plate is suspended vertically in the solvent containing the compounds to be separated (the solvent level or origin), and over time the compounds and solvent migrate up the plate to different heights and are separated. The retention factor (Rf) for compound 1 is calculated as AB/AD, and for compound 2 AC/AD.

7.4   Gas chromatography (GC)

Gas chromatography (GC or, less commonly, GLC) is the most widely used separation technique for volatile samples. The resolution is sufficient to routinely separate components, such as homologous series, saturated from unsaturated fatty acids, terpenoids, triacylglycerols, etc. The use of a mass spectrometer to identify the separated components (GC–MS) is discussed in Section 8.4.

Gas chromatography is more complex than classical column chromatography or TLC, and it is therefore referred to as an instrumental technique. A gas (the *carrier gas*), which is usually hydrogen or helium, is used as the mobile phase. The stationary phase is usually a thin layer lining the inside of a capillary column. Due to the thin stationary phase, only small quantities of samples can be analyzed. Another drawback is that the samples must be sufficiently volatile to be carried in the gaseous mobile phase. This generally limits the analysis to lipids of molecular weight similar to or less than the triacylglycerols, and it is often not possible to directly analyze lipids with polar functional groups. However, by chemically replacing or altering the functionalities using a *derivatization* prior to injection on the column, it is possible to increase the volatility and make many components amenable to analysis (Drozd 1981, Blau and Halket 1993). Commonly used derivatization techniques include *silylation*, using BSTFA (N, O-bis(trimethylsilyl)trifluoroacetamide), often used with 1% TMCS (trimethylchlorosilane) for difficult derivatizations (e.g., Evershed 1993); *methlyation*, using diazomethane

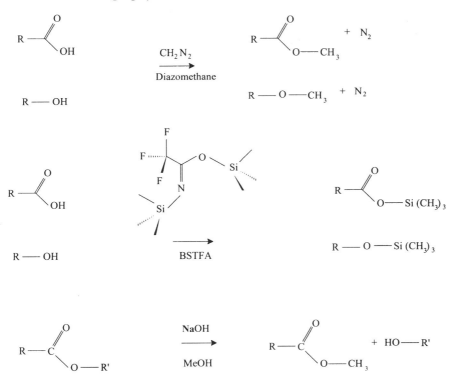

Figure 7.3 Derivatization of organic acid and alcohol compounds by diazomethane (CH_2N_2: top two reactions); by BSTFA (N, O-bis(trimethylsilyl) trifluoroacetamide: middle two reactions), and transmethylation of fatty acid esters by saponification using methanolic sodium hydroxide.

(Fales *et al.* 1973) or BF_3 in methanol; or *transmethylation* during saponification using methanolic sodium hydroxide (Stern *et al.* 2000). The effect of these processes on alcohol or carboxylic acid functionalities is shown in Fig. 7.3.

A schematic drawing of a typical GC system is shown in Fig. 7.4. Samples are dissolved in a small quantity of volatile solvent and injected (up to 1 µl volume) using a special syringe through the injector port of the instrument. There are two common types of injector port. In the on-column injector, the fine needle of the syringe penetrates into the start of the column, therefore the whole sample is available for separation, and there is no discrimination between the components. In the split-splitless injector, the sample is injected into a lined cylinder where the gas either sweeps some of the sample into the column or out of the instrument; the ratios of this split can be altered, and this technique is commonly used for unknown or "dirty" samples. GC originated using wide bore (6 mm diameter) packed columns a few meters in length filled with an inert material coated with a liquid stationary phase, as described for classical column chromatography. This resulted in poor

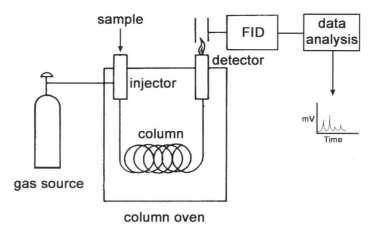

Figure 7.4 Schematic diagram of a gas chromatography (GC) system. The carrier gas enters from the left, and the sample is injected into the gas flow and is carried through the capillary column inside a temperature-controlled oven where the components are separated. Detection here is by flame ionization, where the eluent increases the conductivity of the flame.

resolution, because of the many possible pathways along the column, although these columns are still used for gaseous samples. Modern capillary columns are long (15 to 60 m), narrow internal diameter (0.2 to 2 mm), hollow tubes. The gaseous mobile phase passes through the centre of the column and the stationary phase is coated on the interior surface, where it is often chemically bonded to the wall materials. These were originally glass, but have since been replaced by fused silica, which is inert and highly flexible. Columns are bought preprepared with differing polarities of mobile phase, length, diameter, and thickness of mobile phase – all of which determine the chromatographic resolution, amounts, and types of sample which it is possible to separate, and the analysis time. The column is coiled (to save space) within an accurately temperature-controlled oven, which is commonly programmed to rise in temperature from 50 up to 400°C during the analysis. This rise in temperature aids the chromatographic separation by increasing the volatility of the molecules and encouraging them into the mobile phase. As the components elute from the column, they are measured with a detector. There are many different types of detectors, but the one most commonly used is the flame ionization detector (FID). The FID is attached to the end of the capillary column and burns the eluents in a mixture of hydrogen and air as they emerge. The measurement taken is the conductivity of the resulting flame. The carrier gas alone produces few ions, and therefore a low current will be measured. If an organic component is present in the carrier gas it will produce a greater number of ions, and therefore greater current flow, in proportion to the quantity of eluent. If the current is plotted against time (to produce a *chromatogram*), peaks are observed as components elute, generally with the low molecular weight, low polarity components eluting first (having a shorter retention time).

GC cannot be used to directly identify the molecular species present. It is, however, possible to infer their identity by comparison with known standards. One method involves running the standard alone and comparing the retention time with that of the unknown compound. The same retention time is likely to be caused by the same compound. A more secure method is to analyze the unknown sample, and then to add a known amount of the standard. If the standard corresponds to one of the components of the mixture, a subsequent analysis will then show a corresponding increase in peak area.

Quantification

Unlike previous chromatographic techniques, the response of the GC detector is proportional to the amount of component, and therefore quantification is possible. In practice, quantification is carried out by adding a known weight of standard to a known weight of sample and then comparing the area of the peak for the standard to the unknown peaks. This internal standard method should use a standard which is available in very high purity, and should be chosen so that it does not co-elute with other components. In addition, it should not be so volatile that it is preferentially lost before analysis or insufficiently soluble that it does not dissolve in the solvent (the use of a C_{34} *n*-alkane is commonly reported in the literature). Usually, the standard is added immediately prior to analysis by GC, but it is also possible to add the standard to the sample *before extraction*. This method enables an estimate of the efficiency of the extraction protocol, but must also be combined with the use of a different internal standard. Although the area of each peak is proportional to the quantity of the eluting component, the detector does not have exactly the same response to different functional groups or even within a homologous series. Therefore, unless a relative response factor of one is assumed, it is preferable to use an internal standard of similar functionality and molecular weight to the unknowns. For example, an odd carbon-numbered fatty acid, such as C_{21}, may be a good idea for fatty acid analysis as this odd carbon number is unlikely to occur naturally in the samples and is of similar molecular weight to the commonly found fatty acids. It is also possible to measure the relative response factors of different molecules, by making a test solution of a variety of standards of known weights and then comparing the peak areas.

Chiral compounds

It is possible to use chromatography to separate chiral compounds (enantiomers; see Section 11.6). This technique uses a stationary phase which is often very specific to the compounds to be separated, and achieves this by itself being chiral (but these columns can be expensive). The intermolecular forces which lead to the preferential binding of one enantiomer over another are very weak, and careful optimization of instrumental conditions is required. Both GC and HPLC (below) techniques can be used for chiral separations, and applications include amino acid racemization (Pollard and Heron 1996: 271–301) and separation of isomeric terpenoids.

7.5   High performance liquid chromatography (HPLC)

High performance liquid chromatography (HPLC), sometimes referred to as high *pressure* liquid chromatography, commonly uses liquids for both mobile and stationary phases. In some ways, it is a return to classical column chromatography, but as an instrumental technique. The major advantage over GC is that samples need not be volatile, but only soluble in solvents, making amino acid and drug analysis the major uses. The instrumentation, however, is more complex than GC because of the need to handle a liquid mobile phase (Fig. 7.5). Many systems have the facility for changing the composition of the mobile phase as the run progresses, by mixing solvents from two or more reservoirs (*gradient elution*). The mobile phase is pumped through the column by a device which can give a high pressure liquid and control the flow rate. The sample (dissolved, if possible, in the solvent which comprises the mobile phase) is injected into a microsampling injector valve, which holds the sample in an injection loop, and releases a fixed volume (usually 10 or 20 μl) into the liquid flow at the top of the column. Autosamplers can be used to relieve the tedium and ensure better reproducibility of injection. Columns for HPLC need to be sturdy to withstand the high pressures (up to several hundred atmospheres). They are made of stainless steel, or glass-lined metal for chemical inertness, and are straight, with a length of 10–30 cm. They are usually fitted with a guard column or an in-line filter to prevent unwanted particles entering the column, and are housed in an oven to allow temperature control. Once the liquid has passed through the column and been separated it is fed into a detector which quantifies the eluting compounds. Several types of detector are available, depending on the application, but the two most common types are *ultraviolet-visible spectrophotometers* or *fluorescence* detectors. The UV/visible (UV/vis) detectors come in a variety of forms, but the most common type is a fixed wavelength detector. The mobile phase plus separated compound passes through a detector cell (typically of 2–8 μl capacity) through which is focused radiation of the selected wavelength, and the mobile phase only passes through a reference cell. The absorbance at this wavelength is measured as the difference between the absorbance of the two cells, as determined by a photometer. Many compounds absorb around the 254 nm wavelength, which is one of the wavelengths emitted from a medium

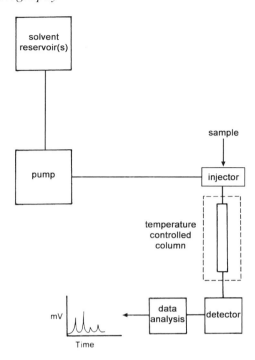

Figure 7.5 Schematic diagram of a high performance liquid chromatography (HPLC) system. The solvent(s) are pumped through the system, and the sample injected just before the column where separation occurs. Detection is often by UV/visible spectrophotometry at a fixed wavelength.

pressure mercury vapor lamp, and so this is usually the wavelength chosen. A fluorescence detector is similar to a UV/vis detector, but the irradiating light illuminates the sample cell and the resulting fluorescence is detected at right angles to it. Since not all compounds exhibit fluorescence to UV/vis radiation, a fluorophor may have to be added to the sample by derivatization prior to injection. The fluorescence detector is generally considerably more sensitive (perhaps by two or three orders of magnitude), but the need to sensitize the sample to the fluorescing radiation may make the sample preparation more complex. It is now possible to connect the output of an HPLC to a mass spectrometer by the removal of the mobile phase (HPLC–MS), so that the vacuum within the mass spectrometer is maintained. *Reverse phase HPLC* is a derivation of the normal HPLC technique in which the polarity of the mobile phase is greater than the stationary phase.

7.6 Sticky messengers from the past – archaeological applications of chromatography
Many of the organic residues found in archaeological contexts are associated with ceramic vessels; the additional data provided by such analyses can,

therefore, supplement more traditional archaeological approaches (e.g., analysis of vessel shape, ceramic type, use wear, etc.) and is the only way to directly determine the organic contents. Important considerations which will determine the applicability of the technique are the properties of the ceramic vessel such as the porosity, slip, burnishing, the extent of use and reuse with different materials, and whether certain contents would leave a residue for analysis. These factors have been discussed by Rice (1987) and Heron and Evershed (1993).

Most commonly, the organic material is observed as a visible residue on the surface of an object, but it may also be absorbed within the porous structure of ceramics, where the small pore size is thought to restrict access to degrading microorganisms. Residues may also be found associated with other objects (such as hafting on axes), or as discrete artifacts or amorphous "lumps". As all of these residues are amorphous, it is not possible to identify them without chemical analysis (unless, of course, Faraday's method of tasting, as described in Section 1.1, is applied!). Archaeological residues often only enable one-off, small-scale sampling; this, therefore, implies that the best available analytical technique should be applied. Of those discussed above, GC (and GC–MS) are the most commonly used for lipid residues, and are the "gold standard" for the separation and identification of complex archaeological organic residues. It is not surprising, therefore, that there are few published analyses of archaeological material using classical column or thin layer chromatography, although these methods have been used for fraction separation prior to further analysis by instrumental chromatography (e.g., Passi *et al.* 1981, Connan *et al.* 1992). Few archaeological analyses have used HPLC (e.g., Passi *et al.* 1981), in part due to the easier applicability of GC to lipid analysis, and also due to the fact that only recently has it been possible to combine HPLC with mass spectral peak identification (HPLC–MS).

Many (if not all) of the following studies rely on the *biomarker* approach. This is the matching of a specific organic compound, or preferably a group of compounds, to that of a contemporary plant or animal product. Such chemotaxonomic distinctions rely on there being distinct molecules and distribution patterns present in different materials. It may also be possible to identify "biomarkers" for the preparation and use of these organic materials. So, for example, to identify resins, one would look for terpenoids; for oils and fats, one would expect to find triacylglycerols, fatty acids, and sterols. Identification of the exact molecular structures is, therefore, crucial. It is also important to examine relevant (and correctly botanically identified) modern examples of the materials (e.g., Gunstone *et al.* 1994) which are believed to have been used in the past, with the additional understanding that there may (or, more likely, definitely will) have been changes in these species over time. Because the preservation potential of lipids is much higher than other organic material (cf. DNA, proteins, carbohydrates, sugars; Eglinton and Logan 1991), lipid analysis techniques have been the most commonly applied in archaeological chemistry. It should be remembered, however, that even lipids are still vulnerable to partial and even complete degradation (approximately 50% of likely vessels yield no recoverable lipids). The processes of degradation, and even preferential losses of one component over another, are still poorly understood, and the resulting low levels of indigenous lipids may be further confused by contamination from the burial matrix and during excavation, storage, and analysis. The complex transformation processes of organic material in and out of pots is shown in Fig. 7.6, which illustrates the "life cycle" of a ceramic vessel from production, through to deposition, excavation, and final organic residue analysis, including various processes and the associated movement of organic material into and out of the pot.

Wine

The literature of the analysis of wine residues provides an interesting case study for organic residue analysis (for a review of ancient Egyptian wine and its analysis see Murray *et al.* 2000). Although there is "traditional" archaeological evidence for wine production (e.g., grape seeds, presses, amphorae, etc.), the direct chemical analysis of wine has often not been carried out and much is based on assumptions – e.g., amphorae of a certain shape are *assumed* to contain wine, and resin linings are *assumed* to be associated with wine contents (Hosetter *et al.* 1994). Wine has, however, been one of a few materials to which a wide range of analytical techniques have been applied – e.g., spot tests, IR spectroscopy (McGovern and Michel 1996, McGovern 1997) and chromatography (TLC, GC, HPLC: Badler *et al.* 1990, Formenti and Duthel 1996, McGovern *et al.* 1996, McGovern 1997). However, many of these lack selectivity and sensitivity and, without the use of combined separation and characterization techniques (e.g., GC–MS, HPLC–MS), misinterpretation of degradation products and contamination leads to false positive results (as discussed in Murray *et al.* 2000). More recently, however, the biomarker approach (tartaric acid – a wine marker rarely found in nature other than in grapes – and syringic acid derived from malvidin from red wine) has been more convincingly applied with HPLC–MS/MS separation and identification (Gausch-Jané *et al.* 2004).

Fatty acids, triacylglycerols, and sterols

Fatty acids are carboxylic acids, often with a long aliphatic tail (long carbon chains), which can be either saturated (all single bonds) or unsaturated. They are biosynthesized from two-carbon units (acetate, CH_3COO^-), and therefore usually have an even number of carbons with a range of C_4 to C_{36}, although C_{16} and C_{18} are dominant. Figure 7.7 shows the structure of octadecanoic acid (slearic acid, $C_{18:0}$), *cis*-9-octadecenoic acid (oleic acid, $C_{18:1}$), and

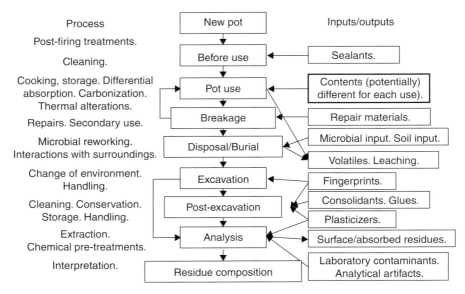

Process		Inputs/outputs
Post-firing treatments.	New pot	
Cleaning.	Before use ←	Sealants.
Cooking, storage. Differential absorption. Carbonization. Thermal alterations.	Pot use ←	Contents (potentially) different for each use).
Repairs. Secondary use.	Breakage ←	Repair materials.
Microbial reworking. Interactions with surroundings.	Disposal/Burial	Microbial input. Soil input. Volatiles. Leaching.
Change of environment. Handling.	Excavation ←	Fingerprints.
Cleaning. Conservation. Storage. Handling.	Post-excavation	Consolidants. Glues. Plasticizers.
Extraction. Chemical pre-treatments.	Analysis ←	Surface/absorbed residues.
Interpretation.	Residue composition	Laboratory contaminants. Analytical artifacts.

Figure 7.6 Possible transformation processes of residues in or on pottery vessels from manufacture through to post-excavation treatments (adapted from Bonfield 1997, by permission of the University of Bradford).

cholesterol. The fatty acids are hydrophobic, although the carboxylic acid functionality, $-COOH$, can ionize to $-COO^-$ making the shorter chain fatty acids slightly water soluble and therefore prone to loss. Saturated fatty acids have a higher melting point due to high degree of packing (e.g., saturated animal fat, such as butter, is semisolid) whilst unsaturated fatty acids, which contain one or more double bonds, usually as the *cis* diastereoisomer (see Section 11.6), have relatively low melting points due to disruption of packing by double bonds (e.g., unsaturated fat, such as vegetable oil, is liquid). *Triacylglycerols* (sometimes referred to by their non-IUPAC name triglycerides) are the main storage form of fats within the body, where their main function is to store energy. Nearly all fats and oils of animal and plant origin consist almost exclusively of triacylglycerols. They consist of a glycerol backbone with three fatty acids linked by ester bonds. *Phospholipids* are abundant in all biological membranes, and contain one phosphoric acid and two fatty acid units. The phosphate group is often linked to a nitrogen-containing molecule. *Steroids* are a type of lipid characterized by a carbon skeleton with four fused rings. Their most important role in most living systems is as hormones. *Sterols* are a subgroup of steroids with a hydroxyl group in the 3-position of the A-ring. *Cholesterol* is a steroid lipid found in the cell membranes of all animal body tissues.

Fatty acids have been reported in a large number of analyses of archaeological residues. They are often associated with cooking vessels (Charters *et al.* 1993), lamps (Evershed *et al.* 1997b), or transport vessels

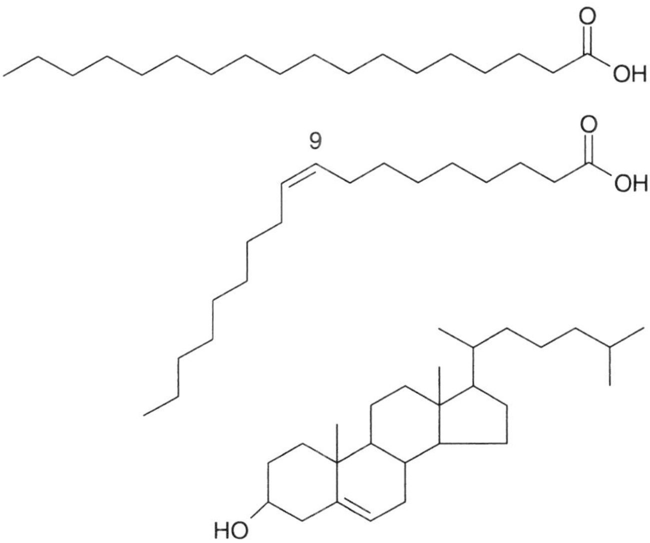

Figure 7.7 Structures of some fatty acids and sterols found in archaeological residues. Upper compound octadecanoic acid (stearic acid, $C_{18:0}$), middle compound *cis*-9-octadecenoic acid (oleic acid, $C_{18:1}$), lower compound cholesterol.

(Condamin *et al.* 1976, Stern *et al.* 2000). Although Condamin *et al.* (1976) identified oil residues from Mediterranean amphorae, their claim of identifying *olive* oil is supported by archaeological evidence alone (similar to the case of wine discussed above), and not by the molecular evidence, which is probably limited to the identification of a generic plant oil. Fatty acids have also been found in preserved human soft tissues (Evershed and Connolly 1988, Evershed 1990) and bones (Evershed *et al.* 1995).

Although fatty acids can be a natural component of a fat or oil (e.g., Gunstone *et al.* 1994), they are also derived from the hydrolysis of triacylglycerols (Dudd *et al.* 1998). It is therefore commonly observed that diacylglycerols, monoacylglycerols, and fatty acids are extracted along with triacylglycerols (e.g., Evershed *et al.* 1990). In addition to hydrolysis, the fatty acids, and in particular the unsaturated fatty acids, are prone to losses caused by bacterial degradation. These will result in the preferential loss of triacylglycerols and the unsaturated fatty acids, with a build-up of odd-carbon numbered and branched fatty acids. Fatty acids may also be lost during the formation of long chain ketones (Raven *et al.* 1997), and from degradation leading to dicarboxylic fatty acids (Passi *et al.* 1993, Regert *et al.* 1998). In the past it has been claimed that it is possible to distinguish animal fat from vegetable oils based on the fatty acids abundances and distributions (Mills and White 1994: 171–2). This is based on the ratio of the $C_{16:0}/C_{18:0}$ fatty acids, which in fresh animal fats ranges from 1 to 2, whilst in plant oils this ratio is greater than 3. However, the archaeological situation may not be so simple, as the $C_{16:0}$ fatty acid is relatively more water soluble than the $C_{18:0}$ fatty acid, and little is known about the loss or generation of either component during degradation. Classification of the origin of archaeological fats cannot be based on fatty acid distributions alone, except perhaps at exceptionally arid sites (Copley *et al.* 2001). In instances where the loss of triacylglycerols is complete (e.g., Stern *et al.* 2000), although the remaining fatty acids may indicate that a plant or animal oil/fat was once present, it is no longer possible to differentiate between the two, let alone attempt to identify the species.

Unlike, for example, the terpenoids, which are limited in their origin and may be associated with a unique source, the fatty acids are ubiquitous in the environment. This means that contamination from associated soil, the fingers of excavators, and laboratory reagents may be a serious problem. This is especially so when the yields of extracted lipids are low, and therefore contamination can be significant. Consequently, it is vital for the researcher to demonstrate that contamination is not a problem by analyzing method blanks. If possible, extracts of associated soil (Heron *et al.* 1991) and vessels from the same contexts but not associated with an organic use, e.g., kiln wasters (Condamin *et al.* 1976), should also be analyzed. The researcher should also show, by demonstrating a gradient of decreasing concentration of the fatty acids from the interior to the exterior, that the exterior surfaces of the vessels are not contaminated (Condamin *et al.* 1976, Stern *et al.* 2000). The distribution of residues within a single vessel can also be informative about vessel use. Charters *et al.* (1993, 1995) extracted lipids (beeswax and animal fat) from different parts of the same vessel (base, body, and rim) from a number of Late Saxon/Early Medieval vessels of different types. The distribution of extracts was found to differ according to the vessel shape, leading to a confirmation that form was related to function.

Soils have also been examined directly, not for evidence of possible contamination, but as a study of manuring practice in medieval to early modern Orkney, Scotland. The sterols campesterol, sitosterol, and 5β-stigmastanol were used as biomarkers for ruminant animal manure and coprostanol for omnivorous animal manure, with hyodeoxycholic acid used to further define the manure as coming from pigs (Bull *et al.* 1999, Simpson *et al.* 1999). It is rare to be able to extract sterols from such samples because their natural abundance is generally low. If they can be found, however, then they are useful as unambiguous biomarkers for either plants or animals.

The possibility of identification of milk production in the archaeological record has been debated for the last 100 years, and although there is archaeological and ethnographic evidence (e.g., bone assemblages, lactose intolerance), the molecular evidence until recently has been unconvincing. Many of the problems associated with the identification of milk residues are due to degradation (Dudd *et al.* 1998). It is now possible to distinguish between ruminant and nonruminant animal fats based on $\delta^{13}C$ isotopic data (using GC–C–IRMS – see Section 8.4) for fatty acids (Evershed *et al.* 1997a, Mottram *et al.* 1999). Dudd and Evershed (1998) have measured the isotopic composition of individual fatty acids and can distinguish milk from adipose (fat) residues. Using this approach, the history of dairying has been charted from the Neolithic in the British Isles (Copley *et al.* 2005a, 2005b, 2005c). The ability to detect milk has been confirmed by Craig *et al.* (2000), who identified it in Iron Age cooking vessels from the Western Isles of Scotland, not from lipid analysis, but by detecting milk-specific proteins (bovine α-casein) using immunochemistry. This finding of 2500-year-old milk proteins has shown that farming in the marginal environment of the Scottish Atlantic coast was surprisingly well developed.

Terpenoids

The terpenoids are the largest family of natural products, with more than 23 000 described. They are secondary products of plants, i.e., they are not involved in primary metabolism, but often have very specific functions and are therefore produced in relatively small quantities. In the past they have been used by humans for a wide range of purposes including perfumes, psychoactives, medicines, flavors, adhesives, and waterproofing agents (Langenheim 1990, Pollard and Heron 1996: 239–70, Lampert *et al.* 2002). They occur in all parts of plants but are often extruded as the major component of resins. Although their biosynthesis is more complicated, the terpenoids can be thought of as being composed from an integral number of isoprene units (C_5H_8, 2-methylbutadiene, Fig. 7.8). Subsequent modification of the structure (rearrangements and functional group changes) gives rise to the wide range of terpenoid types (Table 7.2).

Compared to many other organic materials found in the archaeological record, the terpenoids generally exhibit good preservation (Eglinton and Logan 1991). However, degradation products are often present and the lower molecular weight terpenoids (monoterpenoids and sesquiterpenoids) are often lost due to their volatility (they may be extracted in exceptional circumstances, for example, from the center of a large block of resin). Despite these problems, the terpenoids are relatively easy to solvent extract, separate (by GC), and identify by their characteristic molecular fragmentation (using GC–MS) (Mills and White 1994, Pollard and Heron 1996: 239–70). They can also be excellent biomarkers, if their biosynthesis is limited to a few plants.

Figure 7.8 2-methylbutadiene (C_5H_8), "the isoprene unit" – the basis of the terpenoid family of compounds.

Table 7.2. *Structural formulas of the terpenoid groups, and their construction from basic isoprene units.*

Monoterpenoids	C_{10}	$2 \times$ isoprene unit
Sesquiterpenoids	C_{15}	$3 \times$ isoprene unit
Diterpenoids	C_{20}	$4 \times$ isoprene unit
Triterpenoids	C_{30}	$6 \times$ isoprene unit

Rarely do plants biosynthesize both diterpenoids and triterpenoids, so a simple GC analysis and comparison to authentic samples may indicate which resin type is present, or if mixing has occurred. However, for true identification GC–MS is required to fully identify the molecular components. As discussed below, pitches and tars were processed by heating raw plant materials, and these too may be identified. However, degradation processes can alter the composition, and identification to the species level may not always be possible.

Diterpenoids: e.g., amber, pine resins, and pitches
Amber is a fossilized resin, and contains polymerized monoterpenoids and diterpenoids. Although some free terpenoids may be solvent extracted and analyzed by GC–MS, the polymerized material has too high a molecular weight for such analysis, and much work has been done using IR spectroscopy to identify and provenance amber (see Sections 1.1 and 4.4). *Pinaceae* resin is composed of diterpenoids. The trees which produced amber-forming resin are now extinct, and modern *Pinaceae* resins do not polymerize making the terpenoids amenable to solvent extraction and analysis by GC–MS. Trees may yield as much as 5 kg of resin per year, making *Pinaceae* resin an extremely useful resource which was often traded. In addition to the resin, *Pinaceae* pitch, derived from destructive distillation of the wood, has also been recovered from archaeological contexts. By using GC and GC–MS, it is possible to identify both pitches and resins. These materials have been used to seal porous amphorae, probably to facilitate transport, but also to add to the flavor of wine, as in modern retsina (Heron and Pollard 1988), and also to waterproof ships (caulking: Evershed *et al.* 1985, Robinson *et al.* 1987). This material has been discussed in detail by Pollard and Heron (1996: 239–70).

Triterpenoids: birch bark tar and *Pistacia* resin
Birch bark tar has been reported in finds from the Middle Palaeolithic to Modern times in Europe (Pollard and Heron 1996, Grünberg *et al.* 1999). The uses of birch bark tar are wide ranging, including hafting, waterproofing, caulking, repairing, and even a reported use as a "chewing gum" (Aveling and Heron 1999). Although the process has not been fully elucidated, the

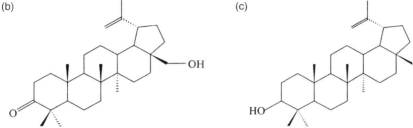

Figure 7.9 Some diagnostic triterpenoid compounds from birch bark tar: (a) betulin ($C_{30}H_{50}O_2$), (b) betulone ($C_{30}H_{49}O_2$), (c) lupeol ($C_{30}H_{50}O$).

destructive heating of birch bark in a sealed container is thought to be involved in the production of the tar. The bark of birch trees (*Betula* spp.) contains a variety of diagnostic triterpenoid compounds including betulin, betulone, lupenone, and lupeol (Ekman 1983, O'Connell *et al.* 1988, Cole *et al.* 1991; Fig. 7.9). The presence of these and other components will identify residues as birch bark tar, and such materials have been identified using GC and GC–MS by a number of workers (Binder *et al.* 1990, Hayek *et al.* 1990, Charters *et al.* 1993, Reunanen *et al.* 1993, Regert 1997, Regert *et al.* 1998, Aveling and Heron 1998, 1999, Urem-Kotsou *et al.* 2002). Due to the presence of components not found in modern birch bark, or in experimentally produced birch bark tar, the mixing of birch bark tar with animal fat (Regert *et al.* 1998, Dudd and Evershed 1999) and other plant tars (Hayek *et al.* 1990, Regert *et al.* 1998) has also been reported.

Pistacia sp. resin is also known as mastic, Chios terpentine and terebinth (in fact the word terpenoid is derived from this). The genus *Pistacia* has four species (*atlantica, khinjuk, lentiscus,* and *terebinthus*), which may have been available in the Mediterranean for the production of resin. However, it is not possible to distinguish the species based on the triterpenoid composition, so evidence for the species used relies on modern evidence, such as the amounts of resin produced by each species and their geographical distributions. The resin is largely composed of triterpenoids, the chemical composition of which has been studied by a variety of workers (cited in Stern *et al.* 2003). The major components (Fig. 7.10) are moronic, oleanonic, *iso*masticadienonic,

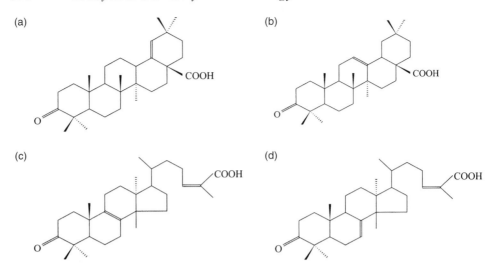

Figure 7.10 Some triterpenoid compounds found in mastic (Pistacia resin): (a) moronic acid, (b) oleanonic acid, (c) *iso*masticadienonic acid, (d) masticadienonic acid.

and masticadienonic acids (isomers of one another). The characteristic composition and distribution of triterpenoids, especially in comparison to modern resins, enable the identification of *Pistacia* resin when found as a residue in an archaeological context (Mills and White 1989). Such analyses have allowed the resins in Canaanite amphorae from the Bronze Age shipwreck at Ulu Burun, off the south coast of Turkey, to be identified as originating from the genus *Pistacia* (Mills and White 1989, Hairfield and Hairfield 1990). Similar analyses from the fourteenth century BC site of Amarna, Egypt, have identified the contents of Canaanite amphorae to be *Pistacia* (Serpico and White 2000). Stern *et al.* (2003) have also identified compositional variations between unheated and heated resins – presumed to be the result of incense burning.

Wax

Waxes are biosynthesized by plants (e.g., leaf cuticular coatings) and insects (e.g., beeswax). Their chemical constituents vary with plant or animal type, but are mainly esters made from long-chain alcohols (C_{22}–C_{34}) and fatty acids with even carbon numbers dominant (Fig. 7.11). They may also contain alkanes, secondary alcohols, and ketones. The majority of wax components are fully saturated. The ester in waxes is more resistant to hydrolysis than the ester in triacylglycerols, which makes waxes less vulnerable to degradation, and therefore more likely to survive archaeologically.

Heron *et al.* (1994) used GC and GC–MS to identify beeswax from a Neolithic (3700–3340 cal. BC) potshard from Ergolding Fischergasse,

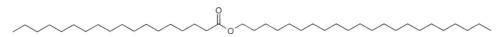

Figure 7.11 C_{40} wax ester, made up of C_{18} fatty acid (octadecanoic acid or stearic acid, $C_{18:0}$) and C_{22} alcohol.

Germany. The GC analysis of modern beeswax showed an almost identical profile to the Neolithic wax, both in the carbon number range of the dominant wax esters and their relative abundance. Minor components were also present in similar distributions, although the distributions of *n*–alkanes and free carboxylic acids were different, which the authors ascribe to combustion of the wax. Evershed *et al.* (1997b) report the extraction of ceramic lamps and conical cups believed to be used as lamps from the Late Minoan I (c. 1600–1450 BC) site of Mocholos, Crete. Instead of the expected olive oil (which would yield triacylglycerides and their degradation products), wax esters, alkanes, and free long-chain alcohols were extracted from the shards. Both the GC distribution and GC–MS identification of wax esters and the long-chain alcohols, derived from hydrolysis of wax esters, indicate that beeswax was present. Further evidence supplied by GC–C–IRMS shows that the $\delta^{13}C$ values of the alcohols were similar to those from modern beeswax and not modern plant waxes (bees biosynthesize the wax and do not collect it from the plants, as they do nectar). Loss of fatty acids and alkanes is attributed to the formation of soluble salts and volatilization caused by heating, respectively. This cannot rule out, however, the preferential loss of one component of a mixture, such as triacylglycerides from fats or oils. As described above, Charters *et al.* (1995) interpreted such mixtures of beeswax and animal fat as evidence that the beeswax was used as a sealant prior to the addition of the fat. Garnier *et al.* (2002) have taken the study of archaeological beeswax further by using conventional GC–MS (as TMS derivatives), and also using electrospray ionization mass spectrometry (see Section 8.1), which reveals (nonderivatized) higher molecular weight biomarkers (such as diesters), which are of too high molecular weight to be analyzed by GC–MS.

Bitumen

Bitumen is a naturally occurring fossil-fuel hydrocarbon deposit. One must, however, be aware of different terminologies being used by different authors (e.g., see glossary in Connan *et al.* 1998). In general, the molecules are significantly more degraded than (the much younger) archaeological residues, with resultant loss of functionalities, double bonds, and an increase in aromatization. However, the biomarker approach still works well on these compounds. Bitumen usually contains a homologous series of *n*-alkanes, with the isoprenes pristane and phytane (Fig. 7.12). These compounds are commonly extracted and ratios such as pristane/phytane, C_{17}/pristane,

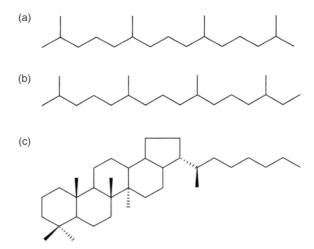

Figure 7.12 Potential biomarkers in bitumen: the isoprenes (a) pristane ($C_{19}H_{40}$) and (b) phytane ($C_{20}H_{42}$), and (c) the hopane $17\alpha(H)$, $21\beta(H)$-pentakishomohopane (22R).

C_{18}/phytane, and CPI (carbon preference index), defined as:

$$CPI = 1/2[(Sum\ odd\ C_{25}\ to\ C_{33})/(Sum\ even\ C_{24}\ to\ C_{32})$$
$$+(Sum\ odd\ C_{25}\ to\ C_{33})/(Sum\ even\ C_{26}\ to\ C_{34})],$$

have been used to characterize the sample (Killops and Killops 2005: 224). These have also been used as an indicator of the original geological depositional conditions, although there are some difficulties with interpretation. Of greater interest are the hopanes. These are biomarker compounds, which can be related to their original biogenic precursors. They are nonaromatic, polycyclic compounds, with relatively high molecular weights. This makes them resistant to photodegradation, biodegradation, and evaporation (Glegg and Rowland 1996, Barakat *et al.* 2001). The hopanes have a complex distribution of stereoisomers, which are characteristic of the origin of the oils, and geochemists have long been applying this approach to the identification of oil–oil correlation, source rock identification, and maturity determinations (e.g., Tissot and Welte 1984, Engel and Macko 1993, Barakat *et al.* 2001, Killops and Killops 2005). It is therefore of no surprise that these correlations are also of use to archaeologists.

Although fossil fuels dominate the modern world, these materials have also been found in archaeological contexts. The use of naturally occurring seeps and floating blocks of bitumen has been described by Nissenbaum (1993), who identifies the earliest use of the Dead Sea bitumen at 9000 BP. This material was put to a wide range of uses, such as the direct carving of objects, coatings for waterproofing or aesthetic reasons, as a mortar and adhesive, in weapons such as Greek fire, medicine, and for mummification (e.g., Connan and Deschesne 1996). In addition, differences in the bitumen composition indicate that the embalmers were not using a single source of bitumen for mummification, and that beeswax and gum-resins were added to the mixture. The identification, provenance, uses, and trade of bitumen has been described by Connan and Dessort (1989), Connan *et al.* (1992, 1998), and Nissenbaum (1992). The identification of the source of the bitumen is based on a number of factors, including comparison of the biomarkers with authentic samples, and more recently, the $\delta^{13}C$ and δD isotopic compositions (see Chapter 8). However, it is important to analyse the asphaltene fraction, rather than the bulk bitumen, because only this is representative of the original bitumen as it is not modified by weathering.

8

MASS SPECTROMETRY

Mass spectrometry is perhaps the ultimate analytical tool – it involves counting the individual ions, and thus it is the most sensitive detection system possible. After an introduction to the basic components of a mass spectrometer (ion source, separation device for charged ions, and ion detector), we review the various types of spectrometer (single focusing, double focusing, quadrupole). We then introduce the systematics relevant to the study of light isotopes (hydrogen, carbon, nitrogen), and outline the role that these isotopes now play in environmental research. Our attention then turns to the quite different systematics relevant to heavy isotope research (lead and strontium). Highlighted applications of isotope archaeology include palaeodietary research from light stable isotopes on human bones and teeth, "provenancing" humans from light stable isotopes and also heavy isotopes in bone and teeth, and the use of lead isotopes to track the circulation of metal artifacts. There are several excellent texts of isotopes in geochemistry and the environmental sciences, including Faure (1986) and Hoefs (1997).

8.1 Separation of ions by electric and magnetic fields

Mass spectrometry in chemistry is widely used as a tool for organic structural analysis, where precise measurement of the mass of the sample and of its fragmentation products is of prime importance. In many ways, however, mass spectrometry is also the ultimate tool as a detector for a wide range of techniques of inorganic chemical analysis, since it allows the counting of individual ions, giving what should be the best possible analytical sensitivity. In this type of application, it is the precise measurement of the intensity of the peaks (i.e., number of ions collected) in the mass spectrum which is important, making it quite different from "traditional" mass spectrometry. It is this application of mass spectrometry which is discussed here. Used in this way, a mass spectrometer can simply be regarded as an ultra-precise detector for the many types of spectrometers used in analytical chemistry – hence the proliferation of the so-called "hyphenated techniques" of analysis, where a mass spectrometer is coupled to another device to improve the detection sensitivity (e.g., ICP–MS, GC–MS, HPLC–MS, etc.). Mass spectrometry is also used in its own right in archaeology, earth, and environmental sciences for the determination of heavy stable isotope ratios such as lead, or for light stable isotopes (hydrogen, carbon, nitrogen, oxygen, and sulfur) as used in dietary and palaeoenvironmental reconstruction. Isotopic measurements using mass spectrometers also form the basis of several dating techniques involving radioactive isotopes (e.g., K-Ar dating) or in accelerator-based methods for radiocarbon dating. These applications are well covered elsewhere (e.g., Faure 1986, Aitken 1990, Hoefs 1997) and are not addressed here.

Mass spectrometry is based on the principle that the trajectory of electrically charged ions or molecules moving through an externally imposed electrical and/or magnetic field is controlled by their atomic masses (strictly, mass to charge ratio, m/z), and this can be used to separate charged particles of different masses. A simple mass spectrometer consists of a source of positively charged ions of equal energy, a magnetic and/or electrostatic deflection system for separating the charged ions, and an ion collector to measure the current flowing in the selected beam. The pressure within the system must be low, to ensure that the ions are not absorbed or deflected by passage through air. As with most analytical instruments, a mass spectro-meter can be broken down into familiar components: a source of charged particles, a monochromator for the separation of these particles, and a charged particle detector. The various possibilities for each of these are discussed separately.

Ion sources
Most spectrometers are designed to handle either a gaseous sample, such as CO_2, or a solid sample deposited on a wire (which is usually made of a high melting point metal such as Ta, Re, or W). Generally speaking, light isotope machines (i.e., those used for measuring the isotopes of H, C, N, O, S) use a gas source, whilst heavy isotope instruments use solid sources. Sampling for plasma source mass spectrometers, including laser ablation, is discussed in Chapter 9. We also discuss briefly a range of techniques developed over the last few years to aid the mass spectrometry of large biomolecules. Most ion sources produce both positively and negatively charged species, and some machines can be switched to work with either. In some cases, it is worth considering which will give the most information.

The most common conventional gas source is an *electron impact* (EI) source. This consists of a metal chamber with a volume of a few cm^3, through which the sample flows in the form of a gas. Electrons produced by thermionic emission from a heated tungsten filament are passed through this gas, and accelerated by a relatively low voltage ($\sim 100\,eV$), causing ionization within the sample gas. A plate inside the chamber carries a low positive potential (the "repeller") which ejects the positive ions into a region which contains a series of plates (called lenses) and slits, which serve to focus, collimate, and accelerate the ion beam into the next part of the system

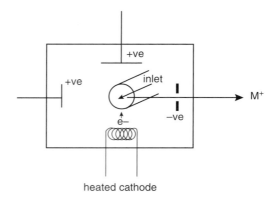

+ve

+ve   inlet

e–   –ve   M⁺

heated cathode

Figure 8.1 Schematic diagram of electron impact (EI) source for mass spectrometry. The sample enters the evacuated chamber as a gas and is intersected by a beam of electrons released from the heated cathode and accelerated towards the positive anode at the top. The impact of the electrons atomizes and ionizes the sample, and the resulting positive ions are attracted towards the annular cathode on the right, passing through it and out of the source towards the mass selection device.

(Fig. 8.1). An alternative ionization procedure is provided by *chemical ionization* (CI). In this technique, the gaseous sample is ionized by collision with positively charged ions, which are themselves produced by electron bombardment of an excess of a reagent gas – often methane (CH_4). In this case, bombardment of methane with electrons produces a range of ions such as CH_4^+, CH_3^+, etc. These ions react with other methane molecules to produce species such as CH_5^+ and $C_2H_5^+$, which, in turn, react with the sample molecules to produce a range of ionic species. It is also possible to produce negatively charged ions for measurement. In general, chemical ionization produces less fragmentation of the sample molecules than does electron impact ionization (sometimes called *soft ionization*). Comparison of the mass spectra of fragments from the same sample, but using different ionization sources, can often give clues about the structure of the target molecule.

These methods require that the sample is either a gas or, at least, a volatile substance which can be easily converted into a gas (this explains the utility of mass spectrometry in the field of organic chemistry). In inorganic chemistry it is often more difficult to obtain a gaseous sample, and so other ionization sources have been developed. If the sample is thermally stable, it may be volatilized by depositing it on a filament and heating the filament (*thermal ionization mass spectrometry* – see below). In restricted cases (e.g., organometallic chemistry), chemical treatment of the sample may give a more volatile sample.

A solid sample may also be *sputtered* by a beam of heavy ions, so that ions are physically knocked off the surface. This is the basis of *secondary ion mass spectrometry* (SIMS), in which a solid sample is bombarded with an argon ion beam. This is mainly a surface analysis technique, and tends to produce large molecular fragments. A modification of this is now widely used for the study of high molecular weight biological samples, called *fast atom bombardment* (FAB). In this technique, the sample is contained in a low molecular weight matrix (such as glycerol), and a beam of fast atoms (i.e., a neutral species) is obtained by passing argon or xenon ions through a chamber at moderate pressures (10^{-5} torr, compared to a high vacuum of 10^{-9} torr). The fast ions undergo electron exchange with the slow gaseous atoms in the partial vacuum, without losing much kinetic energy. The result is a beam of high energy neutral atoms, which sputter a high proportion of parent ions, as well as ion fragments, from the sample, even for high molecular weight biological samples (molecular weights up to 12 500 Daltons have been successfully studied – i.e., small proteins).

For the identification and characterization of very large biological samples (up to 1 Mda), a technique called *electrospray ionization* (ESI) can be used. The sample is dissolved in a polar volatile solvent and pumped through a narrow bore stainless steel capillary tube. A voltage of a few kV is applied to the tip of the tube, and, as the liquid emerges from the tube, it is converted to an aerosol of charged droplets. The whole process is aided by the flow of an inert gas such as nitrogen, some of which is injected co-axially around the capillary tube (nebulizing gas), and some is directed across the stream (drying gas). This serves to aid the production of the aerosol, and to promote the desolvation (drying) process. The solvent evaporates from the droplets to leave a stream of charged particles, which pass through a sampling cone and into regions of increasing vacuum, until they enter the analyzer of the mass spectrometer. Electrospray ionization is a very sensitive analytical technique, and it causes very little fragmentation of the target molecule. It is now the most popular technique for the analysis of nonvolatile lipids, such as triacylglycerols, phospholipids, and glycolipids (Pulfer and Murphy 2003). Proteins and peptides are best analyzed under positive ionization, whereas saccharides and oligonucleotides work best under negative ionization (Mano and Goto 2003).

An alternative approach for thermally sensitive or nonvolatile large biomolecules is *matrix assisted laser desorption ionization* (MALDI). The technique is similar to FAB as described above, except that ionization is brought about by laser irradiation, and the matrix is designed to improve the efficiency of ionization by absorbing the laser energy and transferring it to the analyte, thus reducing the energy needed to ionize the sample. The sample is dissolved in a volatile solvent, and mixed with a solution containing the matrix (e.g., sinapinic acid for protein analysis). This solution is placed on the sample target holder and dried. Ionization is achieved by firing a pulsed laser, causing positive and negative ions to be desorbed, which are then selectively extracted into the mass spectrometer. Again, MALDI is a soft ionization technique, which results in little fragmentation of the target molecule, which helps when interpreting the spectra (Cristoni and Bernardi 2003, Ferranti 2004).

Mass analysis

Once the ions have been injected into the analyzer, it is necessary to separate them according to their mass-to-charge ratio, and therefore identify individual charged species. This is possible because charged particles will follow different paths depending on their mass-to-charge ratios when moving through a space subject to either an electrostatic or a magnetic field, or both. The simplest mass spectrometers have only a single mass analysis device (usually a magnetic sector or a quadrupole), e.g., a single focusing magnetic sector analyzer. Higher resolution can be obtained using double focusing mass analyzers, in which the beam passes first through an electrostatic field, and is then focused via a slit into a magnetic field (Fig. 8.2). For further refinement, mass analyzers can be used sequentially (e.g., quadrupole into quadrupole, or magnetic sector into quadrupole, etc.). This is sometimes known as tandem mass spectrometry, or MS–MS, especially if the interface between the two analyzers contains a collision cell in which an inert gas induces further fragmentation of the particle beam.

An ion of mass m with a charge of e is given a kinetic energy of E when it is extracted from the ion source by an applied voltage V, where:

$$E = eV = 1/2\ mv^2$$

where v is the velocity of the ion. All ions of the same charge leaving the ion source have the same kinetic energy E, but the velocity of the ion will depend on its mass. The velocity of an ion is given by rearranging the above:

$$v = \sqrt{\frac{2eV}{m}}.$$

The equation of motion of a charged particle in a magnetic field of strength B is given by the following, where r is the radius of the circular track taken by the ion:

$$Bev = mv^2/r.$$

Combining these equations to eliminate v gives:

$$Be = mv/r = m\sqrt{\frac{2eV}{m}} \Big/ r$$

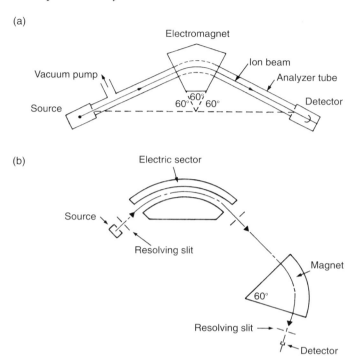

Figure 8.2 Schematic diagrams of (a) single focusing and (b) double focusing mass spectrometers. The single focusing spectrometer has a 60° electromagnet to deflect and separate the ion beam. The double focusing instrument has a 90° electrostatic deflector, followed by a 60° magnet, giving much higher mass resolution. Fig. 8.2(a) from Faure (1986), Fig. 4.9, reproduced by permission of John Wiley & Sons, Inc.; Fig. 8.2(b) adapted from Beynon and Brenton (1982), Fig. 4.9, by permission of University of Wales Press.

rearranging:

$$m/e = B^2 r^2 / 2V$$

or:

$$r = 1.414 \sqrt{V(m/e)} \Big/ B.$$

The radius of the path taken by an ion is dependent on the square root of the accelerating voltage V, and inversely proportional to the magnetic field strength B. Therefore, for ions of the same charge, with fixed values of accelerating voltage V and magnetic field B, the trajectory of the ion is governed solely by its mass (strictly, the square root of its mass). Thus, in a single focusing magnetic sector instrument, for fixed values of V and B, only ions of a particular mass will pass through the magnet and into the detector. If either B or V is varied systematically, ions of different mass will sequentially pass through the instrument. Thus, if one or another of these is scanned, the mass spectrum of the sample can be obtained. In a fixed geometry single magnetic sector instrument, the magnetic field is fixed, so it is usual for the accelerating voltage V to be varied systematically in order to scan through the mass range.

The resolution of a mass analyzer is given as $m/\Delta m$, where m and $m + \Delta m$ are the masses of two equal intensity adjacent peaks just separable by the analyzer ("just separable" is most stringently defined as having a valley between them of $\leqslant 10\%$ of the peak heights). The resolution of a single focusing magnetic sector spectrometer is typically ~ 1000, and is limited by variations in kinetic energy of the ions as they leave the ion source. The resolution can be dramatically improved (by a factor of up to 10) by using a double focusing instrument. This uses an electrostatic selector before the magnetic selector, which has the effect of removing all particles other than those with the required kinetic energy.

A radically different type of mass analyzer is the *quadrupole*. It uses only electrostatic forces to separate the ions, and, although it has lower resolution, it has the advantage of being much smaller and cheaper than the others, and allows the mass spectrum to be scanned through very rapidly. Because it does not require the ions to be accelerated to such high energies as the magnetic sector machines, it can receive ions from sources other than the conventional ion source, and is therefore the detector which is most often used in "hyphenated" techniques. It has, therefore, greatly expanded the applicability of mass spectrometry.

A quadrupole consists of four parallel metal rods (length typically around 20 cm, and diameter 1 cm), as shown in Fig. 8.3, electrically connected together in opposite pairs. The ion beam passes down the center, parallel to the long axis of the rods. If one pair carries a small positive potential and the other pair an equal negative potential, the path down the exact center of the rods is at zero potential. Under these conditions, a beam of positively charged particles will pass down the center without deflection, but the beam is unstable with respect to the negatively charged rods, since a positive beam is attracted to this polarity. In practice, the rods, in addition to this fixed (DC) potential, have an alternating radio frequency (RF) voltage applied to them. By varying these electric fields, only ions of a particular m/z ratio will pass through the quadrupole, and all other ions will be deflected into the rods and lost. The exact trajectory of an ion through a quadrupole is complex, and depends on the magnitudes of the DC and RF voltages and the frequency of the alternating RF potential. The mass spectrum is scanned by varying systematically the magnitude of the DC and oscillating voltages, usually in such a way that their ratio to each other does not change and with the RF frequency fixed at around 1–2 MHz. Because it is a purely electrostatic device, the mass spectrum can be scanned very rapidly – typically 0 to 800

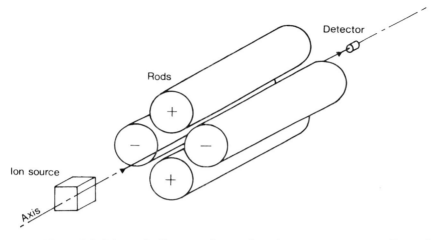

Figure 8.3 Schematic diagram of a quadrupole mass spectrometer. It consists of two pairs of parallel metal rods carrying a DC plus an oscillating voltage, in such a way that only a particular mass-to-charge ratio will pass down the center of the rods for a given setting. The mass spectrum can be rapidly scanned by varying the potentials on the rods. Adapted from Beynon and Brenton (1982), Figs. 4.6 and 4.7, by permission of University of Wales Press.

mass units in a fraction of a second. The normal mode of operation is to scan many times and accumulate an average spectrum in an attached computer, with consequent advantages for improved signal-to-noise. The mass resolution of the machine depends on the length of the rods and the frequency of oscillation, but is generally less than that achievable by the magnetic sector type instruments. The maximum mass range is normally around 4 kDa with a resolution of around 2000. Nevertheless, it is a rapid, relatively cheap, and sensitive detector, and is increasingly used in ICP and chromatography applications, as well as for applications such as secondary ion mass spectrometry and other surface analytical techniques.

Ion detectors
Detectors in mass spectrometry can be relatively simple – all that is required is a sensitive charge collector to integrate the ion currents (which are of the order of 10^{-15}–10^{-8} A). The simplest is a Faraday cup, which is just an earthed metal collector plate. The ions strike the detector and the resulting current is passed to earth through a large resistor, where the voltage developed is measured. The magnitude of the current flowing (as measured by this voltage) is directly proportional to the number of ions being received at the detector.

For many applications in geochemistry and archaeology, the information desired from mass spectrometry is a precise measure of the abundance ratio of two or more isotopes of the same element – $^{12}C/^{13}C$, or $^{16}O/^{18}O$, or $^{206}Pb/^{207}Pb$ and $^{208}Pb/^{207}Pb$ at the heavier end of the mass scale. In these cases, it is better to use multiple collectors, each simultaneously monitoring the current from a particular charged species (e.g., one Faraday cup for the ^{12}C beam, and a second one, at a slightly different angle to the deflecting magnet, to simultaneously record the ^{13}C current). Because the information is gathered simultaneously, the ratio can be continuously monitored, and this compensates to some extent for any fluctuations that might occur in the system as a result of changes in the ionization process, and therefore produces a more precise ratio determination. Light isotope ratio instruments (*isotope ratio mass spectrometers* – IRMS), in particular, tend to have two or three detectors, and are capable of operating in a number of set modes, e.g., for measurement of H/D, $\delta^{13}C$, $\delta^{15}N$, $\delta^{18}O$, and $\delta^{34}S$ (see below for a definition of the delta notation). Thermal ionization mass spectrometers (TIMS), widely used in geochemistry for radiogenic and stable heavy isotope ratio determinations, also routinely have multiple collectors. It should be noted that it is also possible to produce isotope ratios using quadrupole detectors, since the speed of the quadrupole means that a large mass range can be recorded simultaneously, and pairs of isotopes (e.g., $^{86}Sr/^{87}Sr$) can be selectively monitored. It is generally the case, however, that the precision of the isotopic ratio measurements provided in this way is substantially inferior to those obtained by multiple collector measurements on higher resolution machines.

An alternative way of measuring the mass-to-charge ratio and the associated ion current is to monitor the *time of flight* (ToF) of an ion as it passes through a detector. This detector relies on the same physics as described above for the extraction of charged species from the ion source. The ions are generated in a source zone of the instrument, and a potential is applied across the source to extract the ions and accelerate them into the detector, which consists of a field-free "drift" zone. As noted above, all ions leave the source with the same kinetic energy, but with different velocities according to their mass. Thus, the time of flight of the ions through the drift zone will depend only on the mass (and the charge) of the ion. For a reliable mass spectrum to be obtained from measurements of the time of flight, the time of ion extraction must be accurately known. This is a relatively straightforward problem to solve, if the source uses a pulsed ionization technique like laser desorption or MALDI. The most popular application of ToF techniques is coupled with MALDI, in which case, no other mass analyzer is necessary; the laser desorbed sample is injected directly into the time-of-flight tube, which separates out the various masses present, and records their abundance. Alternatively, ToF detectors can be used as second mass analyzers in tandem techniques, where their dual operation as mass analyzer and detector makes them convenient to use. Thus so-called Q–T machines exist, in which a quadrupole mass analyzer is coupled via a gas collider with a ToF detector, giving an effective and compact tandem MS–MS instrument.

The development of "soft ionization" methods (electrospray ionization and matrix-assisted laser desorption ionization, and others not discussed here) has contributed to the remarkable progress seen in mass spectrometry applied to biochemistry and molecular biology research progress, and is beginning to find applications in archaeology.

8.2 Light stable isotopes (δD, δ^{13}C, δ^{15}N, δ^{18}O, and δ^{34}S)

Many light elements (e.g., hydrogen and oxygen) occur naturally in more than one isotopic form. The most common form of hydrogen is a single proton (charge +1, mass 1) orbited by a single electron (charge −1, mass negligible). This is symbolized by ^{1}H. Much less abundant, but naturally occurring and stable, is the heavy isotope ^{2}H, or deuterium (D). This has an additional neutron in the nucleus, with zero charge, but a mass of +1, making it twice as heavy as the lighter isotope. A third isotope (^{3}H, or tritium, T) is even less abundant, and is radioactively unstable. In nature, only 0.0156% of all hydrogen atoms are the heavier isotope ^{2}H (roughly 3 in 20 000 atoms). The most abundant stable isotope of oxygen is ^{16}O, with eight protons and eight neutrons in the nucleus; however, two other heavier stable isotopes exist: ^{17}O, with nine neutrons, and ^{18}O, with ten neutrons. The abundance of ^{17}O is low (0.04%) compared with 0.2% for ^{18}O, but it can be seen that the lighter isotope is still the most abundant (99.76%). A similar pattern is exhibited by most other light stable isotopes.

Carbon and nitrogen isotopes in organic samples are now routinely measured on a continuous flow combustion–IRMS mass spectrometer, and can thus be processed automatically and relatively quickly. Brenna *et al.* (1997) have produced an excellent review of the history of the development and application of high precision continuous flow stable isotope ratio mass spectrometry for biological and organic samples. The solid sample (which often requires little sample preparation) is simply wrapped in tin foil and dropped from a multiturret sample holder into a flash combustion furnace, where the tin and the sample volatalize, and the gases are combusted over an oxidative surface (at 800°C) to CO_2, N_2, NO_x, and H_2O – an elemental copper stage reduces NO_x to N_2, and a dryer removes water vapor. Pressure measurements of the amounts of CO_2, H_2O, and N_2 produced allow the estimation of the percentage C, H, and N in the original sample, as in a conventional combustion C, H, N analyzer. The resulting CO_2 and N_2 are passed through a chromatography column to separate the gases. A GC column bleeds the gases into the mass spectrometer, which is usually a magnetic sector device with two or more detectors, to allow the precise measurement of the required isotope ratios. Most instruments will run automatically, making the routine measurement of δ^{13}C and δ^{15}N (see below) on solid organic samples a relatively straightforward and rapid procedure. δD can also be done automatically, but the much smaller mass of the isotopes means that an additional magnet is needed to make the measurements, and therefore it cannot usually be done at the same time as the carbon and nitrogen measurements. In the last ten years, developments in using laser ablation systems combined with mass spectrometry have led to the capacity to measure sulfur ($^{34}S/^{32}S$), oxygen ($^{18}O/^{16}O$), and carbon isotopes on geological samples (silicates, carbonates, sulfides, and sulfates) with good analytical precision and high spatial resolution (Wagner *et al.* 2002). Of more immediate significance to archaeology has been the development of a method of measuring oxygen isotope ratios in tooth enamel phosphate mineral using laser ablation combined with either combustion IRMS or GC–C–IRMS (Jones *et al.* 1999).

Isotope systematics of the lighter elements have been extensively studied because of their importance in understanding a wide range of environmental, earth science, and bioscience processes (Taylor *et al.* 1991, Griffiths 1998, Pollard and Wilson 2001). For example, as water is cycled around the Earth's system (from atmosphere to ocean to terrestrial rivers), the ratios of both $^{2}H/^{1}H$ and $^{18}O/^{16}O$ change. This is because the increased mass of the heavier isotope renders it slightly less likely to take part in processes such as evaporation, enriching slightly the remaining liquid in the heavier isotope whilst depleting the resulting vapor of the same isotope. Such processes are termed *fractionation*, and the magnitude of the effect depends on the mass difference between the two isotopes. Hydrogen, therefore, shows the largest fractionation, since the heavier isotope is twice the mass of the lighter, whereas in oxygen, it is only heavier by 12.5%. Even for hydrogen, however, the effects are small. The average abundance ratio of ^{2}H to ^{1}H is 0.000156, and therefore any changes due to fractionation are only detected in the last digit of this small number. In order to magnify these small but important effects, isotope geochemists have adopted the δ notation, which is defined for hydrogen as follows:

$$\delta^{2}H = \delta D = \left(\frac{\left(^{2}H/^{1}H\right)_{sample} - \left(^{2}H/^{1}H\right)_{standard}}{\left(^{2}H/^{1}H\right)_{standard}} \right) \times 1000.$$

In this notation, the ratio of ^{2}H to ^{1}H in the sample is compared to the same ratio in an internationally agreed standard material. If the ratio in the sample is identical to that in the standard, then the δ value ($\delta^{2}H$, or δD) is zero. If the sample is isotopically heavier than the standard, the $^{2}H/^{1}H$ ratio in the sample is greater than that in the standard, and δ becomes positive. If the sample is isotopically lighter, then the top line becomes negative, and δ becomes negative. The units (because of the multiplication by 1000) are known as "per mil" (or "parts per thousand"), symbolized as ‰. The beauty of the δ notation is that if δ becomes more positive as it is fractionated, then the sample is getting isotopically heavier, and vice versa. Thus the direction of the fractionation relative to the standard can immediately be discerned from the change in sign. The standard used for hydrogen isotopic measurements in water is SMOW (standard mean ocean water) or SLAP (standard light arctic precipitation). The equations for $\delta^{13}C$, $\delta^{15}N$, $\delta^{18}O$, and $\delta^{34}S$ are identical to that given above, with the appropriate isotope ratio (e.g., $^{18}O/^{16}O$) replacing that of hydrogen. The same standards are used for measurement of oxygen isotope ratios in water, but different standards are used for other isotopes in rocks and biominerals (Ehleringer and Rundel 1988, IAEA 1995).

The importance of oxygen and hydrogen isotope ratios in the water cycle was first demonstrated by Dansgaard (1964), who showed that a simple linear relationship exists between $\delta^{18}O$ in precipitation and the average annual air temperature. Through the isotopic analysis of a large number of meteoric water samples (rainfall and surface water) collected at different latitudes, Craig (1961) had previously demonstrated that a simple relationship existed between $\delta^{18}O$ and δD in precipitation:

$$\delta D = 8 \times \delta^{18}O + 10.$$

This is called the *meteoric water line*. Dansgaard compared the annual mean $\delta^{18}O$ value of precipitation with the average annual air temperature T and obtained a straight line of equation:

$$\delta^{18}O = 0.695T - 13.6.$$

Thus $\delta^{18}O$ in the precipitation becomes increasingly positive (i.e., isotopically heavier) as the average air temperature rises. This relationship has been used to convert the $\delta^{18}O$ record obtained from Greenland (Johnsen *et al.* 1997) and Antarctic (Grootes and Stuiver 1986) ice core records into palaeotemperature records, thus giving a climatic framework for the past 420 000 years.

Carbon has two stable isotopes: ^{12}C, with six protons and six neutrons, and ^{13}C, with seven neutrons. Isotopic fractionation of carbon as it is cycled has been studied in great detail for many years. The internationally agreed standard for carbon is the CO_2 produced from a Cretaceous belemnite rock in South Carolina, called the Pee Dee Formation (PDB). Measurements of $\delta^{13}C$ have become particularly important in archaeology for two reasons. One is that $\delta^{13}C$ measurements are used to correct radiocarbon dates obtained on organic material for fractionation effects, (on the assumption the ^{14}C fractionates twice as much as ^{13}C, because it is two units heavier than ^{12}C rather than one). The other is because $\delta^{13}C$ measurements (often combined with $\delta^{15}N$) made on skeletal and dental collagen (and occasionally skeletal mineral or lipid) can be used to reconstruct the diet of an animal or human. This is explored in more detail below.

Carbon fractionation begins when green plants photosynthesize, and combine CO_2 taken in from the atmosphere through the leaf stomata with H_2O

taken up by the root system to produce sugars and eventually cellulose. Farquhar *et al.* (1982) showed that the carbon isotopic composition of plant material ($\delta^{13}C_p$) as a result of photosynthesis can be expressed as:

$$\delta^{13}C_p = \delta^{13}C_{atm} - a - (b - a)c_i/c_a.$$

where *a* is the discrimination against $^{13}CO_2$ compared to $^{12}CO_2$ during diffusion of CO_2 through air, and *b* is the discrimination in a particular plant species against ^{13}C during the carboxylation reaction. $\delta^{13}C_{atm}$ is the isotopic value of atmospheric CO_2, and c_i and c_a are the partial pressures of CO_2 within the intercellular spaces of the leaf and in the atmosphere, respectively. Typically $\delta^{13}C_{atm}$ has a value of around -7‰ (this changes with latitude and time), *a* is 4.4‰, and *b* varies from species to species, but is typically 30‰. Most terrestrial plants (temperate grasses, and all trees and woody shrubs) photosynthesize using the C_3 metabolic pathway, giving a range of $\delta^{13}C_p$ values between about -19‰ and -29‰, with an average of -26.5‰. A second photosynthetic pathway (C_4) used by many species of subtropical grasses has a different value of *b* in the Farquhar equation, and results in plants with $\delta^{13}C_p$ values of between -12‰ and -6‰, with an average of -12.5‰ (van der Merwe 1992).

Cycling of nitrogen can also be followed isotopically by measuring changes in $\delta^{15}N$, where the international standard is atmospheric nitrogen (AIR). Nitrogen isotope systematics are less well understood than those of carbon, but are frequently used in parallel to carbon to reconstruct diet from the isotopic analysis of skeletal collagen. The nitrogen isotope ratios in bone can also reflect the differential utilization of nitrogen-fixing plants (e.g., legumes) and nonnitrogen fixing plants. The principal variation, however, is between terrestrial and marine ecosystems. Terrestrial mammals and birds have a mean bone collagen $\delta^{15}N$ value of $+5.9$‰, whereas marine mammals have an average value of $+15.6$‰ (Schoeninger *et al.* 1983). Subsequent studies (Wada *et al.* 1991) have shown distinct trophic level discrimination against nitrogen in marine ecosystems. This results in a clear distinction in $\delta^{15}N$ between humans who live predominantly on marine resources (e.g., North American Inuit), who have $\delta^{15}N$ between $+17$ to $+20$‰, and terrestrial agriculturists who have values in the range $+6$ to $+12$‰. When combined with carbon isotope data, this provides a powerful tool.

Sample preparation of collagen from bone and dental samples for isotopic measurement and radiocarbon dating has been improved and standardized over recent years. It is normal to prepare collagen for isotopic measurements to the same standard as that required for radiocarbon dating. The most comprehensive protocol (Bronk Ramsey *et al.* 2000) involves sequential demineralization, dehumification, and reacidification in a continuous flow process, followed by gelatinization at 65°C for 16 hours, filtration through an 8 μm filter, and finally ultrafiltration, to remove the low molecular weight material, normally with a 30 kD cut-off. The retained solution is then freeze-dried (lyophilized), and the resulting solid sample is suitable for direct introduction into a combustion IRMS, and also for radiocarbon dating. Typically about 0.1 to 0.5 g of bone (or dentine) sample (depending on collagen preservation) will give sufficient collagen for all isotopic measurements, as well as for dating by ^{14}C accelerator mass spectrometry, if required.

8.3 Heavy isotopes (Pb, Sr) – thermal ionization mass spectrometry (TIMS)

Until the recent advent of high precision MC–ICP–MS instruments (plasma ion sources, but with magnetic selectors and multiple collectors: see Chapter 9), the standard tool for the measurement of heavy isotope ratios in earth sciences was TIMS (thermal ionization mass spectrometry). In this technique, very small samples (a few milligrams) are chemically deposited on a platinum wire (or similar refractory material). This is then mounted in the sample turret of the mass spectrometer and heated by passing an electrical current, either through the sample wire, or through an adjacent heater wire. This causes the deposited material to be ionized and emitted into the vacuum. Sample turrets can contain up to 20 samples at a time, and run automatically. TIMS machines usually use a double focusing mass analyzer, and have multiple ion collectors – sometimes as many as seven Faraday cups, in addition to other detectors. TIMS instruments are still used for a wide range of heavy isotope ratio determinations, e.g., Sr, Nd, and Pb isotopes, and low abundance measurements for U and Th series dating (cf. alpha counting), as well as for light element isotope determinations at extremely low abundances, such as B, Be, Al, Li, etc.

As discussed in Section 10.3, there are three main radioactive series in nature, starting with the elements uranium and thorium (^{238}U, ^{235}U, and ^{232}Th), and ending in one of the three stable isotopes of lead (^{206}Pb, ^{207}Pb, and ^{208}Pb respectively). Consideration of the behavior of these chains in secular equilibrium (i.e., when the rate of decay of the daughter isotope becomes equal to the rate of decay of the parent, and assuming a closed system) shows that it is possible to consider the decay chain simply in terms of the parent decaying directly to the stable lead end point, with a half-life essentially the same as the longest half-life in the system, which happens to be that of the parent isotope (Faure 1986: 285). Thus, each of the three decay chains can be simplified to the following, which is particularly useful when considering the evolution of the isotopic compositions of terrestrial lead deposits:

$$^{238}\text{U} \rightarrow {}^{206}\text{Pb} \quad T_{1/2} = 4.468 \times 10^9 \text{ years}$$
$$^{235}\text{U} \rightarrow {}^{207}\text{Pb} \quad T_{1/2} = 0.7038 \times 10^9 \text{ years}$$
$$^{232}\text{Th} \rightarrow {}^{208}\text{Pb} \quad T_{1/2} = 14.01 \times 10^9 \text{ years.}$$

The fourth stable isotope of lead (^{204}Pb) is not produced radiogenically, and is therefore termed *primeval* – its existence is the result of it being present at the beginnings of the solar system (from nucleosynthesis during the "big bang"), and therefore being incorporated into the earth as it solidified. The abundance of the three radiogenic isotopes also has a primeval component, to which has been added a radiogenic component. The isotopic ratios ^{206}Pb/^{204}Pb, ^{207}Pb/^{204}Pb, and ^{208}Pb/^{204}Pb for a particular ore body therefore change over a time, in a manner which is dictated by the original isotopic composition of the body (Pollard and Heron 1996: 312–22). Any uranium or thorium present in the ore itself will continuously alter the isotopic composition. Therefore the isotopic "signature" of a particular ore body will be unique, apart from that of ore bodies formed at the same geological time, in the same manner, and in the same country rock. Furthermore, the values of the isotopic ratios are constrained, in that they should conform to theoretically predictable growth curves when plotted appropriately. These constraints mean that isotopic data cannot be treated as if they were randomly distributed variables. All of these factors are particularly important when the measurement of lead isotope ratios is applied to archaeology, as discussed below.

Strontium isotope systematics are rather more straightforward. Strontium has four stable naturally occurring isotopes: ^{84}Sr (0.56%), ^{86}Sr (9.86%), ^{87}Sr (7.0%), and ^{88}Sr (82.58%). Of these, ^{87}Sr is radiogenic, being produced by the decay of the radioactive alkali metal ^{87}Rb, with a half-life of 4.75×10^{10} years. Thus, there are two sources of ^{87}Sr in any mineral: that which formed along with ^{84}Sr, ^{86}Sr, and ^{88}Sr during primordial nucleosynthesis, plus that formed from the subsequent radioactive decay of ^{87}Rb. The isotope ratio ^{87}Sr/^{86}Sr in a mineral is therefore related to the age and original isotopic composition of the mineral. ^{87}Sr/^{86}Sr ratios in minerals and rocks have values ranging from about 0.699 in meteorites and moon rock to greater than 0.74 in carbonate fractions of deep sea sediments (Faure 1986). Because Sr has an atomic radius similar to that of Ca, it readily substitutes for Ca in minerals, including phosphates in bones and teeth. As discussed below, this has been exploited in attempts to "provenance" archaeological humans.

8.4   Combined techniques – GC–MS

As discussed in Chapter 7, gas chromatography (GC) is used to separate complex mixtures of volatile organic compounds. However, unless pure authentic standards are also analyzed to compare retention times, it is not possible to identify the components by GC alone. However, by connecting the output of a GC to a mass spectrometer, and by removing the carrier gas to maintain the low pressures required, it is possible to both separate and identify these complex mixtures. This method is the "gold standard" for the identification of organic samples, if they are sufficiently volatile.

The instrumental design is similar to that of other mass spectrometers described above, with the end of the GC column directly inserted into the ion source. The eluting components are bombarded with high energy electrons (usually 70 eV), resulting in the removal of an electron and the generation of a positive molecular ion, abbreviated as $M^{+\cdot}$. The mass selection can be either by quadrupole or magnetic sector, although quadrupoles are more common, due to their fast scan speeds, typically covering the 50 to 700 amu mass range. This range is sufficient for most organic samples which are amenable to GC separation, although not high enough to measure the molecular ion of triacylglycerides. One major difference of GC–MS to other mass spectrometry techniques is that complex molecules are being ionized; in some instances the resulting molecular ion is stable, but in most cases it is not and will split into a neutral and a positively charged fragment. The neutral fragment will be removed by the vacuum pumps, but the positive ion, of lower mass than the molecular ion, can also be analyzed by the mass spectrometer. This results in a complex *mass spectrum* of mass plotted against intensity for each ion produced by many different fragments of the molecular ion. This will form a reproducible, predictable, and characteristic *fingerprint* of each component, as it elutes from the GC column. Because the mass spectrometer scans across the mass range many times as a component elutes from the column, it is possible to view the data in a number of different ways. The most common use is to scan the entire mass range and to combine the scans to produce a mass spectrum. This results in a *total ion count* (TIC; Fig. 8.4). This is a plot of detector response for all masses against retention time, and is, therefore, similar to a GC chromatogram, and can be used to compare samples run on both instruments. Another use of the data is to produce a *mass chromatogram*, where only selected mass(es) are plotted against retention time. This can be useful for identifying molecules with known fragment ions and homologous series. Figure 8.5 shows a plot for $m/z = 71$ from a sample which is a characteristic *n*-alkane fragment. For components of low abundance, it is possible to set the mass spectrometer to measure only certain masses, and, therefore, increase sensitivity (*selected ion monitoring*, SIM). It is also possible to examine each mass scan as a component elutes to see whether two different compounds are eluting at similar times (co-eluting). It may also be useful to remove background noise – something which may be particularly useful at the end of a run where column bleed (small fragments of the column liner breaking off resulting in a high background intensity) can be significant. Many computerized systems can now compare an unknown mass spectrum to a library of previously recorded mass spectra. These are, however, of limited use for archaeology as most of the data are for fossil fuel or synthetic compounds. It is of more use for the archaeological user to assemble a personal library of mass spectra, through experience of the literature, of related molecules, and from known modern samples or standards.

For interpreting mass spectra there are some general rules, illustrated in Fig. 8.6. The molecular ion ($M^{+\cdot}$), if it is present, will be at the highest mass: it will be an even number unless the molecule contains an odd number of nitrogens. (Nitrogen-containing molecules are rarely found in archaeological extracts.) The

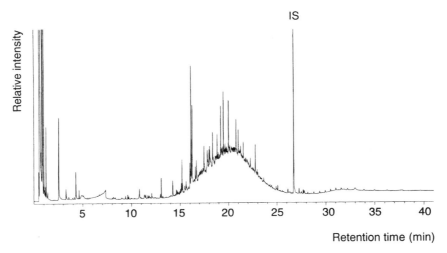

Figure 8.4 Typical total ion count (TIC) of a bitumen extract from the exterior surface of an archaeological shard obtained by GC–MS. IS = internal standard (C_{34} *n*-alkane). This is identical to the output of a GC.

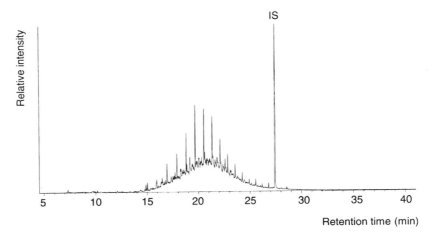

Figure 8.5 Mass chromatogram for $m/z = 71$. This is obtained by running the GC–MS with the mass spectrometer set to register only ions with $m/z = 71$. It shows a homologous series of *n*-alkanes.

molecular ion may be accompanied by a peak at 15 amu less (M-15$^{+\cdot}$), which usually corresponds to the loss of a methyl group (CH_3). The base peak (bp) is the fragment of highest abundance. Other characteristic fragmentation ions are shown in Table 8.1.

8.5   Isotope archaeology – applications of MS in archaeology

The inference of past human behavior from measurements of light and heavy isotopes in material remains has been termed "isotope archaeology" (e.g.,

Table 8.1. *Typical mass fragment ions (including those from contaminants) encountered during GC–MS of organic archaeological compounds.*

Compound	Typical mass fragment ions	Molecular ion
n-alkanes	57, 71, 85, 99 ... M-29	M weak
n-alkenes	97	
n-alcohols (TMS)	57, 75	M-15 strong
Fatty acids (TMS)	73, 117	
Fatty acids (methyl esters) FAMES	74, 87	M weak
TMS fragment	73	
Hopanes and hopenes	191	
Sterols (TMS)	129, M-129	M and M-15
Wax esters (C_{16} acid)	239, 257	M weak
Wax esters (C_{18} acid)	267, 285	M weak
Triacylglycerols ($C_{16}O$)	239	
Triacylglycerols (C_{16} + glycerol)	313	
Triacylglycerols ($C_{18}O$)	267	
Triacylglycerols (C_{18} + glycerol)	341	
Triacylglycerols (C_{16}, C_{16} + glycerol)	551	
Triacylglycerols (C_{16}, C_{18} + glycerol)	577	
Triacylglycerols (C_{18}, C_{18} + glycerol)	607	
Column bleed	207, 281	
Phthalate plasticizers	149, 163, 167	
Dimethyl-polysiloxane (column degradation)	147, 207, 281	
Squalene	69, 81	410
Sulfur (S_8)	64, 96, 128, 160, 192, 256	256
Dichloromethane	84	
Air leak (H_2O, N_2, O_2, Ar, CO_2)	18, 28, 32, 40, 44	

Pollard 1998b). Table 8.2 lists some of the isotope techniques used in archaeology, excluding those used primarily in dating (isotopes used in dating techniques have been reviewed by Pollard [in press b]). In the 1960s and 70s, Robert Brill used lead isotopes (^{204}Pb, ^{206}Pb, ^{207}Pb, and ^{208}Pb) to address questions of provenance, initially of lead-containing glass, but later for metallic silver, lead, and copper (Brill and Wampler 1967). The subsequent use of other isotope systems, such as $\delta^{13}C$, $\delta^{18}O$, and $^{87}Sr/^{86}Sr$, has extended isotopic provenancing of inorganic materials to include marble, obsidian, gypsum, and, most recently, human beings.

At about the same time as this early lead isotope work was taking place, archaeologists were also being introduced to the application of oxygen isotopes for temperature reconstruction from marine sediment cores (Emiliani 1969) and marine molluscs (Shackleton 1969). Most subsequent terrestrial isotope palaeoclimatology studies have been carried out using measurements of δD, $\delta^{13}C$, or $\delta^{18}O$ in peat cores, lake sediments, or tree-rings (e.g., Frenzel 1995). More recently, attempts have been made to interpret stable

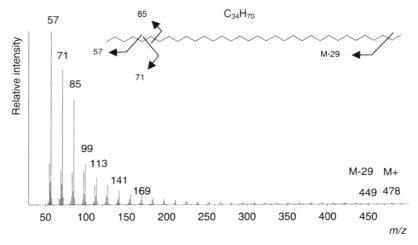

Figure 8.6 Mass spectrum of C_{34} *n*-alkane ($C_{34}H_{70}$). The complete molecule appears at $M^{\bullet+} = 478$ and various fragment ions ($m/z = 57$, 71, etc.) at lower masses. The fragmentation pattern is shown on the molecular structure.

oxygen isotope data from fossil mammalian bone and tooth enamel as a source of climatic evidence (Longinelli 1995). Measurements of $\delta^{18}O$ in modern human bone phosphate have been shown to have a positive correlation with $\delta^{18}O$ in local meteoric water (Longinelli 1995: 61), but temperature reconstructions from medieval human tooth enamel from Greenland (Fricke *et al.* 1995) have proved controversial. Fricke and co-workers attributed a reduction of 3‰ in $\delta^{18}O$ in enamel samples dating to c. AD 1400 as the result of a temperature downturn, corresponding to "the Little Ice Age" of Greenland. Bryant and Froelich (1996) noted that this "downturn" did not appear in the temperature reconstruction from the adjacent Dye 3 Greenland ice core, and concluded that the observation might have a physiological or social explanation. Prompted, perhaps, by this dispute, further work was undertaken which showed that the $\delta^{18}O$ signal in the phosphate mineral component of dental enamel was directly related to the $\delta^{18}O$ signal in drinking water, and thus within a single dentition provided reliable information on short term (seasonal) fluctuations, or as a longer term archive of climatic variation (Fricke *et al.* 1998). Some caution has, however, been expressed about $\delta^{18}O$ measurements from dental enamel carbonate, which is susceptible to diagenetic alteration.

On a global scale, it has been reported that $\delta^{13}C$ measurements on Holocene bone collagen, charcoal, and wood samples from across Europe show a trend from north to south and east to west, which can be linked to latitudinal differences and oceanic influences on climate (van Klinken *et al.* 1994). In bone collagen, for example, the average value of $\delta^{13}C$ for archaeological samples from Spain is $-18.9‰$ compared with $-20.8‰$ for Sweden. Similar trends are reported for charcoal. These observations are based on large data sets accumulated during the

Table 8.2. *Some of the isotopes used in "isotope archaeology"* (from Table 17.1, page 286, in Pollard, A. M. (1998b), with permission).

Element	Isotope ratio[1]	Natural isotopic abundance (%)	Substances studied	Application
Hydrogen	^{2}H/^{1}H	^{1}H = 99.985 ^{2}H (=D) = 0.015	Water, organic matter (cellulose, collagen, lipids, chitin, peat)	Climate, plant water metabolism
Carbon	^{13}C/^{12}C	^{12}C = 98.89 ^{13}C = 1.11	Organic matter, carbonates, biomineralized tissue, soil, CO_2	Diet, plant water-use efficiency, climate and habitat, provenance (ivory, marble)
Nitrogen	^{15}N/^{14}N	^{14}N = 99.633 ^{15}N = 0.366	Organic matter, soil, dissolved NO_3^- and NH_4^+, groundwater	Diet, nitrogen fixation pathways, animal water use, climate, groundwater pollution
Oxygen	^{18}O/^{16}O	^{16}O = 99.759 ^{17}O = 0.037 ^{18}O = 0.204	Water, biomineralized carbonates and phosphates, sedimentary phosphates and carbonates, silicates, organic matter	Climate, plant and animal water metabolism, ocean temperature, provenance (marble), chronostratigraphy
Sulfur	^{34}S/^{32}S	^{32}S = 95.00 ^{33}S = 0.76 ^{34}S = 4.22 ^{36}S = 0.014	Organic matter, hydrocarbons, sulfates, sediments	Diet, pollution
Strontium	^{87}**Sr**/^{86}Sr	^{84}Sr = 0.56 ^{86}Sr = 9.86 ^{87}Sr = 7.02 ^{88}Sr = 82.56	Bone and dental mineral, sediments, seawater	Diet, trophic levels, provenance, dating
Lead[2]	^{208}**Pb**/^{206}**Pb**, ^{207}**Pb**/^{206}**Pb**, ^{206}**Pb**/^{204}Pb	^{204}Pb = 1.4 ^{206}Pb = 24.1 ^{207}Pb = 22.1 ^{208}Pb = 52.4	Geological material, metals, silicates, biominerals, environmental samples	Provenance, pollution sourcing

[1] Isotopes in bold are radiogenic
[2] The isotope ratios given for lead are those usually reported in the archaeological literature, and differ from those used geologically

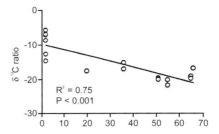

Figure 8.7 Relationship between bone collagen carbon isotope ratio and latitude for modern carnivorous terrestrial mammals. The regression equation is given as $\delta^{13}C = -0.20 \ (\pm 0.03) \times$ latitude $- 9.7 \ (\pm 1.0)$, with $r^2 = 0.75$. Reproduced from Kelly (2000: 7) by permission of the National Research Council Canada Research Press.

routine measurement of $\delta^{13}C$ for the correction of radiocarbon dates. The same publication shows plots of $\delta^{13}C$ from bone collagen, charcoal, and wood against modern day mean July temperatures, sunshine, humidity, and precipitation, which show significant correlations (e.g., $r = 0.84$ between bone collagen $\delta^{13}C$ and total July sunshine). Interestingly, these relationships appear to be as good as those reported elsewhere for the correlation between climate parameters and so-called climate proxies, such as isotopes in tree rings. Similar studies have been made on bone collagen data from modern bird and mammal samples, which confirm the tendency of some isotopic data to vary with latitude (Kelly 2000). For example, $\delta^{13}C$ of bone collagen from carnivorous terrestrial mammals has a correlation of $r^2 = 0.75$ with latitude, although other animal groups show less significant correlation (e.g., African elephant, $r^2 = 0.28$). The numbers of samples are, however, relatively small, and there appears to be some variation in sample extraction procedures. Figure 8.7 shows an example of some of these correlations.

A first attempt to utilize the wealth of accumulated isotope data now routinely captured during the radiocarbon dating of bone and dental collagen as a palaeoclimate indicator has recently been published (Hedges *et al.* 2004). This compiles $\delta^{13}C$ and $\delta^{15}N$ data from equids, bovids, and cervids over the past 40 000 radiocarbon years (Fig. 8.8). The $\delta^{13}C$ pattern clearly shows a drop in $\delta^{13}C$ (of around 1–1.5‰) at the onset of the Holocene, which is very similar in appearance to the oxygen isotope signal obtained from the GRIP (Greenland) ice core. The $\delta^{15}N$ signal shows a drop of 2–3‰ during the period 10–15 ka (radiocarbon years) BP, which is more difficult to interpret as a simple climatic response. This work shows, however, that there is a wealth of untapped proxy palaeoclimatic data residing in various archaeological databanks.

Dietary reconstruction using stable isotopes
The closest we ever come to the physical presence of our ancestors is the excavation and study of human bone, and it is, therefore, not surprising that

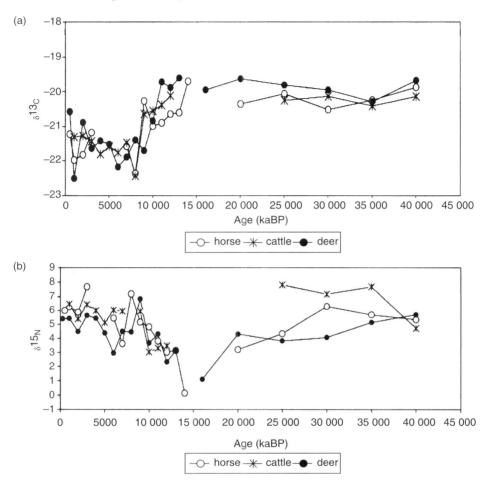

Figure 8.8 Variations in mammalian bone collagen carbon (a) and nitrogen (b) isotope values over the last 40 000 radiocarbon years. The carbon data show a clear shift at c. 10 000 radiocarbon years BP, corresponding to the warming at the onset of the Holocene, but the nitrogen data appear to show a minimum during the last Ice Age. Reprinted from *Quaternary Science Reviews* 23, Hedges, R. E. M., Stevens, R. E., and Richards, M. P., "Bone as a stable isotope archive for local climatic information states", pp. 959–65, copyright 2004, with permission from Elsevier.

human remains have received particular attention in scientific research. The popular saying "you are what you eat" has been taken literally in archaeology for more than 30 years, and dietary reconstruction has been attempted, first by using trace element levels in bone mineral and, more recently, by using stable isotope studies on collagen and mineral in both bone and teeth (e.g., DeNiro 1987, Schwarcz and Schoeninger 1991, Pate 1994). The mineral fraction of the bone is normally described as biological calcium hydroxyapatite or *dahlite*, $Ca_{10}(PO_4)_6(OH)_2$, although it also contains small amounts of carbonate. Bone mineral acts as a reservoir for these ions, and also for the storage of other ingested inorganic elements, such as strontium and lead, and it is these and similar elements which have been studied for their presumed dietary and health significance (Sandford 1993a). However, it was soon realized that the inorganic chemistry of bone was altered to a greater or lesser extent by *post-mortem diagenetic* alteration, the magnitude and significance of which has been extensively debated (e.g., Hancock *et al.* 1989, Price 1989b, Radosevich 1993, Sandford 1993b). Although a number of workers have proposed selective leaching procedures to remove exogenous material from excavated bone, on the assumption that post-mortem contamination is more soluble than endogenous mineral (Sillen and Sealy 1995), these remain disputed. As a consequence, most researchers are very wary of using trace element data alone to predict diet, health, and status from bone and dentine, although enamel is regarded as much more resistant to alteration, and therefore potentially suitable for chemical analysis.

Isotopic studies of the organic fraction (mostly collagen) have been chemically far less controversial. Providing adequate quality assurance procedures are applied to the extracted collagen (as outlined in general terms in Section 13.5), they appear to avoid most of the diagenetic problems encountered with trace elements. Most authors accept the fact that the isotopic ratios appear to be unchanged in bone collagen as a result of burial, providing that more than about 10% of the original collagen survives (estimated from data presented in Ambrose 1990). Thus, the most immediate impact of "isotope archaeology" has been in the area of human dietary reconstruction.

The isotopic method is based on the observation that carbon and nitrogen isotope ratios ($^{13}C/^{12}C$ and $^{15}N/^{14}N$) in bone collagen (and bone mineral carbonate) will reflect the corresponding isotopic ratios in the diet, with some adjustment for fractionation through the system. Because of the relationship between trophic level and isotope value discussed above, in principle these isotope ratios can be used to distinguish between a reliance on terrestrial and marine food resources in human diet. Carbon isotope ratios may further be used to differentiate between the consumption of terrestrial plants which photosynthesize using the C_3 or C_4 pathways described above. Virtually all land plants photosynthesize using the C_3 pathway, but a few plants, mainly tropical grasses, have evolved the C_4 pathway as an adaptation to a hot, dry environment. Archaeologically the most important C_4 plant is maize, which has its origins in central America, and carbon isotope measurements have been used to follow with great success the spread of maize agriculture in prehistoric American cultures (van der Merwe 1992).

In a classic study of the spread of maize (*Zea mays*) agriculture from Central America into eastern and central North America in pre-Columbian times, van der Merwe and Vogel (1977) demonstrated its arrival in the lower

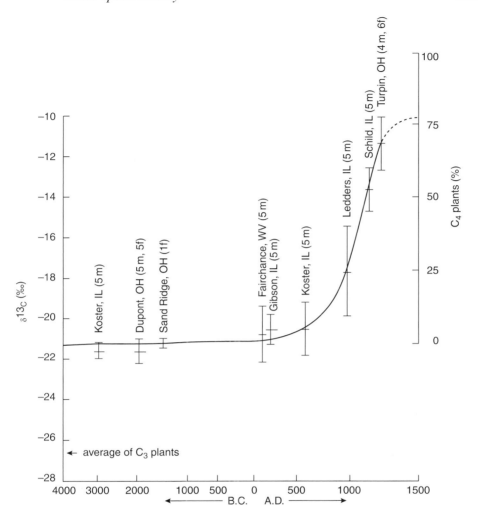

Figure 8.9 Carbon isotope composition of human bone collagen from the lower Illinois Valley, North America. The increase from $\delta^{13}C = -22‰$ to $-10‰$ at c. AD 1000 marks the arrival of maize agriculture at the end of the Late Woodland period (van der Merwe 1982). Reproduced by permission of *American Scientist*.

Illinois Valley by the end of the Late Woodland period (c. 1000 AD: Fig. 8.9). Archaeological opinion, prior to this, was that maize had been introduced into this area by 400 AD or perhaps earlier (van der Merwe 1992). This work is now regarded as one of the great triumphs of scientific archaeology. Because of the ephemeral nature of the direct evidence for agricultural practices, it actually helped to solve a question which, on archaeological grounds alone, was relatively intractable, and also established isotopic human palaeodietary studies as a legitimate research area.

The most comprehensive isotope palaeodietary work to date has been done in southern and eastern Africa, where climatic conditions (resulting in both C_3 and C_4 plants at the base of the food web) and, in some cases, a hunter–gatherer lifestyle, have combined to give what might be regarded as an ideal ecosystem to study (Sealy and van der Merwe 1985, Ambrose and DeNiro 1986). This success can be attributed not only to the suitability of the ecosystem, but also to the research methodology adopted – that of attempting to reconstruct as many levels of the food web as possible, by analyzing bone and tissue from a wide range of plants and animals with known or assumed predator–prey relationships. In less complex societies, it is possible to regard humans as the top predators in the ecosystem, and apply the techniques of isotope ecology used elsewhere in zoology (Wada *et al.* 1991).

Many isotopic studies of bone collagen have been carried out in the USA since the original work of van der Merwe and his colleagues. Matson and Chisholm (1991) demonstrated the spread of maize subsistence during the Basketmaker II phase (c. first century BC) to the Cedar Mesa area of Utah, in contradiction to the previously expected date of AD 800–1000. Buikstra and Milner (1991) investigated the dependence of humans on maize in the central Mississippi and Illinois River valleys between AD 1000 and 1400, which showed a complex pattern of regional and temporal variation. Schurr (1992) studied the relationship between social position (as inferred from burial practice) and diet in the Middle Mississippian (AD 1200–1450) of eastern North America. Larsen *et al.* (1992) investigated human remains from four prehistoric periods (range 1000 BC–AD 1450) and two historic periods from the Georgia Bight (south-eastern coastal US). Increasingly positive $\delta^{13}C$ values were interpreted as greater utilization of maize during the prehistoric period. The accompanying decrease in $\delta^{15}N$ values allowed the authors to discount an alternative possible explanation – the increased exploitation of marine resources. Further evidence for increasing maize consumption was the observation of increased dental caries – maize, being high in sugar, is more cariogenic in general than C_3 diets. One site (Irene), however, dated to the very end of the prehistoric period (AD 1300–1450), showed a marked decrease in $\delta^{13}C$ values, interpreted as a reversion to C_3 subsistence. This is linked to archaeological evidence for a marked decline in social organization in Mississippian cultures in the early fifteenth century – a phenomenon related to climatic deterioration and a reduction in rainfall in the region.

Katzenberg *et al.* (1995) reviewed the isotopic evidence for maize agriculture in human bone from southern Ontario, Canada, dating to the period AD 400–1500. They saw a gradual increase in the importance of maize from AD 650–1250. They also compiled published $\delta^{13}C$ data from human bone collagen from central North America (the Mississippi, Illinois, and Ohio valleys, and the Great Lakes region) between AD 500 and 1300 (about

130 measurements). This showed a general increase in $\delta^{13}C$ from around $-20‰$ in AD 600 to $-10‰$ by AD 1200, but with regional variations, which are counter-intuitive to a simple model for the spread of maize agriculture from the south. Southern states such as Missouri, Arkansas, and Tennessee showed little increase in maize utilization until near the end of the period, whereas Illinois appeared to have early and continued exploitation of maize. This evidence, combined with that of Larsen *et al.* (1992) for a reversion to more traditional agricultural resources during times of social or environmental stress, illustrates not only the complexity of human palaeoecology, but also the value of stable isotope measurements in such studies.

Given this interest in the archaeology of maize cultivation, it is surprising how relatively little dietary reconstruction has been done in Central America, and the almost complete lack of parallel studies in South America. White and Schwarcz (1989) measured trace elements in bone mineral and stable isotope values in human bone collagen from the Lowland Maya site at Lamanai, Belize, covering a date range of pre-Classic (1250 BC–AD 250) to Historic (AD 1520–1670). From $\delta^{13}C$, they estimated a dietary maize input of 50% at the beginning of the pre-Classic period, falling to 37% at the end of this period, rising to 70% in post-Classic times. An observed decline in $\delta^{13}C$ (and an associated decline in dental caries) at the end of the pre-Classic was taken to suggest a reduction in maize production, perhaps as a result of social or climatic change. $\delta^{15}N$ is constant in human collagen (at around $+10‰$) throughout the period, with the exception of one individual – a man, buried together with a female in a high status Early Classic (AD 250–400) tomb burial. His $\delta^{15}N$ value of $+13.2‰$ was taken to indicate a higher consumption of imported coastal dietary resources by the elite. Stable isotope palaeodietary studies of the Maya have recently been reviewed by Tykot (2002).

In South America, van der Merwe *et al.* (1981) established that maize was a significant dietary component along the Orinoco River in Venezuela between 800 BC and AD 400, in contrast to the previously held assumptions about tropical Amazonian ecosystems. They concluded that by around AD 400 the diet consisted of 80% or more of maize, and that this shift in subsistence strategy allowed a 15-fold increase in population density. This conclusion was based on an isotopic shift in $\delta^{13}C$ from $-26‰$ in "pre-maize" humans to $-10‰$ in those exploiting maize. The unusually negative average of $-26‰$ (compared with $-21.5‰$ for prehistoric North American humans with a C_3 diet) was attributed to an extreme depletion in ^{13}C, as a result of carbon recycling in the tropical forest ecosystem (van der Merwe 1992). On the other side of the Andes, Ubelaker *et al.* (1995) used isotopes to assess the dietary relationship between high status individuals and those sacrificed buried in the same tombs. The remains were from six shaft tombs excavated at La Florida, Quito, Ecuador, and dated to the Chaupicruz phase (c. AD 100–450). Although ethnographic evidence from the sixteenth century AD suggested that there might be a higher consumption of animal protein by the elite, this was not observed isotopically. The only difference suggested analytically was a higher consumption of maize by the elite class (average $\delta^{13}C$ $-10.3‰$ in the elite group, $-11.6‰$ in those of lower rank), attributed to a higher consumption of *chicha* (maize beer) by the elite.

The above brief review shows that there has been more than 30 years of research using stable isotope studies on human collagen in the New World and in Africa, and this has had a significant impact on the broader archaeological debate. Until recently, however, the impact of stable isotopes on European archaeology has been considerably less substantial. This is, in large part, because C_4 plants are a relatively recent introduction, and therefore we would not expect to see such large shifts in $\delta^{13}C$ as seen in the Americas and Africa. Isotopic work carried out on human collagen from prehistoric Europe has focused on detecting more subtle differences in the balance between terrestrial C_3 subsistence and exploitation of marine resources, either temporally or geographically. The first was Tauber (1981), who measured $\delta^{13}C$ in human remains dating from the Mesolithic (c. 5200–4000 BC) through to the end of the Iron Age (c. AD 1000) in Denmark, and some historic Inuit samples from Greenland. This work showed a clear transition from the hunter–gatherer lifestyle of the Mesolithic ($\delta^{13}C$ approximately -11 to $-15‰$) to the agricultural lifestyle of the Neolithic and later populations ($\delta^{13}C$ approximately -13 to $-27‰$). In the absence of any C_4 terrestrial dietary component, the higher $\delta^{13}C$ in the Mesolithic was attributed to a subsistence pattern heavily dependent on marine resources. This was supported by similar figures for three pre-contact Inuit from Greenland, with an assumed diet dominated by marine food. In a later study involving measurements of $\delta^{13}C$ and $\delta^{15}N$, combined with dental evidence, Lubell *et al.* (1994) demonstrated a gradual shift from marine exploitation to terrestrial food resources in Portugal at the Mesolithic/Neolithic transition – here dated to around 5000 BC. In this case, $\delta^{13}C$ drops from a range of -15 to $-19‰$ in the Mesolithic to between -19 and $-20.5‰$ in the Neolithic. The interpretation of this as being due to reduced marine input is supported by a concomitant change in $\delta^{15}N$ from greater than $+10‰$ in the Mesolithic to about $+9‰$ in the Neolithic.

The debate intensified recently with the publication of Richards *et al.* (2003), which claimed that, in Britain at least, on the evidence of bone collagen δ^{13}, the transition from the Mesolithic to Neolithic (c. 4000 cal. BC) was a sharp one, with a complete abandonment of marine resources in the Neolithic, even by coastal communities (Fig. 8.10). This was further interpreted as being the result of a very rapid adoption of the Neolithic lifestyle of plant and animal domestication, contrary to earlier views which argued for a gradual shift. Perhaps predictably, this has provoked a sharp debate focusing on both the interpretation of isotopic evidence (Milner *et al.* 2003) and on evidence to the contrary for other parts of Europe (Lidén *et al.* 2003). Milner *et al.* (2003) summarize the assumptions upon which the

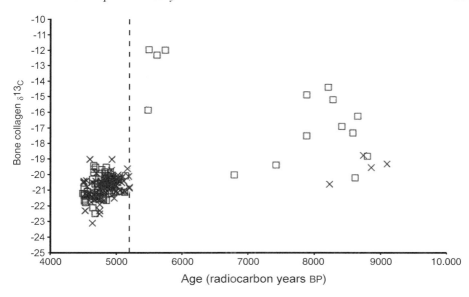

Figure 8.10 Carbon isotope ratios in bone collagen plotted against radiocarbon ages for 183 British Mesolithic and Neolithic humans from coastal (within 10 km of modern coastline; squares) and inland sites (crosses). The sharp change in carbon isotope ratio at around 5200 radiocarbon years BP is interpreted as a shift from a marine diet to one dominated by terrestrial protein. This coincides with the onset of the Neolithic period in Britain. (Reproduced from Richards *et al.* 2003, with permission of Nature Publishing Group and the first author.)

estimation of the proportion of marine food in human diet is estimated from carbon and nitrogen isotopes are based:

- bone collagen composition reflects the average diet over the last 5–10 years of life
- isotopes in collagen reflect only protein inputs into diet
- the offset (fractionation) between dietary protein and bone collagen is 0–1‰ for $\delta^{13}C$ and 3‰ for $\delta^{15}N$
- variations in diet, such as variations in the ratio of protein to carbohydrate, have no effect on the above statements, and
- the dietary "end members" (i.e., pure marine and pure terrestrial inputs) are known in terms of isotopic value.

On the basis of uncertainties in these assumptions and the absence of complete isotopic examinations of the associated food webs, they argue that the data cannot be interpreted in such a clear-cut way. The response from Hedges (2003) accepts that there is some uncertainty in some of these assumptions (particularly related to the metabolic "routing" of different sources of dietary carbon – see also Sillen *et al.* 1989), but reasserts that the overwhelming body of isotopic evidence is for a sharp change in diet towards a more terrestrial subsistence at the onset of the Neolithic. The debate will undoubtedly continue.

Most of the work discussed so far refers to isotopic measurements (almost always $\delta^{13}C$ and $\delta^{15}N$) on collagen extracted from human bone or dentine, or, more strictly, on the acid-insoluble organic matter contained in bone and dentine. It is likely in archaeological material that this is not entirely collagen (Ambrose 1990), unless great care is taken (e.g., ultra-filtration) to remove the various degradation products and intrusive material. However, collagen, being an organic molecule (albeit one protected by a mineral matrix), and one susceptible to hydrolytic degradation, is unlikely to survive in most environments for more than a few thousand years (Smith *et al.* 2001). In order to extend the method into "deep time" (i.e., hundreds of thousands of years, or even millions), measurement has focused on the $\delta^{13}C$ in the carbonate incorporated into mineralized tissue, and especially dental enamel, since this is usually the most resilient mammalian tissue (Lee-Thorp *et al.* 1989, Lee-Thorp and van der Merwe 1991). This has allowed the estimation of diet in a wide range of fossil animals, and, indirectly, dating the emergence of C_4 plants in Pakistan and Kenya to between 10 and 15 Ma (Morgan *et al.* 1994). More important archaeologically, however, has been the study of diet in fossil hominids stretching back to *Australopithecus robustus* at Swartkrans (Lee-Thorp *et al.* 1994), dating to the range 1.8–1 Ma. Comparison of $\delta^{13}C$ in the dental enamel carbonate from eight hominid samples (average value −8.5 ± 1.0‰) with measurements from the teeth of known C_4 grazers (average value c. 0‰) and C_3 browsers (average −11 to –12‰) from Swartkrans suggested that the Australopithecines had a significant component (25–30 %) of C_4 plant material in their diet, either obtained by eating C_4 grasses or, more likely, from consuming grazing animals. This indicates an omnivorous diet, in contradiction to the previously held belief from dental studies that Australopithecines were vegetarian. This shows that isotopic studies on fossil dental enamel have a significant role to play in understanding human evolution.

Isotopes and human mobility

A further substantial extension of this work on dietary reconstruction has been the use of differential information available from within a single skeleton to give an indication of lifetime mobility. This is based on the fact that the continual resorption and remodeling of bone leads to different rates of bone turnover within the skeleton, which, in turn, means that different elements of the skeleton give information from different periods of time prior to death. Turnover rates for different skeletal components in humans are not known precisely, and will also depend on age, but are likely to range up to ten years (Sealy *et al.* 1995). Even more useful is the fact that teeth are formed early in life, and are essentially unaltered after eruption, since there is no major remodeling within dental tissue. Thus, the isotopic composition of the collagen in teeth will represent dietary inputs early in life (up to perhaps 20 or so), but the isotopic composition from rib, for example, may reflect the diet over the last few years prior to death. Thus, an individual who died aged more than 30 or so might be expected to show differences, if he/she spent adult years in a different ecological environment from that of childhood. As with dietary studies, this technique has largely grown out of isotopic studies of other mammals – in this case, the need to trace the movement of elephants in Africa, and to be able to provenance traded ivory (van der Merwe *et al.* 1990, Vogel *et al.* 1990, Koch *et al.* 1995).

Sealy *et al.* (1995) reported the measurement of $\delta^{13}C$ and $\delta^{15}N$ in dentine, enamel, rib, and femur (or humerus) from five individuals excavated in South Africa. Two were prehistoric Khoisan hunter–gatherers, whose isotopic signatures showed similar values in all tissues, indicating no significant movement during their lifetime (or, strictly speaking, no significant residence in a different ecological environment – the extent of movement within an ecozone cannot be determined by this method). Another skeleton was an adult male from Cape Town Fort, probably a European who died at the Cape during the seventeenth century AD. His isotopes also showed no variation, and it was assumed that he was newly arrived in the Cape when he died. A fourth individual, another European from the Dutch East India Company station at Oudespost (occupied between AD 1673 and 1732), did show significant differences between dental and bone measurements – less negative $\delta^{13}C$ values and higher $\delta^{15}N$ figures – a pattern attributed to greater consumption of marine food in adult life. His strontium isotope ratio was similar for all tissues, and indicated a coastal habitation throughout life. The fifth individual was an African woman assumed to be a slave, and dating to the eighteenth century AD. She showed a marked shift in all ratios measured. In early life through to early adulthood she showed $\delta^{13}C$ and $\delta^{15}N$ measurements consistent with a C_4 biome – interpreted as a tropical or sub-tropical inland area. At the end of her life, she had increased $\delta^{15}N$ values, consistent with a more marine diet. Her strontium ratios dropped from 0.732 in canine dentine to 0.717 in the rib, suggesting a move to a coastal environment, consistent with where she was found and the increase in seafood input. This work shows that the whole of an individual's life history is isotopically encoded in the skeleton.

A significant addition to this methodology, as alluded to above, has been the measurement of $^{87}Sr/^{86}Sr$ ratio in mineralized tissue, first suggested by Ericson (1985). This ratio is thought to be characteristic of the local underlying geology, and passes unmodified through the food chain. Migrations which result in the last years of life being spent in a region of different geology from that of the early years should show up in a different strontium isotope ratio between dental enamel and bone tissue. Moreover, because modern data is available for Sr isotope values, it is possible, in principle, to predict where these regions might be. The disadvantage of Sr isotope ratio work is that, until recently, Sr isotopes needed to be determined by TIMS, which is relatively slow and expensive, thus limiting the applicability of the method. It is yet to be seen what effect the emerging technology of high resolution MC–ICP–MS combined with laser ablation will have on this area of research.

Perhaps the most archaeologically significant application of Sr isotopes to date is that of Price and co-workers, who have used this technique to study the Neolithicization of Europe (Bentley *et al.* 2002), and the later spread of the "Beaker Folk" (e.g., Price *et al.* 1994, Grupe *et al.* 1997). The key question to be addressed in both cases is whether it was, in the case of the Neolithic, farming as an idea or farmers as a population who spread through Europe, and the same question in respect to metallurgy for Bell Beakers. In both cases, there are a number of different sources of information to be considered in addition to traditional archaeological culture-change information, including linguistics and genetics. Price *et al.* (1994) focused on strontium isotope ratios in teeth and bone from eight individuals from Bell Beaker burials in Bavaria. The "Beaker Folk" are traditionally seen as a group of people identified by their burial practices (including the characteristic ceramic "beakers") who spread through central and western Europe at the end of the Neolithic (c. 2500 BC), and who may have brought with them the knowledge of metalworking. What is not clear, archaeologically, is whether the "Beaker Folk" themselves moved, or whether "beaker ideas" moved and were simply adopted by indigenous populations. Hence, the importance of an isotopic method which might be capable of detecting the movement of individuals or groups of individuals is apparent. Price *et al.* (1994) plotted total Sr concentration in the bone and teeth against the $^{87}Sr/^{86}Sr$ ratio. Of the eight individuals measured, two showed clear evidence of having moved significantly between adulthood and childhood. In a later study, Bentley *et al.* (2002) applied the same technique to the LBK (Linearbandkeramik) culture, traditionally believed to be the first European farmers (c. 7500 BP). From three different cemeteries, they identified 7 nonlocals from 11 individuals (Flomborn), 9 from 36 (Schwetingen), and 11 from 17 (Dillingen). They suggested that nonlocal females were common in these cemeteries, and that burial practice varied between locals and nonlocals. Overall, they concluded that Sr isotope studies showed that there was a great deal of mobility during the LBK period (especially of females, consistent with genetic evidence for patrilocality), but that the most likely explanation for the spread of the Neolithic was a colonization of south-eastern Europe by farmers, followed by the adoption of farming by the indigenous population in central and northern Europe.

Inherent in all these methodologies, which measure either absolute Sr levels or strontium isotope ratios in mineralized tissue, is the assumption that diagenesis has not altered the signal since death. This has been a matter of some considerable debate (e.g., Nelson *et al.* 1986), but the consensus of current opinion amongst practitioners is that the repeated acid-washing procedures used remove any diagenetic mineral, because it has a higher solubility than biomineralized apatite (Sillen and Sealy 1995). Intuitively, this seems a rather simplistic generalization, although it has to be acknowledged that there is a growing body of evidence to support this position (e.g., Trickett *et al.* 2003). Given the potential archaeological importance of the interpretations now being placed on Sr isotope and abundance measurements in human tissue, this is obviously a crucial point, and one which deserves further rigorous investigation.

One of the major advantages of using Sr isotope measurements, as opposed to simple Sr abundance measurements, is that the data can be compared to modern geochemical maps of geographical variation in Sr isotope values, which gives the method a predictive capacity (the same is true of Pb isotope measurements, discussed below). Another isotope which can be used in this way is $\delta^{18}O$, as measured in the phosphate mineral of bone or, preferably, dental enamel, which is generally the most resistant bodily tissue. The oxygen isotope composition of skeletal mineral is related to that of the source of drinking water (Longinelli 1984). Because the isotope values of meteoric and terrestrial waters have been studied extensively, maps are available of the modern variation in surface water isotopic compositions for several parts of the world. In the British Isles, for example, the oxygen isotope values in rainfall varies from –4.5‰ (against the international standard VSMOW) in the west to –8.5‰ in the northeast (Talbot and Darling [1997] and subsequent publications). Unlike the heavier Sr and Pb isotopes, however, fractionation will occur as the oxygen is incorporated into the body, so that some form of calibration or correction is required before the values measured in human tissue can be compared directly with geochemical data. This has been studied in a range of mammalian species, but the calibration produced by Levinson *et al.* (1987: 369) is widely used for human tissue. For the phosphate in human teeth, this relationship is:

$$\delta_p = 0.46\delta_w + 19.4$$

where δ_p is the oxygen isotope ratio ($^{18}O/^{16}O$) in teeth and δ_w is the ratio in drinking water. If this equation is used to "locate" the geographical origin of an ancient tooth sample by calculating the value of δ_w from the isotopic composition of the tooth and comparison with modern δ_w data, it assumes, of course, that the oxygen isotope ratio of drinking water in that region is the same now as it was in antiquity – a highly questionable assumption.

Oxygen isotopes, sometimes combined with carbon, nitrogen, strontium, and lead isotopic measurements, have been used to study the mobility of diverse human groups such as in Teotihuacán and Oaxaca, Mexico, dating from about 300 BC to AD 750 (Stuart-Williams *et al.* 1996), the Kellis 2 cemetery (c. AD 250) in the Dakhleh Oasis, Egypt (Dupras and Schwarcz 2001), and in Britain (Budd *et al.* 2003).

Lead isotope provenancing

The use of "chemical fingerprinting" to trace metal objects back to their parent ore source has been one of the main goals of archaeological chemistry since the 1930s. Achieving this by chemical analysis has, however, proved difficult. The relationship between the trace element composition of a metalliferous ore and that of a metal object derived from it is complicated by factors such as variations in partitioning due to process and temperature, mixing of ores from different sources, deliberate or accidental addition of metals to modify the working or visual properties of the finished product, and the likely recycling of scrap metal (Wilson and Pollard 2001).

Lead has four stable isotopes, and an unusually large range of natural isotopic compositions, because three of them lie at the end of radioactive decay chains, the decay of which supplements the original (primeval) ratios (see above). The lead isotopic ratio in a metalliferous deposit depends on the geological age of the ore body, and the relative proportions of primeval lead, uranium, and thorium in the original ore-forming fluids (Pollard and Heron 1996: 312). The discovery in the late 1960s that the lead isotope ratios in an archaeological metal object give an indication of the ore source (Brill and Wampler 1967), and are apparently unaffected by anthropogenic processing, was a major breakthrough. This was reinforced when it was realized that it applied not only to lead artifacts (relatively rare archaeologically), but also to the traces of lead left in silver extracted from argentiferous lead ores by cupellation (Barnes *et al.* 1974), and to the lead traces left in copper objects smelted from impure copper ores (Gale and Stos-Gale 1982).

Brill and Wampler (1967) showed that, even with the analytical resolution available from mass spectrometers of the time, it was possible to differentiate between lead from Laurion in Greece, England, and Spain, although they noted that an ore sample from north-eastern Turkey fell into the same "isotope space" as that occupied by three ores from England; this presaged some of the subsequent interpretational difficulties. The majority of archaeological lead isotope analysis has focused on the circulation of metal in the Mediterranean Bronze Age, using the relatively slow and expensive method of TIMS. This work has been extensively reviewed and summarized (Gale 1991, Gale and Stos-Gale 1992, Knapp and Cherry 1994, Pollard and Heron 1996: 329). By the mid 1990s, however, the whole intellectual enterprise had become so mired in controversy (Pollard in press a) that, since then, very little in the way of new archaeological interpretation has been published. There was initially some theoretical speculation that anthropogenic processing of metals might alter the isotopic ratio of the lead (Budd *et al.* 1995a), but this was subsequently shown to be unimportant within the then existing measurement precision. (It remains untested using the higher precision machines now available.) The idea was, however, subsequently and profitably applied to the anthropogenic fractionation of zinc in brass

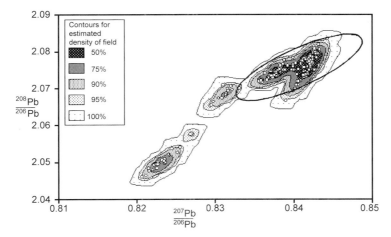

Figure 8.11 Kernel density estimate of the lead isotope data for part of the Troodos orefield, Cyprus (data from Gale *et al.* 1997). The superimposed ellipse is the one used to represent the Cyprus orefield in several publications, and clearly does not encompass the entirety of the data (Scaife *et al.* 1999: 129, with permission from the University of Bradford).

(Budd *et al.* 1999) and tin in bronze (Budd *et al.* 1995b, Gale 1997, Yi *et al.* 1999, Clayton *et al.* 2002).

More significant and contentious were the differences of opinion about the display and interpretation of lead isotope data. Much of this focused on the normality or otherwise of lead isotope data, and the extent to which provenance could and should be assigned from bivariate plots. Subsequent contributions (Baxter and Gale 1998, Scaife *et al.* 1999) have demonstrated quite conclusively that lead isotope data is not, in general, normally distributed, and therefore much of the earlier data interpretation needs to be reevaluated. Scaife *et al.* (1999) clearly showed that lead isotope data can be fully described using kernel density estimation (KDE), without resort to "confidence ellipses" which assume normality, and that previously defined ellipses might, in some cases, be misleading. Figure 8.11 shows a kernel density estimate of two isotope ratios for part of the Troodos orefield, Cyprus (data from Gale *et al.* 1997). The superimposed ellipse is the one conventionally used to represent the Cyprus field in many previous publications. Clearly, the KDE field is non-normal, at least trimodal, and extends well beyond the limits of the ellipse. It is hard to avoid the conclusion that, at least in this case, the orefield in the past has been too conservatively defined, perhaps resulting in the misclassification of samples from the orefield as non-Cypriot.

The net effect of all this controversy was to stifle the application and development of what is, fundamentally, an extremely useful and practical technique. This is unfortunate, because in the last ten years advances in mass spectrometry, particularly the advent of high resolution MC–ICP mass spectrometers (Chapter 9), could have made lead isotope analysis relatively cheap and routine for archaeology. The latest generation of machines has analytical sensitivities an order of magnitude better than conventional TIMS, a vastly increased throughput capacity, and relatively simpler sample preparation requirements (especially if laser ablation is used, although this is more difficult to quantify). Some recent publications, such as Ponting *et al.* (2003) on Roman silver coins, have demonstrated the potential of these instruments in archaeology. This uses high-resolution ICP–MS with sampling by laser ablation, and is a clear example of the way forward, using the new technology available in this area.

9

INDUCTIVELY COUPLED PLASMA–MASS SPECTROMETRY (ICP–MS)

Inductively coupled plasma–mass spectrometry is now such an important technique in archaeology, as elsewhere, that we devote a whole chapter to it. There are now a number of different ICP–MS modes of operation (solution analysis, laser ablation, multicollector, high resolution); this chapter provides a general overview. Further description of the instrumentation for ICP–MS may be found in Harris (1997) and Montaser (1998). Some general applications of solution ICP–MS are discussed by Date and Gray (1989), Platzner (1997), and Kennett *et al.* (2001).

9.1 Types of ICP analysis

Inductively coupled plasma–mass spectrometry (ICP–MS) was first commercialized in 1983, and since then has gradually replaced techniques such as AAS, ICP–OES (Chapter 3), and NAA (Chapter 6) as the method of choice for fast, trace level elemental analysis in a wide range of materials (Fig. 9.1). It offers multielement detection limits below parts per billion (ppb; 10^{-9}), sometimes down to parts per trillion (ppt; 10^{-12}), and can give a rapid throughput of samples (commonly 20–50 per day, depending on the number of elements or isotopes required). Most elements can be analyzed, except some of the light elements (H, He, C, N, O, F, Ne, Cl, Ar), and some actinides. Although this encompasses a wide mass range (i.e., ^{6}Li to ^{238}U), the most common mass selector for basic instruments (the quadrupole) has an inherent bias for producing better data at higher masses. Unlike ICP–OES, which has no isotopic capacity, each elemental measurement in ICP–MS is made on one or more selected isotopes of that element, and so potentially even a quadrupole instrument can provide isotopic ratio measurements for elements of interest to archaeology such as Pb or Sr. However, the combination of plasma instability and quadrupole resolution does not lead to isotope ratio measurements of the precision required for archaeological samples. For such applications, it is preferable to use TIMS or, increasingly, a multicollector (MC–ICP–MS) ICP instrument.

ICP–MS now comes in various guises. The primary differences are in the way in which the sample is introduced into the plasma (either as a solution, or by laser ablation of a solid sample), and in the type of magnetic separation applied to the ions. Whilst the type of magnetic separation is a fixed property of the instrument and cannot therefore be changed, most instruments can accommodate either solution or laser ablation sample presentation.

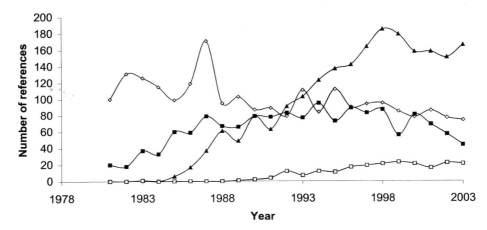

Figure 9.1 The number of published scientific papers (1981–2003) with keywords relating to ICP and NAA (as shown) in their titles or abstract. Data source ISI Web of Knowledge (http://wok.mimas.ac.uk/).

However, each of these requires a different hardware configuration, and therefore specific tuning of the instrument, before use. It is not possible to switch between these modes during the same experimental run.

Solution analysis

The digestion of solid samples to produce a solution is discussed in Section 13.2. For solution-based ICP–MS analysis, the liquid is taken up through a thin tube via a peristaltic pump. This feeds directly into the instrument nebulizer, where argon gas is introduced into the liquid and a fine mist of droplets is expelled from the tip of the nebulizer. This sample aerosol is sprayed into the condenser to reduce the size of the droplets, ensuring an even sample loading and preventing cooling of the plasma. About 1% of the sample solution uptake is transported to the plasma torch, and any unused solution is drained away and may be recycled.

The plasma is maintained at a temperature of 10 000°C by an external radio frequency current, as described in Section 3.3. At this temperature, many molecular species are broken down, and approximately 50% of the atoms are ionized. So far this is identical to ICP–OES, but for ICP–MS we are not interested in the emission of electromagnetic radiation, but rather in the creation of positive ions. To transfer a representative sample of this plasma ion population to the mass spectrometer, there is a special interface between the plasma and the mass spectrometer. This consists of two sequential cones (sampling and skimmer) with narrow apertures. The cones are made from pure nickel, which is resistant to acids, is physically robust, and has a good thermal conductivity (platinum tipped cones are also available for greater inertness, and for resistance to HF, if necessary). The position of the plasma relative to the cone apertures is critical to the quality of the analysis. The bulk plasma in the center of the fireball must impinge on the sample cone, because the boundary layer is much cooler and can form oxides, which would degrade the mass spectrum. To enable this to be achieved, the whole box containing the nebulizer, condenser, and plasma torch can be moved in three perpendicular directions relative to the interface.

The other technical problem to be solved in ICP–MS is maintaining a high vacuum around the mass selector, whilst injecting (extremely hot) plasma through the cones. If not under vacuum, the positive ions would be scattered and the beam attenuated, and the high voltages in the quadrupole and detector would discharge by sparking. Therefore the plasma torch interface and mass spectrometer are pumped to maintain a high vacuum. The design of the interface is, therefore, critical in both sampling the ions produced by the plasma and maintaining a vacuum for the mass spectrometer. In some instruments, an additional vacuum pump (S-option) is provided to increase the vacuum in the interface region, and this can improve the signal-to-noise ratio for heavy mass elements by a factor of ten. This is especially useful for the analysis of the rare earth elements (see below).

Laser ablation (LA–ICP–MS)

Although solution analysis by ICP–MS is rapidly acquiring the status of the "gold standard" for inorganic analysis in the earth and environmental sciences, for many solid samples the generation of solution for analysis is a considerable undertaking. Furthermore, it also loses any spatial information which may be present in the sample (such as diffusion profiles across bone samples). The advantage of laser ablation is that the samples are analyzed in the solid state with minimal preparation. Even so, the sample must fit within the sample chamber (which is typically cylindrical, $\sim$6 cm diameter by $\sim$4 cm depth), which may require subsampling of a larger object. The area for analysis must also be microscopically flat to ensure that the laser can maintain focus during ablation. This may be achieved by polishing a resin-embedded sample, of the type used for other analyses such as SEM and optical microscopy, or by pressing a powder into a pellet, or by fusing the sample into a glassy matrix (lithium metaborate fusion, as described in Section 13.2).

The sample is usually ablated using a Nd-YAG ultraviolet laser ($\lambda = 266$ nm: the theory of laser light is given in Section 4.1). Earlier systems used an infrared laser, but chemical fractionation was found to be a problem (Jeffries *et al.* 1996). A movable stage and integral optical microscope allow

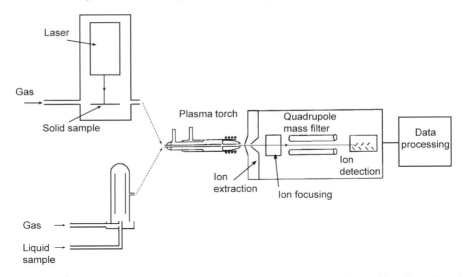

Figure 9.2 Schematic diagram of a quadrupole ICP–MS capable of working in either the solution or laser ablation mode. In the solid mode, a vertical laser ablates material from the sample which is mounted on a moveable horizontal stage. In solution mode, the liquid is sucked up into the injection chamber. In either case, a stream of argon gas carries the sample into the plasma torch, where it is ionized at high temperature and injected into the quadrupole mass selector.

the user to visualize and select the area to analyze. The focused and pulsed laser beam carries sufficient energy to evaporate a discrete area of the sample, the products of which are carried in a stream of argon directly into the plasma torch. The laser can create ablation craters with diameters between 5 and 400 μm. Variable energy levels and flash rates mean that the conditions can (and should) be optimized for each matrix type. In order to move the sampling site, the stage is moved by computer-controlled motors, rather than by steering the laser. As the stage can be moved automatically during the analysis, it is possible to follow a preset pathway (e.g., a transect along a single strand of hair, or across tree rings, or to "raster" a defined area).

Although laser ablation is clearly becoming more popular (as shown in Fig. 9.1), it is difficult to produce fully quantitative data because of problems in matrix matching between sample and standard (see below and Section 13.3). There are also likely to be variations in ablation efficiency in multi-component mixtures, leading to over- or under-representation of particular phases of the sample. It is also unlikely that all ablation products will enter the plasma in the elemental state, or that different particle sizes produced by ablation will have the same compositions. Ablation products may, therefore, not be truly representative of the sample (Morrison *et al.* 1995, Figg *et al.* 1998). Additionally, limits of detection for most elements are approximately

1000 times worse than by solution analysis. This is because not only vaporized ions are swept into the plasma, but also particles of various sizes, which cause the plasma loading to vary over a wider range. This means that the plasma is less controllable than in solution analysis.

To measure all possible elements on a sample by ICP–MS (at least 70), using a beam of approximately 20 μm cross-section, a raster covering an area of approximately 2 mm by 2 mm is needed. For fewer elements a smaller area is required. Even so, this damage can only be seen under the microscope, so the technique may be considered minimally destructive. Because only the surface is sampled, surface concentration or leaching effects and sample heterogeneity on this sampling scale need to be carefully considered. It is possible to preablate a sample (i.e., ablate an area initially to "clean" it, and then repeat for the sample measurement), however Jeffries *et al.* (1996) found that the rise in temperature caused fractionation between the elements. Figure 9.2 shows a schematic diagram of a quadrupole ICP–MS capable of working in either the solution or ablation mode. For more details on laser ablation see Sylvester (2001), and below.

Magnetic selection

Irrespective of the method of introduction of the sample into the plasma, the result of the complex interface between the plasma torch and the mass spectrometer is a stream of positive ions entering a high vacuum magnetic selector device. The lens system following the interface focuses these positive ions into a narrow beam, and the ions are then selected by their mass-to-charge ratio (m/z) using the mass filter (see Section 8.1). Once separated, a charge sensitive detector (at its simplest, a Faraday cup) then records the impact of the ions, amplifying the signal through external circuitry. Quadrupole mass filters are used in most ICP–MS instruments for trace element determination, because they can quickly scan a wide mass range. Quadrupoles can also be used to measure isotopic abundance ratios, but cannot match the better mass resolution of magnetic filters (e.g., TIMS analyses for lead or strontium isotope ratios).

A more recent development of ICP–MS has been the multiple collector ICP–MS (MC–ICP–MS: Fig. 9.3). This uses the same ICP ion source as the quadrupole instrument, but a magnetic selector instead of a quadrupole, and multiple ion beam collectors (detectors). This combines the advantages of the plasma ion source with those of the higher resolution mass filter in terms of mass resolution. The use of more than one detector simultaneously measuring different masses enables greater precision and accuracy in the determination of isotopic ratios by removing problems of instability in the plasma ion source. The net result of these advantages is isotopic ratio measurements of equal sensitivity to those of thermal ionization mass spectrometry (TIMS), but considerably faster, largely because of the need for

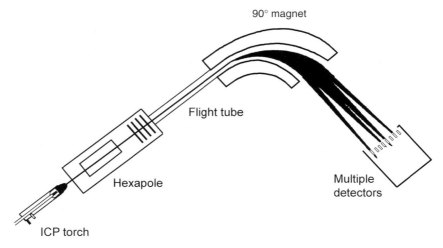

90° magnet

Flight tube

Hexapole

Multiple
detectors

ICP torch

Figure 9.3 Schematic diagram of a multicollector ICP–MS (MC–ICP–MS). This
is a double focusing instrument, with a hexapole (a six-rodded version of the
quadropole) and a 90° magnetic selector, and a multiple bank of ion detectors,
allowing simultaneous measurement of a number of isotopic ratios.

less sample preparation and purification. These advantages, particularly
when combined with laser ablation (LA–MC–ICP–MS), have led to this
technique rapidly overtaking all others in the earth and environmental
sciences, as reviewed by Halliday *et al.* (1998).

9.2   Comparison with other techniques

ICP–MS and neutron activation analysis for trace element determination
Up until the late 1990s, the preferred method for all analyses of trace
elements (in the ppm quantities or less) in earth and environmental science
samples was, generally speaking, neutron activation analysis (NAA; see
Chapter 6). This is because of its sensitivity and reproducibility, as well as the
lack of matrix effects and interferences. Because of the demise of large
sources of neutrons around the world, ICP–MS has gradually replaced NAA
as the method of choice for trace element determinations in a wide range of
samples (Fig. 9.1). It is difficult to carry out a simple comparison of ICP–MS
with NAA, because, as shown above, there is a vast difference between ICP–
MS by solution and LA–ICP–MS. Both ICP–MS and NAA have elements
which they either cannot analyze at all, or have very poor sensitivity for (e.g.,
Pb and Si for NAA, and H, He, C, N, O, F, Ne, Cl, Ar for ICP–MS). For the
majority of the 70 elements measurable by ICP–MS, limits of detection are
quoted as between 0.01 and 0.1 ppt in solution, with a few elements (Ca, Fe,
K, Na, Se) having a higher limit of detection (around 1–100 ppt). A very few
elements have much poorer lower limits (>1 ppb – Si, S, and P).

In the early days of commercial ICP–MS, Ward *et al.* (1990) compared NAA with ICP–MS (solution and laser ablation) for the trace element analysis of biological reference materials. They found that both techniques gave good agreement with certified or published values for 18 elements down to the levels of 30 ppb. The comparison between solid and solution ICP–MS work was, however, described as "fair for most elements". Durrant and Ward (1993) compared LA–ICP–MS with NAA on seven Chinese reference soils. Thirty elements were analyzed, and it was found that 80% of the LA–ICP–MS measurements were within a factor of two of the NAA determinations, although many were considerably closer. Precisions of 2–10% were obtained for most elements by LA–ICP–MS, although the figure deteriorated at lower concentrations. Clearly, in the early 1990s, LA–ICP–MS had some way to go to compete with NAA. Subsequent comparisons have shown that ICP–MS (at least in solution mode) can reproduce INAA measurements to within ±20% at levels of ppb to ppm (although Zheng *et al.* [1997] have observed a systematic error in the ICP–MS determination of Hg). The specific issue of the comparability of NAA and ICP–MS for the analysis of archaeological ceramics is discussed in Section 6.3.

TIMS and multicollectors for heavy element isotopic ratios

Thermal ionization mass spectrometry (TIMS) has been used for over 30 years for heavy (often radiogenic) isotope ratio determination e.g., Rb, Pb, Sr, and U. The sample must be dissolved in acid and separated in ion exchange columns to isolate the element of interest and prevent isobaric interference, e.g., ^{87}Rb and ^{87}Sr which have the same mass. All of this must be carried out in the cleanest of conditions to prevent any contamination. The samples are then loaded onto a metal filament and heated to produce a stream of ions. This is very time consuming and expensive, with approximately 15 isotope measurements made per week. The use of TIMS for archaeological lead isotope provenance studies has been discussed by Ghazi (1994), and Gale and Stos-Gale (2000).

Interlaboratory studies of quadrupole ICP–MS measurements on a range of environmental samples suggests that realistic precisions for lead isotope ratio determinations are 0.3% for ^{206}Pb/^{207}Pb, 0.8% for ^{206}Pb/^{204}Pb and 1.4% for ^{208}Pb/^{204}Pb (Furuta 1991), which are roughly an order of magnitude worse than TIMS. It is now widely accepted, however, that multicollector ICP–MS measurements of lead isotope ratios are sufficiently precise to offer a realistic alternative to TIMS measurements for a wide range of environmental and earth science applications. Walder and Furuta (1993), using a magnetic sector multicollector with seven Faraday cup detectors, have quoted ratios of ^{206}Pb/^{204}Pb = 17.762 ± 0.014 (0.08%), ^{206}Pb/^{207}Pb = 1.1424 ± 0.0009 (0.08%), and ^{208}Pb/^{204}Pb = 37.678 ± 0.034 (0.095%), on a solution containing 82 ppb lead taken from pond sediments (errors quoted at 2 sd). Clearly, this analytical precision is comparable to, if not better than, TIMS.

9.3   Instrument performance

These comments apply to the running of a low resolution quadrupole ICP–MS, capable of both solution and laser ablation analysis, since this is the most widespread form of the instrument. High resolution MC–ICP–MS is, as they say, a whole other ball game!

Stability

The detector on a quadrupole ICP–MS counts the numbers of impacts of ions with a particular mass/charge (m/z) over the time of analysis for each sample. These counts are then averaged and reported as the number of counts per second (CPS). A *tune solution* of 1 ppb (usually containing elements across the mass range e.g., Li, Be, Co, In, Bi, Ba, Pb, Ce, and U) is used before each experiment to ensure that the instrument is set up to achieve the highest CPS across the mass range. The rate of argon flow, position of the plasma on the cones, and lens values are all critical to the response of the detector to this tune solution. An instrument such as the PlasmaQuad 3 is able to achieve at least 20 000 CPS for an element at 1 ppb. However, the CPS will vary for different masses and for the same mass on different days, due to varying instrumental and environmental conditions. Therefore the instrument must be calibrated for each run (see below). Analyses for stability should be performed as a separate experiment to check the performance of the instruments. Any problems can often be reduced by tuning. For a 1 ppb standard solution, the % RSD (relative standard deviation – the standard deviation as a percentage of the mean) should be less than 2–3%. For laser ablation, the stability is worse than for solution analyses (typically 10–15% RSD).

Doubly charged and oxide species

As any mass filter separates the ions produced in the plasma by their mass/charge ratio, it is assumed that such ions are singly charged. However, if doubly charged ions are present, then the detected mass will be halved (e.g., m/z for Ce^+ is 140, but for Ce^{2+} it is 70). This becomes important for elements which have second ionization energies lower than that of the main plasma species, argon, because this is the source of energy for ionization (Fig. 9.4). For example, of the elements of interest archaeologically, barium, cerium, and strontium are susceptible to this. To reduce the "loss" of these elements, the Ba^{2+}/Ba^+ and similar ratios should be less than 6%. In addition, barium and cerium form polyatomic oxides, which will increase the measured mass by 16 (the major isotope of oxygen). The ratio of CeO^+/Ce^+ and BaO^+/Ba^+ should be less than 2%. An adaptation to reduce these problems is to use a plasma

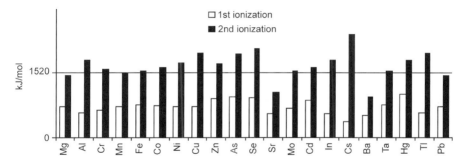

Figure 9.4 The first and second ionization energies for selected elements. The ionization energy of argon is shown by the horizontal line at 1520 kJ/mole.

screen (also called a *plasma shield*). This is a nickel cylinder inserted between the RF coils and the plasma. It can be used in either laser or solution mode, and it allows the plasma to be run at a lower temperature. This is also useful for elements such as Li, Mg, K, Ca, Cr, Mn, Fe, and Cu, as these elements can be susceptible to the formation of polyatomics with argon. Running a "cool plasma" drops the system below the ionization potential of Ar, reducing argon polyatomic interference. Such low temperatures, however, are only useful for particular purposes, since the cooler plasma allows other (nonargon) polyatomics to form, which interfere with the analysis for other elements of interest. It is usual, therefore, to carry out a "normal" run, and then a "cool" run for specific elements such as Ca or Fe.

Interferences

Isobaric interference is still common in ICP–MS, despite the fact that all elements except indium have at least one isotope with a unique mass. This form of interference is due to two different elements having isotopes of the same mass (e.g., $^{40}Ar^+$ and $^{40}Ca^+$, $^{115}Sn^+$ and $^{115}In^+$, etc.). It can often be avoided by selecting nonconflicting isotopes (such as using ^{44}Ca instead of ^{40}Ca), although they may be of lower natural abundance (in this case 2.086% as opposed to 96.94%). Consequently, there is likely to be a loss of analytical sensitivity.

Although the plasma is at an extremely high temperature and most compounds are fully dissociated, in some cooler regions of the plasma and in the interface region between the torch and the magnetic selector, some ions can recombine. Such polyatomic interference can be caused by the argon, the matrix, the residual atmosphere, or species in the sample itself (e.g., $^{40}Ar^{16}O^+$ interferes with $^{56}Fe^+$, $^{14}N_2^+$ with $^{28}Si^+$). The reason for avoiding hydrochloric and sulfuric acids during the sample preparation (Section 13.2) is that chlorine and sulfur ions also generate polyatomic species (e.g., $^{40}Ar^{32}S^+ = {}^{72}Ge^+$, $^{32}S^{16}O^+ = {}^{48}Ti^+$, $^{40}Ar^{35}Cl^+ = {}^{75}As^+$, $^{40}Ar^{37}Cl^+ = {}^{77}Se^+$, $^{35}Cl^{16}O^+ = {}^{51}V^+$). For more examples of interferences, see May and

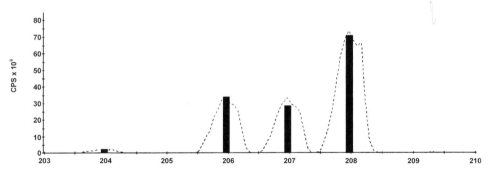

Figure 9.5 ICP–MS survey data from masses 203 to 210. The vertical columns show the expected positions and relative abundances of the four natural isotopes of lead (^{204}Pb, 1.4%; ^{206}Pb, 24.1%; ^{207}Pb, 22.1%; ^{208}Pb, 52.4%). The agreement between the survey data (dotted line) and the actual abundance of lead confirms that lead is present, and that there are no significant interfering elements.

Wiedmeyer (1998). One method of testing for interference is to examine the survey data. In this type of analysis a large number of points are recorded across the mass range, rather than a single measurement taken at a particular mass number for each element. Figure 9.5 shows survey data (dashed line) for masses 203 to 210 on a sample believed to contain lead. The natural lead isotopic abundance is superimposed, shown by filled columns. The proximity of the survey data to the actual abundance of lead indicates that lead is present, and that no interfering elements are present. In this case, a single measurement at mass 208 (which is used for most analyses of lead) is sufficient to quantify lead in the sample.

Limits of detection
Quantification of the limits of detection (LOD), or minimum detectable levels (MDL: statistically defined in Section 13.4), is an important part of any analysis. They are used to describe the smallest concentration of each element which can be determined, and will vary from element to element, from matrix to matrix, and from day to day. Any element in a sample which has a value below, or similar to, the limits of detection should be excluded from subsequent interpretation. A generally accepted definition of detection limit is the concentration equal to a signal of twice (95% confidence level) or three times (99% confidence) the standard deviation of the signal produced by the background noise at the position of the peak. In practice, detection limits in ICP–MS are usually based on ten runs of a matrix matched blank and a standard. In this case:

$$\text{Detection limit } (3\sigma) = \frac{3 \times s \times c}{cps_s - cps_b}$$

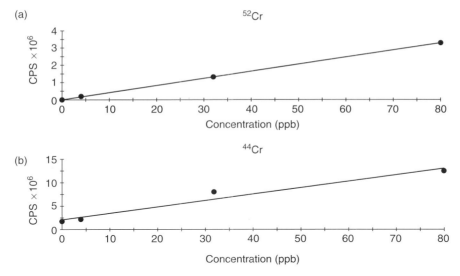

Figure 9.6 Examples of calibration lines produced during ICP–MS analysis. (a) (For ^{52}Cr) produces a good calibration, with a relatively low background intercept (0.032×10^{6} cps), good sensitivity (40 580 cps/ppb), and high correlation (r = 0.999995). (b) (For ^{44}Ca in the same solution) produces a poor curve, with high background intercept (2×10^{4} cps), low sensitivity (1353 cps/ppb) and lower correlation (r = 0.96595).

where s = standard deviation of the blank in CPS, c = concentration of the standard, and cps_s and cps_b are the mean counts per second recorded for the standard and the blank, respectively.

Quantification

Historically, solution-based analytical techniques such as ICP–MS have quantified data using the parts per million/billion (ppm/ppb) system, rather than the SI unit of quantity the mole (see Section 13.1). It is worth repeating that the ppm/ppb system is derived from mass (e.g., 1 ppm is 1 µg in 1000 ml), whilst the mole system is related to number of atoms or molecules (1 mole = 6×10^{23} atoms or molecules).

To perform a quantitative analysis, the response of the detector (in CPS) needs to be converted to a concentration. This is achieved by calibration, as described in more detail in Section 13.4. Where the element to be quantified is present in the calibration solution and an internal standard has been used, the resulting data are termed *fully quantitative*. ICP–MS as a technique is characterized by having a linear relationship between instrument response and concentration over a very wide (i.e., several orders of magnitude) concentration range. Thus, a plot of CPS from known standards against concentration should give a straight line going through or close to the origin (Fig. 9.6). An important consideration for the production of fully quantified

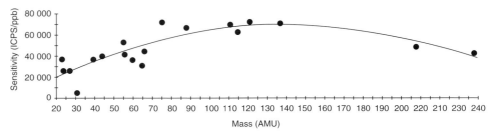

Figure 9.7 Sensitivity (ion counts per second/concentration in ppb) as a function of mass number in ICP–MS analysis. A semiquantitative analysis for elements not available as standards can be carried out by interpolating from such a graph.

data is that the concentrations of the unknowns must be within the range of the calibration solutions and within the range of quantification for the instrument (between approximately 50 ppt and 1 ppm). It may be necessary to carry out further dilution to bring the samples into this range.

A common source of error in ICP–MS is that negative masses are produced for unknown solutions. This occurs when the calibration line crosses the vertical axis at a value significantly above zero (Fig. 9.6(b)), which is often the result of high counts from the instrument blank, usually caused by an uncorrected interference. Any unknown samples which have a CPS below this value will then produce negative masses. One solution to this is to computationally force the line through the origin, or to remove "outliers" from the calibration line, but it is much better to identify the true cause of the problem (i.e., find the interference, if this is the source), and to rerun the samples.

If it is not possible to include a particular element in the calibration solutions, it is possible to perform a *semiquantitative* analysis. This uses the response of those elements which are in the calibration solution, but predicts the sensitivity (defined as cps/concentration) for the missing element(s) by interpolating between the sensitivities of known elements. By plotting sensitivity against mass for all the elements present in the calibration solutions (Fig. 9.7) and fitting a curve through the points, it is possible to predict the sensitivity of the instrument for any particular mass number, and hence use this sensitivity to convert cps to concentration at that mass number. As can be seen from the figure, however, this is a very crude approximation, and any data produced in this way must be treated with some caution.

As described in Section 13.3, using an instrument for a long period can result in variation in instrument calibration, or drift. This can be detected in solution analysis by the addition of a known amount of an internal standard to the sample solutions. This is impossible, however, for LA–ICP–MS analysis of a solid sample. One method of minimizing this is to simultaneously measure a minor isotope of the major element in the sample (e.g., ^{13}C in wood samples, as recommended by Watmough *et al.* 1998, or ^{29}Si in glass samples, etc.). All of the elements of interest can then be ratioed to this peak (effectively using ^{13}C or ^{29}Si as an internal standard), and to calibrate using this ratio rather than the absolute value. In this way, any variations in laser output, ablation efficiency, or drift in detector sensitivity during the course of the analysis will, to some extent, be compensated for.

Matrix effects

A major problem with ICP–MS by laser ablation (and, to a lesser extent, with solution analysis) is that differences in the main component of the sample between samples and standards (or between samples) can affect the composition of the plasma, and, therefore, drastically affect the results. For example, in solution analysis, if the samples are dissolved in a 2% HNO_3 solution but the standards are made up in water alone, then this is likely to be sufficient to compromise the analysis. In laser ablation, for example, if the sample is a strand of hair, but the standards are glass samples, then it would not be surprising if ablation efficiency varied from the sample to the standard, again compromising the quality of the analysis. For solution analysis, this can be controlled by ensuring that the total dissolved solids are not too high, and that all calibration and sample solutions are matrix matched (as described in Section 13.3). For the analysis of solids by LA–ICP–MS, this is almost impossible to achieve. The accepted calibration standards tend to be in the form of glass (described by Pearce *et al.* 1996, Perkins *et al.* 1997), since it is extremely difficult to obtain standards of the required homogeneity and with the correct certified trace element concentrations other than as a glass. Thus, whilst it might be reasonable to expect an acceptable matrix match between the glass standards and unknowns if they are glasses, it is highly unlikely to apply to any other sample form. Whilst it is possible to make your own standards (e.g., Hamilton and Hopkins 1995), there are great difficulties retaining the required elemental concentrations in the final product and in ensuring homogeneity over the small sampling scale required by LA–ICP–MS. Even using powdered samples pressed into pellets, perhaps not surprisingly, does not overcome matrix differences, although semiquantitative analysis has been shown to be effective (Morrison *et al.* 1995). One option is to measure the concentrations of the elements to be determined by LA–ICP–MS in a "type sample" of the same matrix using a different analytical method (most conveniently, by dissolution and ICP–MS of the resulting solution), and then using these to calibrate the LA–ICP–MS (Watmough *et al.* 1998). For any LA–ICP–MS analysis, however, because of the microscale of the laser sampling, there is always going to be a question of homogeneity, even for glass or other commercial standard materials. This issue has also been discussed in Section 6.3 in the context of the intercomparability of ICP–MS and NAA analysis.

Data analysis

ICP–MS produces a great deal of data in a very short time, both in terms of the number of samples analyzed, and also in terms of the number of elements it can, at least in principle, quantify. It is important to be prepared for this, and whilst there are a number of descriptions of how best to analyze analytical data (e.g., Baxter and Buck 2000), it is also important to evaluate the quality of the data before embarking on such numerical investigations. The first step is always to consider the accuracy and precision of the data. This may involve excluding some values for particular elements, such as all results at or below the LOD. It may require the entire data set for one or more elements to be omitted, if the QA procedure showed that a particular element does not agree with the limits of the certified values in the SRMs. It might also include excluding all elements with poor calibration lines, and those which had interference problems or high blank values. It is also important to identify those data which are semiquantitative, in case they are best omitted.

The next stage is to carry out simple statistical procedures, such as the plotting of bivariate scatter diagrams and the calculation of correlation coefficients between all pairs of elements. The behavior patterns of most elements in geochemistry and biochemistry are often well established, and so deviations from these can often reveal important information. Likewise, knowledge of this behavior can often prevent a great deal of time from being wasted in pursuing perfectly predictable patterning, such as the relationship between Ca, Sr, and Ba in human mineralized tissue, or Fe and Ti in clays. If these investigations provide sufficient information to answer the original research question, then it is perfectly acceptable to stop there, without applying further, more elaborate, statistical techniques. Multivariate analysis is, however, likely to be the most appropriate approach for the large amounts of data produced by ICP–MS. A number of well-established texts exist (e.g., Aitchison 1986, Baxter 1994, 2003) which describe the most appropriate methods of numerical analysis for archaeological data. Finally, one of the most important considerations is to relate the analyses to the original samples, and to the original research questions.

9.4   Splitting hairs – archaeological applications of ICP–MS

Applications of ICP–MS in archaeology have mostly centered on determining geological provenance, where different elemental patterns or isotopic ratios have been taken as signatures of different geographical locations (see Section 1.2). A wide range of materials has been analyzed, including ceramics (see Section 3.5), obsidian (Bigazzi *et al.* 1986, Williams-Thorpe 1995, Tykot and Young 1996, Tykot 1998), soils (Middleton and Price 1996, Entwhistle and Abrahams 1997, Entwhistle *et al.* 1998: see Section 4.4), metals and slags (Young *et al.* 1997, Hall *et al.* 1998, Heimann *et al.* 2001). In terms of biomaterials, Budd *et al.* (2000) measured strontium isotope ratios in human tooth enamel and showed that the enamel (but not the dentine and bone) retains the biogenic signal, and English *et al.* (2001) determined the provenance of architectural timber in Chaco Canyon from Sr isotope ratios.

The analysis of solids by laser ablation has been done with ICP–OES (e.g., Brenner and Zander 2000: 1231–2), but the vast majority of such applications now use ICP–MS. Comparisons between ICP–OES, solution, and LA–ICP–MS have been carried out by examining LOD, sensitivities, etc. (e.g., for glass analysis by Moenke-Blankenburg *et al.* 1992). Almost all sample matrices have been investigated, such as obsidian (Gratuze 1999), single vitreous tephra shards (Eastwood *et al.* 1998), metals (Raith *et al.* 1995, Watling *et al.* 1997, Guerra *et al.* 1999), calcified biological structures, such as teeth (Evans and Outridge 1994, Evans *et al.* 1995, Lee *et al.* 1999, Lochner *et al.* 1999), and tree rings (Watmough *et al.* 1996, Garbe-Schonberg *et al.* 1997, Prohaska *et al.* 1998). Laser ablation is particularly suited to the study of laminated materials, where environmental information in the annual growth layers is revealed by LA transects. Other biological matrices such as hair, leaves, etc., present more problems, largely because of the matrix effect and the lack of calibration standards (Durrant 1992, Durrant and Ward 1994). All of these studies emphasize, however, the relative ease of direct solid sampling, and the advantages of "nondestructive" analysis.

Trace elements in human tissue

Inorganic and heavy isotope analysis of human bones and teeth has been used to look directly at a number of archaeological issues, including diet (Lambert *et al.* 1984b, Burton *et al.* 1999), mobility (Budd *et al.* 2000), disease (Yoshinaga *et al.* 1995, Roberts *et al.* 1996), and exposure to heavy metals (Yamada *et al.* 1995, Yoshinaga *et al.* 1998, Oakberg *et al.* 2000). The nature of the samples can cause analytical difficulties in ICP–MS. Having a high calcium matrix and low levels of trace elements results in the need for sample pretreatments, because high dissolved solids can result in clogging of the cones (Outridge *et al.* 1996). There are, however, other serious problems in using bones and teeth for the measurement of trace element and heavy element isotopic ratios. Obviously, to be of any use, the factor which it is desired to understand (e.g., dietary input) must influence the level of the measured element(s) in the bone. This is not necessarily the case, and makes it essential to find the natural variation within modern bone before moving on to archaeological samples (Hancock *et al.* 1989). In addition, different bone types (cancellous, cortical) and skeletal components have different trace element compositions; it is not, therefore, possible to mix the analyses of different bone types. There are also a large number of other factors, such as sex, age, and health status, all of which can affect the composition of bone. However, diagenesis is likely to be the major problem. This makes it essential to use well-preserved samples, if these can be identified. The problem of elements being lost and gained in the burial environment is a serious one, and the papers by the following authors should be considered before any work is undertaken: Lambert *et al.* (1984a), Price *et al.* (1992), Radosevich (1993), Burton and Price (2000). One useful approach of diagenesis is that of Trueman (1999), where differential uptake of the REE (see below) from the environment is used to understand differing taphonomic processes.

Hair (made from the cross-linked protein α-keratin), and in particular its pigment (melanin), acts as a sink for trace metals from the body. Head hair grows at the rate of approximately 1 cm per month, and once formed does not undergo further biogenic turnover, in contrast to other tissue such as bone. It therefore provides a very high resolution environmental record of the last few months before sampling. Trace element analysis of hair has been shown to provide a record of diet, health, toxicology, environment, and even geographical information. Much of this work has been published relating to modern medical and forensic uses of trace element analysis, and this has now been extended to archaeological samples (Wilson *et al.* 2001). Traditional approaches have used solution analysis of digested hair, but elemental distributions along the length of the hair can be achieved with LA–ICP–MS. This involves careful optimizing of ablation conditions and extremely careful work tracking the laser along a single hair length. The resulting data, although not fully quantified because of the difficulties in obtaining standards as described above, gives an elemental profile along the hair length (Fig. 9.8).

Hair is, however, not inert, although it is relatively resistant to degradation because of the cystine disulfide cross-linkages which stabilize the keratin structure. Hair frequently survives when all other soft tissues have disappeared. The key to hair survival is inhibition of keratinolytic microbial activity, which most commonly occurs under extreme conditions of temperature, aridity, anoxia, or by metal ion inhibition. One important factor, often ignored in the study of archaeological hair, and the principal distinguishing factor between medical and archaeological analysis, is again the effect of diagenesis and the burial environment. Considerable uptake of trace elements from the depositional environment has been recorded in hair samples from experimental burials (Wilson *et al.* 2001).

The rare earth elements (REE)

The rare earth elements (REE) are the lanthanides (defined as those elements with valence electrons in $4f$ orbitals), La, Ce, Pr, Nd, (Pm), Sm, Eu, Gd ,Tb, Dy, Ho, Er, Tm, and Yb. Often included for analysis, because they behave in a chemically similar way, although strictly not REE, are the Group 3 transition metals Y and Lu. The radioactive lanthanide element promethium (Pm) is excluded from analysis, since it is not found in samples because of its short half-life.

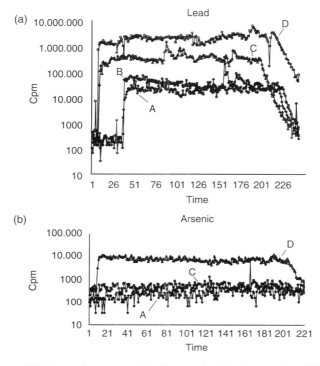

Figure 9.8 Trace element profile along a single hair using LA–ICP–MS. The horizontal axis refers to the tracking time of the laser along the hair, which equates to distance. (a) shows lead along individual hairs from different depositional environments: A is a modern sample, B is an experimentally buried modern sample, C is from a surface-exposed (8 months) forensic case, and D is an archaeological sample (died 1867). (b) shows arsenic from three of these same samples. There is clearly postdepositional uptake of both elements in the archaeological samples, and in these particular examples little evidence of lateral variation.

The interest in the REE results from their presence as a group in trace quantities in many minerals – they are lithophilic, and therefore concentrate in silicates. They have similar chemical and physical properties, having a common +3 oxidation state, with the exception of europium (Eu), which can also form +2, and cerium (Ce), which can also form +4. Despite their chemical similarities, the REE are physically fractionated by rock formation processes and weathering as a result of their gradual increase in size, and therefore their distribution profile may indicate the geological origin of samples. Their analysis is ideally suited to ICP–MS, as the masses are free from most interferences (although not polyatomic oxides; Dulski 1994), and they are often present at concentrations which are within the instrument detection limits. This means that ICP–MS determination of REE requires no special preconcentration or chemical separation, unlike other instrumental techniques such ICP–AES or TIMS (Casetta *et al.* 1990, Balaram 1996).

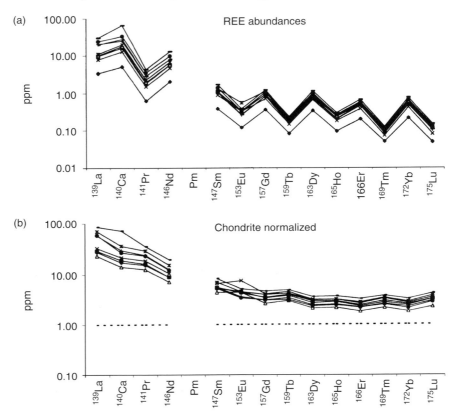

Figure 9.9 REE abundances from archaeological glass, showing the effect of chondrite normalization. (a) shows the raw abundances of the REE measured on a set of English medieval window glasses, with the "saw-tooth" pattern evident, and little indication of differences between any of the samples (apart from perhaps one which has lower overall REE concentrations). (b) shows the same data normalized to the chondrite data (Table 9.1). The "saw-tooth" has largely disappeared, and close inspection suggests that two samples have a positive europium anomaly, possibly indicating a different geographical origin.

Chondrite normalization

The absolute REE distribution from selected archaeological glass samples is shown in Fig. 9.9(a). There is a decreasing abundance of the elements with increasing atomic number, and a predominance of odd over even atomic numbers, giving the characteristic "saw-tooth" distribution when the elements are plotted in the order of increasing atomic number. These data are clearly difficult to interpret as shown. The usual practice is to normalize the data set by dividing the values with a standard REE abundance and plotting on a logarithmic scale, as shown in Fig. 9.9(b). There are a variety of normalization standards to select from (e.g., Henderson 1984), and it is important to specify the one used. One commonly used data set is that of the

Table 9.1. *Abundance of REE in a chondrite meteorite (ppm) used for normalization of REE data (reported in Henderson 1984).*

La	Ce	Pr	Nd	Pm	Sm	Eu	Gd
0.34	0.91	0.121	0.64	–	0.195	0.073	0.26

Tb	Dy	Ho	Er	Tm	Yb	Lu
0.047	0.3	0.078	0.2	0.032	0.22	0.034

REE from chondrite meteorites (Table 9.1). This is taken to be representative of the composition of the early solar system, and is, therefore, unaffected by terrestrial geological and weathering processes. Normalization to this data set is referred to as "chondrite normalization". An alternative common procedure is to normalize the data to a material similar to that of the samples (e.g., shale to normalize a wide range of oil-bearing sediments). The normalization procedure removes any variations between high/low and even/ odd atomic numbers and emphasizes any relative fractionation due to terrestrial processes. Normally a smooth curve is obtained after normalization, but often anomalies (either positive or negative) may be observed for Eu and Ce, indicating that the abundance of these lanthanides is either higher or lower than expected by comparison with the others. Usually this is a result of the variable oxidation state of these elements affecting their solubility or mobility in the rock-forming processes (Henderson 1984). Once normalized, these anomalies may be expressed numerically by calculating the ratios $(Sm+Gd)/2Eu$ and $(La+Pr)/2Ce$ from the abundance data, and the overall slope of the curve as the abundance ratio La/Lu.

An early use of REE profiles in archaeology was by Allen *et al.* (1982), in which they used NAA to determine a limited number of rare earths (La, Nd, Sm, Eu, Gd, Tb, Yb, and Lu) in Predynastic (4000–3100 BC) Egyptian pottery in an attempt to locate the source of the silts used in their manufacture. Conventional REE analysis by ICP–MS requires dissolution of the samples (e.g., Lichte *et al.* 1987, Jarvis 1988), but they have also been analyzed by laser ablation with quantitative results from powder pellets of geological (Jarvis and Williams 1993) and soil samples (Cousin and Magyar 1994). Pillay and Punyadeera (2001) have published an acid digestion procedure suitable for REE determination of archaeological silicate samples, and also discussed the use of REE profiles in determining archaeological provenance. Two types of material have been studied using REE analysis by

ICP–MS – glass and ceramics. Glasses are extremely suitable for REE analysis, since they are made from a mixture of sand and alkali, and it is likely that the REE are characteristic of the sand source used. Similarly, ceramics are also suitable, in that the REE are likely to be characteristic of the clay source. One such study (Ford *et al.* 2005) has studied South Asian finewares, and has used REE profiles to compare similar vessels made at a range of different sites in Sri Lanka and southern India.

PART III

SOME BASIC CHEMISTRY FOR ARCHAEOLOGISTS

10

ATOMS, ISOTOPES, ELECTRON
ORBITALS, AND THE PERIODIC TABLE

This chapter sets out some of the fundamentals of modern chemistry. It chronicles the historical development of our current understanding of the structure of the atom – at least as far as is necessary from a chemistry perspective. (For more information on the history of chemistry, see Partington [1961–70] and Hudson [1992].) The work summarized here was so important that it was honored by the award of numerous Nobel Prizes to some of the most famous chemists. We follow the development of our understanding through the identification of the nature of the proton and electron, and subsequently the neutron. Following a review of the discovery of the various particles emitted during natural radioactivity, we present the basic model of the nuclear atom surrounded by orbital electrons. This model allows us to understand radioactive stability and the existence of isotopes. We then venture into the exotic world of quantum chemistry, in order to explain the stability of the orbital electrons, and the concept of atomic energy levels. (For an introduction to the development of quantum theory see McEvoy and Zarate 1999.) This introduces the concept of quantum numbers, which then leads to a set of simple rules to understand the way in which electron orbitals are filled as the size of the atom increases. This in turn leads to an understanding of the construction of the modern periodic table, which is the key to understanding the chemical behavior of the inorganic elements and compounds. Many of the classic papers referred to in this and other chapters are available in full on the "Classic Chemistry" website compiled by Carmen Giunta at Le Moyne College, Syracuse, NY (http://web.lemoyne.edu/~giunta/papers.html), as well as the invaluable volumes of republished papers in chemistry (Knight 1968, 1970) and physics (Wright 1964).

10.1 The discovery of subatomic particles

Several strands of evidence came together at the beginning of the twentieth century to suggest that the atom, originally envisaged by the Greek philosophers as the smallest indivisible unit of matter, was, in fact, composed of smaller particles, subsequently named *protons*, *neutrons*, and *electrons*. The story begins in the nineteenth century with efforts to identify the atom itself, followed by research which led to the identification of the electron, and the confirmation that the atom was made up of subatomic particles.

Weighing the atom

As noted in Chapter 2, at the beginning of the nineteenth century Dalton interpreted two empirical laws, those of *constant composition* and *multiple proportions*, to mean that all matter is composed of a great number of atoms. Each element has its own distinctive kind of atom, and compounds are made up from atoms which combine together in simple fixed proportions to form "compound atoms", now termed molecules. Dalton wrote that "*When we attempt to conceive the number of particles in an atmosphere, it is somewhat like attempting to conceive the number of stars in the universe; we are confounded by the thought*" (Dalton 1808: 212). He did, however, believe that it was possible to ascertain the relative weights of the different atoms. In the same year that Dalton published the first volume of his *New System of Chemical Philosophy* in Manchester, England, Joseph Louis Gay-Lussac (1778–1850), simultaneously Professor of Physics at the Sorbonne and (from 1809) Professor of Chemistry at the École Polytechnique, published his *Law of the Combination of Gases by Volume*, now known as *Gay-Lussac*'s law (Gay-Lussac 1808). This states that when gases react, they do so in volumes which bear a simple relationship to one another, and to the product, if gaseous. Dalton knew of this, and believed it implied that equal volumes of gases contain equal numbers of atoms. He was unable to reconcile this observation with his own theory, citing as evidence the observation that if equal volumes of oxygen and nitrogen are reacted together, the result is two volumes of nitric oxide (NO). If the reaction is, as he believed:

$$N + O = NO$$

then one particle of nitric oxide is produced for every one of nitrogen and oxygen, but experimentally the resulting volume is twice that of the original oxygen or nitrogen. Thus the number of particles of NO in unit volume must be half that of either oxygen or nitrogen – equal volumes cannot therefore contain equal numbers of atoms.

After some debate between the two, in which Dalton cast doubt on Gay-Lussac's experiments, the conclusion was reached that equal volumes of gas (when measured under the same conditions of temperature and pressure) must contain equal numbers of *molecules*. This statement (Avogadro 1811), attributable to another great scientist, Amedeo Avogadro (1776–1856), from 1820 Professor of Physics at Turin, was consistent with observation, if it is assumed that simple gases such as oxygen and nitrogen are composed of molecules made up of two atoms, and is now known as *Avogadro*'s *hypothesis*. The equation then becomes:

$$N_2 + O_2 = 2NO$$

showing that equal volumes of nitrogen and oxygen combine to form two volumes of nitric oxide, and that these two volumes of nitric oxide contain twice the number of molecules as contained by one volume of either nitrogen or oxygen. Thus equal volumes of gas contain equal numbers of molecules.

This somewhat archaic early nineteenth century dispute is important for two reasons. One is that it fixed clearly the different identities of atoms and molecules, especially in the case of homogeneous molecules, made up of multiple identical atoms. The second is that it led to the discovery of the number of atoms in common substances, and to estimates of the weights and sizes of these atoms. It had been known for some time that hydrogen is the lightest of gases, and the term *relative density* had been coined to denote the ratio of the weight of a particular volume of gas to the weight of an equal volume of hydrogen. Since, according to Avogadro, equal volumes contain equal numbers of molecules, then the relative density is also the ratio of the weight of one molecule of the gas to one molecule of hydrogen. Hydrogen was known to be diatomic (i.e., to exist as H_2) from volumetric experiments similar to those described above, so the relative molecular weight of gaseous substances could be worked out, being numerically twice the relative density on a scale which sets the atomic weight of hydrogen as one. This scheme was extended in 1858 by Stanislao Cannizzaro (1826–1910), who published a method for determining the atomic weights of volatile substances based on vapor density measurements (Cannizzaro 1858). By the last quarter of the nineteenth century, chemistry had been provided with one of its most valuable tools – a systematic tabulation of the relative atomic weights of many elements, together with an understanding of how these elements combine into molecules.

The *gram-molecular weight* of any substance is the molecular weight of that substance expressed in grams. It soon became noticed that the gram-molecular weight (GMW) of simple gases occupied very nearly the same volume when measured under the same conditions of temperature and pressure, that volume being 22.412 liters ($1\,L = 1000\,cm^3 = 1$ cubic decimeter $= 0.001\,m^3$). *Standard temperature and pressure* (STP) was defined as 0°C and 1 atmosphere of pressure, defined as 760 mm of mercury. The modern equivalents are 273.15 K, using the thermodynamically based *Kelvin* or *absolute* scale of temperature, and 101 325 Pa (the SI unit of pressure, where 1 Pascal = a force of 1 newton per meter^2). According to Avogadro, this volume, termed the *gram-molecular volume*, should contain the same number of molecules for each gas, and this number became known as *Avogadro*'s number or *constant*, and is the number which Dalton had declared to be "inconceivable" in 1808. It is a tribute to nineteenth century scientific endeavor that, by the beginning of the next century, this number (N_A, now accepted as $6.02214199 \times 10^{23}$ mol^{-1}) was known with some accuracy. Evidence came from many different observations, each adding strength to the conviction that this huge number represented some physical reality. An early estimate came from the same considerations of the passage of electric charge through a liquid (*electrolysis*) which led to the naming of the electron in 1891 (see below), and subsequently from Jean Baptiste Perrin's (1870–1942) reconsideration (1909) of *Brownian motion* (the random movement of pollen grains suspended in a liquid, first observed by Robert Brown in 1827). The best estimates came from work on the X-ray diffraction of crystals (see Section 5.4) which, between 1928 and 1940, gave a number of estimates close to the modern figure (Murrell 2001).

As with any breakthrough in scientific understanding, many subsequent discoveries follow quickly. Knowing Avogadro's number, and the relative molecular weights, it is simple to obtain estimates of the actual weight of atoms and molecules – a staggering achievement, given that, until very recently, nobody had ever seen an individual atom or molecule. If the gram-molecular weight of hydrogen is 2 g, then these two grams occupy 22.4 L at STP, and contain 6.023×10^{23} molecules. A molecule of hydrogen is made up of two atoms, and therefore:

$$\text{weight of one hydrogen atom} = \frac{1}{6.023 \times 10^{23}} = 1.67 \times 10^{-24}\,\text{g}$$

The first table of atomic weights in recognizable form had been published by the Swedish chemist Jöns Jakob Berzelius (1779–1848) in two papers in the journal *Annals of Philosophy* (Berzelius 1813, 1814), and subsequently revised in his textbook *Lärbok i kemien* (1808–18) (later republished in German as *Lehrbuch der Chemie*, culminating in the fifth edition of 1843–8). He published the atomic weights of 46 elements, together with the formulae for about 2000 compounds, although in early editions the weights were often in error by a factor of two or more due to misunderstandings of the formulae. Dalton had introduced the first systematic notation for the elements based on a series of circles embellished with various lines and dots. In his second (1814) paper in the *Annals of Philosophy*, Berzelius proposed the letter notation for around 50 elements that is essentially the same as is used today, based originally on the first letter of the Latin names for the elements. Even more presciently, he used the simple notation of combined letter symbols to denote compounds, with, originally, a superscript number to the right of the symbol to denote the multiples involved in combining to form molecules. Dalton was outraged: in a letter to Thomas Graham (1805–69) in 1837, he wrote that "*Berzelius's symbols are horrifying, ... a young student in chemistry might as well learn Hebrew as make himself acquainted with them!*" With the exception of the adoption of subscripts rather than superscripts to indicate the stoichiometry of compounds, Berzelius's "horrifying" notation is now firmly established as the language of modern chemistry.

Identification of the electron

According to George Johnstone Stoney (1826–1911), the first identification of the electron as a particle "charged with a minimum quantity of electricity" was made by him in 1874, and subsequently (1891) named by him as the electron (Stoney 1894). This was the result of experiments carried out by Michael Faraday (1794–1867), in which he passed electric currents through various conducting solutions. By placing electrodes of different materials in solutions of different compounds, he was able to observe the various processes which go on when current is flowing – gaseous evolution, dissolution of one of the electrodes, or precipitation of one or more components out of the solution. In 1834 he enunciated the Law of Definite Electrolytic Action, which stated that "*the mass of substance dissolved or liberated in electrolysis is proportional to the quantity of electricity which passes through the electrolyte, and the mass of the different products set free by passing a given quantity of electricity through different electrolytes is proportional to the chemical equivalents of the substances concerned*" (Faraday 1834). The equivalent weight (chemical equivalent) of a substance is defined as that mass of a substance which will combine with or displace eight parts by mass of oxygen, as discussed above. Mathematically, for a constant current of I amperes flowing for t seconds, the mass of substance liberated or deposited (m) is given by:

$$m = e \times I \times t$$

where e is a constant known as the *electrochemical equivalent* of that substance. Furthermore, from the second observation,

$$\frac{m_1}{m_2} = \frac{e_1}{e_2} = \frac{E_1}{E_2}$$

where E is the chemical equivalent of the substance. It follows that the ratio of E/e is a constant for any substance, and is the quantity of electricity which will liberate the gram-equivalent weight of any substance. This quantity is called the *Faraday constant*, F, and is 96 487 coulomb mol^{-1}. The observation made by Stoney in 1874 and von Helmholtz in 1881 (Stoney 1894) was that, if we assume that a mole of substance contains Avogadro's number of particles, the ratio of F/N_A is also a constant, and is the unit of electrical charge associated with each particle, providing each particle only carries one charge unit (the constant is nF/N_A if the particle carries n charges, where n is the *valency*). It is this unit of charge, equivalent to 1.6×10^{-19} coulombs (C), which was termed the electron by Stoney in 1891.

Further information on the electron, including the mass of the particle, and evidence that it was the same electron which was involved in the structure of the atom, came from two other sources – the passage of electric currents through gases in glass tubes under reduced pressures and observations of the particles produced by naturally radioactive substances. Under normal atmospheric pressure, gases will only conduct electricity if the applied potential is so high that an electric discharge occurs, as is the case with natural lightning (voltages of 3 million volts [MV] per meter are required to conduct electricity in air). Under reduced pressures, continuously flowing currents can be produced, and these were the subject of much study in the late nineteenth century. As the pressure is reduced, various patterns of dark spaces and glows are observed, particularly around the *cathode* (the negatively charged terminal) where the *cathode glow* is observed, followed by a dark band known as *Crookes dark space*. With an applied voltage of 10 000 volts (10 kV) and a pressure below 0.001 mm of mercury, the Crookes dark space fills the entire tube except for a faint blue glow around the cathode. It was observed that, under these conditions, a beam of invisible rays was emitted by the cathode, which produced a fluorescence at the opposite end of the tube as the rays struck the glass. These were, therefore, known as *cathode rays*. Experiments showed that these rays traveled in straight lines (opaque solid material such as a metal Maltese cross in their path cast a "shadow" on the glass) and could be deflected by applied electric and magnetic fields, which demonstrated that they carried a negative electrical charge. This suggested to J. J. Thomson (1856–1940) that the rays consisted of a stream of high velocity negatively charged particles, as opposed to electromagnetic radiation, and he termed them *corpuscles* (Thomson 1897). Their properties were independent of the material used to make the cathode, suggesting that they were a fundamental property of all materials.

In 1897, a number of scientists, most famously J. J. Thomson, published a method of estimating the ratio of the charge to mass of these particles. He used a specially designed cathode ray tube (Fig. 10.1) which allowed the rays to pass through a small hole in the anode (the positively charged plate) and to pass a pair of deflector plates carrying an electric charge, and through a region of magnetic field, striking the glass at the end of the tube. The beam is deflected by either the electrostatic charge on the deflector plates or the magnetic field when acting separately, but, by adjusting the electric field to bring the beam back to the straight-through position (Fig. 10.1(a)), and knowing the magnetic flux density (B, in units of tesla) and the magnitude of the electric field (E, in units of volts per meter) it is possible to solve the following set of equations to find e/m, the ratio of charge (e) to mass (m) for the electron:

Force acting due to electric field alone $= Ee$ newtons
Force acting due to magnetic field alone $= Bev$ newtons

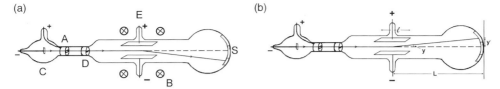

Figure 10.1 J.J. Thomson's method for measuring e/m, the mass-to-charge ratio of an electron (Thomson 1897). Electrons (cathode rays) leave the cathode (C) and are accelerated towards the anode (A), passing through a small hole and a further hole in plate (D) to provide a collimated beam. It then passes through crossed electric (E) and magnetic fields (B) which deflect the beam in the same plane but in opposite directions, and strikes the fluorescent screen at the end. In (a) the strengths of E and B are adjusted to bring the spot back to zero deflection (S). In (b), with electric field only, the deflection from S (y') is measured, and e/m calculated as in the text.

where v is the velocity of the moving particle. When no deflection occurs these forces must be equal and opposite, therefore;

$$Ee = Bev$$

so the velocity v is given by E/B. For typical values of E and B in this experiment, the velocity could be as high as 10^7 m s^{-1}. If the magnetic field is removed (Fig. 10.1(b)), and the deflection of the beam as a result of the electric field E measured, then the following equations apply:

$$Ee = \frac{2my}{t^2}$$

where y is the vertical displacement as the particle leaves the deflector plates and t is the time taken to traverse the electric field. Rearranging,

$$\frac{e}{m} = \frac{2y}{Et^2} = \frac{2yv^2}{El^2}$$

since the time taken to traverse the plates t is equal to the length of the plates l divided by the velocity v. We can substitute for v from the previous experiment, giving:

$$\frac{e}{m} = \frac{2yE^2}{El^2B^2} = \frac{2yE}{l^2B^2}.$$

On the assumption that the motion of the particle can be approximated by assuming a single deflection event in the middle of the plates, we can replace the ratio y/l by d/L, where d is the measured deflection on the end of the tube and L is the distance of the end of the tube from the middle of the deflector plates, since from similar triangles these ratios are the same. Thus:

$$\frac{e}{m} = \frac{2dE}{B^2Ll}.$$

Thus the ratio of the charge to mass for a single electron can be calculated from a simple experiment. The current estimate of e/m is $1.7588 \times 10^{11}\,\mathrm{C\,kg^{-1}}$. Given that the charge on the electron, e, can be estimated from Faraday's work, this provides a crude estimate for the mass of the electron at around $9.1 \times 10^{-31}\,\mathrm{kg}$. More useful, perhaps, the ratio between the mass of the hydrogen atom (or proton) and that of the electron can be calculated as follows – the gram equivalent weight of hydrogen is $1.008\,\mathrm{g}$ (or $1.008 \times 10^{-3}\,\mathrm{kg}$), and from Faraday's law this carries a charge of $96\,490\,\mathrm{C}$, so the charge-to-mass ratio for the proton is $96\,490/1.008 \times 10^{-3}\,\mathrm{C\,kg^{-1}}$, or $9.57 \times 10^{7}\,\mathrm{C\,kg^{-1}}$. Thus the ratio of the mass of the electron (m_e) to that of the proton (m_p), assuming both carry an equal charge, is:

$$\frac{m_e}{m_p} = \frac{9.5724 \times 10^7}{1.7588 \times 10^{11}} = 5.44 \times 10^{-4} = \frac{1}{1838}.$$

In other words, the mass of an electron is roughly $1/2000$th that of a proton.

Natural radioactivity
The final piece of evidence, which identified the proton and the electron as subatomic particles, came from observations of radiation from naturally radioactive compounds, such as uranium ores. The first systematic observation of the radioactive properties of certain natural compounds was in 1896 when Antoine Henri Becquerel (1852–1908) noticed that uranium compounds had the ability to darken photographic paper, even if the paper was contained in lightproof wrappings. Lord Ernest Rutherford (1871–1937), a New Zealand physicist working at the time in the Cavendish Laboratory in Cambridge, England, showed in 1899 that there were two kinds of radiation involved, one of which he termed α-radiation, and the other β-radiation. He showed that these emanations were capable of causing ionization in the air as they passed through it, in the same manner as the recently discovered X-rays (see Chapter 5). This provided a means for monitoring their progress, using an instrument called a *cloud chamber*, in which the tracks of the ionizing radiation are made visible by saturating the air with water vapor, which condenses on the ionized particles as they are produced. Rutherford found that α-radiation caused about 100 times more ionization than β-radiation, but was easily stopped by thin metal foil, whereas the less ionizing β-radiation was about 100 times more penetrating. More remarkably, Rutherford showed that the particles are deflected in different directions if either a magnetic or electric field is applied, suggesting that they carry opposite electrical charges. He published a book on his findings (Rutherford 1904), and was awarded the Nobel Prize for Chemistry in 1908 "*for his investigations into the disintegration of the elements, and the chemistry of radioactive substances*". He was raised to the peerage in the New Year's Honours list of 1931, with the title Lord Rutherford of Nelson. Shortly after

the initial discovery of α- and β-radiation, Paul Villard (1860–1934) in 1900 showed that there was a third component to the radiation from radioactive materials which was not deflected by applied electrical or magnetic fields: these rays, subsequently called γ-rays, had about 10 to 100 times the penetrating power of β-radiation, but caused 100 times less ionization. Pierre Curie (1859–1906) and his wife Marie Sklodowska Curie (1867–1934) coined the term "radioactivity" in 1898, and in the same year demonstrated the radioactive properties of thorium and discovered the highly radioactive element radium. The Curies and Becquerel shared the 1903 Nobel Prize for Physics for "*the brilliant discovery of radioactivity*".

At the beginning of the twentieth century, it became clear that the salts of many radioactive elements produced these α, β, and γ radiations to differing degrees, and that their nature needed to be clarified. This was done using the same sort of equipment and calculations as described above for the ratio of the mass to charge of the electron. Becquerel in 1900 measured the charge per unit mass for β-rays, concluding that they were essentially the same as cathode rays (i.e., electrons), but traveling with much greater velocities. Subsequent, more precise, experiments showed that e/m for β-rays was not, in fact, identical to that ratio for cathode rays, but the difference is attributable to the fact that β-particles can travel at anything up to 99% of the speed of light ($c = 3 \times 10^8$ m s^{-1}), with an average of around 66% of c. At these velocities, relativistic considerations become important, in which the mass of a moving particle increases as the velocity increases towards the speed of light. Inadvertently, this work provided a rigorous test for the emerging postulates of Einstein's Special Theory of Relativity.

Similar experiments were carried out to determine the nature of the α-particles. The direction of deflection in an electrostatic field showed them to carry a positive electric charge, and measurements of their charge per unit mass (termed E/M for α-particles) showed them to have a ratio of 4.787×10^7 C kg^{-1}. If the charge on the particle could be determined, then it would be possible to calculate its mass. In an ingenious experiment, Rutherford and Geiger (1908) managed to estimate the charge on an individual α-particle. Since the passage of charged particles corresponds to the flow of electric current, they were able to calculate the total current carried by all α-particles emitted by a radioactive substance by placing a metal sheet of known area a fixed distance from the source, measuring the current flow as a result of the interception of the α-particles by the sheet, and multiplying this up to correspond to the total current emitted into a full sphere surrounding the source. This allows the current flow per unit solid angle to be known. They then needed to know the number of α-particles carrying this current. By adjusting the gas pressure in the measurement chamber and the distance between the source and the detecting metal sheet, it was possible to arrange it so that the rate of arrival of α-particles at the sheet was as low as three to five per minute, in which case individual pulses of current could be registered, corresponding to the arrival of a single particle. In this way, it was possible to estimate the number of α-particles responsible for the total current measured above, and thus calculate the charge carried per particle. This turned out to be approximately 3.19×10^{-19} C, or twice that on the electron. From the above estimate of E/M for the α-particle, it follows that it carries a positive charge equal to twice that on the electron, and has four times the mass of the hydrogen atom.

Rutherford's work allowed further deductions to be made. From the above experiment, it was calculated that 1 g of radium (the radioactive source used) produced 3.7×10^{10} α-particles per second (the unit of radioactivity is the Becquerel (Bq), which corresponds to the number of radioactive particles produced per second). With regard to the nature of the α-particle, it had been observed by Ramsay and Soddy (1903) that it was similar in mass and charge to the nucleus of the helium atom, and that helium gas is continuously produced from radium. Further evidence is provided by the fact that all radioactive minerals contain helium. Experimental confirmation of the identity of the α-particle was provided by Rutherford and Royds (1909). They sealed a quantity of the radioactive gas radon in a thin-walled glass tube and surrounded it by a second glass vessel, which was evacuated at the beginning of the experiment. The α-particles produced by the radon traveled through the first glass wall, but not through the second. It was observed that the pressure began to rise in the outer vessel as the experiment proceeded, suggesting that the α-particles were converting to a gas, and the chemical identity was confirmed by passing an electric current through the gas, which produced an emission spectrum (see Section 12.3) identical to that of helium. This was sufficient to confirm that the α-particles produced by the naturally radioactive elements were indeed the same as the nuclei of helium.

The third detectable emission from naturally radioactive materials, γ-rays, were shown not to be charged particles, and were subsequently identified as being electromagnetic radiation (see Section 12.2), but with a wavelength even shorter than that determined for X-rays. Rutherford and Andrade (1914) measured the wavelength of the γ-rays using a mineral crystal as a diffraction grating (Section 4.2), and found them to be in the range 10^{-10} to 10^{-13} m, compared to a range of 10^{-8} to 10^{-10} m for X-rays. It is now known that they are emitted by radioactive nuclei which have undergone a radioactive disintegration, as a mechanism of returning the nucleus to its ground state energy (see below).

The neutron

The final piece in this subatomic jigsaw (or, at least, in this simple version) was provided by the discovery of the neutron by James Chadwick (1891–1974) in 1932. Chadwick had been a student of Rutherford's in

Manchester, and worked with him at the Cavendish Laboratory in Cambridge from 1919. In 1920, Rutherford had postulated the existence of a particle which had roughly the same mass as the proton, but no electrical charge, from considerations of the likely structure of the atom, described below. The lack of charge on the neutron made it difficult to detect. In 1930 Bothe and Becker carried out some experiments in which they bombarded atoms of the lighter elements (lithium and beryllium) with α-particles, which resulted in the production of a very penetrating type of radiation, previously unknown. Bothe and Becker assumed it to be very high energy γ-radiation, but in 1932 Irène Curie and Frédéric Joliot showed this unknown radiation was capable of ejecting protons from material, such as paraffin wax. From the theory of elastic collisions, they calculated that the unknown radiation must be of very high energy to eject these protons. The predicted energy (up to 55 MeV, or million electron volts – an electron volt is the unit of energy used in particle physics, and is equivalent to 1.602×10^{-19} joules) is in fact much higher than that normally emitted by radioactive material. Chadwick repeated and modified these experiments, so that they could measure more precisely the energies involved in the various collisions. Using the laws of classical mechanics governing elastic collisions between solid objects (the same laws which govern the game of snooker), they concluded that the unknown radiation was, in fact, due to particles with a mass very close to that of the proton (1.674920×10^{-27} kg compared to 1.672614×10^{-27} kg for the proton), but with no charge: this particle was termed the neutron (Chadwick 1932). Chadwick received the Nobel Prize for Physics in 1935 for his discovery.

10.2. The Bohr–Rutherford model of the atom

The "plum pudding" model

In the atomistic view of matter as espoused by the Greek philosophers and Dalton, the atom was defined as the smallest indivisible particle of matter, and therefore had no structure. By the beginning of the twentieth century, it had become clear that this model was unsustainable. Not the least of the evidence was the existence of radioactively unstable substances, which were capable of ejecting relatively large particles with high energies. The first attempt to explain this and other phenomena was put forward by J. J. Thomson in 1904. From considerations of the cathode ray experiments described above, in which it was observed that the nature of the cathode rays (i.e., electrons) was unaffected by the nature of the material used to make the cathode, he concluded (correctly) that electrons are constituents of all atoms. He envisaged the atom as being composed of a sphere of positive electricity, into which were embedded sufficient electrons to create electrical neutrality – the so-called *plum pudding* model of the atom. Because it was assumed that the mass of the atom was due solely to the presence of these electrons, then even the lightest element, hydrogen, needed 1838 electron "plums" to make a mass of one.

A little earlier, in 1903 (Lenard 1903), Philipp Eduard Anton von Lenard (1862–1947) had carried out some scattering experiments in which he bombarded various metallic foils with high-energy cathode rays. He observed that the majority of electrons passed through the foils undeflected – from this he concluded that the majority of the volume occupied by the metallic atoms must be empty space. This idea was more fully developed by Rutherford (1911), who proposed the nuclear model of the atom which, despite much further elaboration, we still use today for the most basic explanations.

The Rutherford nuclear atom

Rutherford based his model on a refinement of von Lenard's electron scattering experiment carried out by Geiger and Marsden in 1909. They used α-particles, which were known to be much heavier than electrons (more than 7000 times heavier), instead of electrons as the "shells". Using a thin gold foil, they observed that almost all the α-particles went through the foil undeflected, but approximately 1 in 20 000 was reflected back towards the radioactive source. Rutherford, in describing this experiment, is widely quoted as saying *"It was almost as if you fired a 15 inch shell at a piece of tissue paper and it came back and hit you,"* but the source of this quote is obscure.

Such large reflection angles could not be explained using the classical scattering theory applied to multiple scattering events. It must therefore be the result of a single event – the collision of an α-particle with a single metal atom. He concluded that the most likely explanation of such a drastic event was that it was not simply the result of a mechanical collision, but that some electrical repulsion must also be involved. The fact that the α-particle is positively charged therefore required that the target should also carry a positive charge, but it must also be physically small since the majority of α-particles pass straight through. He assumed that the whole of the positive charge on the atom was located in a small *nucleus*, and that electrical neutrality was maintained by the presence of the appropriate number of extranuclear electrons. Being so much lighter, the extranuclear electrons would have little effect on a fast moving α-particle, so the reflection events represent the rare close encounter of an α-particle with the small positive nucleus.

The same experiments could, in fact, be used to predict the size and charge on the nucleus. If we assume that, at the point of impact between an α-particle (charge $+2e$) and the nucleus of a metal atom (charge $+Ze$), the kinetic energy is approximately matched by the force caused by electrostatic repulsion between the two positive charges, we can calculate the following:

$$\text{kinetic energy of } \alpha\text{-particle} = \frac{1}{2}MV^2$$

where M is the mass of the α-particle and V is its velocity, and:

$$\text{potential energy due to electrostatic repulsion} = \frac{2Ze^2}{4\pi\varepsilon_0 r}$$

which is the potential energy of the repulsive force between two like charges of $2e$ and Ze at a separation of r, where $4\pi\varepsilon_0$ represents a constant, equal to $4\pi \times 8.854 \times 10^{-12} \text{kg}^{-1} \text{ m}^{-3} \text{ s}^4 \text{ A}^2$. In this case, r may be taken as the maximum possible radius of the metallic nuclei of charge Ze.

At impact:

$$\frac{1}{2}MV^2 = \frac{2Ze^2}{4\pi\varepsilon_0 r}.$$

From previous calculations, we have values for m, the mass of the α-particle (approximately four times the mass of the proton, or $4 \times 1.67 \times 10^{-27}$ kg), for e, the charge on the electron (1.6×10^{-19} C), V, the velocity of an α-particle (approximately 2×10^7 m s^{-1}), and we can estimate that Z (the number of positive charges in a metallic nucleus: see below) is about 80. Substituting and rearranging gives:

$$r = \frac{4Ze^2}{4\pi\varepsilon_0 mv^2} = \frac{4 \times 80 \times (1.6 \times 10^{-19})^2}{4 \times 3.142 \times 8.854 \times 10^{-12} \times 4 \times 1.67 \times 10^{-27} \times (2 \times 10^7)^2}$$

$$= \frac{20.58 \times 10^{-37}}{743.3 \times 10^{-25}} = 6 \times 10^{-14} \text{m}.$$

This represents an upper limit for the dimensions of the nucleus. Compared with the estimates for the size of the atom, obtained from kinetic theory calculations on gases, which are typically 4×10^{-9} m, we can see that the nucleus is very small indeed compared to the atom as a whole – a radius ratio of 10^{-5}, or a volume ratio of 10^{-15}, which supports Rutherford's observation that most of an atom consists of empty space. We can also conclude that the density of the nucleus must be extremely high – 10^{15} times that encountered in ordinary matter, consistent with density estimates in astronomical objects called pulsars or neutron stars.

In the early part of the twentieth century, then, a simple model of atomic structure became accepted, now known as the Rutherford nuclear model of the atom, or, subsequently, the Bohr–Rutherford model. This supposed that most of the mass of the atom is concentrated in the *nucleus*, which consists of *protons* (positively charged particles) and *neutrons* (electrically neutral particles, of approximately the same mass). The number of protons in the nucleus is called the *atomic number*, which essentially defines the nature of the element, and is given the symbol Z. The number of protons plus neutrons in the nucleus is called the *atomic mass*, given the symbol A. Electrical neutrality in the atom is maintained by a number of negatively charged electrons (equal numerically to the number of protons, but with only a small fraction of the mass) circling the very small dense nucleus like a miniature solar system.

The Bohr theory of electronic orbitals
The Rutherford nuclear model predicts their existence, but gives no indication of the structure of the extranuclear electrons. The first suggestion came in 1913 when Niels Bohr (1885–1962) put forward the idea that these electrons occupy fixed stable orbits around the nucleus, in very much the same way as the planets orbit the sun. This was an empirical observation in the first place, designed to explain the fact that light and other electromagnetic radiation emitted when an atom is excited (the *emission spectrum* – see Section 12.3) consists only of light of discrete wavelengths. Bohr suggested that these wavelengths arose when electrons changed orbits in the electronic structure of the atom, and that these orbits had fixed energy levels. Because the energy difference between orbits with fixed energies must also be fixed, this gives an explanation to the observation of only discrete wavelengths in the emission spectrum, if we assume that wavelength is directly related to energy difference. It also has a number of consequences in terms of the chemical differences between the elements, and leads directly to the construction of the periodic table (see below). The great success of the combined Bohr–Rutherford model of the atom was that it explained some of the experimental observations, such as the unexpected scattering patterns resulting from α-particle collisions with metal foils, and the discrete nature of the emission spectra from simple atoms.

10.3   Stable and radioactive isotopes
Stable isotopes
According to the Bohr–Rutherford model, atoms are made up of a positively charged nucleus surrounded by a "cloud" of electrons in fixed orbitals carrying an equal negative charge. The nucleus contains both positively charged particles (*protons*) and electrically neutral particles (*neutrons*) which are roughly the same mass as the protons. The proton mass (1.673×10^{-27} kg) is given the value of one on the atomic mass *unit* (amu) scale, and is now termed a *Dalton* in recognition of his contribution to the development of chemistry. On this simple model, it is impossible to satisfactorily explain the structure of the nucleus itself, since this concentration of positive charge and mass in a tiny volume ought to make the nucleus itself inherently unstable. This phenomenon cannot be properly explained without resort to quantum

mechanics and subatomic physics, which is far beyond the scope of this book, but it is conventionally stated that the neutrons in the nucleus act as some form of "glue" which prevents the positively charged protons flying apart as a result of electrical repulsion. We will, for the sake of simplicity, adopt this explanation.

The number of protons in the nucleus is called the *atomic number*, and is given the symbol Z. It is this integer which gives all the elements their different chemical characteristics and distinguishes one element from another. Z varies continuously from 1, which is the lightest of all elements, hydrogen, up to 103, which is currently the heaviest known element (lawrencium). Since Z gives the number of units of positive charge in the nucleus, it also dictates the number of electrons orbiting the nucleus. In an electrically neutral atom, the number of electrons must be identical to the number of protons in the nucleus, since the charge on the proton and electron is identical and opposite. The familiar chemical symbols (e.g., H, C, O, Pb, etc.) are effectively a shorthand code for the proton number – thus the symbol Pb (lead) stands for, and is synonymous with, "the element with 82 protons in its nucleus". A full list of the elements can be found in Appendix VII.

All elements, except the simplest form of hydrogen, have some neutrons in their nucleus. For the lightest elements, the number of neutrons is the same (or nearly the same) as the number of protons (e.g., helium, He, has two protons and two neutrons), but as the number of protons increases, there appears to be a need for an excess of neutrons to "hold the nucleus together" (Fig. 10.2). Thus, gold (Au, atomic number 79) has 118 neutrons in its nucleus, giving it a total weight on the atomic scale of 197 Daltons. The number of neutrons is given the symbol N, and the combined number of protons plus neutrons is given the symbol A, the *atomic mass number*. Protons and neutrons are collectively termed *nucleons*, and the following simple relationship holds:

$$A = N + Z.$$

All elements, by definition, have a unique proton number, but some also have a unique number of neutrons (at least, in naturally occurring forms) and therefore a unique atomic weight – examples are gold (Au; $Z = 79$, $N = 118$, giving $A = 197$), bismuth (Bi; $Z = 83$, $N = 126$, $A = 209$), and at the lighter end of the scale, fluorine (F; $Z = 9$, $N = 10$, $A = 19$) and sodium (Na; $Z = 11$, $N = 12$, $A = 23$). Such behavior is, however, rare in the periodic table, where the vast majority of natural stable elements can exist with two or more different neutron numbers in their nucleus. These are termed *isotopes*. Isotopes of the same element have the same number of protons in their nucleus (and hence orbital electrons, and hence chemical properties), but

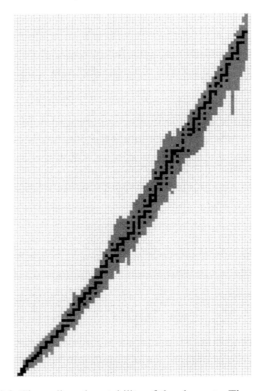

Figure 10.2 The radioactive stability of the elements. The *x* axis is proton number (up to Z = 83, bismuth), the *y* axis the neutron number (N). Stable isotopes are shown in black and radioactive isotopes in grey, indicating the relative excess of radioactive isotopes over stable isotopes in nature, and the fact that as proton number increases, the neutron number has to increase faster to maintain stability. The basic data for this figure are given in Appendix VI.

different numbers of neutrons, and hence different atomic weights (and therefore different kinetic properties). Of the 103 elements known to exist, only 21 are monoisotopic (Greenwood and Earnshaw 1997). This is one reason why the quoted atomic weights of many elements are not whole numbers – they are averages of two or more different isotopes, with the exact value of the average depending on the relative abundance of the various isotopes. For example, natural copper has a quoted atomic mass of 63.54 Daltons, as a result of having two isotopes – one of mass 63 with a relative abundance of 69%, and one of 65, with an abundance of 31%, giving an average of 63.54. It is conventional to denote the various isotopes by using the atomic weight as a preceding superscript – thus these two isotopes of copper are ^{63}Cu and ^{65}Cu. Strictly speaking, the atomic number should also be given as a preceding subscript, but for most purposes this is unnecessary since the symbol "Cu" is synonymous with the element whose atomic number is 29. It can be noted in passing that even elements which have only one isotope do not have an atomic weight which is exactly a whole number, because the actual mass of a nucleus is never exactly equal to the sum of the masses of its constituents, due to the relativistic conversion of a small proportion of the mass into energy, known as the *binding energy*.

For the lightest elements, there are usually only two isotopes which are stable, and the lighter of the two is usually the more common. Thus carbon has two stable isotopes, ^{12}C (six protons and six neutrons, abundance 99% of all naturally occurring carbon) and the heavier ^{13}C (six protons and seven neutrons, abundance approximately 1%). A third isotope, ^{14}C (six protons and eight neutrons), is extremely rare (fractional abundance 10^{-12}) and radioactively unstable, but is, of course, of vital importance to archaeology. Similarly, nitrogen has two stable isotopes, ^{14}N and ^{15}N, with abundances 99.6% and 0.4% respectively. Oxygen has three stable isotopes, ^{16}O, ^{17}O, and ^{18}O, with abundances 99.76%, 0.04%, and 0.20% respectively: this abundance pattern is typical of the slightly heavier "light" elements.

Chemically, all isotopes of the same element behave identically, but varying abundances of the various isotopes are found in different situations. For the light elements (e.g., H, C, N, O, S), some processes can alter the ratio of the isotopes present, which is known as *fractionation* (see Section 8.2). This is because the relative weight differences between the individual isotopes is large. For heavy elements (e.g., Sr, Pb), variable isotopic ratios are not caused by fractionation, but are due to the augmentation of the abundance of a particular isotope by the radioactive decay of another (see below). Typical causes of isotopic fractionation include diffusion (transport through membranes) and biological cycling, especially if repeated frequently. Fractionation is particularly marked in biological processes such as photosynthesis. Fractionation in light isotopes is now widely used as a natural isotopic marker system in biogeochemical cycles (e.g., Lajtha and Michener 1994), and has found extensive application in archaeology as a marker for dietary reconstruction (Section 8.5).

Radioactive isotopes

As atomic weight increases, the tendency to have a large number of stable isotopes also increases. Lead (Z = 82) has four – ^{204}Pb, ^{206}Pb, ^{207}Pb, and ^{208}Pb, with average natural abundances of 1.3%, 26.3%, 20.8%, and 51.5% respectively. The most prolific in this respect is tin (Sn, Z = 50), with ten stable isotopes (112, 114, 115, 116, 117, 118, 119, 120, 122, and 124) and abundances varying from 0.4% up to 33%.

In addition to these stable isotopes, many elements have one or more radioactively unstable isotopes, which are produced either as a result of specific nuclear processes (such as ^{14}C, which is the result of the interaction of neutrons produced by cosmic radiation with ^{14}N in the atmosphere) or as daughter nuclides during the radioactive decay of the heavier unstable elements. Lead, for example, in addition to the four stable isotopes listed above, has at least a further 17 unstable isotopes, ranging from ^{194}Pb up to ^{214}Pb, with half-lives (see section below) which vary from 800 milliseconds to 3×10^5 years. In fact, of the total number of nuclides (atoms with different nuclei) known, which is well in excess of 1700, only 260 are stable, suggesting that radioactive instability is the rule rather than the exception in nature (although some isotopes thought of as stable are in fact radioactively unstable, but with extremely long half-lives, e.g., ^{204}Pb, estimated to have a half-life of 1.4×10^{17} years, and therefore effectively stable on the geological timescale).

In order to maintain stability as the atomic number increases, the ratio of neutrons to protons has to increase from 1:1 in the very light elements up to about 3:1 for the heaviest. Too few or too many neutrons leads to nuclear instability. The reasons for the radioactive instability of some nuclei and not others is rather unclear, but it has been observed that certain combinations of nucleon numbers are more stable than others, giving rise to the concept of *magic numbers* in nuclear stability (Faure 1986: 15). Over half of the stable nuclides known have even numbers of both Z and N. Odd/even and even/odd combinations contribute just over another 100, but only four nuclei with an odd/odd configuration are stable. Furthermore, it has been noted that nuclei which can be imagined as being multiples of the helium nucleus (^{4}He, $A = 2$, $N = 2$) such as ^{12}C, ^{16}O, ^{32}S, and ^{40}Ca are all particularly stable, which gives some indication of the robustness of the helium nucleus, or α-particle, in nuclear physics. Standard tables of nuclides exist; for example Littlefield and Thorley (1979) Appendix C, which lists the nuclear configuration, natural abundances, decay process, and half-life of all known nuclides. New information is constantly being added and can be found on some chemical data websites such as WebElements [http://www.webelements.com/].

Radioactive decay

In order to explain the experimental observations on the behavior of uranium compounds, Rutherford and Soddy (1902) proposed a theory of radioactive disintegration. They suggested that the atoms of the radioactively unstable elements undergo spontaneous disintegration via the emission of either an α- or a β-particle, with the result that a new element is formed (called the *daughter*), which is physically and chemically different from its parent. This new element may itself be radioactive, and disintegrate in its turn. We now know that there are several other processes by which radioactive disintegration can occur, but they all have the effect of creating a new element (*transmutation* – the process which was one of the goals of the alchemists: see Section 2.1). The relationship between the nucleon numbers of parent and daughter is a characteristic of the particular process involved, and can be generalized using the notation that superscript numbers refer to atomic weight (A) and subscripts refer to proton number (Z). It should be noted that the following focuses on only the major particles involved in these events. Other particles, such as *antineutrinos* are necessary for a full quantum understanding of what is involved, but add little to the explanation at this level. Almost all nuclear disintegrations are accompanied by the emission of high energy electromagnetic radiation known as γ-emission, following rearrangement of the daughter nucleus to its lowest possible energy state. These γ-emissions have characteristic energies and can be used to follow the path of the nuclear reactions in neutron activation analysis (Chapter 6).

The following particles are involved in natural radioactive decay.

α-emission

The nucleus of a helium atom ($^4_2$He) is ejected from the parent nucleus, leaving it four mass units lighter, and its charge reduced by two protons:

$$^A_Z X \rightarrow {}^{A-4}_{Z-2} Y + {}^4_2 \text{He}.$$

This results in the transmutation of parent element X into daughter Y, which has an atomic number two less than X. The particular isotope of element Y which is formed is that with an atomic mass of four less than the original isotope of X. Note that, as in chemical reactions, these nuclear reactions must be numerically balanced on either side of the arrow. Many of the heavy elements in the three naturally occurring radioactive decay chains (see below) decay by α-emission.

β-emission

An electron ($^0_{-1}\beta$), for these purposes, is considered to have zero mass (being approximately $1/1840$ of that of the proton), but to carry a single negative charge. It is important to realize that this is still a particle which has been ejected from an unstable nucleus, and not to confuse it with the orbital electrons, which are (initially at least) unaffected by these nuclear transformations. The general equation for β decay is:

$$^A_Z X \rightarrow {}^A_{Z+1} Y + {}^0_{-1}\beta.$$

The effect of the β-emission is to increase the atomic number by 1 (i.e., to transmute parent X into the next heaviest element in the periodic table, daughter Y), but to leave the atomic weight unchanged (a so-called *isobaric* transmutation). Although it does not actually happen like this, it is often useful to think of the process as being the conversion of a neutron into two equal but oppositely charged particles, the proton and the electron, as follows:

$$^1_0 n \rightarrow {}^1_1 p + {}^0_{-1} e.$$

Many of the heavy elements in the three natural radioactive decay chains also decay by β-emission.

Positron-emission

A positron is a positively charged electron (β^+, or $^0_{+1}\beta$). It is annihilated by interaction with normal electrons, once it has lost most of its ejection energy. Its emission leaves the parent nucleus unchanged in mass, but decreased in charge by one:

$$^A_Z X \rightarrow ^A_{Z-1} Y + ^0_{+1}\beta.$$

Atoms which are deficient in neutrons tend to decay via positron-emission, whereas those which have a neutron excess decay via β-emission.

Electron capture

A fourth mode of decay, which results in the nucleus reducing its proton number by one, is called electron capture, whereby a proton from the nucleus "captures" one of the extranuclear (orbital) electrons, converting itself into a nuclear neutron. The daughter is isobaric (same mass) with the parent, but has a proton number which is decreased by one:

$$^A_Z X \xrightarrow{ec} ^A_{Z-1} Y.$$

Nuclear fission

Fission of the nucleus, whereby it splits into two roughly equal halves, is accompanied by a huge release of energy. It was first observed by Hahn and Strassman (1939), who were bombarding uranium with neutrons. Many heavy elements are susceptible to induced fission, but spontaneous fission can occur in some of the heaviest elements, and is thought to be the principal mode of decay for the transuranic elements.

The first four modes of radioactive decay can be plotted on a single diagram (Fig. 10.3), which allows for a prediction of the nature of the daughter nucleus from a parent subject to any one of the above processes.

The radioactive decay of a nucleus is a random process, but the decay of a particular element is characterized by a number known as the *half-life* ($T_{1/2}$), which is the time taken for half of the original material to change into another element by radioactive decay. Half-lives vary from fractions of a second to many billions of years, depending on the isotope. The half-life is only meaningful when considered in terms of the behavior of an assemblage of atoms of the radioactive element – for any particular atom, the probability that it will undergo radioactive decay in any particular time period is essentially unpredictable – it may happen in the next second, or it may not happen for millennia. It is possible that the atom we have selected to watch

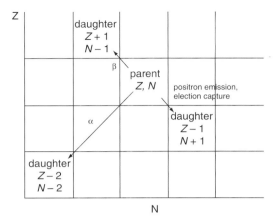

Figure 10.3 Schematic diagram of the four common modes of radioactive decay. N = neutron number, Z = proton number. The atomic number A = Z + N.

will be the last one of all to change to its daughter, many half-lives away in the future. It is, therefore, useful to think not just in terms of the half-life but also the mean lifetime (τ) of the radioactive element. The mean lifetime is the average "life expectancy" of any particular atom in an assemblage of atoms of the radioactive element. It can be used to calculate the number of radioactive disintegrations per second per gram of radioactive material. This is a measurable and useful quantity, and is related to the half-life as follows:

$$T_{1/2} = \frac{0.693}{\lambda}.$$

where λ is the decay constant for the radioactive process. The mean lifetime is then given by:

$$\tau = \frac{1}{\lambda}$$

i.e., the mean lifetime is the reciprocal of the decay constant. A full derivation of these relationships is given in Pollard and Heron (1996, 306).

Because radioactive decay is a nuclear process, the rate of radioactive decay is totally unaffected by any external factors. Unlike chemical reactions, therefore, there is no dependency on temperature, or pressure, or any of the other environmental factors which affect the rate at which normal chemical reactions occur. This is the reason why radioactive decay chronometers, such as ^{14}C, Ar-Ar, and U-series methods, are so important in geology and archaeology – they provide an "absolute clock".

Although many nuclei are naturally radioactive, there are three main radioactive decay chains in nature. These start with the elements uranium and thorium (^{238}U, ^{235}U, and ^{232}Th) and all end in one of the three stable isotopes of lead (^{206}Pb, ^{207}Pb, and ^{208}Pb respectively). Although each chain goes through a large number of intermediate unstable nuclei, the three chains can be summarized as follows:

$$^{235}_{92}U \rightarrow {}^{207}_{82}Pb + 7{}^{4}_{2}He + 4\beta^- + energy$$

$$^{238}_{92}U \rightarrow {}^{206}_{82}Pb + 8{}^{4}_{2}He + 6\beta^- + energy$$

$$^{232}_{90}Th \rightarrow {}^{208}_{82}Pb + 6{}^{4}_{2}He + 4\beta^- + energy.$$

Thus the chain that starts with ^{238}U goes through eight different radioactive decay processes each of which results in the emission of an alpha particle, and six involving beta particles, and the stable end member is ^{206}Pb, at which point the series ends. The ^{206}Pb produced as a result of these radioactive processes is termed *radiogenic*, to distinguish it from any other (nonradiogenic) ^{206}Pb which may exist. In detail, each of these decay chains involves a number of radioactive intermediates, all of which have a particular half-life. Invariably, however, the first step in the chain has by far the longest half-life. Consideration of the behavior of these chains under conditions of *secular equilibrium* (i.e., when the rate of decay of the daughter isotope becomes equal to the rate of decay of the parent, and assuming a closed system), shows that it is possible to consider the decay chain simply in terms of the parent decaying directly to the stable Pb end point, with a half-life essentially the same as the longest half-life in the system, which happens to be that of the parent isotope (Faure 1986: 285). Thus, each of the three decay chains can be simplified to the following, which is particularly useful when considering the evolution of the isotopic compositions of terrestrial lead deposits (see Section 8.3):

$$^{238}U \rightarrow {}^{206}Pb \qquad T_{1/2} = 4.468 \times 10^9 \text{ years}$$

$$^{235}U \rightarrow {}^{207}Pb \qquad T_{1/2} = 0.7038 \times 10^9 \text{ years}$$

$$^{232}Th \rightarrow {}^{208}Pb \qquad T_{1/2} = 14.01 \times 10^9 \text{ years.}$$

10.4 The quantum atom

The Bohr–Rutherford model established that the atom can be considered as a small dense nucleus made up of positively charged protons "glued" together by an equal or greater number of neutrons, surrounded at some distance (relatively speaking) by orbital electrons, the number of which must match exactly the proton number for a neutral atom. A necessary part of this model is that the electrons circling the nucleus are in fixed stable orbits, each of which has a specific energy (i.e., their energies are *quantized*, and the orbitals are sometimes called *energy levels*), similar to the planets around the sun.

However, the classical Newtonian mechanics which explains the universe on the scale to which we are familiar (e.g., falling apples, billiard balls, and planets) does not work at the scale of the atom and an explanation of such orbitals required the development of an entirely new field of physics – quantum theory. Another part of the Bohr–Rutherford model, for reasons explained below, requires each "orbital" or "shell" to contain only a fixed number of electrons. Additional electrons must be added to the next stable orbital above (in energy terms) that which is full. This fixed number of electrons in each orbital was determined to be two in the first level, eight in the second level, eight in the third level (but extendible to eighteen), and so on. Strange though it seems at first sight, this model has allowed chemists to derive the systematic structure underlying the periodic table, and to understand factors such as atomic sizes, the shapes of molecules, and the underlying reason behind the observed periodicity of chemical properties.

Quantum numbers and orbitals
Each orbital (or energy level) is uniquely characterized by a set of *quantum numbers*. The integer which defines the orbital in the above discussion (1, 2, 3, etc.) is called the *principal quantum number*, n. The sublevels described by the letters s, p, d, f (the labels for which are derived from observations of lines in the emission spectra of atoms, and stand for sharp, principal, diffuse, and fundamental – see Section 12.3) are associated with the *azimuthal* (or *angular momentum*) *quantum number*, given the symbol l, with $l = 0$ being labeled the s orbital, $l = 1$ the p orbital, etc. The maximum value of l for any orbital ranges from 0 to $(n - 1)$. Thus, the first orbital ($n = 1$) has only one allowed value of l (i.e., 0), whereas the second ($n = 2$) can have $l = 0$ or 1. The labels for these orbitals combine these two quantum numbers, as $1s$, $2s$, $2p$, etc. Each subshell (s, p, etc.) has a characteristic shape in three-dimensional space (Fig. 10.4) which is important in descriptions of chemical bonding and the shapes of molecules (Section 11.4). The s orbitals are spherically distributed around the nucleus, whereas the three p orbitals are elliptical figure-of-eight lobes at right angles to each other, centered on the nucleus. Some of these orbitals can be split even further, according to a third quantum number m_l (the *magnetic quantum number*), which can take values of 0, ± 1, up to a maximum of $\pm l$. Thus, s orbitals (with $l = 0$) have no sublevels, whereas p orbitals have 3 (with m_l values of -1, 0, and $+1$), d has 5 (-2, -1, 0, $+1$, $+2$), etc. One further quantum number is the spin of an electron (s), which can take one of two values, either spin up ($\uparrow$) or spin down ($\downarrow$). *Pauli's* exclusion principle (Wolfgang Pauli, 1900–58) states that no two electrons in an atom can have the same set of these four quantum numbers (n, l, m_l, s), thus setting the maximum occupancy for a particular orbital (Pauli 1925) – 2 electrons for s-orbitals, 6 for p-orbitals, 10 for d-orbitals, etc.

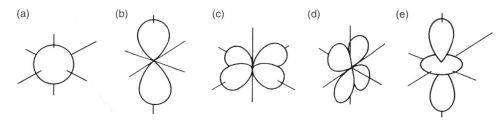

(a)   (b)   (c)   (d)   (e)

Figure 10.4 Shapes of the *s*, *p*, and *d* atomic orbitals. The *s* orbital (a) is spherically symmetrical about the nucleus. The three *p* orbitals (b) are figure-of-eight lobes orientated along the three orthogonal axes (only z axis shown). The five *d* orbitals (c, d, and e) are four quatrefoil lobes, one orientated along the x–y axes, three between the axes, and the fifth (e) a figure-of-eight along the z axis with an additional "donut" around the nucleus. The orbitals are not drawn to the same scale.

We can now begin to understand the way in which the orbital electrons are distributed with increasing atomic number, as we step systematically by proton number through the list of elements. Table 10.1 shows how the *electronic configuration* (the number and distribution of the orbital electrons) of most of the elements can be understood by simply following the above rules for filling up the successive electron orbitals to keep pace with the increasing number of protons in the nucleus. Appendix VII gives a full quantum description of the ground state electronic configuration of all atoms. The 1*s* orbital has no subshells, and is therefore full with only two electrons (one spin up, one spin down). Thus the first two elements (H and He) have electronic configurations signified as $1s^1$ (meaning one 1*s* electron) and $1s^2$ (meaning two 1*s* electrons) respectively. The second shell consists of a 2*s* level (full with two electrons), and also three 2*p* levels (with m_l values of -1, 0, and $+1$), each of which can hold two electrons. Thus, the third element by atomic number (Li) fills the 1*s* orbital with two electrons, and puts the third electron in the next available orbital, the 2*s*. It has an electronic configuration of $1s^2 2s^1$. This filling of the second orbital continues through the elements beryllium (symbol Be, proton number Z = 4; electronic configuration $1s^2 2s^2$), boron (B, Z = 5; $1s^2 2s^2 2p^1$: the 2*s* orbital being full, the next electron must go into the 2*p* orbital), carbon (C, Z = 6; $1s^2 2s^2 2p^2$), nitrogen (N, Z = 7; $1s^2 2s^2 2p^3$), oxygen (O, Z = 8; $1s^2 2s^2 2p^4$), fluorine (F, Z = 9; $1s^2 2s^2 2p^5$), and neon (Ne, Z = 10; $1s^2 2s^2 2p^6$). With neon (like helium, one of the so-called "rare" or "noble gases", because they are chemically relatively unreactive), the 2*p* shell is completely full, and any further electrons must begin to fill the third orbital. We might suspect from this that the chemical unreactivity of the noble gases is linked to the fact that they have completely full outer orbitals (in the case of neon, the second orbital), and also that a full outer orbital is a desirable property for other elements to attain, which they do by losing or gaining electrons. This is the basis of valency and bonding theory, and is discussed in Section 11.2.

Table 10.1. *Definition of electron orbitals in terms of the four orbital quantum numbers* (n, l, m_l, s).

Orbital	Principal quantum no. (n)	Azimuthal quantum no. (l)	Magnetic quantum no. (m_l)	Electron occupancy (spin up or down)
1s	1	0	0	2 (↑↓)
2s	2	0	0	2 (↑↓)
2p	2	1	0, ±1	6 (↑↓)(↑↓)(↑↓)
3s	3	0	0	2 (↑↓)
3p	3	1	0, ±1	6 (↑↓)(↑↓)(↑↓)
3d	3	2	0, ±1, ±2	10 (↑↓)(↑↓)(↑↓)(↑↓)(↑↓)
4s	4	0	0	2 (↑↓)
4p	4	1	0, ±1	6 (↑↓)(↑↓)(↑↓)
4d	4	2	0, ±1, ±2	10 (↑↓)(↑↓)(↑↓)(↑↓)(↑↓)
4f	4	3	0, ±1, ±2, ±3	14 (↑↓)(↑↓)(↑↓)(↑↓)(↑↓)(↑↓)(↑↓)

The next element by atomic number is sodium (Na), with 11 protons in the nucleus, and therefore 11 orbital electrons, which gives the electronic configuration $1s^2 2s^2 2p^6 3s^1$, sometimes written as [Ne]$3s^1$, denoting that it has the same electronic configuration as neon, plus an additional 3s electron (or more simply still as 2,8,1 referring to the total occupancy of levels 1, 2, and 3). This is the lowest energy configuration the neutral sodium atom can have, since all of the possible first and second orbitals are full, and the final spare electron has gone into the 3s level, which is the next available orbital. This configuration is termed the *ground state*, and is the configuration listed for each element in Appendix VII.

Atomic energy levels

Complications arise in heavier atoms, because it turns out that these simple rules for filling orbitals by principal quantum number appear to be broken, but in fact they are not when the relative energy levels of each orbital are considered. Since the closer a positive and negative charge are brought together, the greater the external energy needed to pull them apart again, we can assume that the binding energy (i.e., the energy needed to remove an electron from that orbital) is higher the closer that orbital is to the nucleus. Thus, in this model, we assume that the 1s orbital has a higher binding energy than a 2s orbital because it is closer to the nucleus, and so on. Rather than measure this energy directly, however, we conventionally reference the binding energy of the outer orbitals to that of the innermost orbital (the 1s orbital). By arbitrarily setting the energy of this level to zero, we can show the energies associated with all other orbitals as a positive scale which increases with distance from the nucleus. Although the actual values of the energy levels for atoms of different elements are different, it is possible to

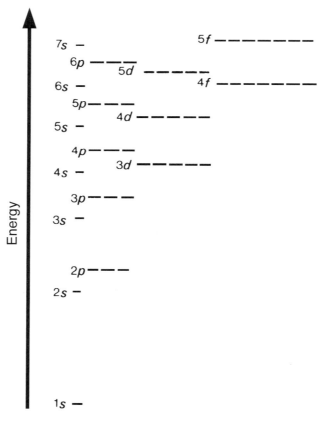

Figure 10.5 Energy levels of atomic orbitals. *n* is the *principal quantum number*, and the *s, p, d* notation indicates the *azimuthal quantum number* (*l*). For *l* = 1 and above the orbital is split into multiple suborbitals (indicated by the number of lines), corresponding to the values of the *magnetic quantum number m_l*. Each of these "lines" can hold two electrons (corresponding to "spin up" and "spin down"), giving rise to the rules for filling up the orbitals. Note that the 3*d* orbital energy is below that of the 4*p*, which explains the electronic structure of the transition (*d*-block) metals. After Fig. A1.1, Pollard and Heron (1996).

represent schematically this sequence, since it is the same for all atoms, as shown in Fig. 10.5. This shows that the 4*s* level has an energy below that of 3*d*. Thus, when the 3*p* orbital is full (the rare gas argon, with $Z = 18$, and configuration $1s^2 2s^2 2p^6 3s^2 3p^6$), the next element (potassium, K, $Z = 19$) has configuration $1s^2 2s^2 2p^6 3s^2 3p^6 4s^1$ rather than $1s^2 2s^2 2p^6 3s^2 3p^6 3d^1$ as would be predicted from the simple numerical sequence. The second available 4*s* orbital is filled in the next element, calcium (Ca, $Z = 20$, $1s^2 2s^2 2p^6 3s^2 3p^6 4s^2$), and then the next available orbital becomes the 3*d*. The next ten elements by atomic number (Sc, $Z = 21$ to Zn, $Z = 30$) fill up these available *d* orbitals (but not quite in a simple sequence), giving rise to the first series of transition metals elements, or *d*-block elements, whose chemical properties are dictated by the behavior of the *d* orbital electrons as well as the outer 4*s* orbitals. Thus, the simple explanation of how the orbital structure of the elements is related to the proton number is still followed, but allowance has to be made for a deviation from the numerical sequence because of the relative energies of the outer orbitals.

It must be emphasized that, in any atom, although the orbital electrons may actually fill only the first two or three orbitals (depending on the number of protons in the nucleus), the other unfilled energy levels still exist, and under certain circumstances an electron from a lower filled state can be promoted to one of the unfilled energy levels. For sodium ($1s^2 2s^2 2p^6 3s^1$), it is possible to promote the outer (3*s*) electron to occupy one of the unfilled higher orbitals, such as the 4*p*, by supplying some energy to this outer electron. The atom is then in an *excited state*, but it will normally de-excite very quickly back to the ground state, when the promoted electron drops back down to the 3*s* level (energetically the most stable configuration), and the energy acquired is released. If enough energy is supplied to the atom, it is possible to remove the electron from the atom completely, and the atom is said to be *ionized*. Because it is now one electron deficient, it has an unbalanced positive nuclear charge, and the resulting entity carries a single positive net charge – in this case, it has become the sodium *ion*, symbolized by Na^+, and with the electronic configuration of the noble gas neon ($1s^2 2s^2 2p^6$).

10.5   The periodic table

Early constructions of the periodic table

The process of science involves, in its early stages, the classification of data. One of the great advances of chemistry came from the systematization of the known chemical elements based on their atomic weights. The ultimate product of this systematization, the periodic table in its current form, was not completed until the mid twentieth century, but, as early as 1817, Johann Wolfgang Döbereiner (1780–1849) observed the existence of *triads*. These are sets of three elements with similar chemical properties and whose atomic weights are related – the weight of the middle member is approximately halfway between the weights of the other members. Döbereiner's triads (1829) include chlorine, bromine, and iodine (now know as the *halogens*), with atomic weights 35.5, 80, and 127 respectively, and calcium (40), strontium (87), and barium (137) (now known as the *alkaline earth* elements). No explanation could be offered for this observation at the time. In 1850, Max Josef von Pettenkofer (1818–1901) went somewhat further, by demonstrating that the atomic weights of lithium (7), sodium (23), and potassium (39) (the *alkali* metals) were linked by the formula:

$$A = 7 + (2n) \times 8$$

where n can take the value 0, 1, or 2, but, again, no explanation was forthcoming.

Following Cannizzaro's publication in 1858 of an accurate method for measuring atomic weights from vapor pressures, progress was considerably more rapid. Between 1863 and 1866, John A. R. Newlands (1837–98) published a series of papers in which he pointed out that if the elements were arranged in order of atomic weight, then there were chemical similarities between those which occupied places in the table which were eight places apart. Thus, the first (hydrogen) resembled the eighth (fluorine) and the fifteenth (chlorine); the second (lithium) resembles the ninth (sodium), etc. Newlands (1865) observed that, by making a "*few slight transpositions, ... the numbers of analogous elements generally differ either by seven or by some multiple of seven.*" He likened these to musical octaves, and his observations became known as the *Law of Octaves*. His audience, however, was unconvinced by the harmony of his ideas!

Very soon afterwards, however, two scientists independently produced the definitive statement on the classification of the elements – Julius Lothar Meyer (1830–95) in Germany and Dmitri Ivanovich Mendeleev (1834–1907) (also spelled Mendeléeff or Mendelejeff) in Russia. It is the latter who is now credited with the construction of the first periodic table. At the age of 35, Mendeleev was Professor of Chemistry at the University of St Petersberg, when he published his first paper (1869) on the periodic system. He was apparently unaware of the work of Newlands or Lothar Meyer, but came to the same conclusions, and was also prepared to go further, and predict that certain elements must remain to be discovered because of discrepancies in his table. Amongst other things, he concluded the following:

- the elements, if arranged according to their atomic weights, exhibit a periodicity of properties;
- elements of similar chemical properties have either very similar atomic weights, e.g., platinum (195), iridium (192), osmium (190), or exhibit a regular increase, e.g., potassium (39), rubidium (85), caesium (133);
- the character of an element is determined by the magnitude of its atomic weight, and certain characteristic properties of the element can be predicted from a knowledge of its atomic weight.

Mendeleev was rapidly supported in his scheme when his predictions of missing elements turned out to be correct. For example, he predicted that there were missing elements with atomic weights of 44, 68, and 72. Furthermore, he predicted that the missing element whose weight was 72 should have a specific gravity of 5.5, would form metal dioxides with oxygen which would have a specific gravity of 4.7, and also similar predictions about its chloride. He was more than gratified to find, in 1886, that Clemens Alexander Winkler (1838–1904) published his discovery of germanium (Ge) with an atomic weight of 72.6, and its oxide (GeO_2) with a specific gravity of 4.7. Subsequent discoveries of gallium (Ga, $A = 69.7$) and scandium (Sc, 45.0) further strengthened belief in his system.

Mendeleev's table did not, however, solve every chemical mystery. He predicted that tellurium (Te, $A = 127.6$) should have an atomic weight less than that of iodine (I, 126.9), which it does not. The so-called "rare" or "noble" gases (helium, neon, argon, krypton, and xenon), discovered at the end of the nineteenth century, had no immediate place in this classification. These anomalies, and the structure behind the periodic table, were clarified by Henry Gwyn Jeffreys Moseley (1887–1915) in 1913 and 1914, who showed, from his work on the X-ray spectra of the elements, that it was not the atomic *weight* (i.e., combined neutron and proton number in the nucleus) but the atomic *number* (proton number only) which was of fundamental importance in constructing the table. If the elements are arranged in atomic number order, then it becomes clear that, for example, tellurium with an atomic number of 52 should lie below iodine (53) despite the fact that it has a higher atomic weight. The explanation of the periodic properties of the elements had, however, still to wait for a fuller understanding of the orbital electronic structure of the elements, as described above.

Interpretation of the modern periodic table
The most common arrangement of the modern periodic table is shown in Fig. 10.6, although this is a condensed version of the "long" or "extended" table where the *f*-block is shown in its correct place with La and Ac below Sc and Y in group 3, with the remaining elements being accommodated by pushing the *d*-block across. The WebElements site [http://www.webelements.com/] has a copy of the periodic table, with links to a great deal of data about the elements.

In the modern periodic table, horizontal rows are known as *periods*, and are labeled with Arabic numerals. These correspond to the principal quantum numbers described in the previous section. Because the outer shells of the elements H and He are *s* rather than *p* orbitals, these elements are usually considered differently from those in the rest of the table, and thus the 1st period consists of the elements Li, Be, B, C, N, O, F, and Ne, and the 2nd Na to Ar. Periods 1 and 2 are known as *short periods*, because they contain only eight elements. From the discussion above, it can be seen that these periods correspond to the filling of the *p* orbitals (the 2*p* levels for the first period, and the 3*p* for the second), and they are consequently referred to as *p*-block elements. The 3rd and 4th periods are extended by an additional series of elements inserted after the second member of the period (Ca and Sr respectively), consisting of an extra ten elements (Sc to Zn in period 3 and Y

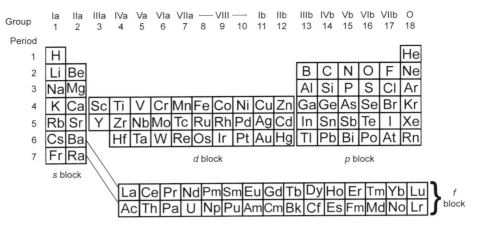

Figure 10.6 The modern "extended" periodic table, showing the older (Roman) and modern (numerical) labeling for the groups. Elements heavier than lawrencium (Z = 103) have been omitted, since they have no naturally occurring isotopes, and the *s*-, *p*- and *d*-blocks have been separated for clarity. Further details of the elements can be found in Appendix VI.

to Cd in period 4), before continuing with the final six members of the period (Ga to Kr and In to Xe). For Sc to Zn this corresponds to filling the 3*d* orbitals after first filling the 4*s* orbitals (K and Ca), before returning to the 4*p* orbitals (Ga to Kr), as described above. The second insertion (Y to Cd) corresponds to the filling of the ten 4*d* orbitals after the two 5*s* (Rb and Sr) but before the six 5*p* orbitals (In to Xe). Period 5 shows a similar ten additional elements (La to Hg, filling the 5*d* orbitals) inserted between the filling of the 6*s* orbitals (Cs and Ba) and the 6*p* orbitals (Tl to Rn). These three insertions (Sc–Zn, Y–Cd, La–Hg) are collectively called the *d-block* or *transition metals*, since they correspond to the filling of the 3*d*, 4*d*, and 5*d* orbitals respectively. In the 5th period (Cs to Rn), there is a second insertion of 14 elements (Ce to Lu) after La and before Hf. This corresponds to the filling of the 4*f* orbitals before completing the 5*d* transition metal sequence. This second insertion into the 5th period, starting with Ce (Z = 58) and concluding with Lu (Z = 71) is called the *f-block* elements, *lanthanides*, which includes the *rare earths*. They have extremely similar chemical properties, and are often used as indicators of the nature of the geochemical processes to which rocks and minerals have been subjected, since their relative abundances are generally more sensitive to physical rather than chemical factors (see Section 9.4). The 6th period begins with Fr and Ra (7*s* outer orbitals), but is incomplete in terms of naturally occurring elements. A fourth *d-block* insertion (6*d*) begins with Ac, but is never completed. Likewise, Ac is followed by a second *f-block* insertion (5*f*), termed the *actinides*, which is complete to lawrencium (Lr), the heaviest of the named elements known to exist.

Vertical columns are known as *groups*, and have historically been labeled with Roman numerals, although IUPAC now recommends numbering with Arabic numerals 1–18. Group I elements consist of H, Li, Na, K, Rb, Cs, and Fr, although H is not normally included with group I elements. At the other end of the table, group VII consists of F, Cl, Br, I, and At, which collectively are termed the *halogens*, or salt-forming elements. Note that H can also be classified here, but is not traditionally included as a halogen. Group O consists of elements which were not known at the time of the compilation of the first periodic table, but which are now known as the *rare* or *noble gases* (Ne, Ar, Kr, Xe, Rn). They are all relatively unreactive gases, but they are not completely inert, nor are they all that uncommon.

The two columns to the left of the table are labeled as groups Ia and IIa. The last two columns of the *d*-block elements (Cu, Ag, Au and Zn, Cd, Hg) are labeled groups Ib and IIb, for reasons which are apparent when the electronic structure of the table is considered, but chemically they behave in a similar manner to the elements in groups Ia and IIa. Likewise, there exist groups IIIa and IIIb, etc. The rationale is that they are related in electronic structure, which influences their chemical properties, and it is convenient to classify them as related. Groups Ia and IIa are called the *s-block* elements, whereas groups IIIb to O are called the *p-block* elements. Together, the *s*- and *p*-block elements are termed *main group elements*, to distinguish them from the *transition* or *d-block* elements.

Periodicity of properties

Chemical properties vary systematically across periods and within groups, and can be explained by the underlying electronic structures discussed above. Group properties are perhaps the most easily appreciated, and of these the most significant (particularly geochemically) is probably size. The size of the atom as measured by its atomic radius increases down the group. Thus in the first group, the *alkali metals* show an increase in size from Li (atomic radius in the metallic state 152 pm, i.e., 152×10^{-12} m) up to Cs (metallic radius 265 pm). Fr, the heaviest of the alkali metals, was predicted to exist by Mendeleev in the 1870s (he called it "eka-caesium"; Mendeleef 1879, 1880) but it was not discovered until 1939 by Marguerite Catherine Perey (1909–75), of the Curie Institute in Paris. It is radioactively unstable and has not yet been isolated in measurable quantities. Many physical properties of the elements are related to the size of the atom or ion, and thus also show systematic group variation – for the alkali metals, for example, the melting point decreases from 180°C for Li down to 29°C for Cs. Group properties also often extend to compounds of the elements. Thus, the group VIb elements S to Po form hydrides (H_2S, etc.) with decreasing chemical stability down the group.

Properties across the periods can also vary systematically. For all periods, elements towards the left-hand side tend to form positively charged ions, whereas those on the right-hand side (excluding group 0) have higher electronegativities (see Section 11.1) and tend to form negative ions. Physical properties, such as melting point and boiling point, change systematically across the period, but not necessarily monotonically. Again, properties of compounds can be predicted from consideration of periodic properties. For example, the oxides of the third period elements (Na to Cl) are strongly basic on the left-hand side (Na_2O), whereas oxides of Cl (Cl_2O, etc.) are strongly acidic in character.

Variation is less marked within the *d*-block elements, but the properties still exhibit periodicity. In the first transition series (Ti to Zn), for example, the melting point of the metals varies from 1668°C for Ti to 1083°C for Cu, but is not linear across the period. Densities, on the other hand, increase from 4.51 g cm^{-3} for Ti up to 8.94 g cm^{-3} for Cu. There are, however, similarities between adjacent elements in the *d*-block. Often three elements in the short group (e.g., group IIb – Zn, Cd, Hg) will have similar chemical properties, although increasing size down the group may moderate this similarity (in this example, Hg is liquid at room temperature). Also, adjacent elements in a period may well have very similar chemical properties, at least in some respects, such as the *platinum group elements* (pges) of Ru, Os, Rh, Ir, Pa, and Pt. Similarity across the period is even more marked in the *f*-block elements, where the first group (the lanthanides or rare earths) show many physical properties which change smoothly across the period – so much so that the chemistries of adjacent elements and their compounds are often virtually indistinguishable (Eu is an exception, often behaving very differently from the other lanthanides, because it can have variable valency).

The modern periodic table represents a pinnacle of the achievement of many nineteenth- and twentieth-century chemists, and is a clear visual expression of our understanding of the structure of the atom. It is not only beautiful, however – it is also supremely useful. It offers a simple key to predicting a wealth of physical and chemical data about the elements and their compounds. It is possible to predict the properties and behavior (biogeochemically, as well as chemically) of hundreds of compounds, from a knowledge of a few. It is the key to understanding modern chemistry.

11

VALENCY, BONDING, AND MOLECULES

This chapter continues the introduction to chemistry, but focuses on the way in which atoms combine to form molecules. The concept of valency is introduced as "combining capacity", but is then explained in terms of electronic orbital theory, leading into a simple explanation of chemical bonding. The three major types of chemical bond (ionic, metallic, and covalent) are introduced, followed by a discussion of the bonding between molecules (van der Waals', dipole–dipole, and hydrogen bonding). This leads into a description of the shapes of molecules. Further discussions of bonding are available in general chemistry textbooks, such as Brady and Hollum (1993) or Atkins and Jones (2002). The final section consists of an introduction to the naming and structure of organic compounds, and the various forms of isomerism in such structures. Again, further details on nomenclature and structure can be found in books such as Streitweiser and Heathcock (1985), and Brady and Hollum (1993).

11.1 Atoms and molecules

Rarely are the chemical elements stable as single isolated atoms. Almost all elements exist as discrete multiatomic atoms (e.g., gases such as O_2, Cl_2) or as larger multiatomic agglomerations such as crystals and metals. By definition, compounds consist of more than one atom combined in some way, either as discrete molecules (e.g., H_2O), or as (effectively) infinitely large crystals such as NaCl. Thus most elements and all compounds have some form of bonding between constituent atoms. Bonding results in the product molecule being more energetically favorable and, therefore, more chemically stable than the original isolated atoms. As contact between atoms occurs in the vicinity of the electrons furthest from the nucleus (the outer shells), the *electronic configuration* (the number and distribution of the orbital electrons, described in Section 10.4) strongly influences the way in which atoms bond, and the shapes of the resulting molecules. There are three principal types of bonding between atoms (*ionic, covalent*, and *metallic*), which differ in the way the outer electrons of the constituent atoms are shared. Sometimes the resulting molecule is (on an atomic scale) infinitely large, such as a crystal of rock salt, or a piece of metal, and no other mechanism is necessary to explain the macroscopic materials we can see and handle. Sometimes, however, molecular entities can themselves form bonds with other molecules to create a macroscopic material. There are three types of this

249

intermolecular bonding; *van der Waals', dipole–dipole,* and *hydrogen-bonds*, and an understanding of such bonding is necessary to explain, for example, why water is a liquid at room temperature. However, before we consider these types of bonds, we must examine the underlying principles which govern the way in which atoms combine.

Valency

Valency is that property of an element which causes it to bond in a certain fixed ratio with another element. For example, two hydrogen atoms (H) will combine with one oxygen atom (O) to form water, H_2O. In the nineteenth century this was described as "combining capacity" and, for each element, it is constant and can be represented by a ratio of simple whole numbers (2:1 for water). Thus the valency of an element was originally determined from a knowledge of the number of hydrogen atoms which combine with or are displaced by one atom of that element. The valency of oxygen is therefore determined to be two, because it forms a dihydride (H_2O). For elements which do not easily combine with hydrogen, the valency can be determined by an extension of this principle. If an oxide forms, the valency of the metal can be calculated from its stoichiometry, and using the fact that the valency of oxygen is known to be two. Magnesium, therefore, has a valency of two because the formula of the oxide is MgO and it therefore has the same "combining capacity" as oxygen. Copper, however, has two valencies, since it can form two oxides (CuO, where the valency is two, and Cu_2O, with valency one), which is difficult to explain at this level. Table 11.1 gives examples of the calculation of the valencies of some common elements by this method.

Electronic structure and bonding

Although this original definition of valency is based on the observation that atoms combine to form molecules in ratios of simple whole numbers, we can provide a more satisfying explanation based on an understanding of the electronic configuration of the atom. As explained in Section 10.5, the periodic table was developed before the discovery of the neutron, and was based on the weights and chemical behavior of the elements, but it is now realized that the arrangement of the elements is dictated by the atomic number of the elements and their electronic configuration. In the older notation (Roman numerals), the numbers above each group (column) in the periodic table (Fig. 10.6 in Section 10.6) show the number of electrons in the outer shell for each element in that group. Even though the structure and properties of the atoms as arranged in the periodic table is perfectly explained by the rules for filling electronic orbitals, the majority of atoms are not chemically stable as single atoms. The most energetically favorable structure for an individual atom is that in which it has a full outer shell of electrons. For most of the common elements, the outer shell can accommodate eight electrons, and this tendency

Table 11.1. *Examples of calculating valency from the combining capacity of some simple compounds.*

Element	Compound	No. of hydrogen atoms	No. of bonds	No. of unpaired electrons	Valency of element
chlorine	HCl	1	1	1	monovalent (1)
oxygen	H_2O	2	2	2	divalent (2)
nitrogen	NH_3	3	3	3	trivalent (3)
carbon	CH_4	4	4	4	tetravalent (4)
copper	CuO	equivalent to 2	2	2	variable
	Cu_2O	equivalent to 1	1	1	valency

towards a full outer shell is, therefore, known as the *octet rule*. The exceptions are hydrogen and helium, which only need two electrons for a complete (*s*) shell. The majority of elements therefore need to lose or gain one or more electrons to achieve an octet, and hence the propensity of most elements to form homogeneous or heterogeneous molecules.

The extreme stability of atoms with full (or "closed") outer orbitals is demonstrated by the almost complete lack of chemical reactivity of the "noble gases" [He ($1s^2$), Ne ($1s^2 2s^2 2p^6$), Ar ([Ne]$3s^2 3p^6$), Kr ([Ar]$3d^{10} 4s^2 4p^6$), Xe ([Kr]$4d^{10} 5s^2 5p^6$), and Rn ([Xe]$5d^{10} 6s^2 6p^6$)]. Since each atom has a full outer *p*-shell structure, it requires no loss, gain, or sharing of electrons to achieve this most stable configuration: consequently, the noble gases exist (unusually in nature) in the nonbonded monatomic state. All other elements need to lose or gain at least one electron to achieve this full outer shell. The halogens, group VII in the periodic table [F ($1s^2 2s^2 2p^5$), Cl ([Ne]$3s^2 3p^5$), Br ([Ar]$3d^{10} 4s^2 4p^5$), and I ([Kr]$4d^{10} 5s^2 5p^5$)], and hydrogen ($1s^1$) are all a single electron short of a full outer orbital, and therefore need to share (covalent bonding) or take (ionic bonding) one of the outer electrons from another atom. The alkali metals [Li ($1s^2 2s^1$), Na ([Ne]$3s^1$), K ([Ar]$4s^1$), Rb ([Kr]$5s^1$), and Cs ([Xe]$6s^1$)], on the other hand, all have a single *s*-orbital electron as the outermost electron, indicating that these elements all have one electron to donate or share with another atom. Consideration of their "combining capacity", as shown above, assigns the halogens and alkali metals a valency of one, and it can now be seen that this must be related to the fact that as a group they are one electron short or one in excess of a full shell. If we assume for the moment that a chemical bond is formed by an electron from one atom being shared with another atom, which in turn shares an electron with the first atom, we can see that a bond is in fact a shared pair of electrons, one from each atom. Thus the halogens and the alkali metals, needing to lose or gain a single electron to complete the outer orbitals, form a single bond with another atom, by sharing one pair of electrons. This gives another definition of valency – it is the potential number of bonds an element can form, or the number of electron pairs involved in bonding.

When going beyond the halogens or the alkali metals in the periodic table, understanding the potential number of bonds an element can form requires a little more appreciation of the behavior of orbital electrons. From the quantum description of orbital electrons (Section 10.4), a full p orbital consists of three sets of paired electrons – one spin up, one spin down – each pair occupying one of the three suborbitals (defined by m_l) in the p shell. If there are only five p electrons, as in the halogens, then one is inevitably an *unpaired electron* – it is this electron which takes part in bonding, and gives it a valency of one. If there are four p electrons (as in oxygen – $1s^2 2s^2 2p^4$), it might be thought that the outer structure would consist of two electron pairs, and no unpaired electrons. This is, however, not the case. Energy considerations mean that it is most favorable to have the four p electrons as widely distributed between the three subshells as possible. Thus the ground state of oxygen has the p electrons existing as one electron pair and two unpaired electrons. We would therefore correctly predict that oxygen is divalent because of these two unpaired p electrons, and that the stable form of oxygen (O_2) is double-bonded ($O = O$) because two of the four p electrons are shared. For the same reasons of energetics, atoms with only three p electrons exist with three unpaired p electrons rather than one pair and an unpaired electron. Thus the diatomic molecule N_2 is triply bonded ($N \equiv N$) because the configuration is $1s^2 2s^2 2p^3$. Each of the three p electrons is shared with those of another nitrogen atom, giving each atom a closed outer shell. It should now be clear that another definition of valency is given by the number of unpaired electrons an element has in its outer shell. Figure 11.1 shows a simple representation of this model of valency and bonding.

These electronic interpretations of valency allow us to interpret the phenomenon of variable valency exhibited by many of the transition metal elements. As shown in Fig. 10.5 (Chapter 10), the transition metals exist because the energy of the outer d orbitals lies between the s and p energy levels of the next lowest orbitals, and thus are filled up in preference to the p orbitals. Copper, for example ($1s^2 2s^2 2p^6 3s^2 3p^6 3d^{10} 4s^1$), has a single outer s electron available for bonding, giving rise to Cu(I) compounds, but it can also lose one of the $3d$ electrons, giving rise to Cu(II) compounds.

Electronegativity
Electronegativity (χ) is an empirical measure of the tendency of an atom in a molecule to attract electrons. The noble gases, therefore, do not have electronegativity values because they do not easily form molecules. The electronegativity value depends primarily on the element, but also on the oxidation state, i.e., the electronegativity of elements with variable valency can be different for each valency – thus that of Fe^{2+} is different from that of

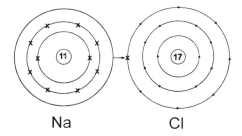

Figure 11.1 Simple model of valency and bonding. The sodium atom (Z = 11) has electronic configuration $1s^2 2s^2 2p^6 3s^1$, drawn simply as (2, 8, 1) (i.e., showing all the $n = 2$ electrons as a single orbital). Chlorine (Z = 17) is $1s^2 2s^2 2p^6 3s^2 3p^5$, drawn as (2, 8, 7). In bonding to form the ionic compound NaCl, the outer ($3s$) electron of Na is "donated" to the outer orbital of Cl, giving both a full outer orbital of eight electrons, and leaving the sodium one electron short (i.e., the Na^+ ion) and chlorine one extra (Cl^-).

Fe^{3+}. There are several ways of defining electronegativity, the simplest being that of Allred and Rochow (1958), which calculates the force experienced by the outer electron from the nucleus using Coulomb's law of electrical attraction:

$$\text{Force} = \frac{(Z^* e)(e)}{r^2}$$

where ($Z^* e$) is the *effective nuclear charge* felt by the outer electron, e is the charge on the electron, r is the mean radius of the orbital, which is taken as the covalent radii. Z^* is the nuclear charge as seen from the outer orbitals, and is less than the proton number Z because of the screening effect of the inner electrons, and can be calculated from a set of shielding parameters. Substituting, the formula becomes:

$$\text{Force} = \chi = 0.359 \frac{Z^*}{r^2} + 0.744.$$

This equation gives a self-consistent set of electronegativity values which range from Cs (least electronegative) with $\chi = 0.7$ to F (most electronegative) with $\chi = 4.0$. Figure 11.2 shows a periodic table with the electronegativity values of the elements inserted.

11.2 Bonds between atoms

The type of bonding in an element or compound is important, as this will determine both the chemical and physical properties of the molecule (literally, the difference between chalk and cheese!). Electronegativity differences between bonding atoms determine the type of bond which will form. Strictly speaking, there is no such thing as a pure ionic bond or a pure covalent bond, just a gradation of character from one extreme to the other, although it is often reasonable to regard many simple compounds as mainly ionically or mainly covalently bonded. There are therefore no explicit values which delineate the boundaries between bond types, but in general the greater the difference in electronegativity values the more ionic character the bond has. The smaller the difference, the more covalent character the bond has. When the electronegativity values themselves are low then the more metallic is the character of the bonding.

Ionic bonding

Ionic bonding occurs as a result of the electrostatic attraction between negative and positive ions. In any ionic compound, the balance of positive and negative charges must be such that the overall structure is not charged. The ions themselves are created by electron transfer between the atoms prior to bonding. A simple example would be the creation of NaCl by the Na atom donating its single outer (3*s*) electron to the singly deficient 3*p* orbital of the Cl atom. The resulting Na^+ and Cl^- ions are mutually electrostatically attractive. In general, for this transfer to occur, there must be a large electronegativity difference between the atoms (generally when the difference is greater than 1.7 the bond is more than 50% ionic). Therefore ionic bonding occurs when a metal (lower left-hand side of the periodic table, Fig. 11.2) reacts with a nonmetal (upper right-hand side of the periodic table). Typical examples are common inorganic compounds such as NaCl, LiF, KCl, CaF_2, MgO, and CaO.

The resulting structures are crystalline, defined by a regular repeating unit cell, which is not limited to a few atoms but can extend to give large crystals (Fig. 11.3). The nondirectional electrostatic attraction between the positive and negative ions results in some of the characteristic properties of crystalline materials. As each ion is surrounded by a large number (the *co-ordination number*) of oppositely charged ions, it requires a large amount of energy to

H 2.1																	He
Li 1	Be 1.5											B 2	C 2.5	N 3	O 3.5	F 4	Ne
Na 0.9	Mg 1.2											Al 1.5	Si 1.8	P 2.1	S 2.5	Cl 3	Ar
K 0.8	Ca 1	Sc 1.3	Ti 1.5	V 1.6	Cr 1.6	Mn 1.5	Fe 1.8	Co 1.8	Ni 1.8	Cu 1.9	Zn 1.6	Ga 1.6	Ge 1.8	As 2	Se 2.4	Br 2.8	Kr
Rb 0.8	Sr 1	Y 1.2	Zr 1.4	Nb 1.6	Mo 1.8	Tc 1.9	Ru 2.2	Rh 2.2	Pd 2.2	Ag 1.9	Cd 1.7	In 1.7	Sn 1.8	Sb 1.9	Te 2.1	I 2.5	Xe
Cs 0.7	Ba 0.9	La 1.1	Hf 1.3	Ta 1.5	W 1.7	Re 1.9	Os 2.2	Ir 2.2	Pt 2.2	Au 2.4	Hg 1.9	Tl 1.8	Pb 1.8	Bi 1.9	Po 2	At 2.2	Rn
Fr 0.7	Ra 0.9	Ac 1.1															

Ce 1.1	Pr 1.1	Nd 1.2	Pm 1.2	Sm 1.2	Eu 1.1	Gd 1.1	Tb 1.2	Dy 1.1	Ho 1.2	Er 1.2	Tm 1.2	Yb 1.1	Lu 1.2
Th 1.3	Pa 1.5	U 1.7	Np 1.3	Pu 1.3	Am 1.3	Cm 1.3	Bk 1.3	Cf 1.3	Es 1.3	Fm 1.3	Md 1.3	No 1.3	Lr

Figure 11.2 Electronegativity values (χ) for the elements. The differences between values, and the magnitude of the values, dictate which sort of bonding will occur between atoms.

(a)   (b)

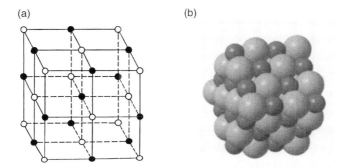

Figure 11.3 Arrangement of atoms in an ionic solid such as NaCl. (a) shows a cubic lattice with alternating Na^+ and Cl^- ions. (b) is a space-filling model of the same structure, in which the small spheres are Na^+ ions, the larger Cl^-. The structure is described as two interlocking face-centred cubic lattices of sodium and chlorine ions.

disrupt the structure, and therefore ionic compounds generally have high melting and boiling points, i.e., they are relatively hard and are usually solid at room temperature. However, if the lattice is dislocated by a blow in the correct plane, then like-charged ions will find themselves neighbors and the resulting repulsion will neatly divide the crystal. They tend to be brittle.

In the solid state, the ions are unable to move freely very easily (they do in fact vibrate, and this motion is what we experience as heat, but the ions are generally confined to their positions within the lattice) and, therefore, although ions are present, they are unable to act as charge carriers and the solid will not conduct electricity. However, if the ions are given enough energy in the form of heat, then the motion allows the ions to move from these fixed positions (the ionic solid melts to form an ionic liquid), then they can transport charge and, therefore, conduct electricity. Similarly, if the ionic lattice can be surrounded by other molecules, in other words dissolved in a solvent, then the free ions will also conduct and the solution is a good electrical conductor. An interesting point to note is that pure water will not conduct electricity, since it has no free charge carriers. It is the contaminants, particularly dissolved ions, which conduct, and therefore measuring the electrical resistance of water is a good way of determining its purity (see Section 13.2).

Metallic bonding
Metallic bonding occurs between atoms which have similar low electro-negativity values. In this form of bonding, each atom shares its valence electron(s) with every other atom in the structure, i.e., the electrons are "pooled", "free", or "delocalized". The electrostatic attraction between the positive ions and the electron pool holds the structure together (Fig. 11.4). As with ionic bonding, each positive ion feels the influence of a large number of

Figure 11.4 Metallic bonding. The atoms of the metal form a regular lattice, the exact nature of which depends on the ionic radius of the metal involved. Each atom donates an electron to the "cloud" which is free to move throughout the structure and holds the ions together.

nondirectional electrostatic attractions, and, therefore, it requires a lot of energy to disrupt the structure. Thus, metals generally have high melting and boiling points. However, as the pool of electrons is free to move throughout the structure, metals are very good conductors of electricity and heat. The luster associated with metals is also due to the free electrons interacting with incoming electromagnetic radiation. Unlike ionic solids, metals will not cleave in certain planes, as all the ions are positively charged and a dislocation has no effect on the bonding. Metals can, therefore, be worked, be malleable (the ability to be hammered), and be ductile (the ability to be drawn into wires) – something that cannot be done with the ionically bonded compounds such as table salt.

As metals tend to have similar ionic radii, it is possible to substitute one metal atom for another in the solid, thereby forming *alloys* (termed *amalgams* with mercury, which is liquid at room temperature), which can have very different physical properties (such as hardness) from the pure metal depending on the degree of substitution. Some examples of alloys include electrum (gold [ionic radius 144 pm] and silver [144 pm]), brass (copper [117 pm] and zinc [125 pm]), bronze (copper [117 pm] and tin [140 pm]). The latter, as is the case with many alloys, cannot form a complete solid solution (i.e., there is a limit on the amount of tin which can be substituted), because it breaks up into several phases due to the larger size of tin. An important substitutional alloy is steel (iron [116 pm] and carbon [77 pm]), but this is an example of interstitial substitution, in which the much smaller carbon sits in the spaces between the iron in the lattice, rather than replacing iron at the lattice points. The majority of the elements in the periodic table are metals, characterized by high electrical conductivity, optical reflectivity, thermal conductivity, and ductility, which arise as a result of the nature of the metallic bond, characterized by delocalized electrons free to move across the whole structure.

Covalent bonding
Covalent bonding occurs when the electronegativity values of the participating atoms are high, but similar in value. Therefore, covalent bonding is electron

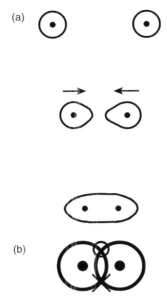

Figure 11.5 Covalent bonding. (a) shows two isolated hydrogen atoms coming together to form a covalently bonded (di)hydrogen molecule. (b) shows a simple model of the bonding in a dihydrogen molecule, with the single 1s orbital electron from each atom being shared by the molecule, to give each atom a closed shell.

sharing, and the atoms sharing the electrons are both attracted to the electrons in the bond. Each atom contributes one electron to the bond, resulting in a covalent bond with two electrons. Most of the *electron density* is between the two atoms (electron density is a probabilistic way of looking at the arrangement of electron orbitals, more suited to the discussion of covalent bonding, and is discussed in more detail in Section 12.2). Figure 11.5 shows the process of the formation of covalent bonding, from two isolated hydrogen atoms to a covalently bonded (di)hydrogen molecule. Initially, the electron density of each atom is spherical (an *atomic s*-orbital), but as the distance between them reduces, they begin to deform and then to merge. In the dihydrogen molecule, the electron density is greatest between the two nuclei, although this may not always be the case (see π-orbitals below), and a new *bonding* orbital has formed. Figure 11.6 shows how the bond energy varies with bond length for the dihydrogen molecule. The initial lowering of energy is caused by the gain of a full outer shell (and the electrostatic attraction of the nuclei for both bonding electrons). However, if the distance between the two nuclei further decreases, the nuclei themselves repel. This takes energy to oppose and, therefore, there is an optimal bond length determined by the energetics of the system.

There is a wide range of molecules which use covalent bonding, and they can exhibit a wide range of physical and chemical properties. Many of these differences result from the scale of the bonding. *Molecular* covalent molecules

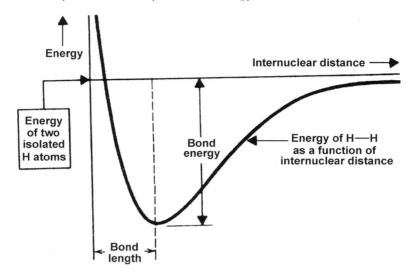

Figure 11.6 Variation of bond energy with interatomic distance for the hydrogen molecule. If the two hydrogen nuclei are close together mutual repulsion occurs, and at greater distances the attractive force becomes weaker. The equilibrium bond length and bond energy occur at the energy minimum.

are discrete molecules, generally containing a small number of bonded atoms e.g., H_2O, N_2, H_2, up to small organic molecules such as caffeine ($C_8H_{18}N_4O_2$). Their physical properties are determined by the nature and arrangement of the atoms and the interactions between molecules (see below). In general, covalent molecules do not conduct electricity as the electrons are not free to move. *Network* or *extended* covalent molecules are formed by a large number of bonded atoms where the repeat unit can be extended over great distances, e.g., diamond, graphite, or polythene. These bonds are directional, and each repeat unit is surrounded by a large number of neighbors which makes them generally solids and insoluble in solvents. Elements in the middle of the periodic table tend to form discrete polyatomic covalent molecules (e.g., P_4, Se_8) or small discrete multiply bonded polymers (e.g., sulfur, which forms ring structures from S_8 up to S_{20}). Other mid-table elements form giant covalent molecules (including B, C, P, S, Si, As, Se, Ge, Sb, Te, Sn, Bi).

11.3   Intermolecular bonds

Intermolecular bonds are much weaker than the bonding types described above. They generally act between atoms and molecules which have already formed internal covalent bonds. They are responsible for the physical properties of the molecules such as melting and boiling points. Although this sounds relatively insignificant, these bonds are vital in holding together the structures of proteins, cell membranes, DNA, and even explain why geckos can walk on ceilings (Autumn *et al.* 2000).

$$\delta^+ \qquad \delta^- \qquad \delta^+ \qquad \delta^-$$

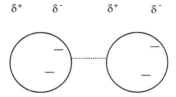

Figure 11.7 van der Waals' bond caused by the creation of an instantaneous dipole. Momentary variations in the electron charge distribution of an atom causes a momentary dipole attraction between the asymmetric negative charge and the positive nuclear charge of another atom.

van der Waals'

These are the weakest of all intermolecular bonds. They result from the random movement of electrons within an atom or molecule. This movement can result in a separation of charge across the atom or molecule (an *instantaneous dipole*: Fig. 11.7). This small separation of charge (indicated by δ^+ and δ^-) will then influence neighboring atoms or molecules, and cause an induced dipole. These van der Waals' bonds (sometimes known as London forces) occur between nonpolar molecules or atoms such as I_2, O_2, H_2, N_2, Xe, Ne, and between the aliphatic chains of lipids (see below).

Dipole–dipole

These intermolecular bonds are caused by a permanent separation of charge across a molecule. This is due to electronegativity differences between two bonded atoms and results in the bond developing a dipole, because the electrons in the bond are nearer to (or spend more time orbiting) the atom with the highest electronegativity. The result is a *polar molecule*. This small separation of charge is indicated by δ^+ or δ^- and neighboring dipolar molecules will align according to this charge and form weak bonds. Dipole–dipole bonds occur between polar molecules such as HCl (Fig. 11.8).

Hydrogen-bonds

If hydrogen is bonded to a small but highly electronegative atom (such as O, N, or F) then permanent dipoles are created as described above. Adjacent molecules align to bring together opposite charges on each dipole, and the result is termed a hydrogen bond. These hydrogen-bonds occur very widely between small molecules such as H_2O, NH_3, and HF, but also are responsible for the bonding between bases in the giant molecule DNA.

Hydrogen-bonding has a huge influence on the physical properties of molecules. Boiling is the conversion of a liquid (where the molecules are free to move, but linked by intermolecular bonds) to a gas, where (in an *ideal* gas) the molecules are so distant from each other that they do not interact. Boiling, therefore, does not break the strong covalent bonds within molecules, but rather the weaker intermolecular bonds between them.

δ^+ δ^- δ^+ δ^-

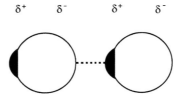

Figure 11.8 Dipole–dipole bonds in polar molecules such as HCl. The hydrogen (black) of one molecule is attracted to the chlorine (white) of another because of the permanent charge imbalance on the molecule.

Figure 11.9(a) shows hydrogen-bonding in water, and Fig. 11.9(b) shows the highly anomalous boiling point of water, which, if it behaved as it should within the group VIb, ought to have a boiling point almost 200°C below its measured value. Because water exists not as isolated H_2O molecules, but as larger water polymers linked by hydrogen-bonding, the effective molecular weight of water is much higher than 18, and thus the boiling point (which is related to molecular weight) is $+100^\circ$C rather than -100°C. A similar anomaly occurs with the melting point of water ice, and this results in water having a wide temperature range over which it is a liquid. The fact that it does has had a great influence on the evolution of life on Earth.

11.4   Lewis structures and the shapes of molecules
Creating the Lewis structures of molecules is a method for determining the sequence of bonding within a molecule and its three-dimensional shape. This works best for covalently bonded molecules, but can also work for ionic compounds. For example, this method can be used to explain why the sequence of bonding in water is H–O–H, rather than H–H–O, and why it has a "bent" structure, rather than linear.

The rules used to draw Lewis structures are as follows:
- count all valence electrons (given by the group number in the periodic table)
- subtract or add electrons for ions
- decide which atoms are bonded to one another (a formula often has the central atom written first)
- place electrons into the bond (two for each bond)
- if the central atom does not have an octet then form double or triple bonds
- any remaining electrons form lone pairs.

As an example, we apply these rules to water, H_2O. Hydrogen (H) is in group 1 of the periodic table and therefore the two hydrogen atoms have one valence electron each to donate to the bonds. Oxygen is in group 6 and it therefore has six valence electrons to donate. The total number of valence electrons is therefore (H [1×2] + O[6]) = 8. Water in this example is a neutral species so we do not need to add (if negative) or subtract (if positive) electrons. Next, we draw some speculative structures showing the sequence of bonding between the atoms (Fig. 11.10). By drawing "–" between the atoms, we are already placing single covalent bonds,

(a)

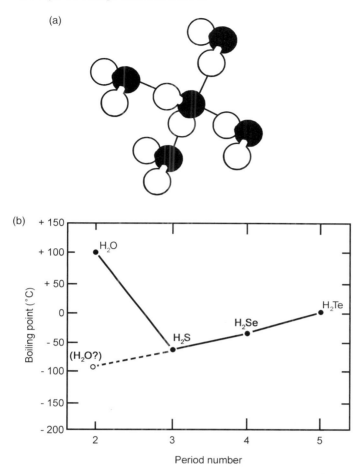

(b)

Figure 11.9 Hydrogen bonding. (a) In water (white spheres are H, black O) hydrogen bonding between O and H from adjacent molecules gives a much higher apparent molecular weight than predicted from the simple formula. (b) This results in a higher boiling point when compared to other hydrides in the same group: from these, a boiling point of around $-100°$C would be predicted.

and each bond will require two electrons (shown as dots). However, at this stage, in either possible structure (Fig. 11.10(a)) we have only placed four of a total eight valence electrons. The remainder could be used as further bonds, or as nonbonding lone pairs on the most electronegative atom, as shown in Fig. 11.10(b). As shown here, by checking that each atom appears to have an octet of electrons (except in this case it is only two for hydrogen, since its outer orbital is only an *s* shell) all but one of these speculative structures can be excluded. The "correct" molecule shows two H–O bonds and two lone pairs on the oxygen. This is, however, only a two-dimensional representation of what is in reality a three-dimensional structure. In three dimensions the

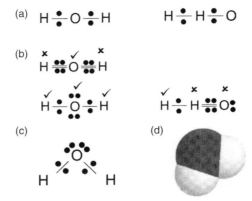

Figure 11.10 Lewis structures of water (H_2O). (a) shows two possible configurations of water, but only H–O–H satisfies the electronic requirements of the oxygen atom. (b) shows three possible bond distributions for this structure, but only one (with a single bond to each of the hydrogens and two "lone pairs" on the oxygen) meets the requirements of all three atoms. (c) shows the "bent" structure of H–O–H which follows from the need to separate the two lone pairs and two single bonds as far as possible in the three-dimensional molecule. (d) shows a space-filling version of this arrangement, where the oxygen is black and the two hydrogens white.

molecule adopts a tetrahedral shape, partly because the two lone pairs need to be as far away from each other as possible, and the two-dimensional structure shown in Fig. 11.10(c) is more representative. This therefore predicts that the structure of H_2O has each H bonded to the central oxygen, and, because of the two additional lone pairs, is a "bent" (as opposed to a linear) molecule, and is also a highly polar molecule. A space-filling model is shown in Fig. 11.10(d).

Bond type, order, length, and resonance structures
As described above for molecular oxygen or nitrogen, it is possible to have more than one bond between atoms (up to a maximum of three for orbital reasons). *Bond order* is simply the number of pairs of electrons shared between two atoms (remember there are two electrons per covalent bond). As the bond order increases the distance between the atoms decreases and the energy required to break the bonds increases.

Figure 11.11 shows there are some molecules which can legitimately be drawn in several different ways using Lewis structures, each conforming to the octet rule. These are *resonance structures*, and are equally valid, but the "true" structure is a hybrid of the two or more possible structures. This is indicated by the double-headed arrow, where the electrons are moved, but the atoms stay in position. However, in this example, the carbon–oxygen bonds are of equal length – they do not rapidly interconvert from one version to another. The true

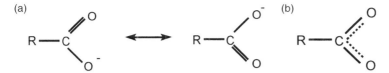

Figure 11.11 The resonance structure of a generalized organic acid RCOO⁻, where R is any organic group and –COO⁻ is the acid radical. (a) shows two possible equivalent forms for this structure, and (b) the resonance structure, which is a mixture of the two.

structure is a blend of both structures, with delocalized electrons no longer restricted between the two atoms, but spread over all the relevant atoms.

Molecular orbitals

As seen in Section 10.4, the quantum numbers determine the electronic configuration of the atom and also the shape of the atomic orbitals (Fig. 10.4). However, these are the shapes of the *atomic* orbitals, i.e., those of isolated atoms, and the process of bonding alters the shapes of these orbitals. We have already seen what happens when two hydrogen atoms bond (Fig. 11.5) – the resulting molecular orbital, which holds two electrons, is a combination of the atomic orbitals. Something similar can be seen in the molecule HF. In this case, one *s*-orbital (from the hydrogen) and one, correctly orientated, *p*-orbital (from the fluorine), each holding only one electron, overlap to create the molecular orbital, where the two electrons form the single covalent bond. The shapes of molecular orbitals are considered further below, in the context of carbon compounds.

11.5 Introduction to organic compounds

As stated in Chapter 2, organic chemistry is the branch of chemistry dealing with carbon compounds. The name "organic" originates from the belief that these compounds could only be produced by living organisms, but in 1828 Wöhler synthesized urea [$CO(NH_2)_2$] from inorganic starting materials, and now many organic compounds can be manufactured. However, it still remains the case that most carbon compounds are largely associated with living, or once living, organisms. Carbon is a major element in biological systems (along with H, N, and O) and is found in all of the molecules important for life (e.g., carbohydrates, proteins, and lipids). Carbon atoms have some unique properties – they form strong covalent bonds with one another (to form rings and long chains) and carbon also bonds strongly with nonmetals (e.g., N, S, O, F, Cl). This variety of possible bonding leads to 95% of all known compounds being organic.

The orbital structure of carbon

The electronic configuration of carbon is $1s^2 2s^2 2p^2$. It is the electrons in the outer shell ($n = 2$) which are in contact with other atoms and hence take part

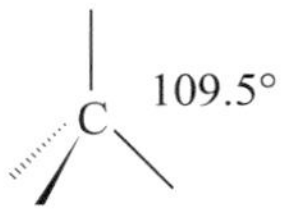

Figure 11.12 The three-dimensional tetrahedral structure of carbon (e.g., in methane, CH_4), with an angle between the bonds of 109.5°. The simple straight lines are in the plane of the paper, the solid tapered line points towards the observer and the dashed line is into the paper.

in bonding. These four electrons ($2s^2 2p^2$) can therefore form four covalent bonds – giving carbon its valency of four. The shape of carbon singly bonded to four other atoms (e.g., as in methane, CH_4) is a tetrahedral structure with an angle between the bonds of 109.5° (Fig. 11.12). As can be seen, however, this shape cannot be created simply by using the atomic orbitals, i.e., one spherical 2s-orbital containing two electrons and two dumb-bell shaped 2p-orbitals with one electron each, and one empty p-orbital – if it were, then one would expect differences in bond lengths and strengths between the four bonds, whereas experimental evidence shows that they are all identical. What happens is that the atomic orbitals combine to create new *hybrid* atomic orbitals prior to bonding (Fig. 11.13). If a hybrid is formed between an s- and one p-orbital, then the result is a linear *sp* hybrid (Fig. 11.13(a)). If it is between one s- and two p-orbitals, then it becomes an sp^2 hybrid, with a plane triangular shape (Fig. 11.13(b)). The tetrahedral structure of methane is therefore a result of the hybridization of the one s-orbital and the three p-orbitals to produce four equivalent sp^3 hybrid orbitals, which have a tetrahedral shape in three dimensions (Fig. 11.13(c)).

When two carbon atoms come together to form a single carbon–carbon bond, each carbon uses one sp^3 hybrid orbital, each containing one electron. A covalent bonding orbital containing two electrons is produced from the two sp^3 hybrids, which is called a σ-bond (sigma). Each carbon then has three remaining sp^3 hybrid orbitals to form a further three bonds with other atoms (usually hydrogen or another carbon). Note that the σ-bond is symmetrical about the bond axis, and therefore the single carbon–carbon bond can rotate. In a double carbon–carbon bond, each carbon provides one sp^2 hybrid orbital and one p-orbital, each containing one electron, i.e., on each carbon, one s- plus two p- gives three sp^2 hybrids, leaving one nonhybridized p-orbital remaining. The two sp^2 hybrids from each carbon overlap to form a σ-bond and the two p-orbitals overlap to produce a π-bond (pi) (Fig. 11.14). Unlike the σ-bond, the π-bond is not symmetrical about the bond axis, having electron density above and below the plane of the bond, not between the two nuclei, and therefore rotation around a double bond is prevented.

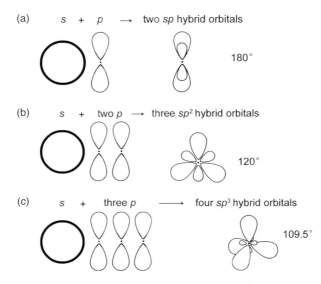

Figure 11.13 Hybridization of *s*- and *p*- atomic orbitals. (a) Linear *sp* hybrid, from one *s*- and one *p*-orbital. (b) *sp*² hybrid, from one *s*- and two *p*-orbitals, with a plane triangular shape. (c) *sp*³ hybrid, from one *s*-orbital and the three *p*-orbitals, which has a tetrahedral shape in three dimensions.

Drawing organic structures

There are different ways of drawing the structures of organic compounds. All are equally valid, but some provide different levels of information and their use will be determined by what is required. Different types of structures may be combined to save space and to highlight the areas of interest. All the structures in Fig. 11.15 are of exactly the same molecule (*n*-hexane). The molecular formula is C_6H_{14}, which gives information about the numbers and type of atoms present in the molecule (six carbon and fourteen hydrogen atoms), but provides no information about which atom is bonded to which, or the arrangement of those atoms in space. Figure 11.15(a) shows one representation of this molecule (i.e., all the tetravalent carbon atoms are shown "flattened", and form a straight chain of six carbons). To save space and time, and without losing any of this structural information, this could be written in a *condensed form* as $CH_3CH_2CH_2CH_2CH_2CH_3$. It could be further simplified to $CH_3(CH_2)_4CH_3$, where the middle (CH_2) unit is shown to be repeated four times. A different representation is shown in Fig. 11.15(b), where each line represents a single carbon–carbon bond. The six carbon atoms are not shown, but are assumed to exist at the ends and at each node (the point where two bonds meet, and the line bends). Furthermore, the C–H bonds are usually "understood" and therefore not shown. Mentally, therefore, we need to add to this picture three hydrogens to each (invisible!) carbon at the ends, and two to each of the four in the chain. Neither of these pictures, however, shows the

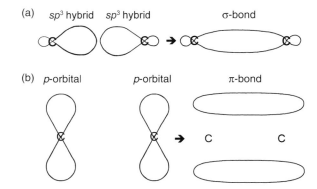

Figure 11.14 σ- and π-bond formation. In (a) two sp^3 hybrids bond to form a σ-bond, in which most of the electron density is between the carbon atoms. In (b) two p-orbitals bond to form a π-bond, in which most of the electron density is above and below the plane of the bond.

three-dimensional structure of the molecule. On a two-dimensional sheet of paper, the convention is to show bonds in the plane of the paper as simple straight lines, bonds pointing out of the paper as solid tapered lines, and bonds into the paper as dashed lines, as illustrated in Fig. 11.15(a). A more realistic diagram is the space filling model (Fig. 11.15(d)), where the volume occupied by each of the atoms is shown by combining solid spheres. There are a number of free software packages which allow molecules to be drawn, and a number of predrawn molecules which include three-dimensional data, thus enabling their true structure to be illustrated. For example, CHIME [http://www.mdli.com/downloads/] is a free plug-in for Netscape so that three-dimensional rotating molecular models can be viewed on the web. The same website gives access to ISIS/Draw 2.4, a free software package which draws and manipulates two-dimensional and three-dimensional molecules.

Nomenclature for organic compounds

There are three main classifications of organic molecules: *aliphatic, aromatic,* and *heteroatomic.* Aliphatic compounds generally contain only carbon and hydrogen. They may include double or triple bonds between some carbon atoms, but they are not *conjugated* (shown by alternating single and double bonds). This means that the electrons are not free to move across the whole molecular structure in extended molecular bonds. Conversely, electrons in aromatic compounds may move across the structure. Figure 11.16 shows the two Kekulé structures of benzene C_6H_6 (both of which can be drawn using the Lewis structure rules described above). However, as explained previously, these are resonance structures and the true structure has a molecular orbital above and below the plane of the ring of carbons, as symbolized by the lower structure, in which the six hydrogens (attached to the six carbons assumed to

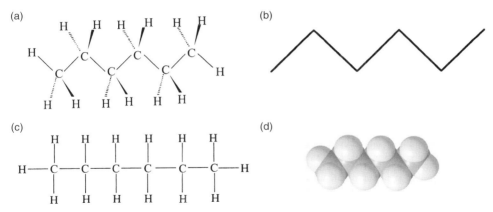

Figure 11.15 Four different representations of the structure of *n*-hexane, C_6H_{14}. (a) is a three-dimensional representation showing all the atoms; (b) reduces the structure to the carbon backbone, in which the hydrogens (three at each end and two at each "joint") are assumed to be present; (c) is a two-dimensional representation; and (d) is a space-filling model in which carbons are grey and hydrogens are white.

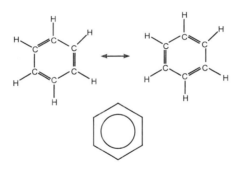

Figure 11.16 The Kekulé structures of benzene (C_6H_6) (upper structures), showing the two possible arrangements of the double bonds around the ring. Below is the aromatic resonance structure with the rotation of the double bonds symbolized by a ring, and the hydrogen atoms assumed to be present at each of the six "corners".

be at the corners of the hexagon) are omitted for clarity. This means that the chemistry of aromatic compounds is very different from that of aliphatic compounds (e.g., Sykes 1986). In fact the name "aromatic" comes from the smells often associated with these molecules. Heteroatomic molecules include atoms other than carbon and hydrogen, and can be either aliphatic or aromatic. The presence of these additional atoms significantly changes the chemical properties of the organic molecule.

As indicated in Chapter 2, many organic compounds have a number of historical or common names, as well as a systematic name (e.g.,

Table 11.2. *Prefix for the number of carbons in the parent chain when naming organic compounds.*

Number of carbons	Prefix
1	meth-
2	eth-
3	prop-
4	but-
5	pent-
6	hex-
7	hept-
8	oct-
9	non-
10	dec-
20	cos-
30	cont-

vinegar = acetic acid = ethanoic acid). These "trivial" names are a result of the history of discovery and the international nature of chemistry. With the continued needs to name new molecules and to prevent confusion, the International Union of Pure and Applied Chemistry (IUPAC) has specified a nomenclature system which should be applied to naming all published molecules [http://www.chem.qmw.ac.uk/iupac/]. However, the trivial names are still in common usage, especially on a day-to-day basis in the laboratory and the organic chemist needs to be familiar with both sets of names, such as chloroform (trichloromethane), acetone (propanone), and toluene (methyl benzene), etc.

The IUPAC nomenclature is allocated according to the following system. Firstly, the parent chain (the longest continuous chain of carbons in the structure) is identified. Any other chains and branching carbons (e.g., $-CH_3$ = methyl, $-CH_2CH_3$ = ethyl) are not counted at this stage. The prefix to the name is then assigned according to the number of carbons in this parent chain using the nomenclature shown in Table 11.2. (For entries not in this table, the numbers can be combined, so for example 18 carbons = octadec-.) The next stage is to identify any functional groups, either on the main chain or elsewhere. These are small structural units within molecules, the presence of which dictates most of the chemical properties and reactions of the molecule. Functional groups generally include heteroatoms (such as O, N, or the halogens), although they can also be just chains or rings of carbon and hydrogen atoms. Once identified, these functional group(s) are named (see Table 11.3) and the family to which the organic molecule belongs can be identified (e.g., an alcohol, an ester, etc.). The position of the functional group along the parent chain is important, so the carbons in the parent chain are numbered. This can obviously be done from either end, but the correct one to use is that which results in the functional group having the lowest number.

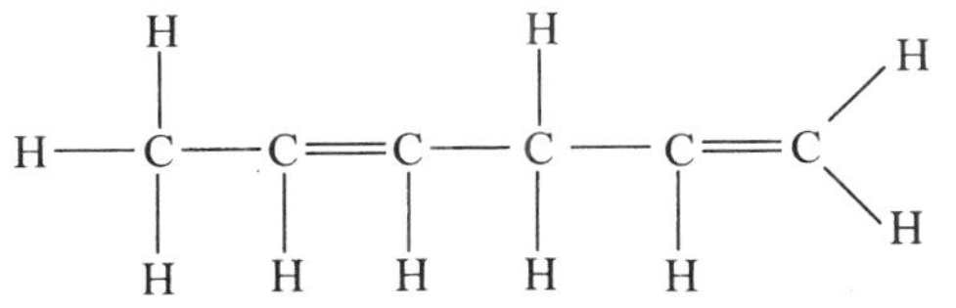

Figure 11.17 Structure of 1,4-hexadiene, showing how the systematic name of an organic compound can be derived from its structure (and vice versa).

However, when writing the names of the functional groups (if there are more than one), they are written in alphabetical order. If there is more than one of the same functional group, then the name need not be repeated, but the prefix di- (for two), tri- (for three) or tetra- (for four) may be added.

As an example, consider the molecule shown in Fig. 11.17. It has a main chain of six carbons – the parent chain, therefore, is labeled *hex* (Table 11.2). There are also two double bonds making the molecule an alkene (Table 11.3), hence *diene*. The positions of the double bonds are either at the 1st and 4th carbon (reading left to right) or 2nd and 5th (reading right to left) – but selecting the lowest numbers results in *1,4*. Therefore combining these results gives the name *1,4-hexadiene*. Note the comma separating the numbers and the hyphen between numbers and letters.

11.6 Isomers

Isomers are compounds which have identical formulas but differ in the nature or sequence of bonding of their atoms or the arrangement of the atoms in space. There is a variety of different types of isomerism.

Conformational isomers
As carbon–carbon single bonds can rotate, structures can differ by rotation about one or more bonds. There are two ways of illustrating these forms – the *sawhorse* or the *Newman* projections. The extreme forms of conformational isomerism for ethane (C_2H_6) are shown in Fig. 11.18. One form (eclipsed) has the three hydrogens on each carbon "pointing" in the same direction when seen end on; the staggered form has one set of three inverted. The eclipsed form has higher energy as the electrons in the adjacent C–H bonds are closer together and will repel one another. These conformations rapidly interconvert and can only be separated at very low temperatures.

Structural isomers
Structural isomers differ by the sequence of bonding of the atoms. Figure 11.19 shows two structural isomers having the molecular formula C_4H_{10}. One has a straight chain of four carbons, and is named butane: the other has a methyl group on the middle carbon of a three-carbon chain – hence, using the rules outlined above, it is termed 2-methylpropane. The chemical properties are very similar because the functional groups are identical. However, as they have

Table 11.3. *Some common organic functional groups, showing the family name, the prefix or suffix used for naming the group, the drawn structure, and the written formula.*

Family	Description	Prefix/suffix	Drawn structure	Written formula
Alkanes	Carbon–carbon single bonds only	-ane	C – C	C_nH_{2n+2}
Alkenes	One or more carbon–carbon double bonds	-ene	C = C	C_nH_{2n}
Alkynes	One or more carbon–carbon triple bonds	-yne	C ≡ C	C_nH_{2n-2}
Cyclic (aliphatic) hydrocarbons	Carbon can form a number of different ring sizes, with 5 and 6 being the most common. Many rings may be fused together.	Cyclo-	□ ⬠ ⬡ there are two conventions for 5 and 6 carbon rings	As with alkenes, closing the ring removes two hydrogens: C_nH_{2n}
Aromatic hydrocarbons	The inner circle indicates the conjugated molecular orbital. Many rings may be fused together to create PAHs (poly aromatic hydrocarbons)	Phenyl -/-benzene	⬡	Usually the aromatic rings are written "together" e.g., for benzene C_6H_6
Alcohols		Hydroxy-/-ol	—OH	OH
Ethers	An oxygen between two carbons	ether	—O—	O
Aldehydes		-al	—C(=O)—H	CHO
Ketones	A carbonyl (C = O) between two carbons	Oxo-/-one	—C(=O)—	CO
Carboxylic acids		-oic acid	—C(=O)—OH	COOH

Esters	-oate		CO_2
Amines	Amino-/-amine		NH_2
Halogeno compounds	fluoro/chloro/bromo-	——F	F, Cl, Br

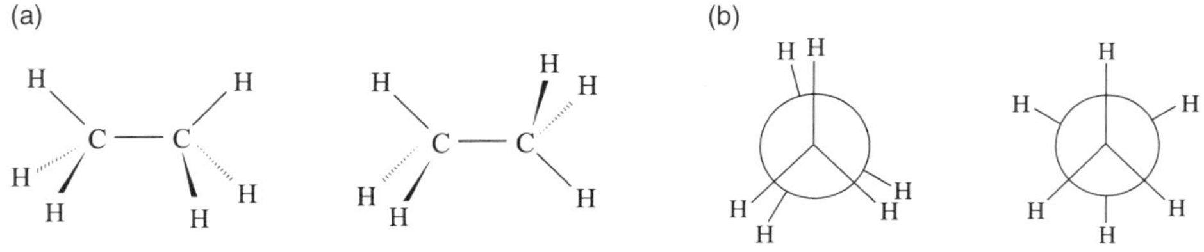

(a)   (b)

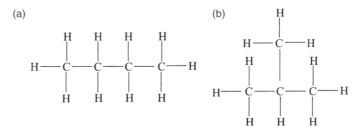

Figure 11.18 Two conformational isomers of ethane, C_2H_6. (a) "Sawhorse" representation and (b) Newman projections.

(a)   (b)

Figure 11.19 Two structural isomers having the molecular formula C_4H_{10}. (a) butane, (b) 2-methylpropane.

different shapes their physical properties are different (butane has a melting point of $-138°C$ and 2-methylpropane $-160°C$). This is because there is less van der Waals' interaction in 2-methylpropane. Interconversion requires breaking and remaking bonds so these isomers are stable under normal conditions.

Stereoisomers

Stereoisomers are compounds which have the same sequence of covalent bonds but differ in the relative position of their atoms in space. There are two forms of stereoisomerism: *diastereoisomers* and *enantiomers*.

Diastereoisomers are stereoisomers which do NOT have a mirror image of one another. Figure 11.20 shows the diastereoisomers of 2-butene (alkenes such as this are sometimes called *geometric isomers* and are a consequence of the prohibition of rotation about double bonds). If a vertical mirror was placed between the two structures in Fig. 11.20 they would not reflect onto one another. If the functionality is on the same side then the isomer is the *cis-* form, if on the opposite side then it is the *trans-* form. The chemical properties are very similar because the functional groups are identical. However, as they have different shapes their physical properties are different. Interconversion requires breaking and remaking bonds so these isomers are also stable under normal conditions.

Enantiomers are stereoisomers which are mirror images of one another, but these images are nonsuperimposable, i.e., they do not fit over one another (e.g., like left- and right-handed gloves). This occurs when a central carbon

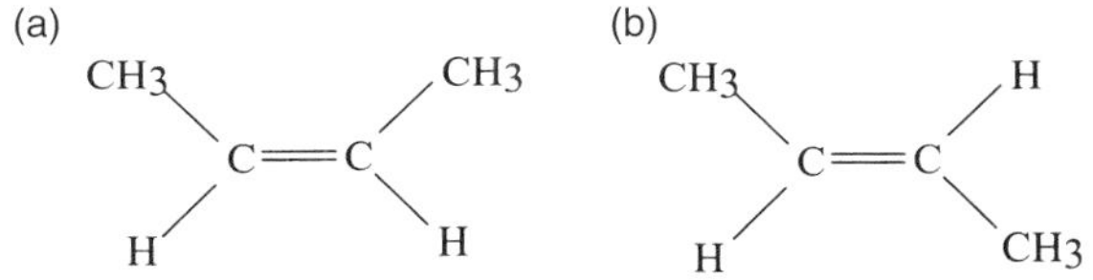

Figure 11.20 Diastereoisomers of 2-butene. (a) *cis*-2-butene, (b) *trans*-2-butene.

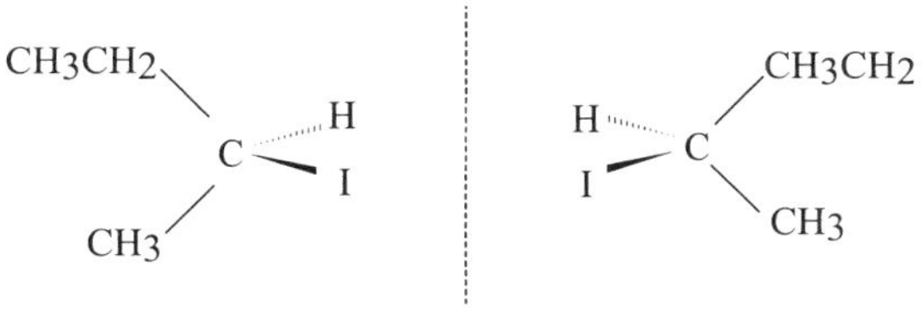

Figure 11.21 Stereoisomerism in 2-iodobutane ($CH_3CH_2CHICH_3$). The dotted line represents a mirror plane between the two structures, showing that one is the mirror image of the other.

atom has four different functional groups attached to it. In Fig. 11.21, which shows the two enantiomers of 2-iodobutane ($CH_3CH_2CHICH_3$), the second carbon of the parent chain of four is a stereocenter (also called a *chiral center*), having four different groups bonded to it. Note that if this atom was not bonded to iodine, it would not exhibit enantiomerism. Most physical properties are identical, such as boiling points, but they generally have different biological activity (aroma, flavor, toxicity, and drug effects). Enantiomers are also known as *optical isomers* because they rotate plane polarized light in different directions. To interconvert, the breaking and reforming of bonds is required and these isomers are generally stable under normal conditions, although interconversion can take place over time, especially if water is present (see below).

Nomenclature of enantiomers
Historically, chemists have used the rotation of polarized light to identify which enantiomer is present. Therefore they use D (dextrorotatory, clockwise, or positive) rotation if a solution containing the enantiomer rotates polarized light to the right, and L (laevorotatory, anticlockwise, or negative) rotation if it rotates to the left, to identify the two forms. This is termed the *relative configuration*. Because biological systems have a preference for one handedness (L) over the other, most biomolecules in living things are the L form. In the geological environment, however, there is no preference) most non-biomolecular enantiomers exist with equal amounts of L and D forms – termed a *racemic mixture*). Thus when a living creature dies, the L biomolecules begin to convert (*racemize*) to the D-form, and the ratio of

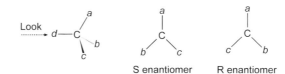

Figure 11.22 Determination of absolute configuration of a stereoisomer. The functional groups are labeled *a* to *d*, in order of decreasing atomic weight. The molecule is arranged with the lightest group (*d*) pointing towards the observer, and the order of the remaining three groups noted. If it goes *a* → *b* → *c* in a clockwise fashion, the absolute configuration is R. If it is anticlockwise, it is S.

D/L enantiomers increases with time. This racemization of amino acids is used for amino acid racemization dating (see Pollard and Heron 1996, 271–301).

IUPAC uses the *absolute notation*, or *Cahn-Ingold-Prelog* convention of R (*rectus*, right) and S (*sinister*, left). This nomenclature, which relates to structure and not to the rotation of light, unfortunately cannot always be simply related to the traditional D and L system. To use this (Fig. 11.22), the four substituents attached to the chiral carbon atom are labeled *a*, *b*, *c*, and *d* in decreasing order of atomic weight (i.e., the heaviest group is labeled *a*, in sequence to the lightest, which is *d*). The molecule is then imagined as if the lightest group (*d*) is pointing towards the observer, and the orientation of the remaining three groups is noted. If it has the sequence *a* → *b* → *c* in a clockwise fashion, the absolute configuration of the molecule is R. If it is anticlockwise, it is S. Although absolute configurations are becoming more standard in organic chemistry, the majority of the literature on stereochemistry in archaeology, geology, and forensic sciences still uses the relative terminology.

12

THE ELECTROMAGNETIC SPECTRUM

This chapter introduces some of the basic concepts of physics necessary to appreciate instrumental methods of chemical analysis. We first consider the behavior of waves from a general point of view, and then specifically relating to electromagnetic (EM) waves. We then present one of the most astonishing results of quantum mechanics – the fact that light can be considered either as a wave, or as a stream of particles (photons), depending on the way in which we choose to observe it. The next section looks at one of the important consequences of quantized electronic orbitals in atoms and molecules – the fact that they absorb and emit energy (including visible light) at specific wavelengths, rather than as a continuous spectrum, and also that the pattern of these wavelengths is unique to each element. Moreover, using an equation (Beer's law) for the absorption of electromagnetic radiation by matter, we show that it is possible to quantify the amount of each element present in a sample. This is the basis of many forms of chemical analysis. By considering the range of energies covered by the different wavelengths within the electromagnetic spectrum (from high energy, short wavelength γ-rays to low energy, long wavelength radio waves), we can see that different energy levels within the atom are probed by different types of radiation. X-rays, for example, give information of inner-shell transitions within heavy atoms, whereas infrared radiation (heat) probes the vibrational states of molecular bonds, giving information on the nature of the chemical groupings present in molecules. Thus, the EM spectrum presents us with a complete toolkit for chemical analysis. Finally, we introduce a relatively new source of high energy EM radiation across the entire spectrum – the synchrotron. This offers the chemist a very powerful tool for determining structure and chemical analysis for a wide range of samples.

12.1 Electromagnetic waves

When a wave, such as that on the sea, travels in a particular direction, we can characterize it by a number of parameters – the velocity of travel, its amplitude (the height of the waves), its wavelength (distance between adjacent peaks), and its frequency (the number of waves per unit time). The simplest form of wave to consider is a sine wave, the equation for which is:

$$y = A \sin(\omega t + \phi)$$

where y is the displacement of the wave at time t, A is the wave amplitude, ω is the angular velocity, and ϕ is the phase angle between this wave and some arbitrary reference wave. The angular velocity (ω) is given by $\omega = 2\pi v$, where v is the frequency of the wave. Thus:

$$y = A \sin(2\pi v t + \phi).$$

It is important to note that the *velocity of the wave* in the direction of propagation is not the same as the *speed of movement* of the medium through which the wave is traveling, as is shown by the motion of a cork on water. Whilst the wave travels across the surface of the water, the cork merely moves up and down in the same place – the movement of the medium is in the vertical plane, but the wave itself travels in the horizontal plane. Another important property of wave motion is that when two or more waves traverse the same space, the resulting wave motion can be completely described by the sum of the two wave equations – the *principle of superposition*. Thus, if we have two waves of the same frequency v, but with amplitudes A_1 and A_2 and phase angles ϕ_1 and ϕ_2, the resulting wave can be written as:

$$y = A_1 \sin(2\pi v t + \phi_1) + A_2 \sin(2\pi v t + \phi_2).$$

The nature of the resulting wave depends on the phase difference ($\phi_1 - \phi_2$) between the two waves. If ($\phi_1 - \phi_2$) is 0 degrees, or 360 degrees, then the two waves are said to be *in phase*, and the maximum amplitude of the resultant wave is $A_1 + A_2$. This situation is termed *constructive interference*. If the phase difference is 180 degrees, then the two waves are *out of phase*, and *destructive interference* occurs. In this case, if the amplitudes of the two waves are equal (i.e., if $A_1 = A_2$), then the two waves cancel each other out, and no wave is observed (Fig. 12.1). *Standing waves*, such as those seen when the string on a musical instrument vibrates, are caused when the reflected waves (from the bridge of the instrument) are in phase and thus interfere constructively.

An important corollary of the principle of superposition is that a wave of any shape can be described mathematically as a sum of a series of simple sine and cosine terms, which is the basis of the mathematical procedure called the *Fourier transform* (see Section 4.2). Thus the square wave, frequently used in electronic circuits, can be described as the sum of an infinite superposition of sine waves, using the general equation:

$$y = A \left(\sin 2\pi v t + \frac{1}{3} \sin 6\pi v t + \frac{1}{5} \sin 10\pi v t \ldots\ldots \right).$$

This is the Fourier transform of a square wave. The dots in the bracket imply that the terms in the bracket go on indefinitely in the pattern established by

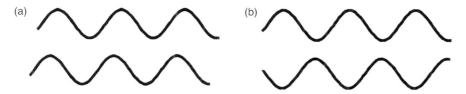

Figure 12.1 Constructive and destructive interference. (a) shows two in-phase sine waves of equal amplitude, which add together to form a sine wave with double the amplitude. (b) shows the same two waves but exactly 180° out-of-phase, which cancel each other out.

the first few. It is an *infinite series*. The adequacy of the fit between the transformed terms and the original square wave depends on the number of terms used in the brackets, since, in practice, the infinite series has to be limited to a fixed number of terms. The more terms that are used, the closer the resultant transform is in appearance to a square wave.

In 1864, James Clerk Maxwell (1831–79) calculated that the speed of propagation of an electromagnetic field is approximately the same as the speed of light. He proposed that light is therefore an electromagnetic phenomenon: "We can scarcely avoid the conclusion that light consists in the transverse undulations of the same medium which is the cause of electric and magnetic phenomena." Thus light and other forms of electromagnetic radiation are transmitted by simultaneous oscillations of electrical and magnetic fields. These oscillations can be described as a pair of in-phase sine waves at right angles to each other traveling through space at the speed of light. If the direction of travel is considered to be the x axis as defined by normal rectangular co-ordinates, then we may consider the electric wave to be oscillating in the xy plane, and the magnetic field to be in the zx plane (Fig. 12.2), as follows:

$$E_y = E_o \sin 2\pi vt$$
$$B_z = B_o \sin 2\pi vt.$$

These equations correspond to a *plane polarized* electromagnetic wave traveling in the x direction. In a normal (i.e., nonpolarized) beam of radiation, the orientation of the plane of the electric oscillation (and hence that of the magnetic oscillation, since it is always orthogonal to the electric plane) can rotate freely about the x axis. Thus a normal beam of light consists of a very large number of waves, all of which can have random orientation about the direction of travel. Only if the beam is plane polarized will all the waves have the same orientation. There are other forms of polarization. As light passes through some specific solutions, the plane of polarization can be rotated either to the left or to the right. The measurement of the degree of rotation is called the *optical activity* of the solution, and is one way of

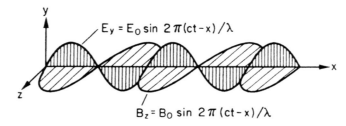

Figure 12.2 Sine wave representation of electromagnetic radiation. It consists of two in-phase waves, with oscillation of the electric field in the *xy* plane, and the magnetic field perpendicular to it, in the *xz* plane.

measuring the chirality of compounds (Section 11.6). Other forms include *right-circularly* polarized, which is when, if viewed from behind, the plane of polarization rotates continuously in a clockwise direction as the wave progresses. Likewise, continuous rotation in an anticlockwise direction as seen gives *left-circular polarization*.

The relationship between the speed of travel of light (or any electromagnetic radiation) through a vacuum c, the frequency of the radiation (ν) and its wavelength (λ) is given by:

$$\nu = \frac{c}{\lambda} = c\bar{\nu}$$

where $\bar{\nu}$ is known as the *wavenumber* (with dimensions of inverse length, m^{-1}). The speed of light in a vacuum is $3 \times 10^8\,m\,s^{-1}$. If electromagnetic radiation travels through any other medium, it is observed that its velocity is always less than that *in vacuo*. The ratio of the speed of light *in vacuo* to that in a particular medium (v_i) is a property of that medium, and is termed the *refractive index* (n_i), which, for a given wavelength, is defined as follows:

$$n_i = \frac{c}{v_i}$$

Two other definitions are important: the power P of radiation is the energy of the beam that reaches a given area per second. The intensity I is the power per unit solid angle in a particular direction. Both are related to the square of the amplitude, and are often used interchangeably, but they are not synonymous.

It is now understood that the electromagnetic spectrum covers a very wide range of wavelengths (from 10^{-12} to $10^3\,m$), and is conventionally classified into a large number of spectral regions (Fig. 12.3). These regions differ widely in the way in which they interact with matter (see below), and are commonly thought of as unconnected entities (e.g., radio waves are thought of as different from light, which is in turn different from X-rays, etc.). However, these differences arise solely as a result of the wide range of wavelengths involved (and hence energy, as shown below), not because of any fundamental differences in properties.

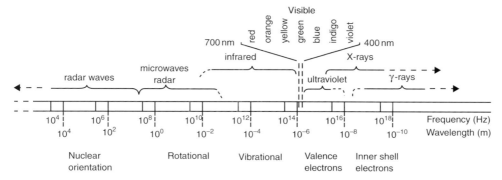

Figure 12.3 Regions of the electromagnetic spectrum in terms of both frequency (hertz) and wavelength (m). The visible region is a very narrow band between 400 and 700 nm. The lower labels show which part of the atom the various radiations correspond to, i.e., X-rays result from reorganization of the inner shell electrons, UV from the valence electrons, etc. From PSSC PHYSICS, second edition, copyright © 1965 by D. C. Heath and Company. Used by permission of Houghton Mifflin Company.

12.2   Particle–wave duality

The above description shows that we may define visible light as that part of the electromagnetic spectrum to which the human eye is sensitive. The wave nature of light can be demonstrated by experiments which show diffraction and interference phenomena (i.e., characteristic wave behavior), such as Young's slits (Fig. 12.4), in which a single beam of light is split into two by passing it through two holes, and, if the spacing of the holes is correct, a series of light and dark lines are seen as a result of constructive and destructive interference. In 1886 and 1887, however, Heinrich Rudolph Hertz (1857–94), whilst experimenting with electrically charged metal spheres (with which, more famously, he produced the first transmission and reception of electromagnetic waves–see Hertz 1893), noticed that sparks jumped more readily between two spheres when their surfaces were illuminated by ultraviolet light from another spark (Hertz 1887). Further work showed that electrons were emitted from metal surfaces as a result of illumination by light, and that the maximum speed of the emitted electron depends only on the frequency of the incident light.

This experimental observation was completely inexplicable by conventional wave theory, and it required a radical new mode of thinking. This came in 1905, when Albert Einstein (1879–1955), whilst still working at the patent office, gave the correct explanation for this effect by suggesting that light could be thought of not only as a continuous wave, but also as discrete bundles or quanta, called *photons*, with an energy E given by:

$$E = \frac{hc}{\lambda}$$

(a)   (b)

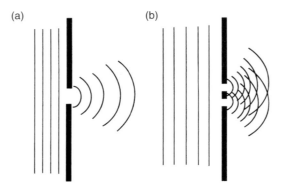

Figure 12.4 Young's slits. (a) shows light as plane waves approaching from the left a single slit of dimensions similar to the wavelength of the light, and being diffracted as they pass through the hole. (b) shows light approaching a double slit. As the light passes through and is diffracted, the two wave fronts show constructive and destructive interference, which is seen as dark and light fringes when viewed from the right. This experiment demonstrates the wave nature of light.

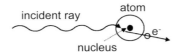

Figure 12.5 The photoelectric effect. Light with photons of energy hc/λ approaches from the left, strikes the atoms in the metal, and ejects a photoelectron with a kinetic energy equal to the photon energy minus the work function of the metal. This demonstrates the particulate nature of light.

where λ is the wavelength of the light, h is Planck's constant and c is the speed of light in a vacuum. The kinetic energy of the ejected electron is given by $\frac{1}{2}mv^2$, where m is the mass of the electron and v is its velocity. If ϕ is the *work function* (the energy required to remove an electron from the metal surface), then the kinetic energy (KE) is given by (Fig. 12.5):

$$\text{KE} = \frac{1}{2}mv^2 = \frac{hc}{\lambda} - \phi.$$

This became known as the *photoelectric effect*, for which Einstein received his Nobel Prize in Physics in 1921. This equation was verified by experimental observation, confirming that, at least in this experiment, light can be considered to consist of a stream of particles termed photons, the energy of which is related to the classical wavelength of light as discussed above. How can these two apparently contradictory views be reconciled? The answer is that both are adequate descriptions of the nature of electromagnetic radiation, and the contradiction, it appears, lies in the nature of the experiment carried out to determine the nature of the light. If an experiment is set up to detect the wave nature of light (e.g., Young's slits), then it manifests itself as an electromagnetic wave. If, on the other hand, a photon-based experiment is conceived, such as the detection of photoelectrons, then it appears as a stream of photons. This remarkable result of quantum theory is summarized by the term *particle–wave duality*. In practice, it presents no real problems. It is easy to switch between expressions for the two manifestations, and, with practice, it becomes easy to live with such ambiguity.

12.3   Emission lines and the Rydberg equation

The emission spectrum of an element is defined as light (or any other EM radiation) which is emitted when an element is excited by heat or electrical energy. If this light, however, is dispersed into its contributory wavelengths (using a prism or a similar device), it turns out that the emission spectrum is not a continuous rainbow of light, but is in fact a series of discrete wavelengths. In 1860 Kirchoff and Bunsen demonstrated that the alkalis and alkaline earth elements all had a characteristic spectrum – i.e., the series of discrete wavelengths observed are the same for all samples of the same element, but the pattern differs from element to element. Johann Jacob Balmer (1825–98) and Janne Robert Rydberg (1854–1919) subsequently empirically derived the laws governing these emission spectra for a number of simple elements, but these patterns were not fully explained until 1913, when Bohr used these observations to successfully establish his theory of quantized electron orbital structure (as described in Section 10.4).

As shown in Fig. 12.6, if a glass discharge tube is filled with hydrogen gas and a high voltage applied between the metal plates, a series of discrete lines is obtained when the emitted light is decomposed into its component wavelengths using a prism. In the visible region, this consists of four main lines at 656.3 nm (red), 486.1 nm (blue), 434.0 and 410.2 nm (violet). Empirically, Balmer (1885) showed that these lines could be described using the following formula:

$$\frac{1}{\lambda} = \bar{\nu} = R\left(\frac{1}{2^2} - \frac{1}{n^2}\right)$$

where R is the Rydberg constant and n is an integer which can have the value $n = 3, 4, 5, 6, 7$, to ∞. This equation was generalized by Rydberg (1897) and Ritz (1908) to cover more of the emission lines in the hydrogen spectrum, i.e., those outside the visible region, by replacing the 2 in the first denominator with the general integer n_1:

$$\bar{\nu} = R\left(\frac{1}{n_1^2} - \frac{1}{n_2^2}\right)$$

where $n_1 < n_2$ and n_2 has values $n_1 + 1, n_1 + 2, n_1 + 3, \ldots \infty$.

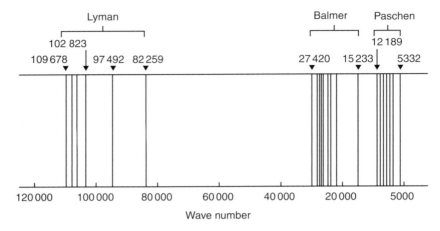

Figure 12.6 The emission spectrum of hydrogen in the UV, visible and near infrared, showing the "families" of lines labeled Lyman ($n = 1$), Balmer ($n = 2$), and Paschen ($n = 3$).

This equation describes the emission spectrum of hydrogen, not only in the visible region of the spectrum but also out to the ultraviolet and infrared. It predicts several "families" of emission lines – one set calculated using the value of $n_1 = 1$, a second using $n_1 = 2$ (the original Balmer equation), and so on. Classical mechanics, however, cannot explain the observation that the emission spectrum of a simple atom like hydrogen shows discrete lines – an orbiting negatively charged electron should lose energy continuously and spiral into the positively charged nucleus. From the above empirical equation, Bohr concluded that only orbital electrons with quantized angular momentum states are permissible and stable. He postulated that only those orbits whose angular momentum could be expressed as whole multiples of $h/2\pi$ could exist, i.e.:

$$mvr = \frac{nh}{2\pi}$$

where m is the mass of the electron traveling at a velocity v in an orbit of radius r around the nucleus, and h is Planck's constant. The integer n can have values 1, 2, 3, etc., and is now identified as the *principal quantum number*, the use of which in defining electron orbital structure was introduced in Section 10.4.

Using this model, electrons which stay in these fixed orbitals are stable and lose no energy (*contra* the classical model), but when an electron moves from one orbit to a higher one (defined by increased principal quantum number, n) then energy is required to cause this promotion. Conversely, if an electron drops down from a higher to a lower energy level, then excess energy is emitted. The energy absorbed or emitted can be calculated as the energy difference (ΔE) between the two stable energy levels E_1 and E_2:

$$\Delta E = h\nu = E_2 - E_1.$$

This now allows a clearer interpretation of the empirical Rydberg equations given above. We may now interpret n_1 as the principal quantum number of the lower of the two energy levels involved (i.e., the orbital from which the promoted electron originates), and n_2 as that of the upper level (i.e., the orbital to which the promoted electron goes). Hence n_2 may have any integer value greater than $n_1 + 1$, up to infinity, when the electron has been lost from the atom, and the atom becomes ionized. In the hydrogen spectrum, the series of emission lines corresponding to transitions from and to the principal quantum number n_1 are called *spectral series*, and have historically been assigned the following names:

$n_1 = 1$ Lyman series – lines appear in far UV region of EM spectrum
$n_1 = 2$ Balmer series – visible region of spectrum
$n_1 = 3$ Paschen series – infrared region of spectrum
$n_1 = 4$ Brackett series – infrared region of spectrum
$n_1 = 5$ Pfund series – infrared region of spectrum

This interpretation of the Rydberg equation for hydrogen was extremely influential (indeed, seminal) in allowing Bohr to establish his quantized electron orbital model, and thus complete the simple nuclear model of the atom that is still used today. Naturally, the next step was to attempt to generalize these rules from the case of hydrogen, with only a single $1s$ orbital electron, to multielectron atoms. The easiest case ought to be the generalization to the alkali metals, which are multielectron, but all have a single outer s orbital electron in the ground state (e.g., Na with 11 orbital electrons, in the configuration $1s^2 2s^2 2p^6 3s^1$). Even with this simple generalization, however, there are considerable difficulties. Table 12.1 and Fig. 12.7 show the wavelength of the major spectral lines (in nm) in the emission spectrum of sodium, arranged in series which are analogous to those in hydrogen, and labeled *sharp, principal, diffuse*, etc.

Rydberg (1897) modified the above equation for hydrogen to fit these emission lines for sodium by introducing two further parameters α and β:

$$\bar{\nu} = R \left[\frac{1}{(n_1 - \alpha)^2} - \frac{1}{(n_2 - \beta)^2} \right]$$

where n_1 and n_2 are the principal quantum numbers of the two orbitals involved, and α and β are fractional correction factors known as *quantum defects*. They are interpreted as being corrections necessary in multielectron atoms to account for the shielding effect of the other orbitals, the magnitude of which depends on the shape of the subshells. As shown in Section 10.4, the shape of the orbital is dictated by the second (angular momentum) quantum

Table 12.1. *The wavelengths of the major spectral lines (nm) in the emission spectrum of sodium, arranged in series which are analogous to those in hydrogen.*

Principal	589.3	330.3	285.3	268.0	259.4
Sharp	1139.3	615.8	575.1	435.0	
Diffuse	818.9	568.5	498.1	466.7	
Fundamental	1845.9	1257.8			

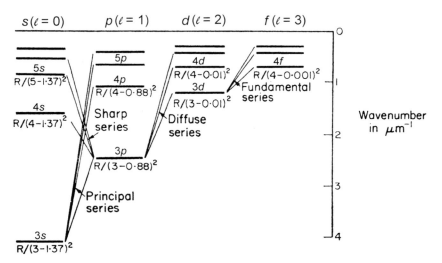

Figure 12.7 Electronic transitions giving rise to the emission spectrum of sodium in the visible, as listed in Table 12.1. The principal series consists of transitions from the 3s level to 3p or a higher p orbital; the sharp series from 3p to 4s or a higher s orbital; diffuse from 3p to 3d or above; and the fundamental from 3d to 4f or higher. The terms below the lines [(R/(3–1.37)^2, etc.] are the quantum defect corrections referred to in Section 10.4.

number *l*. For the third level in sodium, the values are 1.373 for the *s* orbital (α) and 0.883 for *p* orbitals (β). The following equation has, therefore, been empirically derived for the first of these emission series (principal) corresponding to a transition from 3s to one of the higher *p* orbitals (3p or higher):

$$\text{Principal series} \quad \bar{v} = R\left[\frac{1}{(3-1.373)^2} - \frac{1}{(n-0.883)^2}\right].$$

If we substitute *n* = 3 into this equation (i.e., assume we are dealing with a 3s–3p transition), we obtain:

$$\bar{v} = R\left[\frac{1}{1.63^2} - \frac{1}{2.12^2}\right] = 1689\,\text{mm}^{-1}$$

or:

$$\lambda = 592.1 \, \text{nm}$$

which is close to the measured value of 589.3 nm, and is the strong yellow line in the sodium emission spectrum (the line which gives old-fashioned street lamps their characteristic color).

Thus, the energy difference between the $3s$ and the $3p$ orbital in the neutral sodium atom corresponds to light with a wavelength of 589 nm. If, therefore, the atom receives quanta of energy greater than or equal to:

$$E = \frac{hc}{\lambda} = \frac{hc}{589 \times 10^{-9}} = 1.125 \times 10^{-19} \, \text{J}$$

then the $3s$ electron can be promoted to the $3p$ state. It will then return to the $3s$ level, emitting a photon of wavelength 589 nm, in the yellow region of the visible spectrum. This is called *resonance* or *fluorescence* radiation. If enough energy is available, a $3s$ electron can be promoted to the $4p$ level or higher, depending on a set of *selection rules*, which can be derived from the Bohr model. These selection rules define which electron transitions are allowed (although "forbidden" transitions do, in fact, occur, but usually with much lower intensity). These can be summarized in the general case as:

$$\Delta n \geq 1$$
$$\Delta l = \pm 1$$
$$\Delta m_l = 0, \pm 1.$$

However, in the sodium atom, $\Delta n = 0$ is also allowed. Thus the $3s \rightarrow 3p$ transition is allowed, although the $3s \rightarrow 4s$ is forbidden, since in this case $\Delta l = 0$ and is forbidden. Taken together, the Bohr model of quantized electron orbitals, the selection rules, and the relationship between wavelength and energy derived from particle–wave duality are sufficient to explain the major features of the emission spectra of all elements. For the heavier elements in the periodic table, the absorption and emission spectra can be extremely complicated – manganese and iron, for example, have about 4600 lines in the visible and UV region of the spectrum.

As a final note, closer inspection of the emission lines from Na shows that most emission lines are not, in fact, single lines, but are closely spaced doublets or triplets – for example, the strong yellow line discussed above at 589.3 nm is composed of two separate lines at 589.0 and 589.6 nm. This is termed *fine structure*, and is not predictable from the Bohr model of the atom. It is addressed in the Bohr–Sommerfield model, and is the result of a quantum mechanical interaction, known as *spin–orbit coupling*, further discussion of which is not necessary for this volume.

12.4   Absorption of EM radiation by matter – Beer's law

When electromagnetic radiation passes through transparent matter, some of it is absorbed. Strong absorption will occur if there is a close match between the frequency of the radiation and the energy of one of the possible electronic or molecular absorption processes characteristic of the medium. A plot of absorbance (A) against wavelength (λ) or frequency (v) for a particular material is termed an *absorption spectrum*. The complexity of the absorption spectrum depends on whether atomic (simple, with a few sharp absorption bands) or molecular (complex, with many broad bands) processes are responsible.

For monochromatic radiation, the reduction in power as the beam travels through the material is proportional to the number of absorbing particles in the path of the beam, i.e.,

$$\frac{dP}{dn} = -kP$$

where dP is the amount of power P absorbed by a change in the number of absorbing particles dn, and k is a constant of proportionality. Integrating:

$$\ln\frac{P}{P_o} = -kN$$

where P_o is the power of the incident radiation as it enters the absorbing medium, and N is the number of absorbing entities encountered by the beam as it travels through the medium. This number is given by:

$$N = b \times c$$

where b is the path length of the beam through the medium and c is the concentration of absorbing entities (atoms or molecules with the relevant absorption bands) per unit cross-sectional area. Thus:

$$\ln\frac{P}{P_o} = -k'bc$$

where the constant k' has dimensions of mass per unit area of cross-section.

If we invert the logarithmic quotient to remove the negative sign on the right-hand side, and convert for convenience from natural to base ten logarithms, we may reexpress this relationship as follows:

$$\log\frac{P_o}{P} = \log\frac{1}{T} = A = abc$$

where the constant a is called the *absorptivity* and is a property of the medium, whilst the logarithmic term is given the symbol A, the *absorbance*. The ratio P/P_o is given the symbol T, the *transmittance*. This is a statement of

Beer's law (Beer 1852), which, because it builds on earlier observations by Bouguer and Lambert, is also known as the *Beer–Lambert law*.

Absorbance (*A*) is a property of the particular sample, and will vary with the concentration of absorbing species within the material and the dimensions of the sample. It is also a function of wavelength, and may vary quite sharply for small changes in λ, depending on whether the wavelength is above or below that required to excite a particular absorption process. Absorbance at a particular wavelength is additive in multi-component mixtures, but this strictly only applies to dilute solutions (≃0.01 M), since above this the different absorbing species within the mixture tend to chemically react or otherwise influence each other. Absorptivity (*a*) is a property of the absorbing species, and is also a function of wavelength, and will also vary for the same species in solution from solvent to solvent.

The simplest application of Beer's law using visible radiation is in *colorimetry*. This term applies only to absorption measurements in the visible region of the spectrum: elsewhere in the electromagnetic spectrum, it is termed *spectrophotometry*. A colored solution absorbs strongly in its complementary color, so the concentration of cobalt, which gives a strong blue color in aqueous solution, may be determined by measuring the absorbance of the solution in the yellow region of the spectrum. Samples which give transparent solutions may still be determined by colorimetry, if they can be quantitatively complexed (linked) with a chromophore (colored chemical) to produce a colored solution, which may then be measured. An important example in archaeology is the colorimetric determination of soil phosphorus in solution by the production of the blue phosphomolybdate complex (e.g., Bethell and Máté 1989, Heron 2001: see Section 4.4).

In order to use absorbance as an effective tool in chemical analysis, it is beneficial to work in a concentration range where the change in absorbance (ΔA) of a particular substance (for example, a solution) is maximized for a small change in power of the transmitted radiation (ΔP). If the solution is too strong, then it becomes opaque, and insensitive to small changes in transmitted power. Similarly, if it is too dilute, then errors in readings are likely to mask the actual measurement. Expressed mathematically, we need to minimize the ratio of $\Delta A/A$ for greatest accuracy in absorption measurements. By differentiating Beer's law twice, and setting the second differential to zero, it is possible to calculate the transmittance value at which $\Delta A/A$ is a minimum (Ewing 1985: 43). Perhaps surprisingly, this calculation is independent of the nature of the absorbing solution or of the wavelength of the transmitted radiation, and gives the optimum setting at which all transmittance measurements should aim to be made. Calculation gives this value as $A = 0.4343$, which, using the relationship between *A* and *T* above, corresponds to a transmittance *T* of 36.8%. More detailed consideration of the typical shape of an absorption curve shows that for optimum analytical sensitivity, measurements of absorption should be made so that T is in the range 15–65%, i.e., values of A between 0.8 and 0.2. This is a useful guideline for the best absorption conditions when carrying out any absorbance measurements on liquids (such as phosphorus determinations by colorimetry), or when setting up an atomic absorption spectrometer (see Section 3.2).

12.5   The EM spectrum and spectrochemical analysis

Electromagnetic radiation interacts with matter across the whole of the spectrum, from very damaging high energy X-rays to long wavelength, low energy radio waves. The nature of interaction is governed by the photon energy of radiation, given by:

$$E = \frac{hc}{\lambda} = h\nu$$

where λ is the wavelength, ν the frequency, h Planck's constant and c the speed of light. The wavelength of the radiation emitted or absorbed depends on the difference in the energy levels involved. Radiation of high energy (short wavelength), such as X-rays, arises from transitions deep within the electronic structure of the heavier atoms, where the energy differences between orbitals are extremely large. Low energy (long wavelength) radiation, such as microwaves, is the result of transitions between states with very little energy differentiation, such as the rotational and vibrational frequencies of molecules, which are still quantized, although the energy differences between successive states are so small that, to all intents and purposes, they appear unquantized.

Table 12.2 shows the origin (in electronic orbital terms) of the various regions of the electromagnetic spectrum (also indicated on Fig. 12.3). It shows clearly the linkage between nuclear, atomic, and molecular structure and the wavelengths of the radiation which result from transitions at these different levels. Because absorption and emission energies are identical, it also shows which parts of the EM spectrum can probe the different levels of atomic and molecular structure. Thus, as noted above, infrared radiation has its origin in the relatively low energy transitions found in molecular bonding. Conversely, therefore, infrared spectroscopy is primarily used to study molecular bonding and functional groups. Examination of the same molecules by, for example, X-rays, having much higher energy, would not give the same information, because they would only excite transitions deep in the atomic orbital structure. Furthermore, because high energy radiation, such as X-rays, originate from the inner shells of heavier atoms, an X-ray spectrum is relatively insensitive to the state of chemical bonding of the atom, which only involves the outer electron orbitals. This explains why the X-ray spectrum of iron, for

Table 12.2. *Relationship between the wavelength and source of electromagnetic radiation (see also Fig. 12.3).*

Radiation	Wavelength (m)	Origin
Gamma rays	$<10^{-12}$	Nuclear reorganization
X-rays	10^{-12} to 10^{-8}	Inner shells of heavy atoms
Far UV	10^{-8} to 4×10^{-7}	Middle shell electrons
Near UV/visible	$4-7.5 \times 10^{-7}$	Valence (outer) shell electrons
IR	7.5×10^{-7} to 10^{-3}	Molecular vibrations and rotations
Microwave	10^{-3} to 1	Molecular rotations
Radio waves	$1-2 \times 10^{3}$	Nuclear magnetic resonance

example, is the same whether the target is metallic iron, or a compound of iron in either the Fe(II) or Fe(III) valency states, or any other form.

We are now in a position to consider in more detail the general forms of analytical spectroscopy used in archaeology and other analytical sciences. Many are based in one way or another on the quantitative measurement of the absorption or emission of a part of the electromagnetic spectrum by matter – solid, liquid, or (more rarely in analytical chemistry) a gas. Most methods of inorganic (and some organic) chemical analysis can be described in outline quite quickly, since many techniques follow a general pattern. The prime characteristic of any method is defined by the frequency of the EM radiation used, since, as described above, the frequency governs the type of information which can be obtained. Secondly comes the choice of using either emission or absorption. In emission, the sample must be induced to emit radiation of the required wavelength, usually requiring the input of some form of energy (heat, light, or electrical power). In absorption mode, a sample is subjected to a beam of radiation of the required wavelength, which usually requires a spectral source of some sort – a lamp or a spark. Some techniques and instruments can be switched between absorption and emission mode. Finally, the instrument needs a detector sensitive to the wavelength of the radiation being used, either to record quantitatively the intensity of the emission at a particular wavelength, or to record relatively the intensity of the radiation absorbed by the sample. Depending on the nature of the detector, some instruments need a monochromator to resolve the radiation into its component wavelengths before allowing it to fall on the detector (many modern detectors, such as solid state X-ray detectors, can resolve incident radiation by energy as well as quantify the intensity, and therefore do not need separate monochromators). Finally, all instruments require data collection equipment. Invariably now, this is done using a dedicated computer, and often the same computer allows automatic (or semiautomatic) calibration and calculation of results (see Section 13.4

The benefits of this are obvious, but also, alas, are the pitfalls – just because a computer generates a number doesn't mean that it is necessarily right.

12.6   Synchrotron radiation

Despite the possible appearance of the title, synchrotron radiation is not a new form of radiation, or an obscure part of the electromagnetic spectrum. It refers to the astonishing capability of a single (albeit very large) instrument – a synchrotron – to produce extremely intense beams of radiation of all frequencies throughout the electromagnetic spectrum, from gamma rays to infrared. Because of the combination of high intensity with extremely fine beam dimensions (a beam cross-section of a few tens of microns), synchrotron radiation (SR) is becoming increasingly used as a source for a wide range of analytical techniques.

Synchrotron radiation is the consequence of one of the observations made above – in classical electromagnetic theory, an orbiting electron should radiate electromagnetic radiation continuously, because it is constantly being accelerated towards the center by centripetal forces. The fact that, in an atom, this does not happen, and that electrons in stable orbits do not radiate, was the origin of the theory of quantized atomic energy levels. However, if a beam of electrons (or other charged particles) is accelerated around a circular path, then the electrons will continuously radiate electromagnetic radiation of all frequencies. This is known as synchrotron radiation, and was first seen at the General Electric Research Laboratory in Schenectady, New York, in 1947 (Elder *et al.* 1947).

The Synchrotron Radiation Source (SRS) at Daresbury, Cheshire (UK), was the first machine in the world dedicated to the production and use of synchrotron radiation. The whole machine consists of three separate stages – a linear accelerator to produce high energy electrons which are injected into the booster synchrotron where they are accelerated to almost the speed of light, at which stage they are injected into a storage ring (Fig. 12.8). This is a circular tube of 96 m circumference under high vacuum, within which the electrons are "stored", and are capable of producing synchrotron radiation for 10 or 20 hours. The storage ring consists of 16 bending magnets, which keep the electrons in a circular orbit. At each magnet, because the electron beam is deflected (accelerated), it emits an intense beam of electromagnetic radiation according to Maxwell's equations, known as synchrotron radia-tion. Because of the very high velocity of the electrons, the emitted beam forms a narrow cone in front of the electrons, like a searchlight. Synchrotron radiation is thus "tapped off" at each of the magnets, and is fed in to more ˙an 30 experimental stations. At each station, the portion of the ˙tromagnetic spectrum that is needed for a particular experiment is ˙ted, and the station is provided with the specialist instruments, detectors, ˙omputers needed to carry out the experiment. Thus, one station might

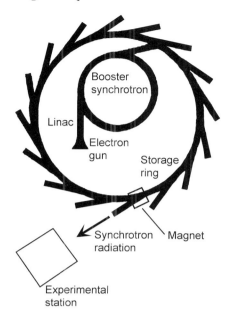

Figure 12.8 Schematic plan of a synchrotron. The storage ring at Daresbury is 96 m in diameter, and contains a 250 mA current of 2 GeV electrons. Synchrotron radiation is emitted as a result of acceleration of the beam at each of the 16 magnets, and is "tapped off" and fed to a number of experimental stations, each of which is equipped to carry out a particular set of experiments.

use X-rays to investigate the structure of proteins with a variety of specialized X-ray diffraction devices, whilst another will use ultraviolet light for the spectroscopic investigation of atoms or molecules.

The wavelength and intensity of the synchrotron radiation depends on the energy and type of the emitting particle – i.e., whether there are electrons or protons in the storage ring. The amount and energy of the radiation depend on the speed of the emitting particles and the magnetic field strength. For a particle moving at velocity v with a total energy E:

$$E = \gamma m_o c^2$$

where m_o is the rest mass of the particle (the electron), c is the velocity of light, and the special relativity factor, γ, is a measure of the closeness of v to c:

$$\gamma = \frac{1}{\sqrt{1 - \frac{v^2}{c^2}}}.$$

The half-angle of the cone of radiation produced ($\Delta\phi$) can be shown to be related to γ as:

$$\Delta\phi = \frac{1}{\gamma}.$$

Thus, as the velocity of the circulating electrons approaches the speed of light, the beam becomes more and more tightly collimated. The radiation emitted by a circulating charged particle consists of a series of short pulses, the separation of which corresponds to the time taken for the particle to complete one circuit of the flight tube. Fourier analysis shows that the wavelength spectrum of the synchrotron radiation produced is related to the frequency of revolution and higher harmonics (2ω, 3ω, etc.). In practice, however, synchrotron radiation sources produce photons with a continuum of energies throughout the spectrum, from infrared to X-rays, because the circulating electrons oscillate in position and energy around the mean flight path.

Because of its intensity and focus, synchrotron radiation can be used as the source of electromagnetic radiation for any of the analytical techniques described here or elsewhere. For example, X-ray diffraction experiments carried out using a synchrotron source are usually described as SXRD, and so on. Although the synchrotron has numerous advantages as a radiation source, it also has disadvantages – the most obvious being the cost of the instrument, and the consequent high cost of access. There are a handful of such instruments in Europe and North America, and most countries have access arrangements through their Research Councils (or equivalent) to allow bone fide researchers free access to suitable synchrotron resources for approved experiments. Although it may take several months to schedule a particular experiment into the required station on a synchrotron, and all samples have to be ready to analyze at whatever time this might be, the intensity of the beamline often means that huge amounts of data can be collected in a short time. Typically, an SXRD experiment might collect, in a few seconds, as much data as would be obtained in several months of conventional XRD. For some types of work, where synchrotron techniques are an option, but not a necessity, there is an obvious cost–benefit analysis problem to be evaluated, but for others, synchrotron sources provide the only possibility of carrying out some types of analysis. An example might be in microanalysis with high spatial resolution, where only the synchrotron can provide sufficient beam intensity on a small enough scale to carry out the analysis. Another might be in heat-sensitive samples such as proteins, where the synchrotron can carry out very rapid analyses, because of the high intensity of the source, before a sample has time to alter.

Synchrotron applications in archaeology date back to 1986 (Harbottle *et al.* 1986), and have been subsequently documented on a dedicated website at Daresbury [http://www.srs.ac.uk/srs/]. The majority of the early applications use SR as a source for X-ray fluorescence microanalysis on a variety of materials, including glass (Schofield *et al.* 1995, Janssens *et al.* 1996), ink and paper (Mommsen *et al.* 1996), dental calculus (Capasso *et al.* 1995), and bone (Janssens *et al.* 1998b). The repertoire has been expanded to include X-ray micro-diffraction on materials such as iron (Dillmann *et al.* 1997), bone, wood (Kuczumow *et al.* 2000), and Egyptian cosmetics (Martinetto *et al.* 2001). More recent applications have included SAXS (small angle X-ray scattering) to study the alterations of shape and size of bone mineral crystals, as a result of diagenetic and microbial attack (Wess *et al.* 2002). Arguably, it has taken 20 years for archaeologists and SR specialists to begin to identify applications of the technique which genuinely use the potential of the tool to answer questions of real archaeological significance. Now that this has begun, we can anticipate a fruitful period of the application of SR techniques in archaeology.

13

PRACTICAL ISSUES IN ANALYTICAL CHEMISTRY

Producing a good chemical analysis, particularly of difficult materials such as those often encountered in archaeology, is as much an art as a science. It requires experience, ingenuity, perseverance, and, often, luck. There are, however, a number of steps which can be taken to minimize the dependence on the element of luck. These include well-thought-out and appropriate sampling procedures, high quality standards matched to the material being analyzed, a rigorous approach to calibration, and, above all, a laboratory dedicated to good quality assurance procedures. Here we outline some of the procedures used for the preparation of solutions for inorganic trace element and organic residue analysis, and give a series of basic "recipes". A more comprehensive treatment can be found in Mester and Sturgeon (2003). We then discuss in detail the types of analytical standards used to calibrate analytical instruments (synthetic, primary, secondary, and internal). The meaning of the terms accuracy and precision is explained, together with some mathematical procedures for calculating the errors associated with the analysis, particularly those arising from linear regression, which is almost invariably used to quantify analytical data. The classic work on quantifying errors of measurement is Topping (1972), and Barford (1985) and Miller and Miller (1993) present much of the basic mathematics necessary to deal with the statistical side of analytical chemistry. The last section discusses appropriate overall quality assurance procedures – essential to ensure (and demonstrate) that the analytical data are fit for purpose.

13.1 Some basic procedures in analytical chemistry

One of the most basic requirements in analytical chemistry is the ability to make up solutions to the required strength, and to be able to interpret the various ways of defining concentration in solution and solids. For solution-based methods, it is vital to be able to accurately prepare known-strength solutions in order to calibrate analytical instruments. By way of background to this, we introduce some elementary chemical thermodynamics – the equilibrium constant of a reversible reaction, and the solubility and solubility product of compounds. More information, and considerably more detail, on this topic can be found in Garrels and Christ (1965), as well as many more recent geochemistry texts. We then give some worked examples to show how the strengths of aqueous solutions can be calculated. Finally, the all-important subject of laboratory safety is outlined. Chemistry laboratories can be dangerous places, and it is essential that aspiring analysts learn how to work safely and also how to handle dangerous materials.

Solution chemistry

This section covers the practical considerations involved in reporting the concentration of a dissolved *species* in solution. The term species is a generic one, and can include anything from an element in aqueous solution (e.g., copper in solution), to a dissolved compound (e.g., dissolved nitrate), to neutral species in solution, to large complexes such as proteins in solution.

Solubility and solubility product

It is easily appreciated that different elements or compounds have different solubilities in water (often termed *in aqueous media*). For example, copper sulfate crystals are reasonably soluble in water at $25°C$; 22 g of the hydrated compound ($CuSO_4.5H_2O$) will dissolve in 100 g of water. Copper nitrate ($Cu(NO_3)_2.6H_2O$) is even more soluble – 150 g will dissolve in 100 g of water. We can see from this, incidentally, that the form the copper takes (nitrate, sulfate, etc.) is important in controlling the solubility. Not all copper compounds, however, are as soluble as this – copper(I) chloride (CuCl) has a solubility of only 0.02 g in 100 g of water. Copper(I) bromide (CuBr) is deemed to be practically insoluble at $25°C$. The term *insoluble* needs treating with some care. In practical terms, it is easy to appreciate that some compounds are insoluble, but the extremely limited solubility of some compounds can be important over long (i.e., archaeological and, especially, geological) time periods. For example, silica (SiO_2 – quartz, or the mineral which makes up pure beach sand) has a very low solubility (0.012 g per 100 g of water), but this solubility is extremely important in explaining the geological process of fossilization, or the formation of flint nodules in chalk deposits. Even more insoluble are compounds such as galena (lead sulfide, PbS) and sphalerite (zinc sulfide, ZnS), and yet their limited solubility is important in explaining the movement of these minerals through host rocks during mineralization processes via hot ore-bearing fluids.

In general, solubilities increase with temperature – often, markedly so. For example, potassium nitrate (KNO_3) has an aqueous solubility of about 14 g per 100 g at $0°C$, rising to over 140 g per 100 g above $70°C$. Other compounds show different or anomalous behavior. Sodium chloride (NaCl, common salt) has a solubility which changes little across the normal temperature range, varying only slightly from 36 g per 100 g. Sodium sulfate has a solubility which increases from about 7 g per 100 g at $0°C$ up to a maximum of just over 50 g per 100 g at $32°C$, and then actually declines to just above 40 g per 100 g around $90°C$. This can be explained in terms of changing hydration patterns, but is, nevertheless, a curious phenomenon. Some compounds, such as calcium ethanoate [(CH$_3$COO)$_2$Ca, calcium acetate], have solubilities which simply decrease with increasing temperature.

The solubility of a compound can simply be expressed, as above, in terms of grams of compound which will dissolve in 100 grams of water at a specified temperature. A more useful concept is the *solubility product*, which is defined as follows. If a compound (generically termed MX, where M^{n+} is any metal ion and X^{n-} is any anion) is present in a solution in excess of its solubility, then an equilibrium is set up between the dissolved species and the undissolved solid, as follows:

$$MX_{(s)} \Leftrightarrow M^{n+}{}_{(aq)} + X^{n-}{}_{(aq)}$$

(assuming for simplicity that MX dissolves by forming positive and negative ions [of charge n] in solution). The subscript $_{(s)}$ means that MX is an undissolved solid, and $_{(aq)}$ that the ions are dissolved species. This is a reversible chemical equation, and the amount of MX that dissolves depends on the balance (or "equilibrium") of the equation between the left- and right-hand sides. This is expressed as the equilibrium constant (K), which we can write for this reaction as follows:

$$K = \frac{\left[M^{n+}{}_{(aq)}\right]\left[X^{n-}{}_{(aq)}\right]}{\left[MX_{(s)}\right]}$$

where, following the normal convention, square brackets denote measures of concentration of the species enclosed. Again, following the normal convention, providing the solid is present in excess, the term in the denominator can be disregarded from this discussion, and we can redefine the equilibrium constant to be the solubility product, K$_{sp}$:

$$K_{sp} = \left[M^{n+}{}_{(aq)}\right]\left[X^{n-}{}_{(aq)}\right].$$

For sparingly soluble compounds, the solubility product can be used in a number of ways. It predicts the point at which a particular compound will cease to be soluble, and therefore precipitate out of solution. It also predicts which compounds will precipitate first out of waters with a range of dissolved species present, and even what will be the effect on a particular species if the concentration of something else changes in the same solution. This is the starting point for the *geochemical modeling* of the behavior of natural waters, which is beginning to find archaeological application as a way of predicting the interaction between a buried object and its depositional environment (see Section 1.3).

Measures of solution concentration
There is a plethora of ways of reporting the strength of a solution, and it is important to be able to interpret each correctly, and translate between equivalent measures. There are essentially two approaches – measurement in

terms of mass of solute per volume of solvent, or measurement of mass of solute per mass unit of solvent. (*Solute* is the term for the substance which is dissolved, and *solvent* is the substance which does the dissolving – for the current consideration, this is water.) Mass per volume (w/v) measures tend to be simpler: volumes of solvent can be measured reasonably precisely with pipettes or volumetric flasks, but suffer from the problem that for all but the most dilute solutions the volume of the solvent will change as the solute is added. Mass per mass measures (w/w) are unaffected by such volume changes, or changes in volume due to temperature. With a good analytical balance, they can also be made more precisely than mass per volume measures.

Despite this, mass per volume measures are the most common, and come in four types:

- *grams* of solute *per liter* (properly termed *per cubic decimeter*) of solvent – ($g\,l^{-1}$ or $g\,dm^{-3}$)
- *kilograms* of solute *per cubic meter* of solvent, $kg\,m^{-3}$ (note that $1\,g\,dm^{-3} = 1\,kg\,m^{-3}$)
- *mole* of solute *per liter* (*per cubic decimeter*) of solvent ($mol\,l^{-1}$, or $mol\,dm^{-3}$). The *mole* is the molecular weight (or formula weight) of the compound expressed in grams. A table of atomic weights is given in Appendix VI, from which the molecular weights can be calculated. This unit is termed the *molarity* of a solution, and given the symbol M ($1\,M = 1\,mol\,dm^{-3}$).
- The *normality* of a solution is still referred to in older European texts, and in current US texts. A 1 Normal (1 N) solution is one which contains the gram-equivalent of an element per liter (cubic decimeter) of solvent. The *equivalent weight* of an element is defined as that weight which will combine with or displace 8 g of oxygen, but for a compound it is often better to define its equivalent weight as that which contains 1 g of replaceable hydrogen (for an acid), or is produced by the replacement of 1 g of hydrogen from its parent acid (for a salt).

Thus, a 1 molar solution of hydrochloric acid (HCl, molecular weight 36.5) is that which contains 36.5 g HCl in 1 liter (cubic decimeter) of water; a 1 N solution is the same, since there is 1 g of replaceable hydrogen in 36.5 g of HCl, and, therefore, in this case molarity and normality are the same. For sulfuric acid (H_2SO_4, with approximate molecular weight 98), 1 M is 98 g H_2SO_4 in 1 liter of water, but, since H_2SO_4 contains 2 g of replaceable hydrogen in 98 g, the gram-equivalent is 49, and so 1 N is 49 g of H_2SO_4 in a liter. Thus, a 1 M solution of H_2SO_4 is the same strength as a 2 N solution.

Mass per mass units come in three varieties:

- grams of solute per 100 g of solvent, often simply expressed as a *percentage*. Thus a "3% salt solution" is 3 g of NaCl dissolved in 100 g of water. A variant of this is the measure of *parts per million (ppm)*, which, by extension, implies 1 g per 1 000 000 g of solvent, i.e., 1 g per metric tonne (1000 kg), or 1 µg of solute per gram of solvent.
- The *mole fraction* is the ratio of the number of moles of solute to the total number of moles of solute plus solvent. This is the same as the ratio of the number of molecules of solute to the total number of solute plus solvent molecules.

- The *molality* (m) of a solution is the number of moles of solute per kilogram of solvent ($mol\,kg^{-1}$).

The relationship between all these different measures is best illustrated by example. Consider the following:

1   An aqueous sodium chloride (NaCl) solution is made up by dissolving 11.7 g pure NaCl in water, and making up the total volume to 1 liter (i.e., $1000\,cm^3$, or $1\,dm^3$). This gives a salt solution of concentration *11.7 g dm^{-3}*.

2   The approximate gram molecular weight of NaCl is 23 + 35.5 = 58.5 g. Thus $1\,dm^3$ of solution contains $\frac{11.7}{58.5}$, or 0.200 mol dm^{-3}, i.e., *0.200 M*.

3   From (1), we know that $100\,cm^3$ solution contains 1.17 g NaCl. The density of the solution at 20°C is known to be $1.006\,g\,cm^{-3}$. Since density $= \frac{mass}{volume}$,

$$100\ cm^3 \text{ of the solution has a mass of } 100 \times 1.006\ g = 100.6\ g$$

$$100.6\ g \text{ of solution contains } 1.17\ g\ NaCl$$

$$\text{or} \quad 100\ g \text{ solution contains} \frac{1.17 \times 100}{100.6} = 1.16\ g\ NaCl$$

there is 1.16 g solute in 100 g solution, which is a 1.16% solution (1.16% is equivalent to 11 600 *ppm*, since 1% = 10 000 ppm).

4   From (2), the solution contains $0.2\,mol\,dm^{-3}$ NaCl, or $11.7\,g\,dm^{-3}$. If the density is 1.006, then $1\,dm^3$ has a mass of 1006 g. $1\,dm^3$, therefore, contains 1006 − 11.7 g of water, or 994.3 g. Since the gram molecular weight of water is 18 g, this indicates that there are:

$$\frac{994.3}{18} = 55.2\ mol\,dm^{-3}\ H_2O.$$

By definition, the *mole fraction* of NaCl in this solution is $= \frac{0.2}{0.2 + 55.2} = 0.0036$. (Note the number of *significant figures* [see Section 13.4] reported here: taking the density of the solution as 1, and calculating the weight of water therefore as 1000 g would not have affected this calculation. The density correction could, therefore, have been omitted. Also, as a rule of thumb, 1 liter of water can be approximated as $55\,mol\,H_2O$.)

5   Since from (4) we have 0.2 mol NaCl in 994.3 g solvent, from the definition:

$$molality = \frac{0.2 \times 1000}{994.3} = 0.201\,m.$$

Of these different definitions, the most important usually are g dm^{-3}, molarity, mole fraction, and percentage (or ppm, for dilute solutions). It is often important in analytical chemistry to be able to convert easily between mass per volume measures (g dm^{-3}, or the equivalent often used units µg ml^{-1}, micrograms per milliliter) and mass per unit mass measures, most often parts per million (ppm).

If:

1 ppm = 1 g solute in 1 000 000 g solution,

or:

1 ppm = 1 µg solute in 1 g solution

then, assuming the density of the dilute solution to be 1.000 g cm^{-3}, this becomes:

1 ppm = 1 µg solute in 1 cm^3 solution.

or, since 1 cm^3 is the same as 1 milliliter, using the notation used commercially in aqueous analytical standards:

1 ppm = 1 µg ml^{-1} of solution.

This approximation applies to most dilute aqueous solutions at room temperature, where the density can be taken as 1.000 g cm^{-3}. This is a reasonable assumption for ppm strength solutions, since these are very dilute. As shown above, a 0.2 M NaCl solution is equivalent to an 11 600 ppm NaCl solution, where the density is 1.006. If the density cannot be taken as 1.000, or for very accurate work, then the above equation should be modified as follows:

1 ppm = (1 × density) µg ml^{-1} of solution.

As a final note, it is worth stating that in advanced chemical calculations dealing with the thermodynamics of nonideal solutions (both liquid and gaseous), the correct measure of concentration becomes the *activity* (or, for gases, the partial pressure or *fugacity*). The activity of a substance is a dimensionless ratio, and is given the symbol a. As the concentration of the substance in solution decreases, however, the activity a converges on its mole fraction, as defined above. It is quite common in the geochemical modeling of dilute aqueous systems, such as natural surface waters and groundwaters, to approximate the activity of the various components using the relevant mole fractions. Only in situations where substances become more concentrated, such as natural brines and ore fluids, does it become essential to use activities. Such considerations are beyond the scope of this volume.

The definition of pH
One particular example of solution strength has an important meaning in chemistry – that of the dissolved hydrogen ion, which relates to the acidity or

alkalinity of a solution, and is expressed as pH. Our perception of an acid has changed since the original understanding of the behavior of an acid in the alchemical period. Johannes Brønsted and Thomas Lowry independently proposed in 1923 the definition of an acid as a substance which donates protons (i.e., hydrogen ions) to other substances (Brønsted 1923, Lowry 1923). By extension, a *base* is defined as any substance which acts as a proton acceptor. These definitions are preferred to the more simple ideas of an acid being a substance which yields H^+ ions in aqueous solutions, and a base being one which similarly yields OH^- ions, since they can be applied to nonaqueous media. A more recent definition, due to Lewis, has defined acids as substances which act as electron acceptors, and bases as electron donors. This, although even more general, and chemically more useful, is also beyond the scope of the current discussion.

According to the Brønsted and Lowry definition, water itself can act as both an acid and a base as the result of *autodissociation*:

$$H_2O \Leftrightarrow H^+ + OH^-.$$

The equilibrium constant for this reaction, K, is:

$$K = \frac{[H^+][OH^-]}{[H_2O]} = [H^+][OH^-]$$

since the concentration of undissociated water is essentially a constant. This equilibrium constant is given the symbol K_w, the *ionic product of water*, and has the value of approximately $1 \times 10^{-14} mol^2 dm^{-6}$ at 25°C. The significance of this is explained below. In fact, the concept of the free proton (H^+) existing in any aqueous media is unrealistic. Because of the small size of a "bare" proton (typically 10^{-4} times smaller than any other ion), the charge densities around it would destroy any other ion in its vicinity. In fact, it appears to behave as if it were the *hydronium ion*, H_3O^+, which results from the association of the proton with an undissociated water molecule. Nevertheless, for theoretical purposes, it is convenient to retain the notion of the bare hydrogen ion as being stable in solution.

Any substance which increases the concentration of hydrogen ions in an aqueous solution above the level provided by the autodissociation of water itself is, by Brønsted and Lowry's definition, an acid. For pure water, the ionic product (K_w) suggests that at equilibrium at 25°C, the following holds true:

$$[H^+] = [OH^-] = 1 \times 10^{-7} \text{ mol dm}^{-3}$$

i.e., at equilibrium, the concentrations of hydrogen and hydroxyl ions are equal, with a value of $10^{-7} \text{ mol dm}^{-3}$. If we define the following logarithmic functions:

$$pH = -\log[H^+] \quad \text{and} \quad pOH = -\log[OH^-]$$

then, at equilibrium, the values are:

$$pH = pOH = -\log(1 \times 10^{-7}) = 7.$$

The logarithmic operator pH is, therefore, simply a measure of the hydrogen ion concentration in solution. If the concentration increases because some compound has released hydrogen ions into solution (by definition, an acid), then $[H^+]$ will increase, and pH will fall: e.g., if $[H^+]$ rises by a factor of 100 to 1×10^{-5}, then the new pH is $-\log(1 \times 10^{-5})$, or 5. Thus, a fall of 2 in pH units is the result of a 100-fold increase in the hydrogen ion concentration. Small changes in pH can therefore reflect rather large changes in ionic concentration. Note, too, that pOH always changes as a result of changes in pH. Because K_w is a constant at a particular temperature, then a change to pH 5 will result in a decrease in pOH, as follows:

$$K_w = 10^{-14} = [H^+][OH^-]$$

$$[OH^-] = \frac{10^{-14}}{[H^+]} = \frac{10^{-14}}{10^{-5}} = 10^{-9}$$

$$\text{or } pOH = 9.$$

This can be more simply calculated by noting from the definitions that:

$$pH + pOH = 14.$$

Because of the definition of acidity and pH, we can conclude that liquids with a pH of less than 7 are acidic, and have excess hydrogen ions, and that pHs greater than 7 are basic, with excess hydroxyl ions. Because of the autodissociation of water, however, the concentrations of hydrogen ions and hydroxyl ions (i.e., pH and pOH) are inextricably linked, but calculable through the above simple formula.

Health and safety in the laboratory

Chemistry laboratories can be dangerous places. The health and safety of the analyst (or anybody else using or visiting the laboratory) are not to be compromised. Lack of time or money are not reasons for risking illness, disability, or even death (especially in the eyes of the law). Some hazards are the same as in any other building environment (e.g., fire, lifting heavy objects, electricity, etc.), but many are specific to the laboratory environment. There are a few principles underlying general safe practice in the laboratory which, if understood, will reduce the majority, if not all, of what appears to be a long list of "dos and don'ts" to common sense. Some of these are listed in Appendix IX. All laboratories should have safety manuals and standard operating procedures (SOPs) which cover what is generally called "good practice in the laboratory". These address practical issues such as the safe handling and disposal of chemicals, the use of safety equipment, and emergency procedures. Appendix IX gives a generalized version of what should be covered in such manuals.

Control of Substances Hazardous to Health (COSHH) regulations

In the UK, the use of almost all chemicals or substances is governed by the Control of Substances Hazardous to Health (COSHH) regulations, and similar legislation applies in most other countries. This publication (Health and Safety Executive 2002, 2004) contains the Approved Code of Practice (ACOP) to the Control of Substances Hazardous to Health Regulations 2002, which revokes all previous regulations. It also includes supporting guidance on the control of carcinogenic substances, provisions relating to work with biological agents, and the control of substances that cause occupational asthma. Generally, if a warning label is present on a chemical packaging then a COSHH form should be completed. In practice, many people complete a COSHH form even for a procedure using no hazardous chemicals. Although this may seem unnecessary, it highlights the main purpose of completing a COSHH assessment – it is an assessment of the hazards, gives details of how to carry out the procedure safely, and documents what to do in an emergency.

There are no specified designs for COSHH forms (see Appendix IX for the chemical and biological COSHH form used at the Department of Archaeological Sciences, University of Bradford, UK). However, they generally follow the layout indicated which uses the eight COSHH requirements as headings (see *COSHH, a brief guide to the regulations* [http://www.hse.gov.uk/pubns/indg136.pdf]). It is vital that the process is a proactive one, carried out by those involved in the work. Simply cutting and pasting hazard data from the web in order to complete a form does not promote understanding of the hazards. COSHH (and equivalent regulations) can sometimes seem a bureaucratic paper chase, but it is designed to ensure that the person who does the work also carries out the risk assessment, and is responsible for minimizing such risks. If approached properly, it is an aid to good experimental work, and, above all, it ensures the safety of all those working in laboratories.

13.2   Sample preparation for trace element and residue analysis

The high sensitivity of modern instrumental techniques such as ICP–MS (Chapter 9) means that in many cases only small samples (typically, a hundred milligrams or less) need be taken for destructive analysis. However, this also means that the amounts of some individual elements may be very low, and problems of contamination can be significant. Common external contaminants include Al from deodorants, Pb from paint or car exhausts, Zn from skin particles (and therefore from dust), and Na from sweat. The levels of contamination for each batch of samples will be revealed by the *sample blanks* (solutions prepared using exactly the same procedure as applied to the samples, but without any sample: see below), and will be different for each element. It is, therefore, recommended that sample preparation be carried out in a *clean laboratory*. This might be a laboratory subject only to normal levels of cleanliness requirements, or it could be an ultraclean purpose-built lab with, for example, no metal fittings, over-pressure air supply to keep out unfiltered external air, air-locks or air showers and sticky mats on entry, and the need to wear full containment suits. The level needed depends on the degree of cleanliness required. In any case, sample containers should be of Teflon, PTFE, or glass and should be acid leached and soaked in deionized water before use. Reagents should be of the highest purity and freshly produced. Deionized water (with $18\,M\Omega$ resistance) should be used to prepare solutions.

Weight is generally a more accurate measure than volume, but in practice it is often easier to make solutions up to a fixed final volume (e.g., in a grade A volumetric flask). Micropipettes are used to transfer solutions for dilution; fixed volume pipettes are more accurate than variable volume pipettes. Techniques such as solution ICP–MS require that the samples be fully dissolved, since any undissolved particles may block the nebulizer, and for the analytical reason that the solution would not be representative of the original sample. *Total dissolved solids* (TDS) in the solution should not be greater than 0.1% by weight (e.g., 0.1 g sample dissolved and made up to a final volume of 100 ml). Older analytical techniques, such as AAS, are less sensitive to high levels of dissolved solids in solution, but also have much poorer levels of detection (see Section 3.4). The minimum sample volume required for ICP solution analysis is $\sim 5\,ml$, but it is usually better to prepare larger volumes if possible. Small volumes only require small amounts of sample, which may be difficult to weigh accurately and there may be problems in ensuring that the sample is representative and homogeneous.

The *matrix* is the major component of the solution (or of the solid if using laser ablation or SEM). Matrix differences between standards and samples or between samples may result in differences of elemental sensitivity. Therefore, it is desirable that all the blanks, calibration standards, and samples have the same matrix (i.e., are *matrix matched*). This is relatively easy to achieve in solution, but can be a major problem with the analysis of solid samples.

General inorganic trace element preparation methods
In general, acid digestion is used to convert solid samples into dilute liquid solutions for analysis. A range of methods for general sample types is indicated in Appendix VIII. Totland *et al.* (1992) have a table comparing the advantages and disadvantages of the methods discussed there. Although written specifically for atomic absorption spectrometry, a useful general reference for sample preparation of typical archaeological samples is

Hughes *et al.* (1976). Sample digestion procedures should be tested and refined by the digestion of a certified reference material of similar matrix to the samples before embarking on an analytical program. Repeated digestions may be needed to achieve complete dissolution of some samples. Hydrochloric acid (HCl) and sulfuric acid (H_2SO_4) are to be avoided, because the chlorine and sulfur will generate polyatomic interfering species (see Chapter 9). Nitric acid (HNO_3) does not have these effects, and, when concentrated, is a powerful oxidizing agent. It is, therefore, the acid of choice for most sample dissolution procedures. Silicate materials (e.g., glass and ceramics), however, are resistant to most mineral acids and require the use of hydrofluoric acid (HF), which is one of the most hazardous chemicals in common use. Unless the analytical instrument has been specially adapted (e.g., the use of special cones in an ICP spectrometer: see Chapter 9) any HF must be removed by evaporation before analysis. Even if nitric acid is not used for the initial digestion, it is often used at a final volume of 1.5–3 % to keep the elements in solution (reflecting the high solubility of nitrates). Further discussion of sample preparation techniques may be found in Holmes *et al.* (1995).

The method used to dissolve samples may have an important impact on the quality of the data for some elements. Obviously, if the sample has not been fully dissolved, then quantification will give less than the true yield for some or all elements. Some individual elements may also form insoluble species or complexes during dissolution (e.g., Sn, Cr), and special precautions are necessary to ensure that such complexes are dissolved. Mercury in solution will often be absorbed onto the surface of glass vessels. Quantification will also be less than expected where volatile elements or their compounds are lost; a process which may be aggravated if heating in an open vessel.

Sample preparation for organic residue analysis

There are three main types of samples we can examine for organic residue analysis: *visible residues* (usually associated with a ceramic vessel shard), *ceramic absorbed residues*, and the depositional *matrix* (usually soil). Sampling can be carried out in the field or museum, but it is generally easier to sample under controlled conditions in a dedicated laboratory. This is because the amounts of archaeological organic residues are generally low and precautions are needed to avoid contamination (see below). The origins and mass spectra of typical organic contaminants are listed by Middleditch (1989).

Visible residues

Generally, only a very small amount of visible organic residue is required for analysis. If it is pure organic material (e.g., if it has the same appearance as a modern resin or bitumen), then a pinhead sized piece (a few milligrams) is usually sufficient. With samples on this scale, however, heterogeneity within the sample can be a problem. Appendix VIII also gives an outline of the sampling methodology for visible residues.

Ceramic absorbed residues and soil matrix

The preservation of organic residues is generally better if they are absorbed into a protective ceramic matrix. For the extraction of these lipids, about 0.1 g of powder (an area of approximately 1×1 cm) must be removed from the shard. This can be done from the center of the shard if it is required for reconstruction of the vessel. A small drill fitted with a tungsten carbide abrasive bit (solvent-cleaned between samples) is most commonly used. The resulting powder is collected on a sheet of aluminum foil before transferring to a glass vial. In the past up to 100 g was taken (e.g., Condamin *et al.* 1976), but with improved instrumental sensitivity, this is generally no longer necessary. Some workers (e.g., Charters *et al.* 1995) recommend removal of the exterior surfaces prior to sampling to exclude contamination, whilst others extract the whole shard section (e.g., Evershed *et al.* 1990) but Stern *et al.* (2000) suggest sampling to a depth of 2 mm without removal of the outer ceramic and have found that the highest concentration of indigenous lipids are in fact in this surface layer. By including the exterior surface in the sample, contamination from the soil matrix and handling can be accounted for. In addition, a "concentration gradient" of lipids from the interior to the exterior of the vessel can be established if 2 mm slices are taken through the entire shard. The lipids in the powdered shard are then extracted as described below.

It is always good practice to examine a sample of the burial matrix from alongside the shard in order to detect the potential migration of external contamination into the shard. If possible, the original soil adhering to the shard is most suitable.

Solvent extraction

The next step is to chemically extract the lipids from the visible residue, powdered shard, or soil. A number of novel and "conventional" sample extraction techniques have been compared by Stern *et al.* (2000). There are two main methods routinely employed, but the exact conditions may vary between different laboratories.

In the conventional method, the shard powder (or visible residue, or soil) is extracted with three separate aliquots of c. 0.5 ml DCM:MeOH (dichloromethane:methanol; 1:1, v/v), with ultrasonication for 5 minutes to break up any particle aggregates and to aid dissolution. The solvent is separated from any insoluble material (including the ceramic) with centrifugation (5 minutes at 1000 rpm) and each of the three solvent aliquots is combined into a new clean vial. The solvent is then removed by placing the sample under a stream of nitrogen on a warm hotplate to aid evaporation, leaving the extracted lipids. This method extracts the "free" lipids, i.e., those which are not chemically bound to the ceramic or contained within a larger organic polymer.

Saponification (see Section 7.4) is carried out to extract more recalcitrant lipids, and the yields are higher than for conventional solvent extraction (Stern *et al.* 2000). 3 ml of 0.5 M methanolic NaOH is added to 0.1 g of the shard powder and heated at 70°C for 3 hours in a sealed glass vial. After cooling, the supernatant is acidified with HCl and extracted with three aliquots of 3 ml *n*-hexane. The hexane will not mix with the methanolic solution (unlike the DCM:MeOH used above), but will absorb the lipids and can be transferred into a new clean vial. The removal of excess hexane is carried out as above. Saponification will hydrolyze and methylate any ester functionalities, which removes the requirement to derivatize the samples (Section 7.4) unless other molecules are suspected of being present. However, any wax esters or triacylglycerols will also be hydrolyzed to their fatty acid methyl esters and alcohols; therefore, if information on their composition is required, then conventional solvent extraction is recommended as a first step. For subsequent characterization of the lipid extract, see Chapter 7.

13.3   Standards for calibration

Almost all methods of chemical analysis require a series of calibration standards containing different amounts of the analyte in order to convert instrument readings of, for example, optical density or emission intensity into absolute concentrations. These can be as simple as a series of solutions containing a single element at different concentrations, but, more usually, will be a set of multicomponent solutions or solids containing the elements to be measured at known concentrations. It is important to appreciate that the term "standard" is used for a number of materials fulfilling very different purposes, as explained below.

Synthetic (calibration) standards

For solution-based analyses, it is normal to make up a set of synthetic standards from commercial calibration solutions (normally supplied as 1000 ppm stock solutions, e.g., from Aldrich, BDH, Fisons, or ROMIL). These are available to different degrees of purity, and it is necessary to use the level of purity commensurate with the sensitivity of the analytical technique to be used; it is, however, better not to use the highest purity in all circumstances, since these are very expensive. Ideally each element to be determined in the sample should be calibrated against a standard solution containing that element, although interpolation is sometimes possible between adjacent elements in the periodic table, if some elements are missing. For most techniques, it is better to mix up a single standard solution containing the appropriate concentrations of each element to be measured, so that any *matrix effects* (interferences between the components of multicomponent mixtures) which might affect the samples will also be reflected in the calibration standards. Unless addition techniques are used, it is also important to have a range of concentrations going beyond (both higher and lower than) the range to be determined in the samples, for each element to be measured. This can be done by making a single standard solution containing all the elements to be measured at a concentration higher than expected in the samples, and then diluting down subsamples to give a series of lower concentration standard solutions. It is better, however, to make up independently more than one calibration solution, since any errors in making up a single calibration solution will not become apparent if all the standards are simply diluted versions of the original solution.

Primary standards

There are internationally agreed standard reference materials (SRMs), also called certified reference materials (CRMs), which meet the requirements of ISO guidelines (see below). They have been accurately and repeatedly analyzed, often using different techniques, in different laboratories. The results are fully documented, although not always for all elements. Data on SRMs are available from websites such as National Institute of Standards and Technology (NIST) [http://www.nist.gov/] and US Geological Survey (USGS) [http://www.usgs.gov/]. Such standards are commercially available, but are often expensive (and, therefore, too costly to use in each analytical run), and occasionally they run out (e.g., Pee Dee Belemnite, PDB, which was the international standard for carbon isotope measurements in rocks). It is important to match the chemistry of the standard material to that of the samples as closely as possible. For example, because of different matrix effects, it is not very effective to use a geological rock standard to calibrate an analysis of medieval glasses, since the concentration ranges of some elements (e.g., Al_2O_3) are substantially different.

Secondary standards

Because of the cost of primary standards, it is normal to use them very sparingly (certainly not as calibration standards), but to include them as unknowns in the analytical run as a measure of the quality of the analysis (see QA, below). Even so, this becomes prohibitively expensive, and it is common to use materials which can be included in each analysis, which may not be fully certified, but whose values can be related to a primary standard. These are often referred to as in-house standards, although they may be more generally available. They can be home-made, providing sufficient attention has been paid to homogenizing the material thoroughly. A simple example is the use of modern ceramic plant pot material as a secondary standard for the analysis of ancient ceramics.

For solution analyses, a good protocol involves calibration against a series of independent and freshly made synthetic solutions (standards have a habit of going off), and including a substantial number of replicates of one or more in-house standards throughout the analysis. If available, one or more internationally recognized reference materials should also be included. It is important to appreciate, however, that the calibration line (see below) is constructed only using the values from the synthetic solutions. The other standards are treated as if they were unknown samples, and are primarily used for quality assurance purposes, to detect drift in the machine, either within-run or between runs. It is also good practice (and should be essential) to publish the data obtained on the SRMs (and preferably also any in-house standards used) alongside the analytical data obtained for the unknowns. This allows others to evaluate the quality of the data.

In the analysis of solid samples (e.g., LA–ICP–MS, SEM), synthetic standards cannot easily be prepared to the required concentrations, and accurate calibration of such techniques is often challenging. In some cases (e.g., SEM) pure element or single mineral standards are used, ideally with an appropriate standard for each element to be quantified. (It is possible in SEM, within limits, to use fewer standards than the number of elements to be determined, with the calibration for other elements being predicted from the response of the nearest element.) More often, however, multielement primary standards are used as the means of calibrating the instrument, e.g., for LA–ICP–MS of glasses, volcanics, and ceramics, two glass standards, NIST 610 and 612 (Pearce *et al.* 1996), are often used. It is always advisable to use more than one multielement standard in order to cover as wide a range of concentrations as possible, and to use at least one additional independent reference material as an unknown, for quality assurance purposes (see below).

Internal standards
During a single run, which may take all day if a large number of samples are to be analyzed, the instrument may "drift" from its optimum settings. To detect this drift in solution-based techniques, and also to compensate for some matrix effects, a known amount of an element may be added to each sample before analysis. This internal standard (also called a *spike*) is added to all the samples and blanks, with the exception of the instrument blank (which is defined as zero concentration for all elements: see below). It is important that the element (or isotope) chosen as the spike is not an element which is to be determined in the samples, and preferably which does not occur naturally in the samples. It must not be an element which will cause, or suffer from, interference with the other elements to be determined. In solution ICP–MS,

usually the mid-mass element ^{115}In is chosen at a concentration of 10 ppb, though occasionally for the measurement of low masses ^{45}Sc or ^{89}Y, or for higher masses ^{232}Th or ^{209}Bi, may be used. The determined concentration of the spike can be monitored from sample to sample, which allows any drift to be detected, and remedial action taken.

Blanks

Two types of blanks need to be prepared with each batch of samples. To subtract background levels of contamination occurring during instrumental analysis, an *instrument blank*, which consists of a matrix-matched solution with no internal standard, is made. Generally, an instrument blank is run at the start of the analysis and will be included in the calibration with assigned concentrations of zero for all elements to be measured, so, in effect, this is subtracted from all the subsequent samples.

Sample blanks are prepared using exactly the same methodology as the samples, but they do not contain any sample. However, they will have the same amounts of reagents and internal standard, and therefore can be used to determine the levels of introduced contamination. Repeated analyses of the sample blank (typically ten) are used to calculate the limits of detection for each element analyzed (see below).

13.4 Calibration procedures and estimation of errors

In science, the word "error" has a very specific meaning; it does not mean "mistake". All experimental measurements will differ, to some degree, from the accurate or "real" value of the quantity being measured. The difference between the observed value of a physical quantity and the "accurate" value is called the error. It is very important to consider all the possible sources of errors in experimental measurements. Every experimental measurement reported should be accompanied by an estimate of the error – scientifically speaking, measurements without accompanying error estimates are worthless.

Systematic and random errors

Experimental errors come from two different sources, termed *systematic* and *random* errors. However, it is sometimes difficult to distinguish between them, and many experiments have a combination of both types of error.

Systematic errors usually arise from specific shortcomings in the measuring instrument, the observer, or the way in which the measurement is taken. Sources of systematic error include a badly calibrated measuring device, a faulty instrument movement, an incorrect action by the experimenter (e.g., misreading a volume measurement), or the parallax effect when incorrectly viewing a scale. Repeating the measurement does not necessarily help, because the error may be repeated, and the analyst may not realize that there is an error unless the final result is checked by a different experimental method, different apparatus or experimenter, or against theory.

Random errors arise in all measurements and are inevitable, no matter what the experiment, the quality of the instrument, or of the analyst. They are a consequence of the limitations of experimental, observations. For example, an instrument reading can only be taken within the limits of accuracy of the scale, as read by a particular observer. The position of the pointer between two division marks may be estimated to one fifth of a division by a skilled experimenter, but only to one half a division by another. Such skill may be improved with practice, but will never be totally perfected. Random errors cannot be eliminated, but can be reduced by using more sensitive measuring instruments or an experienced experimenter. The magnitude of random errors can be estimated by repeating the experiment.

Estimating errors in single and repeated measurements
Here we assume that systematic errors have been eliminated, and show how a reasonable estimate may be made of the likely random error in a simple measurement. When using a meter ruler, the height of a vessel is measured at 2.3 cm. Inspection of the ruler, marked in mm, suggests that the maximum error possible to make using this ruler is $\pm$ 0.1 cm, so, at the very worst, the answer might be 2.2 or 2.4 cm. Hence the possible error is $\pm$ 0.1 cm and the height should be reported as 2.3 $\pm$ 0.1 cm. The percentage error in the measurement is calculated as $\pm$ (0.1/2.3) $\times$ 100 = $\pm$ 4%. If, instead of a ruler, we had used vernier callipers capable of measuring to $\pm$ 0.01 cm, the height of the same vessel might have been read as 2.36 $\pm$ 0.01 cm. In this case, the percentage error is $\pm$ (0.01/2.36) $\times$ 100 = $\pm$ 0.4%. Not surprisingly, a ten-fold increase in measurement precision results in a ten-fold reduction in the estimated error for a single measurement.

If a large number of readings of the same quantity are taken, then the mean (average) value is likely to be close to the true value if there is no systematic bias (i.e., no systematic errors). Clearly, if we repeat a particular measurement several times, the random error associated with each measurement will mean that the value is sometimes above and sometimes below the "true" result, in a random way. Thus, these errors will cancel out, and the average or mean value should be a better estimate of the "true" value than is any single result. However, we still need to know how good an estimate our mean value is of the "true" result. Statistical methods lead to the concept of *standard error* (or *standard deviation*) around the mean value.

The mean value ($\bar{x}$) of n individual observations ($x_1, x_2, x_3 \ldots x_n$) is given by:

$$\bar{x} = \frac{\sum x_i}{n}$$

where the Greek capital letter $\sum$ (sigma) means "the summation of", and implies that all the terms following it should be added together. In other words, all n of the individual values are added together, and the total divided by n. The standard deviation (s) is given by:

$$s = \sqrt{\frac{1}{(n-1)} \sum (x_i - \bar{x})^2}.$$

In this case the summation is the sum of the squares of all the differences between the individual values and the mean. The standard deviation is the square root of this sum divided by $n - 1$ (although some definitions of standard deviation divide by n, $n - 1$ is preferred for small sample numbers as it gives a less biased estimate). The standard deviation is a property of the *normal distribution*, and is an expression of the *dispersion* (spread) of this distribution. Mathematically, (roughly) 65% of the area beneath the normal distribution curve lies within ± 1 standard deviation of the mean. An area of 95% is encompassed by ± 2 standard deviations. This means that there is a 65% probability (or about a two in three chance) that the "true" value will lie within $\bar{x} \pm 1s$, and a 95% chance (19 out of 20) that it will lie within $\bar{x} \pm 2s$. It follows that the standard deviation of a set of observations is a good measure of the likely error associated with the mean value. A quoted error of $\pm 2s$ around the mean is likely to capture the true value on 19 out of 20 occasions.

However, it is sometimes simpler to adopt a procedure for estimating the maximum error likely, i.e., the *possible error*, by combining the errors from the various components of the measurement. This is described below and is suitable for many experimental purposes.

Combining errors
The result of an experiment is usually calculated from an expression containing the different quantities measured during the experiment. The combined effect of the errors in the various measurements can be estimated. The rules for combining errors depend on the mathematical procedure being used, as follows.

Sum
If the quantity Q we require is related to quantities a and b, which we have measured, by the simple equation $Q = a + b$, then the total possible error in Q is the sum of the possible error in a plus the possible error in b. For example, if a vessel is 2.3 ± 0.1 cm high and the lid is 0.5 ± 0.1 cm high, then the total combined height and estimated error would be 2.8 ± 0.2 cm. That is, in the

worst case, if both readings are 0.1 cm too high, the total height would be 3.0 cm, but if both are too low then the total height would be 2.6 cm.

Difference

If $Q = a - b$, then the same rule applies for calculating the possible error, i.e., the total possible error in Q is the possible error in a plus the possible error in b. Thus, if we wished to estimate the height of the pot lid from the difference between the total height of the vessel plus lid and the vessel alone, it would be 0.5 ± 0.2 cm, which represents a significant percentage error (± 40%), and demonstrates that this is a poor way of estimating the height of the lid.

Product and quotient

If the individual measurements have to be either multiplied or divided, it can be shown that the total percentage possible error equals the sum of the separate percentage possible errors, i.e.;

Percentage error in Q = percentage error in a + percentage error in b.

For example, the volume, V, of a cylindrical vessel of height h and radius r is given by:

$$V = \pi r^2 h.$$

Therefore the total percentage possible error in volume is:

percentage error in r^2 + percentage error in h.

or:

$2 \times$ (percentage error in r) + percentage error in h.

If the height of a vessel is 5.3 ± 0.1 cm and the radius is 2.1 ± 0.1 cm, the total percentage possible error in V is:

$$(0.1/5.3) \times 100 + (0.1/2.1) \times 100 + (0.1/2.1) \times 100$$
$$= 1.89 + 4.76 + 4.76$$
$$= 11.4\%.$$

Since $V = (2.1)^2 \times 5.3 \, \text{cm}^3$, the estimate of the volume is 73 ± 8 cm^3 – a surprisingly high uncertainty, given the relatively small uncertainties in the measurement of height and radius. This shows the cumulative properties of errors.

When any experimental measurements are plotted on a graph, the errors should also be plotted, using a pair of *error bars*. These extend on either side of the point in both x and the y direction and give a visual impression of the size of the errors for that particular measurement. If the errors for all the points on the graph are roughly the same, it is acceptable to mark this as a single set of error bars somewhere away from the actual points.

Accuracy and precision

These terms have completely different meanings in analytical chemistry, and cannot be used interchangeably, unlike in common parlance. *Precision* is the degree of reproducibility between replicate measurements on the same sample. It is often qualified to specify the time period covered by the estimate: *within-run* precision means the degree of reproducibility obtained on replicates during the same run of the instrument. Variations of precision between runs, or from day to day, or over longer time periods, are often substantially larger than the figures quoted for within-run precision, and are sometimes termed the *repeatability* of a measurement. *Accuracy*, on the other hand, refers to the closeness of the experimental result to the "true" value. Precision is, therefore, an internal measure of analytical quality, whereas accuracy relates to an absolute measure.

Precision can be evaluated from the repeated analysis of any material which is included in the analysis as an unknown, and which is reasonably close in composition to the samples being analyzed. Often, in-house standards are used to determine precision; it is not strictly necessary to know the composition of the in-house standard, other than to know that it is reasonably close to the unknown material. A good example is the repeated use of samples from modern milk bottles or window glass when analyzing ancient glasses. These are cheap, homogeneous, and readily available materials which can be repeatedly analyzed without incurring excessive costs, as would be the case if international reference materials were used. Accuracy, on the other hand, can only be determined relative to the values of an internationally recognized standard reference material.

The detection of long-term variations in either accuracy or precision (analytical drift) is part of the purpose of quality assurance. It is not always the case that good precision and good accuracy go together. As shown in Fig. 13.1, it is possible to have a situation where high precision analyses have poor accuracy, or low precision analyses have good accuracy. Poor accuracy and poor precision are clearly undesirable; good data are generated from high precision analyses with good accuracy.

Following a determination of the relative error in an experimental measurement it is possible to address the concept of *spurious accuracy*. The relative magnitude of the error will indicate how many *significant figures* it is reasonable to quote in the measurement. It is, sadly, commonplace to see results from a computer quoted to 12 decimal places, when the magnitude of the error is such that only the first three decimal places are known with any certainty – the rest are "noise". Conventionally, the reliability of a measurement is indicated by the number of digits used to represent it. Results should be written so that only the final digit is subject to uncertainty. For example, if four significant figures are quoted, the first three should be known with certainty, and the last one is uncertain. Zeros at the end of a number are

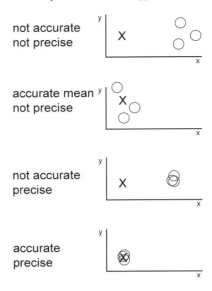

Figure 13.1 Illustration of the terms *accuracy* and *precision* in analytical chemistry. In each case, for a pair of hypothetical measured elements x and y, the cross shows the "true" value, the circles the results of three replicate analyses.

counted as significant figures. Therefore, a result of 1.453 ± 0.01 cm is not justified, because the error term shows that the result can only be accurate to 0.01 cm. The correct expression is 1.45 ± 0.01 cm. When combining significant figures, the result should have the same number of decimal places as the quantity with the lowest number of decimal places. Appendix II shows how to round up or down expressions with too many decimal places.

Estimation of errors in linear calibration
Calibration is the procedure by which we determine how change in one variable is related to variation in another. In instrumental analysis, we need to know how the instrumental response (e.g., spectral intensity, counts per second) is related to the change in concentration of an element in a particular sample (the *analyte*). If there is a good quantifiable relationship between the two, then we can predict the concentration of the analyte in an unknown sample from its instrumental response. Two-dimensional scatterplots are a means of displaying the relationship between the two variables. For analytical purposes, we usually plot the instrument response as the y (vertical) axis against concentration in a standard material along the x (horizontal axis). Table 13.1 shows some typical calibration data, such as might have been generated from a set of synthetic standards using an ICP or AAS instrument. Figure 13.2 is a bivariate plot of these data. This shows that there is a linear relationship between the two, but in order to evaluate the strength of the relationship, we must calculate the *correlation* between the

Table 13.1. *Some hypothetical analytical calibration data.*

Concentration in standard (μg ml^{-1})	Instrument response
0	2.1
2	5.0
4	9.0
6	12.6
8	17.3
10	21.0
12	24.7

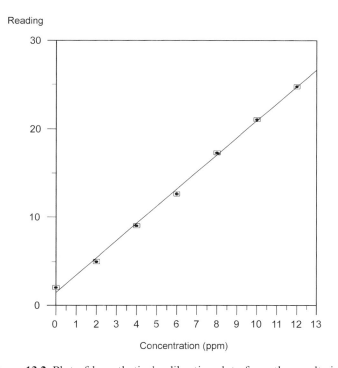

Figure 13.2 Plot of hypothetical calibration data from the results in Table 13.1.

two variables. The most common measure of correlation is the *Pearson's product-moment correlation coefficient*, given the symbol r, and usually simply referred to as the correlation coefficient. The definition of r is as follows, although this is not the best formulation for calculation:

$$r = \frac{\sum_i \{(x_i - \bar{x})(y_i - \bar{y})\}}{\sqrt{\left(\sum_i (x_i - \bar{x})^2\right)\left(\sum_i (y_i - \bar{y})^2\right)}}.$$

Because of the way r is defined, its value always lies between 0 and ± 1. Values close to ± 1 indicate a strong relationship, whereas values near zero imply little relationship. It is possible to use a version of the *Student's t-test* (Miller and Miller 1993) to see if the observed correlation is significant at a particular level of confidence (usually 95%), or to conclude that such a correlation may have occurred by chance. The equation for this is:

$$t = \frac{|r|\sqrt{n-2}}{\sqrt{1-r^2}}$$

where n is the *number of pairs* of observations used to calculate r. (The vertical lines around r mean "the absolute value", i.e., the value of the number without the sign.) The degrees of freedom of t (v) are given by $v = n - 2$, and the test is two-tailed. Critical values of v are shown in Table 13.2. If the value of t exceeds the critical value of t for the appropriate number of pairs of observations, then the value is significant at the 95% level of confidence, and is not the result of chance. In other words, it is safe to use the relationship as a calibration curve.

Once it has been established that a significant relationship exists between a pair of variables, the next step is to quantify this relationship. The usual approach is to "fit" a curve to the data points. The simplest curve is a straight line, which implies that a *linear relationship* exists between the two variables. Unless there is some theoretical reason for expecting a nonlinear relationship, the safest approach is always to use a linear regression, and not to attempt "fitting" a higher order curve, just because it looks better.

The general equation of a straight line relationship between an independent variable x and a dependent variable y is given by:

$$y = bx + a$$

where b is interpreted as the *gradient* of the line (the rate at which y changes per unit change in x) and a is the *intercept* (the value of y when $x = 0$). (These parameters are sometimes called m and c respectively.) The process of calculating the *line of regression* for two variables involves finding the values of a and b for the data, using the following definitions (again, these are not the simplest equations to use in calculations):

$$b = \frac{\sum (x_i - \bar{x})(y_i - \bar{y})}{\sum (x_i - \bar{x})^2}$$

and

$$a = \bar{y} - b\bar{x}.$$

The symbols $\bar{x}$ and $\bar{y}$ are the means of all the x and y values, respectively. For the data shown in Table 13.1, the value of r^2 is 0.998, giving a value of

Table 13.2. *Critical values of t at the 95% confidence interval.*

No. of degrees of freedom	t_{crit}
1	12.71
2	4.30
3	3.18
4	2.78
5	2.57
6	2.45
7	2.36
8	2.31
9	2.26
10	2.23
12	2.18
14	2.14
16	2.12
18	2.10
20	2.09
30	2.04
50	2.01
∞	1.96

$r = 0.999$, which is a very high correlation ($t = 47.2$, well above the critical value of 2.57 for $v = 5$ in Table 13.2). The regression equation is:

$$y = 1.93x + 1.518.$$

The purpose of calculating correlation and linear regression is to allow unknown values of x (the concentration of the analyte in an unknown sample) to be predicted from a measured value of y (the instrument response). The easiest way of doing this is to invert the equation for the linear regression given above, i.e.:

$$x = \frac{(y - a)}{b}.$$

The same result can be achieved graphically by drawing lines on Fig. 13.2, but usually with less accuracy. Thus, if an unknown sample gives a reading of $y = 7.0$, the corresponding value of x is:

$$x = \frac{(7.0 - 1.518)}{1.93} = 2.84 \ \mu g \ ml^{-1}.$$

This is usually as far as most analysts (or automatic calibration programs) go in terms of processing the data, but it gives no indication of the error associated with the measurement arising from uncertainties in the calibration curve. It might be expected that, with a correlation coefficient approaching 1, these errors are likely to be small, but also that they will increase rapidly as the correlation coefficient falls away from this ideal value. In fact, even this is not the case. In order to estimate the errors associated with the predicted value, we need to apply some further analysis to the regression calculations. We define:

$$s_{y/x} = \sqrt{\frac{\sum_i \left(y_i - \dot{y}_i\right)^2}{n-2}}$$

where $s_{y/x}$ is called the *standard deviation of the regression* (and spoken as "s y upon x") and is the *residual* for the point y_i. It is calculated as the difference between the measured value of y_i and the value that would be predicted (y) for the corresponding value of x_i. These equations can be used not only to predict an unknown value of x (x_0) from a measured value of y (y_0) as shown above but also to predict the *confidence interval* (CI, i.e., error) associated with the estimate. If the standard deviation of the estimate of x_0 is s_{x_0} then the following equation is a reasonable approximation:

$$s_{x_0} = \frac{s_{y/x}}{b} \sqrt{1 + \frac{1}{n} + \frac{(y_0 - \bar{y})^2}{b^2 \sum_i (x_i - \bar{x})^2}}$$

and therefore the 95% CI of

$$x_0 = x_0 \pm t s_{x_0}, \textit{where it is read from a table of critical values, as before.}$$

Using the above calibration data, and an unknown sample which gives us an instrument response of 7.0 (i.e., $y_0 = 7.0$), we have already shown that this corresponds to a value of 2.84 µg/ml. Using the above equations for s_{x_0} and $s_{y/x}$, we get:

$$s_{x_0} = \frac{0.4329}{1.03} \sqrt{1 + \frac{1}{7} + \frac{(7.0 - 13.1)^2}{1.93^2 \times 112}}$$

$$s_{x_0} = \frac{0.4329}{1.03} \sqrt{1.232} = 0.467 \, \mu g \, ml^{-1}.$$

To estimate the 95% confidence interval of the predicted value x_0, we use:

$$95\% \ CI = x_0 \pm t s_{x_0} = 2.84 \pm 2.57 \times 0.467 = 2.84 \pm 1.20 \, \mu g \, ml^{-1}.$$

In other words, the predicted value is not 2.84 µg ml^{-1}, but somewhere between 1.64 and 4.04 µg ml^{-1}, at the 95% level of confidence. This is a substantially different result, and is somewhat surprising given the apparent quality of the calibration data. It just shows that you can't always believe what comes out of a computer!

Minimum detectable level (MDL)

The minimum detectable level, or *detection limit*, is defined as that concentration of a particular element which produces an analytical signal equal to twice the square root of the background above the background. It is a statistically defined term, and is a measure of the lower limit of detection for any element in the analytical process. (This definition corresponds to the 95% confidence interval, which is adequate for most purposes, but higher levels, such as 99% can be defined by using a multiplier of three rather than two.) It will vary from element to element, from machine to machine, and from day to day. It should be calculated explicitly for every element each time an analysis is performed.

It can be calculated most straightforwardly from the data generated by the linear regression used above to calibrate the machine. The signal y_{mdl} value is calculated as:

$$y_{mdl} = a + 2\sqrt{a}$$

and the MDL is thus given as:

$$MDL = \frac{y_{mdl} - a}{b}$$

or:

$$MDL = \frac{2\sqrt{a}}{b}.$$

In the above example, this would give an MDL value of $1.28\,\mu g\,ml^{-1}$. It should be remembered that, in the example given here, which is the analysis of a solution, the MDL is for that element in solution, and should be converted into an MDL in the original solid sample to give a true picture of the MDL for the analysis. For the analysis of solids, the MDL can be interpreted directly without any further calculation.

13.5 Quality assurance procedures

Quality assurance (QA) is a generic term for all activities required to maintain quality in analytical results. These include laboratory management structures and sample documentation procedures, as well as the more practical sample preparation and analysis requirements (as described above). The ISO (International Organization for Standardization) develops standards across a wide range of areas, from screw threads to banking cards. The majority of ISO standards are specific to certain areas; they are "documented agreements containing technical specifications or precise criteria to be used consistently as rules, guidelines, or definitions of characteristics to ensure that materials, products, processes and services are fit for their purpose" [http://www.iso.org/iso/en/ISOOnline.openerpage].

ISO has two important functions in analytical chemistry. The first is to publish descriptions of accepted methods. These are effectively "industry standard methods" for particular protocols. The second is in laboratory accreditation. For a laboratory to be ISO accredited, compliance with international QA standards must be confirmed by an initial assessment and subsequently from repeated audits by an independent assessor. Since ISO has no legal or regulatory powers, the standards are voluntary. It is unlikely, however, that a forensic analysis which did not conform to an ISO standard would be upheld in court, for example. Most commercial laboratories need to be accredited to remain competitive and to deal with regulatory authorities. Most university labs are not accredited, mainly due to the time and costs involved, and also to the nonroutine nature of much university research. However, university accreditation may become a requirement in the near future, especially for publicly funded research in the UK. The details of laboratory accreditation are discussed by Christie *et al.* (1999) and Dobb (2004).

An outline laboratory QA procedure would need to include the following. In addition to the use of freshly made synthetic calibration standards, in-house standards, internationally recognized reference materials, and method blanks, as described above, it should include:

- Record keeping carried out not only by the analyst in laboratory notebooks, but also in logbooks for each instrument. After completion, these should be archived for at least ten years. Records should include the type of sample (with a unique identification number), collection method, location, date, description of sample, preparation and analysis method, and instrumental conditions, original data files, and the name of the person responsible.
- Written standard operating procedures (SOP) to ensure that each method is carried out in an identical way.
- Repeat analysis (at the same laboratory) on a random basis to ensure reproducibility (~5% of the samples, or 1 in 20).
- Random laboratory duplicates should be prepared and analyzed (~5%).
- Occasionally, samples should be sent for comparative analysis to a different laboratory (~5%).
- Data verification, also called quality control (QC), to verify the results before reporting, including statistical analysis of duplicates, standards, and blanks.

The financial cost of accreditation is undoubtedly substantial. It has been estimated that the additional cost of being a fully accredited laboratory might add around 30% to the cost of an analysis. Some laboratories state that they work to ISO standards, but without submitting themselves for accreditation, thus avoiding the substantial cost of the external assessment procedure necessary for obtaining certification. It is self-evident that a laboratory which adheres to ISO standards (whether certificated or not) ought to routinely produce better quality data than one which does not. Whether, on a particular day and for a particular set of samples, this is always true is less self-evident. Some laboratories would argue that, because they are always "pushing the boundaries" of what is analytically possible, they could not possibly implement a restrictive QA procedure. A case of "horses for courses", or *caveat emptor*?

EPILOGUE

Hopefully this volume has served to illustrate the diversity of applications of chemistry in archaeology. It utilizes the full armory of analytical techniques, from the humble thin layer chromatography plate to the fearsome power of the synchrotron. The range of materials available for analysis is also vast – ranging from little black sticky messes on the rims of pot shards, through the stable isotopes in human collagen, to the prize museum bronze statue, or marble figurine. It should also be clear that, because of the nature of archaeological materials, there is rarely such a thing as a "routine analysis". Each project presents its own challenges, either because of the limited size of the sample available, the potential degradation or contamination of the sample as a result of burial and excavation, or the hovering presence of the museum curator watching as samples are removed from some precious object which is destined to return to the display case.

Although some of the earliest applications of analytical chemistry in archaeology were focused on organic materials (particularly amber), the bulk of the effort over the last hundred years and more has been devoted to the analysis of inorganic materials – primarily pottery and metal, but also glass, obsidian, flint, and other lithic materials. Often the question has been one of provenance – identifying the source of the raw materials used, with the underlying objective of determining patterns of trade and exchange. Sometimes these have been successful, but occasionally the project has faltered under the sheer weight and complexity of analytical data produced, or because of the lack of a coherent archaeological theory to test. In this context, we must remember Gar Harbottle's phrase (1982: 15): "with a very few exceptions, you cannot unequivocally source anything." Rather, the goal should be to "help arbitrate between competing cultural hypotheses" (Cherry and Knapp 1991: 92). This highlights the constant tension within analytical chemistry applied to archaeology – the need to achieve the twin goals of high quality analytical science and high quality archaeological theory. A project can fail if either falls below the required standard.

Although chemical analysis of archaeological materials for purposes of identification and provenance is now well established, there are still many challenges ahead for the inorganic chemist in archaeology. The field of lead

322

isotope analysis, bogged down for so long in controversy, is now more than ripe for reinvigoration with the availability of high resolution, high throughput mass spectrometers (LA–MC–ICP–MS). Other heavy isotopes, such as strontium, are also being used to tackle previously intractable issues such as the provenance of glass, as well as to address the question of the provenancing of humans. Inorganic chemistry is, however, also at the heart of one of the major current challenges for archaeological science – understanding the factors which control the preservation or otherwise of archaeological materials, and in particular the need to be able to predict how the preservational status of a whole suite of archaeological materials (including buildings, inorganic, and organic artifacts) will change as a result of changing environmental conditions. Predicting the future of archaeological deposits is beginning to be a critical need.

If, historically, the majority of work in the field has been devoted to the analysis of inorganic materials, then the balance has shifted drastically towards organic analysis in the last 20 years or so. There have been two main foci of research – the chemical and isotopic study of human remains, and the extraction and identification of organic residues, principally in ceramics, but also in soils, and other contexts. The initial interest in human remains (principally bone, but also teeth, and, where it survives, soft tissue, hair, and nails) was for the reconstruction of diet from the stable isotope composition (δ^{13}C and δ^{15}N) of collagen, but quite quickly this became more sophisticated, using dietary variation as a proxy for other parameters such as status, nutrition, and mobility. Parallel research using the inorganic trace element composition of bone has fallen away somewhat because of difficulties due to post-mortem contamination. As with many scientific breakthroughs, initial results were spectacular (the identification of the spread of maize agriculture through North America), but subsequent progress has been more hard-won. Collagen, however, does not survive in most burial environments for more than a few tens of thousands of years. In order to extend the method backward in time, therefore, it became necessary to move from bone to teeth, and from the organic phase to the mineral phase. Using this approach, it has proved possible to begin to study the diets of some of our earliest ancestors in southern and eastern Africa.

The reconstruction of diet from carbon and nitrogen stable isotopes in bulk collagen can only give a long-term average of broad dietary balance. Some archaeological questions require more refined information – for example, the Mesolithic–Neolithic transition in western Europe appears to be accompanied by a complete withdrawal from the use of marine resources. Can this be true – what would be the impact on the dietary indicators of a small component (say, 20%) of marine protein? This desire for greater resolution has led some researchers to measure the isotopic composition of individual amino acids within the collagen. This has considerable potential, particularly bearing in mind that some amino acids, referred to as "essential", cannot be biosynthesized and are therefore incorporated into body tissue directly from the diet. As always, however, the story turns out to be more complicated than originally thought. Not all "non-essential" (i.e., biosynthesizable) amino acids are completely produced by biosynthesis – some are incorporated directly under certain circumstances. There are considerable uncertainties in the routing of dietary protein, lipids, and carbohydrates into bone protein amino acids. The techniques for the measurement of the isotopic ratios on individual amino acids are still being developed. Some researchers are also looking at other isotopes (δD and $\delta^{34}S$) in bone collagen, and also considering the potential of other bone biomolecules such as cholesterol to extend the technique. There will undoubtedly be no diminution of effort in this area over the next few years.

The second focus of research on organic materials has been the detection of trace residues from food and drink products in and on ceramics, and, more generally, in the identification of a wide variety of natural products (gums, waxes, resins, etc.) in a wide variety of archaeological contexts. Although the antecedents of this research go back to the 1970s, the explosion of remarkable findings over the last 20 years is due partly to the development of increasingly sensitive analytical techniques for biomolecular analysis, and also to the increasing willingness of archaeological chemists to look for trace remains of biological materials. Interpretative sophistication has increased significantly over this time – undoubtedly many of the early reports of the identification of residues would not now be sufficiently specific to be accepted. There have also been a number of controversies over the years – not least the identification or otherwise of blood residues on stone tools. Nevertheless, the development of biomolecular methods for archaeology has undoubtedly opened up a whole new field of research, which continues to produce a stream of influential findings.

This book set out to provide an introduction to the applications of analytical chemistry to archaeology. The intention was not, however, to provide a simple narrative of what has been done and what might be done. Specifically, it aimed to introduce advanced students of archaeology to some mainstream chemistry, in the hope that some, at least, would become sufficiently enthused by the possibilities that they would want to learn more. Ultimately, we hope they will become true archaeological chemists – students capable of dealing equally with the complexities of social behavior as evidenced by a very partial archaeological record, and the rigors of the chemistry laboratory.

It might be argued by some that this is overambitious. Can a student of archaeology with little if any recent formal training in the sciences really become a competent analytical scientist? In our experience, the answer, overwhelmingly, is yes. Not, obviously, in the same sense as one who has had years of formal training through the conventional route. But, by hard work and targeted learning, it is possible – indeed, we have seen it happen several times. Of course, a little learning can be a dangerous thing, and one of the prime requirements of a student who chooses to follow this path is a keen sense of self-criticism and the ability to recognize the limits of one's own knowledge. The first step on this path, of course, is to appreciate that simply reading a book such as this does not make one an archaeological chemist! It used to be argued that nobody could seriously learn enough geology and chemistry (or biology and chemistry) to become a geochemist – and yet it is now a totally accepted area of specialism. The trick is to become competent at the elements of both geology and chemistry that are relevant to the field. The same must be true of archaeological chemistry.

A common myth is that it is easier to teach a chemist enough archaeology to understand the issues than it is to teach an archaeologist to understand chemistry. This is nothing more than academic arrogance. Archaeology, although a subject of endless fascination to the general public, is a widely misunderstood academic discipline. It is not about things – these are merely sources of evidence. Nor is it solely about excavation – this is the data-recovery phase of archaeological research (important as this is, since the data includes contextual and environmental evidence crucial to the interpretation of the site). It is, as pointed out by Renfrew and Bahn (1996: 17) "concerned with the full range of past human experience," and this of necessity makes it an infinitely complex and fascinating subject. At a meeting in the British Museum some time ago, the technical difficulties associated with obtaining high quality radiocarbon dates for archaeological research were being discussed at length, largely by radiocarbon specialists. After some hours of intricate technical discussion, a patient but obviously irritated senior archaeologist stood up and said "Archaeology is difficult, too!" Stunned silence descended – clearly this was an aspect which had been lost sight of in the welter of technical detail. We must ensure that this lesson is not forgotten in archaeological chemistry.

APPENDIX I SCIENTIFIC NOTATION

Symbol	Prefix	Multiple	
T	tera-	10^{12}	1 000 000 000 000
G	giga-	10^{9}	1 000 000 000
M	mega-	10^{6}	1 000 000
k	kilo-	10^{3}	1 000
d	deci-	10^{-1}	0.1
c	centi-	10^{-2}	0.01
m	milli-	10^{-3}	0.001
μ	micro-	10^{-6}	0.000 001
n	nano-	10^{-9}	0.000 000 001
p	pico-	10^{-12}	0.000 000 000 001

APPENDIX II SIGNIFICANT FIGURES

The reliability of a piece of data is indicated by the number of digits used to represent it. Digits that result from measurement are written so that the last digit only is subject to uncertainty, e.g., four significant figures means that three are known and the last one is uncertain. Zeros within the number are significant, and a zero at the end of a number, if included, is counted as a significant figure.

The following rules apply:

Addition and subtraction: the answer should have the same number of decimal places as the quantity with the fewest number of decimal places.

Multiplication and division: the answer should not contain a greater number of significant figures than the number in the least precise measurement.

Rounding: when rounding, examine the number to the right of the number that is to be the last. Round up if this number is >5, round down if <5. If the last number is equal to 5 then round up if the resulting number is even, if odd then round down. For example, 5.678 becomes 5.68 to 3 significant figures, but 5.673 becomes 5.67. 5.675 becomes 5.68, but 5.665 becomes 5.66.

APPENDIX III SEVEN BASIC SI UNITS

Physical quantity	Name	Symbol
Length	meter	m
Time	second	s
Mass	kilogram	kg
Electric current	ampere	A
Temperature	kelvin	K
Luminous intensity	candela	cd
Amount of substance	mole	mol

APPENDIX IV PHYSICAL CONSTANTS

Symbol	Quantity	Value and units
g	gravitational constant	6.672×10^{-11} N m^2 kg^{-2}
c	speed of light in a vacuum	2.997925×10^8 m s^{-1}
h	Planck constant	6.626176×10^{-34} J s
e	charge on the electron	1.602189×10^{-19} C
m_e	mass of the electron	9.109534×10^{-31} kg
m_n	mass of the neutron	1.674954×10^{-27} kg
m_p	mass of the proton	1.672648×10^{-27} kg
eV	electron volt	1.602×10^{-19} J
N_A (L)	Avogadro constant	6.022045×10^{23} mol^{-1}
k	Boltzmann constant	1.380662×10^{-23} J K^{-1}
π	pi	3.1415927
Ci	curie	3.7×10^{10} s^{-1}
R_H	Rydberg constant	109 678 cm^{-1}

APPENDIX V GREEK NOTATION

Lower case symbol	Upper case symbol	Name	Example of scientific use
α	A	alpha	α-particles
β	B	beta	β-particles
γ	Γ	gamma	γ-rays
δ	Δ	delta	charge separation, isotopic ratios, change
ε	E	epsilon	
ζ	Z	zeta	
η	H	eta	
θ	Θ	theta	diffraction angle
ι	I	iota	
κ	K	kappa	
λ	Λ	lambda	wavelength, decay constant of radioactive nucleus
μ	M	mu	micro (10^{-6})
ν	N	nu	frequency
ξ	Ξ	xi	
o	O	omicron	
π	Π	pi	$3.14\ldots$, π-bond
ρ	P	rho	density
σ	Σ	sigma	summation, σ-bond
τ	T	tau	mean lifetime of radioactive element
υ	Υ	upsilon	
ϕ	Φ	phi	work function
χ	X	chi	electronegativity
ψ	Ψ	psi	electron density function
ω	Ω	omega	resistance

330

APPENDIX VI CHEMICAL SYMBOLS
AND ISOTOPES OF THE ELEMENTS

Name	Symbol	Atomic number	Atomic mass	Naturally occurring isotopes[1]	Radioactive isotopes
Actinium	Ac	89	227.0278	227	224–229
Aluminum	Al	13	26.98154	27	24,25,26,28,29,30
Americium	Am	95	243.0614	243	237–245
Antimony	Sb	51	121.75	121,123	117,118,119,120, 122,124,125,126, 127,128,129
Argon	Ar	18	39.948	36,38,40	35,37,39,41,42,43,44
Arsenic	As	33	74.92159	75	68,69,70,71,72,73,74, 76,77,78,79
Astatine	At	85	209.9871	-	207–211
Barium	Ba	56	137.327	130,132,134,135, 136,137,138	128,129,131,133, 139,140
Berkelium	Bk	97	247.0703	-	245–250
Beryllium	Be	4	9.012182	9	6,7,8,10,11,12,13
Bismuth	Bi	83	208.9804	209	205,206,207,208,210
Bohrium	Bh	107	262.1229	-	260–267
Boron	B	5	10.811	10,11	8,9,12,13
Bromine	Br	35	79.904	79,81	72,73,74,75,76,77, 78,80,82,83,84,85
Cadmium	Cd	48	112.411	106,108,110,111, 112,113,114,116	107,109,115,117
Calcium	Ca	20	40.078	40,42,43,44,46,48	41,45,47,49,50,51,52
Californium	Cf	98	251.0796	-	248–255
Carbon	C	6	12.011	12,13	9,10,11,14,15,16,17
Cerium	Ce	58	140.115	136,138,140,142	134,135,137,139,141, 143,144
Caesium	Cs	55	132.9054	133	129,130,131,132,134, 135,136,137
Chlorine	Cl	17	35.4527	35,37	36,38,39,40,41,42,43
Chromium	Cr	24	51.9961	50,52,53,54	48,49,51,55,56
Cobalt	Co	27	58.9332	59	55,56,57,58,60,61,62
Copper	Cu	29	63.546	63,65	59,60,61,62,64,66,67, 68,69
Curium	Cm	96	247.0703	-	240–250
Darmstadtium	Ds	110	ca. 271	-	267–273,280,281

Appendix VI *(Cont.)*

Name	Symbol	Atomic number	Atomic mass	Naturally occurring isotopes[1]	Radioactive isotopes
Dubnium	Db	105	262.1138	-	255–263
Dysprosium	Dy	66	162.5	156,158,160,161, 162,163,164	152,153,154,155,147, 159,165,166
Einsteinium	Es	99	252.0829	-	249–255
Erbium	Er	68	167.26	162,164,166,167, 168,170	160,161,163,165,169, 171,172
Europium	Eu	63	151.965	151,153	145,146,147,148, 149,150,152,154, 155,156
Fermium	Fm	100	257.0951	-	251–257
Fluorine	F	9	18.9984	19	17,18,20,21,22,23
Francium	Fr	87	223.0197	-	210–227
Gadolinium	Gd	64	157.25	152,154,155,156, 157,158,160	146,147,148,149,150, 151,153,159
Gallium	Ga	31	69.723	69,71	64,65,66,67,68,70,72, 73,74,75
Germanium	Ge	32	72.61	70,72,73,74,76	64,65,66,67,68,69,71, 75,77,78
Gold	Au	79	196.9665	197	194,195,196,198,199
Hafnium	Hf	72	178.49	174,176,177,178, 179,180	172,173,175,181,182
Hassium	Hs	108	ca. 265	-	263–269
Helium	He	2	4.002602	3,4	6,8
Holmium	Ho	67	164.9303	165	161,162,163,164,166,167
Hydrogen	H	1	1.00794	1,2	3
Indium	In	49	114.82	113,115	109,110,111,112,114
Iodine	I	53	126.9045	127	120–126,128–135
Iridium	Ir	77	192.22	191,193	188,189,190,192
Iron	Fe	26	55.847	54,56,57,58	52,53,55,59,60,61,62
Krypton	Kr	36	83.8	78,80,82,83,84,86	74,75,76,77,79,81,85, 87,88,89
Lanthanum	La	57	138.9055	138,139	132,133,134,135,136, 137,140,141,142
Lawrencium	Lr	103	260.1053	-	255–262
Lead	Pb	82	207.2	204,206,207,208	200,201,202,203,205, 210,211,212
Lithium	Li	3	6.941	6,7	8,9,11
Lutetium	Lu	71	174.967	175,176	169,170,171,172,173, 174,177
Magnesium	Mg	12	24.305	24,25,26	22,23,27,28,29
Manganese	Mn	25	54.93805	55	51,52,53,54,56,57
Meitnerium	Mt	109	ca. 268	-	265–271
Mendelevium	Md	101	258.0986	-	255–260
Mercury	Hg	80	200.59	196,198,199,200, 201,202,204	194,195,197,203

Name	Symbol	Atomic number	Atomic mass	Naturally occurring isotopes[1]	Radioactive isotopes
Molybdenum	Mo	42	95.94	92,94,95,96,97,98,100	90,91,93,99
Neodymium	Nd	60	144.24	142,143,144,145, 146,148,150	138,139,140,141, 147,149
Neon	Ne	10	20.1797	20,21,22	18,19,23,24,25
Neptunium	Np	93	237.0482	-	234–239
Nickel	Ni	28	58.69	58,60,61,62,64	56,57,59,63,65,66
Niobium	Nb	41	92.90638	93	89,90,91,92,94,95,96,97
Nitrogen	N	7	14.00674	14,15	12,13,16,17,18,19,20
Nobelium	No	102	259.1009	-	253–259
Osmium	Os	76	190.2	184,186,187,188, 189,190,192	182,183,185,191,193,194
Oxygen	O	8	15.9994	16,17,18	14,15,19,20,21,22
Palladium	Pd	46	106.42	102,104,105, 106,108,110	100,101,103,107,109, 111,112
Phosphorus	P	15	30.97376	31	29,30,32,33
Platinum	Pt	78	195.08	190,192,194, 195,196,198	191,193,197
Plutonium	Pu	94	244.0642	-	236–246
Polonium	Po	84	208.9824	-	206–210
Potassium	K	19	39.0983	39,40,41	37,38,40,42,43,44,45, 46,47,48,49
Praseodymium	Pr	59	140.9077	141	137,138,139,140,142, 143,144,145
Promethium	Pm	61	146.9151	-	143–151
Protactinium	Pa	91	231.0359	-	228–234
Radium	Ra	88	226.0254	-	223–228
Radon	Rn	86	222.0176	-	210–222
Rhenium	Re	75	186.207	185,187	182,183,184,186,188,189
Rhodium	Rh	45	102.9055	103	99,100,101,102,104,105
Roentgenium	Rg	111	ca. 272	-	272,279,280
Rubidium	Rb	37	85.4678	85,87	81,82,83,84,86,87
Ruthenium	Ru	44	101.07	96,98,99,100, 101,102,104	95,97,103,105,106
Rutherfordium	Rf	104	261.1087	-	255–263
Samarium	Sm	62	150.36	144,147,148, 149,150,152,154	145,146,151,153,155,156
Scandium	Sc	21	44.95591	45	43,44,46,47,48,49,50
Seaborgium	Sg	106	263.1182	-	258–266
Selenium	Se	34	78.96	74,76,77,78, 80,82	70,71,72,73,75,79,81,83,84
Silicon	Si	14	28.0855	28,29,30	26,27,31,32,33,34
Silver	Ag	47	107.8682	107,109	103,104,105,106,108,110, 111,112,113
Sodium	Na	11	22.98977	23	21,22,24,25,26

Appendix VI *(Cont.)*

Name	Symbol	Atomic number	Atomic mass	Naturally occurring isotopes[1]	Radioactive isotopes
Strontium	Sr	38	87.62	84,86,87,88	80,81,82,83,85,89,90,91,92
Sulfur	S	16	32.066	32,33,34,36	30,31,35,37,38,39,40
Tantalum	Ta	73	180.9479	180,181	177,178,179,180,182,183
Technetium	Tc	43	98.9063	-	93–99
Tellurium	Te	52	127.6	120,122,123,124, 125,126,128,130	116,117,118,119, 121,127,129
Terbium	Tb	65	158.9253	159	153,154,155,156,157, 158,160,161
Thallium	Tl	81	204.3833	203,205	200,201,202,204
Thorium	Th	90	232.0381	232	227–234
Thulium	Tm	69	168.9342	169	165,166,167,168, 170,171,172
Tin	Sn	50	118.71	112,114,115,116,117,118, 119,120,122,124	110,111,113,121,123, 125,126,127
Titanium	Ti	22	47.88	46,47,48,49,50	44,45,51,52
Tungsten	W	74	183.85	180,182,183,184,186	178,179,181,185,187,188
Ununbium	Uub	112	ca. 285	-	277,283,284,285
Uranium	U	92	238.0289	234,235,238	230–238
Vanadium	V	23	50.9415	50,51	47,48,49,52,53
Xenon	Xe	54	131.29	124,126,128,129,130, 131,132,134,136	122,123,125,127,133,135
Ytterbium	Yb	70	173.04	168,170,171,172, 173,174,176	166,167,169,175,177
Yttrium	Y	39	88.90585	89	85,86,87,88,90,91,92,93
Zinc	Zn	30	65.39	64,66,67,68,70	60,61,62,63,65,69,71,72
Zirconium	Zr	40	91.224	90,91,92,94,96	86,87,88,89,93,95,96,97

[1]Note. Not all naturally occurring isotopes are stable – some are radioactive but with long half-lives. See (for example) WebElements [http://www.webelements.com/webelements/index. html] for abundance ratios of naturally occurring isotopes and half-lives of radioisotopes.

APPENDIX VII ELECTRONIC CONFIGURATION OF THE ELEMENTS (TO RADON, Z = 86)

Z	Element	Symbol	n 1 / l s	2 s	2 p	3 s	3 p	3 d	4 s	4 p	4 d	4 f	5 s	5 p	5 d	5 f	6 s	6 p
1	Hydrogen	H	1															
2	**Helium**	**He**	**2**															
3	Lithium	Li	[He]	1														
4	Beryllium	Be	[He]	2														
5	Boron	B	[He]	2	1													
6	Carbon	C	[He]	2	2													
7	Nitrogen	N	[He]	2	3													
8	Oxygen	O	[He]	2	4													
9	Fluorine	F	[He]	2	5													
10	**Neon**	**Ne**	**2**	**2**	**6**													
11	Sodium	Na			[Ne]	1												
12	Magnesium	Mg			[Ne]	2												
13	Aluminum	Al			[Ne]	2	1											
14	Silicon	Si			[Ne]	2	2											
15	Phosphorus	P			[Ne]	2	3											
16	Sulfur	S			[Ne]	2	4											
17	Chlorine	Cl			[Ne]	2	5											
18	**Argon**	**Ar**	**2**	**2**	**6**	**2**	**6**											
19	Potassium	K					[Ar]		1									
20	Calcium	Ca					[Ar]		2									
21	Scandium	Sc					[Ar]	1	2									
22	Titanium	Ti					[Ar]	2	2									
23	Vanadium	V					[Ar]	3	2									
24	Chromium	Cr					[Ar]	5	1									
25	Manganese	Mn					[Ar]	5	2									
26	Iron	Fe					[Ar]	6	2									
27	Cobalt	Co					[Ar]	7	2									
28	Nickel	Ni					[Ar]	8	2									
29	Copper	Cu					[Ar]	10	1									
30	Zinc	Zn					[Ar]	10	2									
31	Gallium	Ga					[Ar]	10	2	1								
32	Germanium	Ge					[Ar]	10	2	2								
33	Arsenic	As					[Ar]	10	2	3								
34	Selenium	Se					[Ar]	10	2	4								
35	Bromine	Br					[Ar]	10	2	5								
36	**Krypton**	**Kr**	**2**	**2**	**6**	**2**	**6**	**10**	**2**	**6**								
37	Rubidium	Rb								[Kr]			1					
38	Strontium	Sr								[Kr]			2					
39	Yttrium	Y								[Kr]	1		2					
40	Zirconium	Zr								[Kr]	2		2					
41	Niobium	Nb								[Kr]	4		1					
42	Molybdenum	Mo								[Kr]	5		1					

335

Appendix VII (*Cont.*)

Z	Element	Symbol	n	1	2	2	3	3	3	4	4	4	4	5	5	5	5	6	6
			l	s	s	p	s	p	d	s	p	d	f	s	p	d	f	s	p
43	Technetium	Tc									[Kr]	5		2					
44	Ruthenium	Ru									[Kr]	7		1					
45	Rhodium	Rh									[Kr]	8		1					
46	Palladium	Pd									[Kr]	10							
47	Silver	Ag									[Kr]	10		1					
48	Cadmium	Cd									[Kr]	10		2					
49	Indium	In									[Kr]	10		2	1				
50	Tin	Sn									[Kr]	10		2	2				
51	Antimony	Sb									[Kr]	10		2	3				
52	Tellurium	Te									[Kr]	10		2	4				
53	Iodine	I									[Kr]	10		2	5				
54	**Xenon**	**Xe**		2	2	6	2	6	10	2	6	10		2	6				
55	Caesium	Cs													[Xe]			1	
56	Barium	Ba													[Xe]			2	
57	Lanthanum	La													[Xe]	1		2	
58	Cerium	Ce											1		[Xe]	1		2	
59	Praseodymium	Pr											3		[Xe]			2	
60	Neodymium	Nd											4		[Xe]			2	
61	Promethium	Pm											5		[Xe]			2	
62	Samarium	Sm											6		[Xe]			2	
63	Europium	Eu											7		[Xe]			2	
64	Gadolinium	Gd											7		[Xe]	1		2	
65	Terbium	Tb											9		[Xe]			2	
66	Dysprosium	Dy											10		[Xe]			2	
67	Holmium	Ho											11		[Xe]			2	
68	Erbium	Er											12		[Xe]			2	
69	Thulium	Tm											13		[Xe]			2	
70	Ytterbium	Yb											14		[Xe]			2	
71	Lutetium	Lu											14		[Xe]	1		2	
72	Hafnium	Hf											14		[Xe]	2		2	
73	Tantalum	Ta											14		[Xe]	3		2	
74	Tungsten	W											14		[Xe]	4		2	
75	Rhenium	Re											14		[Xe]	5		2	
76	Osmium	Os											14		[Xe]	6		2	
77	Iridium	Ir											14		[Xe]	7		2	
78	Platinum	Pt											14		[Xe]	9		1	
79	Gold	Au											14		[Xe]	10		1	
80	Mercury	Hg											14		[Xe]	10		2	
81	Thallium	Tl											14		[Xe]	10		2	1
82	Lead	Pb											14		[Xe]	10		2	2
83	Bismuth	Bi											14		[Xe]	10		2	3
84	Polonium	Po											14		[Xe]	10		2	4
85	Astatine	At											14		[Xe]	10		2	5
86	**Radon**	**Ra**											14		[Xe]	10		2	6

APPENDIX VIII SOME COMMON INORGANIC AND ORGANIC SAMPLE PREPARATION METHODS USED IN ARCHAEOLOGY

This appendix describes briefly the dissolution procedures for some of the more common inorganic sample types. The use of an internal standard is discussed in Section 13.3.

Acidification for the preparation of water samples
Water samples are amongst the simplest to prepare, simply requiring acidification to keep the sample elements in solution and to matrix-match with the calibration solutions, and the addition of an internal standard. The procedure is as follows.

- Centrifugation or filtration to remove suspended particles
- Add 2 ml of super purity acid (SPA) (or equivalent) nitric acid
- Add internal standard
- Make up to 100 ml in volumetric flask.

Open vessel digestion (HNO_3) for bones, teeth, hair, and soil
This is a standard preparation for most organic samples. In the case of soils, nitric acid will not fully dissolve all of the sample, but this method is sufficient to examine the total *"available"* elements.

- Accurately weigh c. 0.1g of finely powdered sample in Teflon beaker
- Add 2 ml of SPA nitric acid
- Heat gently until digested
- Allow to cool
- Add internal standard
- Make up to 100 ml in volumetric flask.

Open vessel digestion ($HF:HClO_4$) for ceramics, glass, rocks, and soil
These acids should completely dissolve most materials. HF removes the silica (as volatile SiF_4), which reduces the total dissolved solid content and therefore reduces interferences, and ClO_4^- produces perchlorates, which are soluble (but explosive if dried out). The use of hydrofluoric and perchloric acids therefore has considerable safety risks and requires specialized fume hoods, handling equipment, and safety equipment. The hydrofluoric and perchloric acids are removed by a later evaporation stage unless the analytical instrument and safety considerations have been specially adapted.

- Accurately weigh c. 0.1 g of finely powdered sample in a Teflon beaker
- Add 4 ml of 2:1 mixture of SPA hydrofluoric and perchloric acids

- Heat gently until evaporated to dryness (three to four hours)
- Allow to cool
- Add 2 ml of SPA nitric acid then a few ml of deionized water and warm until all solids dissolved
- Allow to cool
- Add internal standard
- Make up to 100 ml in volumetric flask.

Closed vessel microwave digestion for bones, teeth, hair, and soil

Specially designed closed pressurized Teflon vessels may be used for microwave digestion. Teflon is transparent to microwaves, which enhances the effect of the acids by raising the temperature and pressure within the vessel. In addition the closed vessels will retain any volatile components (e.g., Si) in solution. It must, however, be emphasized that any sealed vessels must only be heated if they have been designed for the purpose. Examples of applications include Kingston and Walter (1992), Baldwin *et al.* (1994), Sheppard *et al.* (1994), and Tamba *et al.* (1994).

- Accurately weigh c. 0.1g of finely powdered sample into microwave-designed sealed Teflon beaker
- Add 2 ml of SPA nitric acid
- Microwave program
- Allow to cool
- Add internal standard
- Make up to 100 ml in volumetric flask.

Lithium metaborate (LiBO$_2$) fusion for glass, rocks, and soils.

This fusion method produces an acid-soluble glass bead which is dissolved in nitric acid. It avoids the use of hydrofluoric and perchloric acids. The disadvantages are the cost of platinum labware, and the large quantities of LiBO$_2$ used to produce the glass bead increase the total dissolved solids and may contribute to polyatomic species. Dilution to counter these effects may reduce the elements of interest below the instrumental detection limits.

- Accurately weigh c. 0.1 g powdered sample and c. 0.5 g anhydrous lithium metaborate in platinum, graphite, or pure aluminum oxide crucible, and mix (platinum rod)
- Fuse at 1100°C for 30 min.
- Allow to cool, then pour into 40 ml 2% SPA nitric acid
- Make up to 100 ml.

An outline sampling procedure for organic residues

- Have a prepared "sampling kit" – solvent cleaned glass vials, tweezers, spatulas, scalpels, nitrile gloves, aluminium foil, sticky labels, and pens. Once cleaned, wrap the vials, etc., in a strip of the foil, both to keep them clean and to identify them as such.
- Avoid anything plastic, including para-film and plastic sample bags. If zip-loc sample bags are used, then wrap the sample in aluminum foil first.

- Avoid contamination by modern high lipid samples, e.g., keep ancient samples separate from modern samples (store and post separately) and avoid contact with other sources of oil (lunch, car engines, cigars, etc.!) whilst sampling.
- Use solvent cleaned spatula, scalpel, or tweezers to put the residue in a glass vial.
- Work over a fresh sheet of aluminium foil to catch any "escapee" sample.
- Solvent clean the spatula between samples to avoid cross contamination.
- If possible, avoid handling the ceramic shard (and especially the area to be sampled). Wear nitrile gloves or use tweezers. Washing hands before sampling will also reduce the potential of contamination by skin lipids.
- If there are different colored residues on different areas of the shard, e.g., the interior compared to the exterior, sample and label separately.

APPENDIX IX GENERAL SAFE PRACTICE IN THE LABORATORY

There are a few underlying principles which, if understood, will reduce the majority, if not all, of a long list of "dos and don'ts" to common sense.

- Consider in advance the work to be undertaken – plan what is needed in terms of chemicals, glassware, movement about the laboratory, and specific training. Include a plan for what to do in the event of something going wrong.
- Consider the risks – are they covered by general good laboratory practice, or are more rigorous controls necessary (e.g., COSHH)?
- Check that you fully understand what you are about to do, and, if not, ask for help. An experienced worker will not complain if asked for instruction, or to observe as you carry out a procedure for the first time (but they will if you injure yourself, others, or cause damage).
- A relaxed atmosphere in a laboratory with lots of activity is a productive and enjoyable place to work, but there is a distinction between this and an environment which is so untidy as to be dangerous. An untidy laboratory is also likely to lead to increased levels of contamination.
- Never work alone, or out of earshot of somebody else. Always work during normal office hours, unless special arrangements have been made for you to be accompanied.
- Take responsibility for your own safety and of those around you. Be aware of all the work taking place in the lab, and warn others immediately if you see something you consider to be dangerous. Breakages and breakdowns of equipment occur regularly in laboratories. Embarrassing as this may be, if you are the cause, do not walk away leaving a hazard for somebody else to find.
- Many chemicals are toxic, and very often their main route into the body is via the mouth. Therefore smoking, eating, and drinking are not allowed in laboratories. Pipetting solutions by mouth is forbidden. Washing hands with soap and water when leaving the laboratory is good practice.
- To protect the body, and especially the eyes, from splashes of chemicals or flying glass, buttoned up laboratory coats and safety glasses should be worn at all times. This includes times when you personally are not working with chemicals, as there may be a hazard from someone else. Ordinary spectacles do not provide the same protection as safety glasses, as they do not cover the side of the eye, and goggles should be worn over them. Ordinary clothing also provides some protection, so open-toed shoes, shorts, or similar clothing should never be worn. Loose clothes, dangling earrings, scarves, etc. must be avoided, and long hair should be tied back.
- Although it may appear cool to have the dirtiest and tattiest lab coat, it provides little protection and may be a source of contamination. Laboratory coats should not be worn outside the laboratory. Personal protection equipment, such as gloves and safety glasses, should not be removed from the lab.
- Always test that fume cupboards and other pieces of equipment are working before using them. Also check gloves (inflate and check for leaks) before use.
- Chemicals must always be handled in a safe manner. Do not pick up by the lid or the neck, as this is the weakest point. Always use specialist holders or trolleys for transporting chemicals.

340

- In addition to being harmful to the individual, many chemicals are hazardous to the environment, so waste chemicals must not be put down the sink or into the rubbish bins unless this is stated to be safe. Waste solvent and reagents must be put into appropriate waste bottles. Chlorinated and nonchlorinated solvents are usually kept separately and then sent for disposal by external contractors. Broken glass or needles and scalpels are to be disposed of in "sharps" containers.
- All used glassware must be rinsed and left to dry at the end of the experiment. Do not leave any dirty glassware or any glassware containing unidentified substances for others to remove. If chemicals are left, identify what they are and who is responsible for them, and write on the date.
- There should be established emergency procedures for dealing with spillage or uncontrolled release, including the use of absorbing sand, calcium carbonate for acid spill, or washing to drain using excess water. (Small spillages may be treated differently from large spillages.)
- Laboratory fire procedures must be understood by all in the laboratory. Fires may be extinguished using carbon dioxide, water, or foam fire extinguishers, but it is critical that the right extinguisher is used in each situation.
- For personal exposure, treatment will vary for inhalation, eyes, skin, or ingestion etc., and the appropriate procedures should be known by all in the lab. Some chemicals require special equipment to be on hand, such as HF antidote, and it may be necessary to warn the local hospital that certain chemicals are being used.
- All laboratory personnel should know the correct shutdown procedure for lab equipment, in the event of the operator being rendered incapable.

APPENDIX X COSHH ASSESSMENTS

Step 1 Assess the risks

A COSHH form may be completed for each chemical used, but the easiest method is to complete a form for an entire procedure, which includes details of all the substances used and formed (and their quantities) during the experiment. An assessment should include the title and aim of the work, and location of the work, and name the personnel involved (including their status and experience). The hazard description (e.g., explosive, oxidizing, etc.) and occupational exposure standard, maximum exposure limit, or similar occupational exposure limit should be listed for all substances. For archaeological material, it is also necessary to include an assessment of the samples themselves; for example, dust from a lead coffin may be hazardous. More recently, biological hazards have been included in the COSHH regulations. For archaeologists, this means that an assessment has to be made of the hazards of exposure to soil, which may be contaminated by animal fecal material, fungal spores, bacteria, and viruses. It is necessary to consider what microorganisms might be present, the possible route of infection, virulence, transmissibility, and whether it is active via a toxin or gives rise to an allergy. Some groups of people may be more sensitive to exposure than others (e.g., pregnant women, immuno suppressed, diabetics, etc.). Some chemicals also lead to enhanced sensitivity with extended exposure. The hazards associated with a chemical will be identified by the chemical supplier on material safety data sheets (MSDS). Hazard information can also be obtained from online databases (e.g., http://physchem.ox.ac.uk/MSDS/) or published sources (Weiss 1980, Clydesdale 1990). These sources will also include information concerning safe disposal and emergency procedures. Any biological material must be correctly disposed of. A reference list of the information sources used should be included in the assessment (e.g., attach any hazard data sheets to the form). All COSHH forms should be accessibly stored in the lab, as well as included in the worker's lab notebook.

Step 2 Decide what precautions are needed

The description of the method to be used should include details of all practical precautions which will be taken to limit risk, such as the need for ventilation, minimization of inhalation of particulates or aerosols, using fume cupboards or safety screens, and wearing gloves, laboratory coat, and safety spectacles. Handling procedures, packaging for transit, and disposal of unused reactants or products all need to be considered.

Step 3 Prevent or adequately control exposure

Are there any alternative chemicals which can be used to eliminate hazards (e.g., the use of lithium metaborate fusion rather than hydrofluoric acid as a dissolution procedure)? The protocol should include details of any required checks on the control measures to be adopted, and their frequency (e.g., cleaning of protective clothing, washing down of fume cupboards).

Step 4 Ensure that control measures are used and maintained

It is the responsibility of the employer to ensure that control measures are properly applied, and that all equipment is maintained in working order. For a procedure which is carried out repeatedly, it is necessary to carry out regular reassessment, usually on a yearly basis. This prevents laboratory workers from becoming complacent, and methods may change, quantities may increase, etc.

Step 5 Monitor the exposure

It may be necessary to monitor the environment within the laboratory (e.g., a low oxygen alarm, to warn if the air in a room is becoming oxygen-starved). Separate regulations govern the use of certain classes of material, such as radiochemicals and biological hazards.

Step 6 Carry out appropriate health surveillance

Where assessment shows this to be necessary, or where COSHH sets specific requirements, regular medical checks, such as blood lead levels, might be needed.

Step 7 Prepare plans and procedures to deal with accidents, incidents, and emergencies

These should be written down, and the procedures and equipment tested at regular intervals.

Step 8 Ensure employees are properly informed, trained, and supervised.

The COSHH process also requires details of any specific training requirements that might be necessary to carry out a particular procedure (e.g., safe handling of HF). Such training should be documented, as well as the details of any specific supervisory arrangements.

Procedure no longer in use	ASSESSMENT REFERENCE CODE
Signed:	. . . .
Date:	**Review Date:** *12 months from current date* Procedure NOT to be used if date expired

ASSESSMENT OF HEALTH RISK ASSOCIATED WITH A PROPOSED SCHEME OF WORK

TITLE OF WORK

Control of Substances Hazardous to Health (COSHH) Regulations

BIOLOGICAL AND CHEMICAL

A signed copy of this form should be available at the location of the work and a copy filed centrally.

SECTION A

Department:
Location of work: *Building and room number(s)*
Personnel involved (including status) in proposed work:
*Names of **all** those who will be doing the work, and status (e.g. UG student). Include supervisor's name if appropriate*
Title of proposed work:
Overall title of the procedure you will be carrying out (same as on front cover)
Aim of the work:
Aim of the procedure you will be carrying out

New experiment procedure Y/N	Established Experiment/procedure Y/N
Established by whom: *Give reference*	When:

CHEMICAL AGENTS			Hazard (CHIP descriptions)												Quantities (numerical value)	
Substances used or formed during experiment	Substance code (CAS#)	Form	Explosive	Oxidising	Extremely flammable	Highly flammable	Very toxic	Toxic	Carcinogen	Mutagen	Harmful	Corrosive	Irritant	Dangerous for the environment	OES	Amounts used
List separately each substance used or formed. Include the risks associated with the use of combined or sequential exposure. Also list any hazards from your samples (e.g. lead, dust)	*CAS number (look up on hazard data sheet)*	*e.g. Solid Liquid Gas Dust Mist Fume*	*Tick each hazard*												*The Occupational Exposure Standard, maximum exposure limit, or similar occupational exposure limit (mg/m^3)*	*The amounts per sample, the number of samples and therefore the total amount to be used (mg, g, kg, mL, L)*

BIOLOGICAL AGENTS			Quantities (numerical value)
	Hazard	Hazard Group	Max volume to be handled
Nature of the specimen to be used (include direct work and indirect exposure (e.g. agriculture)) *What micro-organisms might be present? Names of the organisms to be used: e.g. Staphylococcus aureus* *Nature of biological risk: e.g. potential contamination of soil by animal faeces*	*Route of infection for the micro-organisms, virulence, transmissibility. Is it active via a toxin or does it give rise to an allergy?*		*Quantities to be used. In general there will not be a dose relationship, but consideration should be made to replication and infection.*

Information sources used:
References. It is also useful to photocopy and attach the chemical data sheets and any other relevant information to the back of this form.

Anticipated frequency of the work (and duration of exposure): *e.g. Daily (3 hrs), Weekly, Monthly, Once only*

PROCEDURE:

Give exact practical details of the proposed procedure (use separate sheets if necessary). You should include any practical tips/hints gained through personal experience.

Ensure that Good Laboratory Practice is adhered to.

Ensure the personal protective equipment outlined under control measures on page 4 of this assessment is worn and that instructions are adhered to.

Are quantities and dilutions described above as well as Good Laboratory Practice sufficient to negate any risk to health ? *(YES or NO)*

- If the answer to the above is '**YES**' then no further assessment under COSHH is necessary. However, it is considered Good Practice to complete this assessment form.
- If the answer to the above is '**NO**' then complete the whole form, then sign and pass to appropriate supervisor.

Are there less hazardous alternatives available - *YES* or *NO*. If '**YES**', give reason for not using:

Control measures to be adopted

e.g. Informing named staff. Ventilation. Using fume cupboard, gloves, safety screen. (Laboratory coat and safety spectacles as for good laboratory practice.)

Biological risk: Containment, location of work, i.e. does this need level 2? Do these samples need to be opened in a cabinet?

Biological risk: Mitigation of risk: handling procedures, packaging for transit, minimization of inhalation of particulates or aerosols.

Required checks and their frequency, on the adequacy and maintenance of control measures during the course of the experiment/procedure:

e.g. Gloves checked for leaks before use. Fume cupboard flow checked before use. Checking apparatus every hour. Cleaning of protective clothing, fume cupboards, etc.

Is health surveillance necessary? (See A.C.O.P.) *YES or NO*

If '**YES**' state type and send copy to University Health Service:

SECTION B

Additional relevant information. Including other hazards not covered by COSHH regulations:
e.g. Flammability, explosion, asphyxiant, high or low pressure, noise, heat, cold, radiation.
Arrival into department, handling and (secure?) storage.
The need to protect individuals who may be at increased risk (e.g. pregnancy, asthma, dermatitis). Display of warning signs.
Lead and asbestos are covered by separate legislation which must be adhered to.

SECTION C

Disposal procedures during and at the end of proposed work.
*In detail: how to **routinely** dispose of any starting materials (e.g. unused chemicals), end products. This is **not** emergency procedure.*
Biological risk: need to correctly identify correct waste route, who is going to see that the waste goes through the whole process (i.e. marked bag for disposal is not sufficient).

SECTION D: EMERGENCY PROCEDURES

Spillage/uncontrolled release:
Action to be taken. Include references where appropriate.
Chemical or infectious material
e.g. Absorb using sand, calcium carbonate. Wash to drain using excess water. Small spillages may be treated differently from large spillages.
Fire:
Action to be taken. Include references where appropriate.
e.g. Carbon dioxide, water, foam fire extinguisher – include which NOT to use.

Personnel exposure - Treatment to be adopted:
Action to be taken. Include references where appropriate.
Detailed treatment for each (they may be different for each route):
skin contact and absorption
eye contact
breathing fumes or vapours
ingestion (e.g. swallowing liquids/solids)
Removal of contaminated clothing, Seek medical attention

Shutdown procedure for equipment/machinery etc.
e.g. Reference to handbook/instruction manual.

Emergency contact: Telephone number:

Security Ext.

HOME: *XXX*   WORK: *XXX*

Name of assessor: *Your name*   Co-ordinator/compiler/recorder of COSHH

Status: . . . .   assessments

Signed: . . . .

Date:. . . . .   Signed: . . . .

Date:. . . . .

SECTION E

Re-assessment to be carried out at *as on front cover* monthly intervals. Or when no longer valid due to significant change or the results of engineering tests, exposure, health surveillance, or complaints.

Assessor	Date	Signed (Co-ordinator/compiler/ recorder):	Date	Comments

REFERENCES

Abraham, M. H., Grime, G. W., Marsh, M. A., and Northover, J. P. (2001). The study of thick corrosion layers on archaeological metals using controlled laser ablation in conjunction with an external beam microprobe. *Nuclear Instruments and Methods in Physics Research B* **181** 688–692.

Ahuja, S. (2003). *Chromatography and Separation Science*. Amsterdam, Academic Press.

Aitchison, J. (1986). *The Statistical Analysis of Compositional Data*. London, Chapman and Hall.

Aitken, M. J. (1990). *Scientific Dating Techniques in Archaeology*. London, Longman.

Akesson, K., Grynpas, M. D., Hancock, R. G. V., Odselius, R., and Obrant, K. J. (1994). Energy-dispersive X-ray-microanalysis of the bone mineral content in human trabecular bone – a comparison with ICP-ES and neutron-activation analysis. *Calcified Tissue International* **55** 236–239.

Alfassi, Z. B. (ed.) (1990). *Activation Analysis*. 2 vols. Boca Raton, CRC Press.

Allen, R. O. (ed.) (1989). *Archaeological Chemistry IV*. Advances in Chemistry Series 220, Washington, DC, American Chemical Society.

Allen, R. O., Rogers, M. S., Mitchell, R. S., and Hoffman, M. A. (1982). A geochemical approach to the understanding of ceramic technology in Predynastic Egypt. *Archaeometry* **24** 199–212.

Allred, A. L. and Rochow, E. G. (1958). A scale of electronegativity based on electrostatic force. *Journal of Inorganic and Nuclear Chemistry* **5** 264–268.

Al-Saad, Z. (2000). Technology and provenance of a collection of Islamic copper-based objects as found by chemical and lead isotope analysis. *Archaeometry* **42** 385–397.

Al-Saad, Z. (2002) Chemical composition and manufacturing technology of a collection of various types of Islamic glazes excavated from Jordan. *Journal of Archaeological Science* **29** 803–810.

Ambrose, S. H. (1990). Preparation and characterization of bone and tooth collagen for isotopic analysis. *Journal of Archaeological Science* **17** 431–451.

Ambrose, S. H. (1993). Isotopic analysis of paleodiets: methodological and interpretative considerations. In *Investigations of Ancient Human Tissue*, ed. Sandford, M. K., Langhorne, Pennsylvania, Gordon and Breach, pp. 59–130.

Ambrose, S. H. and DeNiro, M. J. (1986). Reconstruction of African human diet using bone collagen carbon and nitrogen isotope ratios. *Nature* **319** 321–324.

Ambrose, S. H. and Katzenberg, A. M. (eds.) (2000). *Biogeochemical Approaches in Paleodietary Analysis*. London, Plenum.

Ambrose, S. H. and Norr, L. (1993). Experimental evidence for the relationship of the carbon isotope ratios of whole diet and dietary protein to those of bone collagen and carbonate. In *Prehistoric Human Bone: archaeology at the molecular level*, eds. Lambert, J. B. and Grupe, G., Berlin, Springer Verlag, pp. 1–37.

Andrade, E., Pineda, J. C., Zavala, E. P., *et al.* (1998). IBA analysis of a possible therapeutic ancient tooth inlay. *Nuclear Instruments and Methods in Physics Research B* **136–138** 908–912.

Appoloni, C. R., Quinones, F. R. E., Aragao, P. H. A., *et al.* (2001). EDXRF study of Tupi-Guarani archaeological ceramics. *Radiation Physics and Chemistry* **61** 711–712.

Ardika, I. W. and Bellwood, P. (1991). Sembiran: the beginnings of Indian contact with Bali. *Antiquity* **65** 221–232.

Asaro, F. and Perlman, I. (1973). Provenience studies of Mycenean pottery employing neutron activation analysis. In *Acts of the International Archaeological Symposium "The Myceneans in the Eastern Mediterranean", Nicosia 27th March–2nd April 1972*, Cyprus, Nicosia, Department of Antiquities, pp. 213–224.

Aspinall, A. and Feather, S. W. (1972). Neutron activation analysis of prehistoric flint mine products. *Archaeometry* **14** 41–53.

Aspinall, A., Warren, S. E., Crummett, J. G., and Newton, R. G. (1972). Neutron activation analysis of faience beads. *Archaeometry* **14** 27–40.

Aston, F. W. (1920). Isotopes and atomic weights. *Nature* **105** 617–619.

Atkins, P. W. (2001). *The Elements of Physical Chemistry*. Oxford, Oxford University Press (3rd edn.).

Atkins, P. W. and Beren, J. A. (1992). *General Chemistry*. New York, Scientific American Books (2nd edn.).

Atkins, P. W. and Jones, L. (2002). *Chemical Principles: the quest for insight*. New York, Freeman (2nd edn.).

Autumn, K., Liang, Y. A., Hsieh, S. T., *et al.* (2000). Adhesive force of a single gecko foot-hair. *Nature* **405** 681–685.

Aveling, E. M. and Heron, C. (1998). Identification of birch bark tar at the Mesolithic site of Star Carr. *Ancient Biomolecules* **2** 69–80.

Aveling, E. M. and Heron, C. (1999). Chewing tar in the early Holocene: an archaeological and ethnographic evaluation. *Antiquity* **73** 579–584.

Avogadro, A. (1811). D'une manière de déterminer les masses relatives de molécules élémentaires des corps, et les proportions selon lesquelles elles entrent dans ces combinaisons. *Journal de Physique* **LXXIII** 58–76.

Badler, V. R., McGovern, P. E., and Michel, R. H. (1990). *Drink and be merry! Infrared spectroscopy and ancient near eastern wine*. MASCA Research Papers in Science and Archaeology, Philadelphia, University of Pennsylvania **7** 25–36.

Baffier, D., Girard, M., Menu, M., and Vignaud, C. (1999). Color at the Grande Grotte, Arcy-Sur-Cure (Yonne, France). *Anthropologie* **103** 1–21.

Bakraji, E. H., Othman, I., Sarhil, A., and Al-Somel, N. (2002). Application of instrumental neutron activation analysis and multivariate statistical methods to archaeological Syrian ceramics. *Journal of Trace and Microprobe Techniques* **20** 57–68.

Balaram, V. (1996). Recent trends in the instrumental analysis of rare earth elements in geological and industrial materials. *Trends in Analytical Chemistry* **15** 475–486.

Baldwin, S., Deaker, M., and Maher, W. (1994). Low volume microwave digestion of marine biological tissues for the measurement of trace-elements. *Analyst* **119** 1701–1704.

Balmer, J. J. (1885). Notiz über die Spectrallinien des Wasserstoffs. *Annalen der Physik und Chemie (Neue Folge)* **25** 80–87.

Barakat, A. O., Qian, Y., Kim, M., and Kennicutt, M. C. (2001). Chemical characterization of naturally weathered oil residues in arid terrestrial environment in Al-Alamein, Egypt. *Environmental International* **27** 291–310.

Barber, D. J. and Freestone, I. C. (1990). An investigation of the origin of the colour of the Lycurgus Cup by analytical transmission electron microscopy. *Archaeometry* **32** 33–45.

Barford, N. C. (1985). *Experimental Measurements: precision, error and truth*. London, Addison-Wesley.

Barnard, T. W., Crockett, M. I., Ivaldi, J. C., *et al.* (1993). Solid-state detector for ICP-OES. *Analytical Chemistry* **65** 1231–1239.

Barnes, I. L., Shields, W. R. S., Murphy, T. J., and Brill, R. H. (1974). Isotopic analysis of Laurion lead ores. In *Archaeological Chemistry*, ed. Beck, C. W., Advances in Chemistry Series 138, Washington, DC, American Chemical Society, pp. 1–10.

Baugh, P. J. (ed.) (1993). *Gas Chromatography: a practical approach*. Oxford, Oxford University Press.

Baxter, M. J. (1994). *Exploratory Multivariate Analysis in Archaeology*. Edinburgh, Edinburgh University Press.

Baxter, M. J. (2003). *Statistics in Archaeology*. London, Arnold.

Baxter, M. J. and Buck, C. E. (2000). Data handling and statistical analysis. In *Modern Analytical Methods in Art and Archaeology*, eds. Ciliberto, E. and Spoto, G., Chemical Analysis Series 155, New York, Wiley, pp. 681–746.

Baxter, M. J. and Gale, N. H. (1998). Testing for multivariate normality via univariate tests: a case study using lead isotope ratio data. *Journal of Applied Statistics* **25** 671–683.

Bayman, J. M. (1995). Rethinking redistribution in the archaeological record – obsidian exchange at the Marana Platform Mound. *Journal of Anthropological Research* **51** 37–63.

Beardsley, F. R., Goles, G. G., and Ayres, W. S. (1996). Provenance studies on Easter Island obsidian: an archaeological application. In *Archaeological Chemistry: organic, inorganic and biochemical analysis*, ed. Orna, M. V., ACS Symposium Series 625, Washington, DC, American Chemical Society, pp. 47–63.

Beck, C. W. (ed.) (1974). *Archaeological Chemistry*. Advances in Chemistry Series 138, Washington, DC, American Chemical Society.

Beck, C. W. (1986). Spectroscopic investigations of amber. *Applied Spectroscopy Reviews* **22** 57–110.

Beck, C. W. (1995). The provenience analysis of amber. *American Journal of Archaeology* **99** 125–127.

Beck, C. W. and Shennan, S. (1991). *Amber in Prehistoric Britain*. Oxford, Oxbow.

Beck, C. W., Wilbur, E., and Meret, S. (1964). Infrared spectra and the origins of amber. *Nature* **201** 256–257.

Beck, C. W., Wilbur, E., Meret, S., Kossove, D., and Kermani, K. (1965). The infrared spectra of amber and the identification of Baltic amber. *Archaeometry* **8** 96–109.

Becquerel, A. H. (1896). Sur les radiations émises par phosphorescence. *Comptes Rendus hebdomadaires des Séances de l'Académie des Sciences* **122** 420–421.

Becquerel, A. H. (1900). Déviation du rayonnement du radium dans un champ électrique. *Comptes Rendus hebdomadaires des Séances de l'Académie des Sciences* **130** 809–815.

Beer, A. (1852). Bestimmung der Absorption des rothen Lichts in farbigen Flüssigkeiten. *Annalen der Physik und Chemie (Poggendorff)* **86** 78–88.

Behrens, H. and Stuke, A. (2003). Quantification of H_2O contents in silicate glasses using IR spectroscopy – a calibration based on hydrous glasses analysed by Karl-Fischer titration. *Glass Science and Technology* **76** 176–189.

Bentley, R. A., Price, T. D., Lüning, J., *et al.* (2002). Prehistoric migration in Europe: strontium isotope analysis of early Neolithic skeletons. *Current Anthropology* **43** 799–804.

Bertoncello, R., Milanese, L., Russo, U., *et al.* (2002). Chemistry of cultural glasses: the early medieval glasses of Monselice's hill (Padova, Italy). *Journal of Non-Crystalline Solids* **306** 249–262.

Berzelius, J. (1813, 1814). Essay on the cause of chemical proportions, and on some circumstances relating to them: together with a short and easy method of expressing them. *Annals of Philosophy* **2** 443–454 (1813), **3** 51–2, 93–106, 244–225, 353–364 (1814).

Berzelius, J. (1814, 1815). Experiments to determine the definite proportions in which the elements of organic nature are combined. *Annals of Philosophy* **4** 409–510, **5** 93–101, 174–184, 260–275.

Bethell, P. and Máté, I. (1989). The use of soil phosphate analysis in archaeology: a critique. In *Scientific Analysis in Archaeology*, ed. Henderson, J., Monograph 19, Oxford, Oxford University Committee for Archaeology, pp. 1–29.

Bethell. P. H. and Smith, J. U. (1989). Trace-element analysis of an inhumation from Sutton Hoo, using inductively coupled plasma emission-spectrometry – an evaluation of the technique applied to analysis of organic residues. *Journal of Archaeological Science* **16** 47–55.

Bethke, C. (2003). *The Geochemist's Workbench™* Version 6. Urbana-Champaign, University of Illinois (www.rockware.com).

Beynon, J. H. and Brenton, A. G. (1982). *An Introduction to Mass Spectrometry*. Cardiff, University of Wales Press.

Beynon, J. D. E. and Lamb, D. R. (eds.) (1980). *Charge-coupled Devices and their Applications*. London, McGraw-Hill.

Bichler, M., Egger, H., Preisinger, A., Ritter, D., and Strastny, P. (1997). NAA of the "Minoan pumice" at Thera and comparison to alluvial pumice deposits in the Eastern Mediterranean region. *Journal of Radioanalytical and Nuclear Chemistry* **224** 7–14.

Bieber, A. M. Jr., Brooks, W. D., Harbottle, G., and Sayre, E. V. (1976). Application of multivariate techniques to analytical data on Aegean ceramics. *Archaeometry* **18** 59–74.

Bigazzi, G., Meloni, S., Oddone, M., and Radi, G. (1986). Provenance studies of obsidian artifacts: trace elements analysis and data reduction. *Journal of Radioanalytical and Nuclear Chemistry* **98** 353–363.

Binder, D., Bourgeois, G., Benoit, F., and Vitry, C. (1990). Identification de brai de bouleau (Betula) dans le Néolithique de Giribaldi (Nice, France) par la spectrométrie de masse. *Revue d'Archéométrie* **14** 37–42.

Bishop, R. L. and Blackman, M. J. (2002). Instrumental neutron activation analysis of archaeological ceramics: scale and interpretation. *Accounts of Chemical Research* **35** 603–610.

Blau, K. and Halket, J. M. (eds.) (1993). *Handbook of Derivatives for Chromatography*. Chichester, Wiley.

Blau, S., Kennedy, B. J., and Kim, J. Y. (2002). An investigation of possible fluorosis in human dentition using synchrotron radiation. *Journal of Archaeological Science* **29** 811–817.

Bohr, N. (1913). On the constitution of atoms and molecules. *Philosophical Magazine Series 6* **26** 1–25.

Bonfield, K. M. (1997). *The Analysis and Interpretation of Lipid Residues Associated with Prehistoric Pottery: pitfalls and potential.* Unpublished Ph.D. thesis, University of Bradford, UK.

Boss, C. B. and Fredeen, K. J. (1999). *Concepts, Instrumentation and Techniques in Inductively Coupled Plasma Optical Emission Spectrometry.* Norwalk, CO, Perkin Elmer (2nd edn.).

Bothe, B. and Becker H. (1930). Künstliche Erregung von Kern-γ-Strahlen. *Zeitschrift für Physik* **66** 289–306.

Bowman, S. (ed.) (1991). *Science and the Past.* London, British Museum Press.

Brady, J. E. and Hollum, J. R. (1993). *Chemistry: the study of matter and its changes.* New York, Wiley.

Brenna, J. T., Corso, T. N., Tobias, H. J., and Caimi, R. J. (1997). High-precision continuous-flow isotope ratio mass spectrometry. *Mass Spectrometry Reviews* **16** 227–258.

Brenner, I. B. and Zander, A. T. (2000). Axially and radially viewed inductively coupled plasmas – a critical review. *Spectrochimica Acta B* **55** 1195–1240.

Brill, R. H. and Wampler, J. M. (1967). Isotope studies of ancient lead. *American Journal of Archaeology* **71** 63–77.

Brody, R. H. (2000). *Applications of FT-Raman Spectroscopy to Biomaterials.* Unpublished Ph.D. Thesis, UK, University of Bradford.

Brody, R. H., Edwards, H. G. M., and Pollard, A. M. (2001). Chemometric methods applied to the differentiation of Fourier-transform Raman spectra of ivories. *Analytica Chimica Acta* **427** 223–232.

Bronk Ramsey, C., Pettitt, P. B., Hedges, R. E. M., Hodgins, G. W. L., and Owen, D. C. (2000). Radiocarbon dates from the Oxford AMS system, Archaeometry datelist 30. *Archaeometry* **42** 459–479.

Bronk, H., Rohrs, S., Bjeoumikhov, N., *et al.* (2001). ArtTAX- a new mobile spectrometer for energy-dispersive micro X-ray fluorescence spectrometry on art and archaeological objects. *Fresenius Journal of Analytical Chemistry* **371** 307–316.

Brønsted, J. N. (1923). Some remarks on the concept of acids and bases. *Recueil des Travaux Chimiques des Pays-Bas* **42** 718–728.

Brothwell, D. and Higgs, E. (eds.) (1963). *Science in Archaeology: a survey of progress and research.* London, Thames and Hudson (2nd edn. 1969).

Brothwell, D. and Pollard, A. M. (eds.) (2001). *Handbook of Archaeological Sciences.* Chichester, Wiley.

Brown, M. A. and Blin-Stoyle, A. E. (1959). Spectrographic analysis of British Middle and Late Bronze Age finds (including reprint of "A sample analysis of British Middle and Late Bronze Age material, using optical spectrometry", from *Proceedings of the Prehistoric Society.*) Supplement to *Archaeometry* **2**.

Brown, R. (1827). *A Brief Account of Microscopical Observations.* (Reprinted in *Edinburgh New Philosophical Journal* 358–837 (July–September 1828)).

Brown, W. H. (2000). *Introduction to Organic Chemistry*. Fort Worth, Saunders College (2nd edn.).

Bryant, J. D. and Froelich, P. N. (1996). Oxygen-isotope composition of human tooth enamel from medieval Greenland – linking climate and society – comment. *Geology* **24** 477–478.

Budd, P., Pollard, A. M., Scaife, B., and Thomas, R. G. (1995a). The possible fractionation of lead isotopes in ancient metallurgical processes. *Archaeometry* **37** 143–150.

Budd, P., Haggerty, R., Pollard, A. M., Scaife, B., and Thomas, R. G. (1995b). New heavy isotope studies in archaeology. *Israel Journal of Chemistry* **35** 125–130.

Budd, P., Haggerty, R., Pollard, A. M., Scaife, B., and Thomas, R. G. (1996). Rethinking the quest for provenance. *Antiquity* **70** 168–174.

Budd, P. D., Lythgoe, P., McGill, R. A. R., Pollard, A. M., and Scaife, B. (1999). Zinc isotope fractionation in liquid brass (Cu-Zn) alloy: potential environmental and archaeological applications. In *Geoarchaeology: exploration, environments, resources*, ed. Pollard, A. M., London, Geological Society Special Publication, pp. 147–153.

Budd, P., Montgomery, J., Barreiro, B., and Thomas, R. G. (2000). Differential diagenesis of strontium in archaeological human dental tissues. *Applied Geochemistry* **15** 687–694.

Budd, P., Millard, A., Chenery, C., Lucy, S., and Roberts, C. (2003). Investigating population movement by stable isotope analysis: a report from Britain. *Antiquity* **78** 127–141.

Buikstra, J. E. and Milner, G. R. (1991). Isotopic and archaeological interpretations of diet in the central Mississippi valley. *Journal of Archaeological Science* **18** 319–329.

Bull, I. D., Simpson, I. A., van Bergen, P. F., and Evershed, R. P. (1999). Muck 'n' molecules: organic geochemical methods for detecting ancient manuring. *Antiquity* **73** 86–96.

Buoso, M. C., Fazinic, S., Haque, A. M. I., *et al.* (1992). Heavy element distribution profiles in archaeological samples of human tooth enamel and dentin using the proton-induced X-ray-emission technique. *Nuclear Instruments and Methods in Physics Research B* **68** 269–272.

Burton, J. H. and Price, T. D., (2000). The use and abuse of trace elements for palaeodietary research. In *Biogeochemical Approaches to Palaeodietary Analysis*, eds. Ambrose, S. and Katzenberg, M. A., New York, Kluwer Academic/Plenum, pp. 159–171.

Burton, J. H., Price, T. D., and Middleton, W. D. (1999). Correlation of bone Ba/Ca and Sr/Ca due to biological purification of calcium. *Journal of Archaeological Science* **26** 609–616.

Bussell, G. D., Pollard, A. M., and Baird, D. C. (1981). The characterisation of Early Bronze Age jet and jet-like material by X-ray fluorescence. *Wiltshire Archaeological Magazine* **76** 27–32.

Butcher, D. J. and Sneddon, J. (1998). *A Practical Guide to Graphite Furnace Atomic Absorption Spectrometry*. Chichester, Wiley.

Buxeda i Garrigos, J., Kilikoglou, V., and Day, P. M. (2001). Chemical and mineralogical alteration of ceramics from a Late Bronze Age kiln at Kommos, Crete: the effect on the formation of a reference group. *Archaeometry* **43** 349–371.

Cahill, T. A., Kusko, B. H., Eldred, R. A., and Schwab, R. N. (1984). Gutenberg's inks and papers: non-destructive compositional analyses by proton milliprobe. *Archaeometry* **26** 3–14.

Caley, E. R. (1949). Klaproth as a pioneer in the chemical investigation of antiquities. *Journal of Chemical Education* **26** 242–247; 268.

Caley, E. R. (1951). Early history and literature of archaeological chemistry. *Journal of Chemical Education* **28** 64–66.

Caley, E. R. (1964). *Analysis of Ancient Metals.* Oxford, Pergamon.

Caley, E. R. (1967). The early history of chemistry in the service of archaeology. *Journal of Chemical Education* **44** 120–123.

Calligaro, T., Colinart, S., Poirot, J. P., and Sudres, C. (2002). Combined external-beam PIXE and mu-Raman characterisation of garnets used in Merovingian jewelry. *Nuclear Instruments and Methods in Physics Research B* **189** 320–327.

Cannizzaro, S. (1858). Sunto di un corso de filosofia chimica. *Nuovo Cimento* **VII** 321–366.

Canti, M. G. and Davis, M. (1999). Tests and guidelines for the suitability of sands to be used in archaeological site reburial. *Journal of Archaeological Science* **26** 775–781.

Capasso, D. J. T., Capasso, L., Di Tota, G., Jones, K. W., and Tuniz, C. (1995). Synchrotron radiation microprobe analysis of human dental calculi from an archaeological site: new possible perspective on paleonutrition studies. *International Journal of Osteoarchaeology* **5** 282–288.

Carnot, A. (1892a). Recherche du fluor dans les os modernes et les os fossils. *Comptes Rendus hebdomadaires des Séances de l'Académie des Sciences* **114** 1189–1192.

Carnot, A. (1892b). Sur la composition des ossements fossils et la variation de leur teneur fluor dans les différents étages géologiques. *Comptes Rendus hebdomadaires des Séances de l'Académie des Sciences* **115** 243–246.

Carnot, A. (1892c). Sur une application de l'analyse chimique pour fixer l'âge d'ossements humains préhistoriques. *Comptes Rendus hebdomadaires des Séances de l'Académie des Sciences* **115** 337–339.

Carter, G. F. (ed.) (1978). *Archaeological Chemistry II. Advances in Chemistry Series 171,* Washington, DC, American Chemical Society.

Casetta, B., Giaretta, A., and Mezzacasa, G. (1990). Determination of rare earth and other trace elements in rock samples by ICP-mass spectrometry: comparison with other techniques. *Atomic Spectroscopy* **11** 222–228.

Chabas, A. and Lefevre, R. A. (2000). Chemistry and microscopy of atmospheric particulates at Delos (Cyclades-Greece). *Atmospheric Environment* **34** 225–238.

Chadwick, J. (1932). Possible existence of a neutron. *Nature* **129** 312.

Chang, S. C. and Jackson, M. L. (1957). Fractionation of soil phosphorus. *Soil Science* **84** 133–144.

Charters, S., Evershed, R. P., Goad, L. J., *et al.* (1993). Quantification and distribution of lipid in archaeological ceramics: implications for sampling potsherds for organic residue analysis and the classification of vessel use. *Archaeometry* **35** 211–223.

Charters, S., Evershed, R. P., Blinkhorn, P. W., and Denham, V. (1995). Evidence for the mixing of fats and waxes in archaeological ceramics. *Archaeometry* **37** 113–127.

Cherry, J. F. and Knapp, A. B. (1991). Quantitative provenance studies and Bronze Age trade in the Mediterranean: some preliminary reflections. In *Bronze Age Trade in the Mediterranean,* ed. Gale, N. H., Studies in Mediterranean Archaeology XC, Jonsered, Åströms, pp. 92–119.

Chippindale, C. (1991). Editorial. *Antiquity* **65** 6–9.

Christensen, M., Calligaro, T., Consigny, S., *et al.* (1998). Insight into the usewear mechanism of archaeological flints by implantation of a marker ion and PIXE analysis of experimental tools. *Nuclear Instruments and Methods in Physics Research B* **136** 869–874.

Christian, G. D. (1994). *Analytical Chemistry.* New York, Wiley (5th edn.).

Christie, W. W., Dobson, G., and Shepherd, T. (1999). Laboratory accreditation in a lipid analysis context. *Lipid Technology* **11** 118–119.

Ciliberto, E. and Spoto, G. (eds.) (2000). *Modern Analytical Methods in Art and Archaeology.* New York, Wiley.

Clark, R. J. H., Curri, L., Henshaw, G. S., and Laganara, C. (1997). Characterization of brown-black and blue pigments in glazed pottery fragments from Castel Fiorentino (Foggia, Italy) by Raman microscopy, X-ray powder diffractometry and X-ray photoelectron spectroscopy. *Journal of Raman Spectroscopy* **28** 105–109.

Clayton, R., Andersson, P., Gale, N. H., Gillis, C., and Whitehouse, M. J. (2002). Precise determination of the isotopic composition of Sn using MC-ICP-MS. *Journal of Analytical Atomic Spectrometry* **17** 1248–1256.

Climent-Font, A., Demortier, G., Palacio, C., *et al.* (1998). Characterisation of archaeological bronzes using PIXE, PIGE, RBS and AES spectrometries. *Nuclear Instruments and Methods in Physics Research B* **134** 229–236.

Clydesdale, A. (1990). *Chemicals in Conservation: a guide to possible hazards and safe use.* Edinburgh, Scottish Society for Conservation and Restoration (2nd edn.).

Coghlan, H. H. and Case, H. J. (1957). Early metallurgy of copper in Ireland and Britain. *Proceedings of the Prehistoric Society* **23** 91–123.

Cole, B. J. W., Bentley, M. D., and Hua, Y. (1991). Triterpenoid extractives in the outer bark of *Betula lenta* black birch. *Holzforschung* **45** 265–268.

Coles, J. M. (1979). *Experimental Archaeology.* London, Academic Press.

Collins, M. J., Neilsen-Marsh, C. M., Hiller, J., *et al.* (2002). The survival of organic matter in bone: a review. *Archaeometry* **44** 383–394.

Condamin, J., Formenti, F., Metais, M. O., Michel, M., and Blond, P. (1976). The application of gas chromatography to the tracing of oil in ancient amphorae. *Archaeometry* **10** 195–201.

Connan, J. (1999). Use and trade of bitumen in antiquity and prehistory: molecular archaeology reveals the secrets of past civilizations. *Philosophical Transactions of the Royal Society B* **354** 33–50.

Connan, J. and Deschesne, O. (1996). *Le Bitume à Suse: collection du Musée du Louvre.* Paris, Réunion des Musées Nationaux.

Connan, J. and Dessort, D. (1989). Dead sea asphalt in the balms of an Egyptian mummy: identification by molecular criteria. *Comptes Rendus de l'Académie des Sciences Serie II* **309** 1665–1672.

Connan, J., Nissenbaum, A., and Dessort, D. (1992). Molecular archaeology: export of Dead Sea asphalt to Canaan and Egypt in the Chalcolithic-Early Bronze Age (4th-3rd Millennium BC). *Geochimica et Cosmochimica Acta* **56** 2743–2759.

Connan, J., Lombard, P., Killick, R., *et al.* (1998). The archaeological bitumens of Bahrain from the Early Dilmun period (c. 2200 BC) to the sixteenth century AD: a problem of sources and trade. *Arabian Archaeology and Epigraphy* **9** 141–181.

Constantinescu, B. and Bugoi, R. (2000). Archaeometrical studies on silver coins and ancient glassy materials using the Bucharest cyclotron. *Acta Physica Hungarica New Series-Heavy Ion Physics* **11** 451–461.

Cook, J. P. (1995). Characterization and distribution of obsidian in Alaska. *Arctic Anthropology* **32** 92–100.

Copley, M. S., Rose, P. J., Clapham, A., *et al.* (2001). Processing palm fruits in the Nile valley – biomolecular evidence from Qasr Ibrim. *Antiquity* **75** 538–542.

Copley, M. S., Berstan, R., Dudd, S. N., *et al.* (2005a). Dairying in antiquity. I. Evidence from absorbed lipid residues dating to the British Iron Age. *Journal of Archaeological Science* **32** 485–503.

Copley, M. S., Berstan, R., Straker, V., Payne, S., and Evershed, R. P. (2005b). Dairying in antiquity. II. Evidence from absorbed lipid residues dating to the British Bronze Age. *Journal of Archaeological Science* **32** 505–521.

Copley, M. S., Berstan, R., Mukherjee, A. J., *et al.* (2005c). Dairying in antiquity. III. Evidence from absorbed lipid residues dating to the British Neolithic. *Journal of Archaeological Science* **32** 523–546.

Corbridge, D. E. C. (1995). *Phosphorus: an outline of its chemistry, biochemistry and uses.* Amsterdam, Elsevier (5th edn.).

Cotton, F. A., Wilkinson, G., and Gaus, P. L. (1995). *Basic Inorganic Chemistry.* Chichester, Wiley (3rd edn.).

Cousin, H. and Magyar, B. (1994). Precision and accuracy of laser ablation-ICP-MS analysis of rare earth elements with external calibration. *Mikrochimica Acta* **113** 313–323.

Cox, M. and Mays, S. (eds.) (2000). *Human Osteology in Archaeology and Forensic Science.* London, Greenwich Medical Media.

Craig, H. (1961). Standards for reporting concentrations of deuterium and oxygen-18 in natural waters. *Science* **133** 1833–1834.

Craig, O., Mulville, J., Parker Pearson, M., *et al.* (2000). Detecting milk proteins in ancient pots. *Nature* **408** 312.

Cristoni, S. and Bernardi, L. R. (2003). Development of new methodologies for the mass spectrometry study of bioorganic macromolecules. *Mass Spectrometry Reviews* **22** 369–406.

Cronyn, J. M. (1990). *The Elements of Archaeological Conservation.* London, Routledge.

Cronyn, J. M. (2001). The deterioration of organic materials. In *Handbook of Archaeological Sciences*, eds. Brothwell, D. R. and Pollard, A. M., Chichester, Wiley, pp. 627–636.

Crowther, J. (1997). Soil phosphate surveys: critical approaches to sampling, analysis and interpretation. *Archaeological Prospection* **4** 93–102.

Cullity, B. D. (1978). *Elements of X-ray Diffraction.* Reading, Mass., Addison-Wesley (2nd edn.).

Curie, I. and Joliot, F. (1932). Émission de protons de grande vitesse par les substances hydrogénées sous l'influence des rayons γ très pénétrants. *Comptes Rendus hebdomadaires des Séances de l'Académie des Sciences* **194** 273–275.

Curie, P. and Curie, S. (1898). Sur une substance nouvelle radio-active, continue dans la pechblende. *Comptes Rendus hebdomadaires des Séances de l'Académie des Sciences* **127** 175–178.

Dalton, J. (1808, 1810, 1827). *A New System of Chemical Philosophy*. 3 vols. Manchester, Bickerstaffe, Manchester, Wilson (Vol I Republished 1965, London, Owen).

Damon, P. E., Donahue, D. J., Gore, B. H., *et al*. (1989). Radiocarbon dating of the Shroud of Turin. *Nature* **337** 611–615.

Damour, M. A. (1865). Sur la composition des haches en Pierre trouvées dans les monuments celtiques et chez les tribus sauvages. *Comptes Rendus hebdomadaires des Séances de l'Académie des Sciences* **61** 313–321, 357–368.

Dansgaard, W. (1964). Stable isotopes in precipitation. *Tellus* **16** 436–468.

Darling, J. A. and Hayashida, F. M. (1995). Compositional analysis of the Huitzila and La Lobera obsidian sources in the southern Sierra-Madre Occidental, Mexico. *Journal of Radioanalytical and Nuclear Chemistry* **196** 245–254.

Das, H. A. and Zonderhuis, J. (1964). The analysis of electrum coins. *Archaeometry* **7** 90–97.

Date, A. R. and Gray, A. L. (1989). *Applications of Inductively Coupled Plasma Mass Spectrometry*. London, Blackie.

Davidson, D. A. and Simpson, I. A. (2001). Archaeology and soil micromorphology. In *Handbook of Archaeological Sciences*, eds. Brothwell, D. and Pollard, A. M., Chichester, Wiley, pp. 167–177.

Davy, H. (1815). Some experiments and observations on the colours used in painting by the ancients. *Philosophical Transactions of the Royal Society* **105** 97–124.

de Benedetto, G. E., Catalano, F., Sabbatini, L., and Zambonin, P. G. (1998). Analytical characterisation of pigments on pre-Roman pottery by means of spectroscopic techniques part I: white coloured shards. *Fresenius Journal of Analytical Chemistry* **362** 170–175.

de la Cruz Baltazar, V. (2001). *Studies on the State of Preservation of Archaeological Bone*. Unpublished Ph.D. Thesis, UK, University of Bradford.

DeAtley, S. P. and Bishop, R. L. (1991). Toward an integrated interface for archaeology and archeometry. In *The Ceramic Legacy of Anna O. Shepard*, eds. Bishop, R. L. and Lange, R. W., Boulder, CO, University Press of Colorado, pp. 358–380.

Dedina, J. and Tsalev, D. L. (1995). *Hydride Generation Atomic Absorption Spectrometry*. Chichester, Wiley.

Demortier, G. (1997). Accelerator-based analysis of gold jewelry items and experimental archaeology. *Annali Di Chimica* **87** 103–112.

Demortier, G., Fernandez-Gomez, F., Salamanca, M. A. O., and Coquay, P. (1999). PIXE in an external microbeam arrangement for the study of finely decorated Tartesic gold jewellery items. *Nuclear Instruments and Methods in Physics Research B* **158** 275–280.

Dempster, A. J. (1918). A new method of positive ray analysis. *Physical Review* **11** 316–325.

DeNiro, M. J. (1985). Postmortem preservation and alteration of in vivo bone collagen isotope ratios in relation to paleodietary reconstruction. *Nature* **317** 806–809.

DeNiro, M. J. (1987). Stable isotopy and archaeology. *American Scientist* **75** 182–191.

Descantes, C., Neff, H., Glascock, M. D., and Dickinson, W. R. (2001). Chemical characterization of Micronesian ceramics through instrumental neutron activation analysis: a preliminary provenance study. *Journal of Archaeological Science* **28** 1185–1190.

Dillmann, P., Populus, P., Fluzin, P., *et al.* (1997). Microdiffraction of synchrotron radiation – identification of non-metallic phases in ancient iron products. *Revue De Metallurgie-Cahiers d'Informations Techniques* **94** 267–268.

Dillmann, P., Neff, D., Mazaudier, F., *et al.* (2002). Characterisation of iron archaeological analogues using micro diffraction under synchrotron radiation. Application to the study of long term corrosion behaviour of low alloy steels. *Journal de Physique IV* **12** 393–408.

Dobb, F. P. (2004). *ISO 9001:2000 Quality Registration Step-by-Step*. Amsterdam, Elsevier.

Döbereiner, J. W. (1829). An attempt to group elementary substances according to their analogies. *Annalen der Physik und Chemie* **15** 301–307.

Drozd, J. (1981). *Chemical Derivatization in Gas Chromatography*. Amsterdam, Elsevier.

Druc, I. C., Burger, R. L., Zamojska, R., and Magny, P. (2001). Ancón and Garagay ceramic production at the time of Chavín de Huántar. *Journal of Archaeological Science* **28** 29–43.

Dudd, S. N. and Evershed, R. P. (1998). Direct demonstration of milk as an element of archaeological economies. *Science* **282** 1478–1481.

Dudd, S. N. and Evershed, R. P. (1999). Unusual triterpenoid fatty acyl ester components of archaeological birch bark tars. *Tetrahedron Letters* **40** 359–362.

Dudd, S. N., Regert, M., and Evershed, R. P. (1998). Assessing microbial lipid contributions during laboratory degradations of fats and oils and pure triacylglycerols absorbed in ceramic potsherds. *Organic Geochemistry* **29** 1345–1354.

Duffy, K. I., Carlson, J. H., and Swann, C. P. (2002). A study of green-glazed ware from England and South Carolina, USA (1760–1780). *Nuclear Instruments and Methods in Physics Research B* **189** 369–372.

Dulski, P. (1994). Interferences of oxide, hydroxide and chloride analyte species in the determination of rare earth elements in geological samples by inductively coupled plasma-mass spectrometry. *Fresenius Journal of Analytical Chemistry* **350** 194–203.

Dupras, T. L. and Schwarcz, H. P. (2001). Strangers in a strange land: stable isotope evidence for human migration in the Dakhleh Oasis, Egypt. *Journal of Archaeological Science* **28** 1199–1208.

Durrant, S. F. (1992). Multi-element analysis of environmental matrices by laser ablation inductively coupled plasma mass spectrometry. *Analyst* **117** 1585–1592.

Durrant, S. F. and Ward, N. I. (1993). Rapid multielemental analysis of Chinese reference soils by laser ablation inductively coupled plasma mass spectrometry. *Fresenius Journal of Analytical Chemistry* **345** 512–517.

Durrant, S. F. and Ward, N. I. (1994). Laser ablation-inductively coupled plasma-mass spectrometry (LA-ICP-MS) for the multielemental analysis of biological materials: a feasibility study. *Food Chemistry* **49** 317–323.

Eastwood, W. J., Pearce, N. J. G., Westgate, J. A., and Perkins, W. T. (1998). Recognition of Santorini (Minoan) tephra in lake sediments from Gölhisar Gölü, southwest Turkey by laser ablation ICP-MS. *Journal of Archaeological Science* **25** 677–687.

Edwards, H. G. M. (2000). Art works studied using IR and Raman spectroscopy. In *Encyclopaedia of Spectroscopy and Spectrometry*, eds. Lindon, J. C., Tranter, G. E., and Holmes, J. L., London, Academic Press, pp. 2–17.

Edwards, H. G. M., Farwell, D. W., Holder, J. M., and Lawson, E. E. (1997). Fourier transform Raman spectra of ivory III: identification of mammalian specimens. *Spectrochimica Acta Part A* **53** 2403–2409.

Edwards, R. (1996). The effects of changes in groundwater geochemistry on the survival of buried metal artifacts. In *Preserving Archaeological Remains In-Situ*, eds. Corfield, M., Hinton, P., Nixon, T., and Pollard, A. M., London, Museum of London Archaeology Service, pp. 86–92.

Efremov, I. A. (1940). Taphonomy: new branch of palaeontology. *Pan-American Geologist* **74** 81–94.

Eglinton, G. and Logan, G. A. (1991). Molecular preservation. *Philosophical Transactions of the Royal Society of London B* **333** 315–328.

Ehleringer J. R. and Rundel P. W. (1988). Stable isotopes: history, units and instrumentation. In *Stable Isotopes in Ecological Research*, eds. Rundel, P. W., Ehleringer, J. R., and Nagy, K. A., New York, Springer-Verlag, pp. 1–15.

Eiland, M. L. and Williams, Q. (2001). Investigation of Islamic ceramics from Tell Tuneinir using X-ray diffraction. *Geoarchaeology* **16** 875–903.

Einstein, A. (1905). Über einen die Erzeugung und Verwandlung des Lichtes betreffenden heuristischen Gesichtspunkt. *Annalen der Physik (Vierte Folge)* **17** 132–148.

Ekman, R. (1983). The suberin monomers and triterpenoids from the outer bark of *Betula verrucosa* Ehrh. *Holzforschung* **37** 205–211.

Elder, E. R., Gurewitsch, A. M., Langmuir, R. V., and Pollock, H. C. (1947). Radiation from electrons in a synchrotron. *Physical Review* **71** 829–830.

Elekes, Z., Biro, K. T., Uzonyi, I., Rajta, I., and Kiss, A. Z. (2000). Geochemical analysis of radiolarite samples from the Carpathian basin. *Nuclear Instruments and Methods in Physics Research B* **170** 501–514.

Emeleus, V. M. (1958). The technique of neutron activation analysis as applied to trace element determination in pottery and coins. *Archaeometry* **1** 6–15.

Emeleus, V. M. and Simpson, G. (1960). Neutron activation analysis of ancient Roman potsherds. *Nature* **185** 196.

Emerson, T. E. and Hughes, R. E. (2000). Figurines, flint clay sourcing, the Ozark Highlands, and Cahokian acquisition. *American Antiquity* **65** 79–101.

Emiliani, C. (1969). The significance of deep-sea cores. In *Science in Archaeology*, eds. Brothwell, D. and Higgs, E., London, Thames and Hudson, pp. 109–117 (2nd edn.).

Engel, M. H. and Macko, S. A. (1993). *Organic Geochemistry: principles and applications*. New York, Plenum.

English, N. B., Betancourt, J. L., Dean, J. S., and Quade, J. (2001). Strontium isotopes reveal distant sources of architectural timber in Chaco Canyon, New Mexico. *Proceedings of the National Academy of Sciences of the United States of America* **98** 11891–11896.

Entwistle, J. A. and Abrahams, P. W., (1997). Multi-element analysis of soils and sediments from Scottish historical sites. The potential of inductively coupled plasma-mass spectrometry for rapid site investigation. *Journal of Archaeological Science* **24** 407–416.

Entwhistle, J. A., Abrahams, P. W., and Dodgshon, R. A. (1998). Multi-element analysis of soils from Scottish historical sites. Interpreting land-use history through physical and geochemical analysis of soil. *Journal of Archaeological Science* **25** 53–68.

Ericson, J. E. (1985). Strontium isotope characterization in the study of prehistoric human ecology. *Journal of Human Evolution* **14** 503–514.

Erlandson, J. M., Robertson, J. D., and Descantes, C. (1999). Geochemical analysis of eight red ochres from western North America. *American Antiquity* **64** 517–526.

Evans, J. (1989). Neutron activation analysis and Romano-British pottery studies. In *Scientific Analysis in Archaeology*, ed. Henderson, J., Monograph No. 19, Oxford, Oxford University Committee for Archaeology, pp. 136–162.

Evans, R. D. and Outridge, P. M. (1994). Applications of laser ablation inductively coupled plasma mass spectrometry to the determination of environmental contaminants in calcified biological structures. *Journal of Analytical Atomic Spectroscopy* **9** 985–989.

Evans, R. D., Richner, P., and Outridge, P. M. (1995). Micro-spatial variations of heavy metals in the teeth of Walrus as determined by laser ablation ICP-MS: The potential for reconstructing a history of metal exposure. *Archives of Environmental Contamination and Toxicology* **28** 55–60.

Evershed, R. P. (1990). Lipids from samples of skin from seven Dutch bog bodies: preliminary report. *Archaeometry* **32** 139–153.

Evershed, R. P. (1993). Advances in silylation. In *Handbook of Derivatives for Chromatography*, eds. Blau, K. and Halket, J. M., New York, Wiley, pp. 51–108 (2nd edn.).

Evershed, R. P. and Connolly, R. C. (1988). Lipid preservation in Lindow man. *Naturwissenschaften* **75** 143–145.

Evershed, R. P., Jerman, K., and Eglinton, G. (1985). Pine wood origin for pitch from the Mary Rose. *Nature* **314** 528–530.

Evershed, R. P., Heron, C., and Goad, L. J. (1990). Analysis of organic residues of archaeological origin by high-temperature gas chromatography and gas chromatography-mass spectrometry. *Analyst* **115** 1339–1342.

Evershed, R. P., Heron, C., and Goad, L. J. (1991). Epicuticular wax components preserved in pot sherds as chemical indicators of leafy vegetables in ancient diets. *Antiquity* **65** 540–544.

Evershed, R. P., Turner-Walker, G., Hedges, R. E. M., Tuross, N., and Leyden, A. (1995). Preliminary results for the analysis of lipids in ancient bone. *Journal of Archaeological Science* **22** 277–290.

Evershed, R. P., Mottram, H. R., Dudd, S. N., *et al.* (1997a). New criteria for the identification of animal fats preserved in archaeological pottery. *Naturwissenschaften* **84** 402–406.

Evershed, R. P., Vaughan, S. J., Dudd, S. N., and Soles, J. S. (1997b). Fuel for thought? Beeswax in lamps and conical cups from Late Minoan Crete. *Antiquity* **71** 979–985.

Ewing, G. W. (1985). *Instrumental Methods of Chemical Analysis*. New York, McGraw-Hill (5th edn).

Ewing, G. W. (ed.) (1997). *Analytical Instrumentation Handbook*. New York, Marcel Dekker (2nd edn.).

Fales, H. M., Jaouni, T. M., and Babashak, J. F. (1973). Simple device for preparing ethereal diazomethane without resorting to codistillation. *Analytical Chemistry* **45** 2302–2303.

Fang, Z. (1995). *Flow Injection Atomic Absorption Spectrometry*. Chichester, Wiley.

Faraday, M. (1834). Experimental research in electricity. 7th series. *Philosophical Transactions of the Royal Society* **124** 77–122.

Farnum, J. F., Glascock, M. D., Sandford, M. K., and Gerritsen, S. (1995). Trace-elements in ancient human bone and associated soil using NAA. *Journal of Radioanalytical and Nuclear Chemistry* **196** 267–274.

Farquhar, G. D., O'Leary, M. H., and Berry, J. A. (1982). On the relationship between carbon isotope discrimination and the intercellular carbon dioxide concentration in leaves. *Australian Journal of Plant Physiology* **9** 121–137.

Faure, G. (1986). *Principles of Isotope Geology*. Chichester, Wiley (2nd edn.).

Fazeli, H., Coningham, R. A. E., and Pollard, A. M. (2001). Chemical characterization of Late Neolithic and Chalcolithic pottery from the Tehran Plain, Iran. *Iran* **XXXIX** 1–17.

Feigl, F. (1954). *Spot Tests*. Amsterdam, Elsevier (4th edn.).

Ferranti, P. (2004). Mass spectrometric approach for the analysis of food proteins. *European Journal of Mass Spectrometry* **10** 349–358.

Ferrence, S. C., Betancourt, P. P., and Swann, C. P. (2002). Analysis of Minoan white pigments used on pottery from Kommos, Palaikastro, Mochlos and Knossos. *Nuclear Instruments and Methods in Physics Research B* **189** 364–368.

Fifield, F. W. and Kealey, D. (2000). *Principles and Practice of Analytical Chemistry*. Oxford, Blackwell Science (5th edn.).

Figg, D. J., Cross, J. B., and Brink, C. (1998). More investigations into elemental fractionation resulting from laser ablation inductively coupled plasma mass spectrometry on glass samples. *Applied Surface Science* **129** 287–291.

Fiorini, C. and Longoni, A. (1998). Application of a new noncryogenic X-ray detector in portable instruments for archaeometric analyses. *Review of Scientific Instruments* **69** 1523–1528.

Fleming, S. J. (1975). *Authenticity in Art: the scientific detection of forgery*. London, Institute of Physics.

Fleming, S. J. and Swann C. P. (1992). Recent applications of PIXE spectrometry in archaeology 2. Characterization of Chinese pottery exported to the Islamic world. *Nuclear Instruments and Methods in Physics Research B* **64** 528–537.

Fleming, S. J. and Swann C. P. (1993). Recent applications of PIXE spectrometry in archaeology. 1. Observations on the early development of copper metallurgy in the Old-World. *Nuclear Instruments and Methods in Physics Research B* **75** 440–444.

Fleming, S. J. and Swann C. P. (1994). Roman onyx glass – a study of production recipes and colorants, using PIXE spectrometry. *Nuclear Instruments and Methods in Physics Research B* **85** 864–868.

Fleming, S. J. and Swann C. P. (1999). Roman mosaic glass: a study of production processes, using PIXE spectrometry. *Nuclear Instruments and Methods in Physics Research B* **150** 622–627.

Ford, L. A., Coningham, R. A. E., Pollard, A. M., and Stern, B. (2005). A geochemical investigation of the origin of Rouletted and other related South Asian fine wares. *Antiquity* **79** 909–20.

Formenti, F. and Duthel, J. M. (1996). The analysis of wine and other organics inside amphoras of the Roman period. In *The Origins and Ancient History of Wine*, eds. McGovern, P. E., Fleming, S. J., and Katz, S. H., Langhorne, PA, Gordon and Breach, pp. 79–85.

Freestone, I. C. (2001). Post-depositional changes in archaeological ceramics and glasses. In *Handbook of Archaeological Sciences*, eds. Brothwell, D. R. and Pollard, A. M., Chichester, Wiley, pp. 615–625.

Frenzel, B. (ed.) (1995). *Problems of Stable Isotopes in Tree-rings, Lake Sediments and Peat-bogs as Climatic Evidence for the Holocene*. Strasbourg, European Science Foundation.

Fresenius, C. R. (1841). *Anleitung zur qualitativen chemischen Analyse*. Bonn (2nd–17th edns., Brunswick 1842–1896).

Fresenius, C. R. (1843). *Elementary Instruction in Chemical Analysis* (trans. J. Lloyd Bullock). London, Churchill.

Fresenius, C. R. (1845). *Anleitung zur quantitativen chemischen Analyse*. Brunswick (2nd–6th edns. 1847–1887).

Fricke, H. C., O'Neil, J., and Lynnerup, N. (1995). Oxygen isotope composition of human tooth enamel from medieval Greenland – linking climate and society. *Geology* **23** 869–872.

Fricke, H. C., Clyde, W. C., and O'Neil, J. R. (1998). Intra-tooth variations in $\delta^{18}O$ (PO$_4$) of mammalian tooth enamel as a record of seasonal variations in continental climate variables. *Geochimica et Cosmochimica Acta* **62** 1839–1850.

Furuta, N. (1991). Interlaboratory comparison study on lead isotope ratios determined by inductively coupled plasma mass spectrometry. *Analytical Sciences* **7** 823–826.

Gale, N. H. (1991). Copper oxide ingots: their origin and their place in the Bronze Age metals trade in the Mediterranean. In *Bronze Age Trade in the Mediterranean*, ed. Gale, N. H., Studies in Mediterranean Archaeology 90, Astroms, Jönsered, pp. 197–239.

Gale, N. H. (1997). The isotopic composition of tin in some ancient metals and the recycling problem in metal provenancing. *Archaeometry* **39** 71–82.

Gale, N. H. and Stos-Gale, Z. A. (1982). Bronze Age copper sources in the Mediterranean: a new approach. *Science* **216** 11–19.

Gale, N. H. and Stos-Gale, Z. A. (1992). Lead isotope studies in the Aegean (The British Academy Project). In *New Developments in Archaeological Science*, ed. Pollard, A. M., Proceedings of the British Academy 77, Oxford, Oxford University Press, pp. 63–108.

Gale, N. H. and Stos-Gale, Z. A. (2000). Lead isotope analysis applied to provenance studies. In *Modern Analytical Methods in Art and Archaeology*, eds. Ciliberto, E. and Spoto, G., Chemical Analysis Series 155, New York, Wiley, pp. 503–584.

Gale, N. H., Stos-Gale, Z. A., Maliotis, G., and Annetts, N. (1997). Lead isotope data from the Isotrace Laboratory, Oxford: Archaeometry data base 4, ores from Cyprus. *Archaeometry* **39** 237–246.

Gale, N. H., Woodhead, A. P., Stos-Gale, Z. A., Walder, A., and Bowen, I. (1999). Natural variations detected in the isotopic composition of copper: possible applications to archaeology and geochemistry. *International Journal of Mass Spectrometry* **184** 1–9.

Garbe-Schonberg, C. D., Reimann, C., and Pavlov, V. A. (1997). Laser ablation ICP-MS analyses of tree-ring profiles in pine and birch from N Norway and NW Russia – a reliable record of the pollution history of the area? *Environmental Geology* **32** 9–16.

Garcia-Heras, M., Blackman, M. J., Fernandez-Ruiz, R., and Bishop, R. L. (2001). Assessing ceramic compositional data: a comparison of total reflection X-ray fluorescence and instrumental neutron activation analysis on Late Iron Age Spanish Celtiberian ceramics. *Archaeometry* **43** 323–347.

Garnier, N., Cren-Olivé, C., Rolando, C., and Regert, M. (2002). Characterization of archaeological beeswax by electron ionization and electrospray ionization mass spectrometry. *Analytical Chemistry* **74** 4868–4877.

Garrels, R. M. and Christ, C. L. (1965). *Solutions, Minerals, and Equilibria*. New York, Harper and Row.

Gausch-Jané, M. R., Ibern-Gómez, M., Andrés-Lacueva, C., Jáuregui, O., and Lamuela-Raventós, R. M. (2004). Liquid chromatography with mass spectrometry in tandem mode applied for the identification of wine markers in residues from ancient Egyptian vessels. *Analytical Chemistry* **76** 1672–1677.

Gay-Lussac, J. L. (1808). Memoir on the combination of gaseous substances with each other. *Mémoires de la Société d'Arçeuil* **II** 207.

Geiger, H. and Marsden, E. (1909). On a diffuse reflection of the α-particles. *Proceedings of the Royal Society of London A* **82** 495–500.

Gernaey, A. M., Minnikin, D. E., Copley, M. S., *et al.* (1999). Correlation of the occurrence of mycolic acids with tuberculosis prevalence in an archaeological population. In *Tuberculosis Past and Present*, eds. Pálfi, G., Dutour, O., Deák, J., and Hutás, I., Szeged, Hungary, Golden Book Publisher Ltd. and Tuberculosis Foundation, pp. 275–282.

Gersch, H. K., Robertson, J. D., Henderson, A. G., Pollack, D., and Munson, C. A. (1998). PIXE analysis of prehistoric and protohistoric Caborn-Welborn phase copper artifacts from the lower Ohio River Valley. *Journal of Radioanalytical and Nuclear Chemistry* **234** 85–90.

Ghazi, A. M. (1994). Lead in archaeological samples: an isotopic study by ICP-MS. *Applied Geochemistry* **9** 627–636.

Giauque, R. D., Asaro, F., Stross, F. H., and Hester, T. R. (1993). High-precision nondestructive X-ray-fluorescence method applicable to establishing the provenance of obsidian artifacts. *X-Ray Spectrometry* **22** 44–53.

Gillard, R. D., Hardman, S. M., Thomas, R. G., and Watkinson, D. E. (1994). The mineralization of fibres in burial environments. *Studies in Conservation* **39** 132–140.

Giumlia-Mair, A., Keall, E. J., Shugar, A. N., and Stock, S. (2002). Investigation of a copper-based hoard from the Megalithic site of al-Midamman, Yemen: an interdisciplinary approach. *Journal of Archaeological Science* **29** 195–209.

Glascock, M. D. (1991). *Tables for Neutron Activation Analysis*. Colombia, University of Missouri.

Glascock, M. D. (1994). Nuclear reaction chemical analysis: prompt and delayed measurements. In *Chemical Analysis by Nuclear Methods*, ed. Alfassi, Z. B., Chichester, Wiley, pp. 75–99.

Glascock, M. D. (1998). Activation analysis. In *Instrumental Multi-element Chemical Analysis*, ed. Alfassi, Z. B., Dordrecht, Kluwer Academic, pp. 93–150.

Glascock, M. D. (2000). The status of activation analysis in archaeology and geochemistry. *Journal of Radioanalytical and Nuclear Chemistry* **244** 537–541.

Glascock, M. D. and Neff, H. (2003). Neutron activation analysis and provenance research in archaeology. *Measurement Science and Technology* **14** 1516–1526.

Glascock, M. D., Spalding, T. G., Biers, J. C., and Corman, M. F. (1984). Analysis of copper-based metallic artefacts by prompt gamma-ray neutron activation analysis. *Archaeometry* **26** 96–103.

Glegg, G. A. and Rowland, S. J. (1996). The Braer oil spill: hydrocarbon concentrations in intertidal organisms. *Marine Pollution Bulletin* **32** 486–492.

Godfrey, I. M., Ghisalberti, E. L., Beng, E. W., Byrne, L. T., and Richardson, G. W. (2002). The analysis of ivory from a marine environment. *Studies in Conservation* **47** 29–45.

Goffer, Z. (1980). *Archaeological Chemistry: a sourcebook on the applications of chemistry to archaeology*. New York, Wiley-Interscience.

Goldschmidt, V. M. (1954). *Geochemistry*. London, Oxford University Press.

Golightly, D. W. and Montaser, A. (1992). *Inductively Coupled Plasmas in Analytical Atomic Spectrometry*, New York, VCH Publishers (2nd edn.).

Gomez, B., Neff, H., Rautman, M. L., Vaughan, S. J., and Glascock, M. D. (2002). The source provenance of Bronze Age and Roman pottery from Cyprus. *Archaeometry* **44** 23–36.

Gordus, A. A. (1967). Quantitative non-destructive neutron activation analysis of silver in coins. *Archaeometry* **10** 78–86.

Gosser, D. C., Ohnersorgen, M. A., Simon, A. W., and Mayer, J. W. (1998). PIXE analysis of Salado polychrome ceramics of the American Southwest. *Nuclear Instruments and Methods in Physics Research B* **136–138** 880–887.

Gratuze, B. (1999). Obsidian characterization by laser ablation ICP-MS and its application to prehistoric trade in the Mediterranean and the Near East: sources and distribution of obsidian within the Aegean and Anatolia. *Journal of Archaeological Science* **26** 869–881.

Gratuze, B., Blet-Lemarquand, M., and Barrandon, J. N. (2001). Mass spectrometry with laser sampling: a new tool to characterize archaeological materials. *Journal of Radioanalytical and Nuclear Chemistry* **247** 645–656.

Greenwood, N. N. and Earnshaw, A. (1997). *Chemistry of the Elements*. Oxford, Butterworth-Heinemann (2nd edn.).

Griffiths, H. (ed.) (1998). *Stable Isotopes: integration of biological, ecological and geochemical processes*. Oxford, Bios.

Grootes, P. M and Stuiver, M. (1986). Ross Ice Shelf oxygen isotopes and west Antarctic climate history. *Quaternary Research* **26** 49–67.

Grünberg, J. M., Graetsch, H., Baumer, U., and Koller, J. (1999). Untersuchung der mittelpalaolithischen Harzreste von Königsaue, Ldkr. Aschersleben-Stafurt. *Jahresschrift für mitteldeutsche Vorgeschichte* **81** 7–38.

Grupe, G., Price, T. D., Schröter, F., *et al.* (1997). Mobility of Bell Beaker people revealed by strontium isotope ratios of tooth and bone: a study of southern Bavarian skeletal remains. *Applied Geochemistry* **12** 517–525.

Guerra, M. F., Sarthe, C-O., Gondonneau, A., and Barrandon, J-N. (1999). Precious metals and provenance enquiries using LA-ICP-MS. *Journal of Archaeological Science* **26** 1101–1110.

Gunstone, F. D., Harwood, J. L., and Padley, F. B. (1994). *The Lipid Handbook*. London, Chapman and Hall.

Hahn, O. and Strassmann, F., (1939). Über den Nachweis und das Verhalten der bei der Bestrahlung des Urans mittels Neutronen entstehenden Erdalkalimetalle. *Die Naturwissenschaften* **27** 11–15.

Hairfield, H. H. Jr. and Hairfield, E. M. (1990). Identification of a Late Bronze Age resin. *Analytical Chemistry* **62** 41–45.

Hall, E. T. (1960). X-ray fluorescent analysis applied to archaeology. *Archaeometry* **3** 29–35.

Hall, E. T., Schweizer, F., and Toller, P. A. (1973). X-ray fluorescence analysis of museum objects: a new instrument. *Archaeometry* **15** 53–78.

Hall, M. E., Brimmer, S. P., Li, F. H., and Yablonsky, L. (1998). ICP-MS and ICP-OES studies of gold from a Late Sarmatian burial. *Journal of Archaeological Science* **25** 545–552.

Halliday, A., Lee, D.-C., Christensen, J. N., *et al.* (1998). Applications of multiple collector-ICPMS to cosmochemistry, geochemistry and palaeoceanography. *Geochimica et Cosmochimica Acta* **62** 919–940.

Hamilton, D. L. and Hopkins, T. C. (1995). Preparation of glasses for use as chemical standards involving the coprecipitated gel technique. *Analyst* **120** 1373–1377.

Hancock, R. G. V., Millet, N. B. and Mills, A. J. (1986). A rapid INAA method to characterize Egyptian ceramics. *Journal of Archaeological Science* **13** 107–117.

Hancock, R. G. V., Grynpas, M. D., and Pritzker, K. P. H. (1989). The abuse of bone analysis for archaeological dietary studies. *Archaeometry* **31** 169–179.

Hancock, R. G. V., Aufreiter, S., Moreau, J.-F., and Kenyon, I. (1996). Chemical chronology of turquoise blue glass trade beads from the Lac-Saint-Jean region of Quebec. In *Archaeological Chemistry: organic, inorganic and biochemical analysis*, ed. Orna, M. V., ACS Symposium Series 625, Washington, DC, American Chemical Society, pp. 23–36.

Hancock, R. G. V., Pavlish, L. A., Farquhar R. M., and Knight, D. (1999a). The analysis of brass samples from the Ball and Warminster sites in southern Ontario, Canada. In *Metals in Antiquity*, eds. Young, S. M. M., Pollard, A. M, Budd, P., and Ixer, R. A., BAR International Series 792, Oxford, Archaeopress, pp. 341–347.

Hancock, R. G. V., Aufreiter, S., Kenyon, I., and Latta, M. (1999b). White glass beads from the Auger site, southern Ontario, Canada. *Journal of Archaeological Science* **26** 907–912.

Harbottle, G. (1970). Neutron activation analysis of potsherds from Knossos and Mycenae. *Archaeometry* **12** 23–34.

Harbottle, G. (1976). Activation analysis in archaeology. In *Radiochemistry Vol. 3*, ed. Newton, G. W. A., London, Chemical Society, pp. 33–72.

Harbottle, G. (1982). Chemical characterization in archaeology. In *Contexts for Prehistoric Exchange*, eds. Ericson, J. E. and Earle, T. K., New York, Academic Press, pp. 13–51.

Harbottle, G. (1986). 25 years of research in the analysis of archaeological artifacts and works of art. *Nuclear Instruments and Methods in Physics Research B* **14** 10–15.

Harbottle, G. (1990). Neutron activation analysis in archaeological chemistry. *Topics in Current Chemistry* **157** 57–91.

Harbottle, G., Gordon, B. M., and Jones, K. W. (1986). Use of synchrotron radiation in archaeometry. *Nuclear Instruments and Methods in Physics Research B* **14** 116–122.

Harris, D. C. (1997). *Quantitative Chemical Analysis*. New York, Freeman.

Hart, F. A. and Adams, S. J. (1983). The chemical-analysis of Romano-British pottery from the Alice Holt forest, Hampshire, by means of inductively-coupled plasma emission-spectrometry. *Archaeometry* **25** 179–185.

Hart, F. A., Storey, J. M. V., Adams, S. J., Symonds, R. P., and Walsh, J. N. (1987). An analytical study, using inductively coupled plasma (ICP) spectrometry, of Samian and colour-coated wares from the roman town at Colchester together with related continental Samian wares. *Journal of Archaeological Science* **14** 577–598.

Hartmann, G., Kappel, I., Grote, K., and Arndt, B. (1997). Chemistry and technology of prehistoric glass from Lower Saxony and Hesse. *Journal of Archaeological Science* **24** 547–559.

Haswell, S. J. (ed.) (1991). *Atomic Absorption Spectrometry: theory, design and applications*. Amsterdam, Elsevier.

Hatcher, H., Hedges, R. E. M., Pollard, A. M., and Kenrick, P. M. (1980). Analysis of Hellenistic and Roman fine pottery from Benghazi. *Archaeometry* **22** 133–151.

Hatcher, H., Tite, M. S., and Walsh, J. N. (1995). A comparison of inductively-coupled plasma emission spectrometry and atomic absorption spectrometry analysis on standard reference silicate materials and ceramics. *Archaeometry* **37** 83–94.

Hayek, E. W. H., Krenmayr, P., Lohninger, H., *et al.* (1990). Identification of archaeological and recent wood tar pitches using gas chromatography/mass spectrometry and pattern recognition. *Analytical Chemistry* **62** 2038–2043.

Health and Safety Executive (2002). *Control of Substances Hazardous to Health*. Sudbury, HSE Books (4th edn.).

Health and Safety Executive (2004). *A Step by Step Guide to COSHH Assessment*. Sudbury, HSE Books (2nd edn.).

Hedges, R. E. M. (1979). Analysis of the Drake Plate: comparison with the composition of Elizabethan brass. *Archaeometry* **21** 21–26.

Hedges, R. E. M. (2003). Isotopes and red herrings: comments on Milner *et al.* and Lidén *et al. Antiquity* **78** 34–37.

Hedges, R. E. M. and Millard, A. R. (1995). Bones and groundwater: towards the modelling of diagenetic processes. *Journal of Archaeological Science* **22** 155–164.

Hedges, R. E. M., Millard, A., and Pike, A. W. G. (1995). Measurements and relationships of diagenetic alteration of bone from three archaeological sites. *Journal of Archaeological Science* **22** 201–209.

Hedges, R. E. M., Stevens, R. E., and Richards, M. P. (2004). Bone as a stable isotope archive for local climatic information. *Quaternary Science Reviews* **23** 959–965.

Heimann, R. B., Kreher, U., Spazier, I., and Wetzel, G. (2001). Mineralogical and chemical investigations of bloomery slags from prehistoric (8th century BC to 4th century AD) iron production sites in upper and lower Lusatia, Germany. *Archaeometry* **42** 227–252.

Hein, A., Mommsen, H., and Maran, J. (1999). Element concentration distributions and most discriminating elements for provenancing by neutron activation analyses of ceramics from Bronze Age sites in Greece. *Journal of Archaeological Science* **26** 1053–1058.

Hein, A., Tsolakidou, A., Iliopoulos, I., *et al.* (2002). Standardisation of elemental analytical techniques applied to provenance studies of archaeological ceramics: an inter laboratory calibration study. *Analyst* **127** 542–553.

Henderson, J. (2000). *The Science and Archaeology of Materials: an investigation of inorganic materials*. London, Routledge.

Henderson, P. (1984). Rare earth element geochemistry. In *Developments in Geochemistry*, ed. Henderson, P., Amsterdam, Elsevier, pp. 1–29.

Heron, C. (1996). Archaeological science as forensic science. In *Studies in Crime: an introduction to forensic archaeology*, eds. Hunter, J., Roberts, C., and Martin A., London, Batsford, pp. 156–170.

Heron, C. (2001). Geochemical prospecting. In *Handbook of Archaeological Sciences*, eds. Brothwell, D. R. and Pollard, A. M., Chichester, Wiley, pp. 565–573.

Heron, C. and Evershed, R. P. (1993). The analysis of organic residues and the study of pottery use. In *Archaeological Method and Theory*, ed. Schiffer, M. B., Tucson, AZ, University of Arizona Press, pp. 247–286.

Heron, C. and Pollard, A. M. (1988). The analysis of natural resinous materials from Roman amphoras, In *Science and Archaeology, Glasgow 1987*, eds. Slater, E. A. and Tate, J. O., British Series 196, Oxford, British Archaeological Reports, pp. 429–447.

Heron, C., Evershed, R. P., and Goad, L. J. (1991). Effects of migration of soil lipids on organic residues associated with buried potsherds. *Journal of Archaeological Science* **18** 641–659.

Heron, C., Nemcek, N., Bonfield, K. M., Dixon, D., and Ottaway, B. S. (1994). The chemistry of Neolithic beeswax. *Naturwissenschaften* **81** 266–269.

Hertz, H. (1887). Ueber einen Einfluss des ultrvioletten Lichtes auf die electrische Entladung. *Annalen der Physik und Chemie* **31** 983–1003.

Hertz, H. (1893). *Electric Waves*. London, Macmillan and Co. (trans. Jones, D.E.).

Herz, N. and Garrison, E. G. (1998). *Geological Methods for Archaeology*. Oxford, Oxford University Press.

Hocart, C. H., Fankhauser, B., and Buckle, D. W. (1993). Chemical archaeology of kava, a potent brew. *Rapid Communications in Mass Spectrometry* **7** 219–224.

Hoefs, J. (1997). *Stable Isotope Geochemistry*. Berlin, Springer.

Hollocher, K. and Ruiz, J. (1995). Major and trace-element determinations on NIST glass standard reference material-611, material-612, material-614, and material-1834 by inductively-coupled plasma-mass spectrometry. *Geostandards Newsletter* **19** 27–34.

Holmes, L. J., Robinson, V. J., Makinson, P. R. and Livens, F. R. (1995). Multi-element determination in complex matrices by inductively coupled plasma-mass spectrometry (ICP-MS). *Science of the Total Environment* **173** 345–350.

Hosetter, E., Beck, C. W., and Stewart, D. R. (1994). A bronze stitula from tomb 128, Valle Trebba: chemical evidence of resinated wine at Spina. *Studi Etruschi Bretschneider* **LIX** 211–225.

Hudson, J. (1992). *The History of Chemistry*. Basingstoke, Macmillan.

Hughes, M. J., Cowell, M. R., and Craddock, P. T. (1976). Atomic absorption techniques in archaeology. *Archaeometry* **18** 19–37.

Hughes, M. J., Northover, J. P., and Staniaszek, B. E. P. (1982). Problems in the analysis of leaded bronze alloys in ancient artefacts. *Oxford Journal of Archaeology* **1** 359–363.

Hughes, M. J., Cowell, M. R., and Hook, D. R. (1991). *Neutron Activation and Plasma Emission Spectrometric Analysis in Archaeology*. Occasional Paper 82, London, British Museum.

Hult, M. and Fessler, A. (1998). Sr/Ca mass ratio determination in bones using fast neutron activation analysis. *Applied Radiation and Isotopes* **49** 1319–1323.

Hunter, F. J., McDonnell, J. G., Pollard, A. M., Morris, C. R., and Rowlands, C. C. (1993). The scientific identification of archaeological jet-like artifacts. *Archaeometry* **35** 69–89.

Hunter, J. R., Roberts, C. A., and Martin, A. (eds.) (1997). *Studies in Crime: an introduction to forensic archaeology*. London, Routledge.

IAEA (1995). *Reference and Intercomparison Materials for Stable Isotopes of Light Elements*. IAEA TECDOC Series No. 825. Vienna, International Atomic Energy Agency. [http://www-pub.iaea.org/MTCD/publications/PDF/te_825_prn.pdf].

Jackson, K. W. (1999). *Electrothermal Atomization for Analytical Atomic Spectrometry*. Chichester, Wiley.

Jakes, K. A. (ed.) (2002). *Archaeological Chemistry: materials, methods, and meaning*. ACS symposium series no. 831, Washington, DC, American Chemical Society.

James, W. D., Dahlin, E. S., and Carlson, D. L. (2005). Chemical compositional studies of archaeological artifacts: comparison of LA-ICP-MS to INAA measurements. *Journal of Radioanalytical and Nuclear Chemistry* **263** 697–702.

Janssens, K., Aerts, A., Vincze, L., *et al.* (1996). Corrosion phenomena in electron, proton and synchrotron X-ray microprobe analysis of Roman glass from Qumran, Jordan. *Nuclear Instruments and Methods B* **109–110** 690–695.

Janssens, K. H., Deraedt, I., Schalm, O., and Veeckman, J. (1998a). Composition of 15th–17th century archaeological glass vessels excavated in Antwerp, Belgium. *Mikrochimica Acta Suppl.* **15** 253–267.

Janssens, K., Vincze, L., Vekemans, B., *et al.* (1998b). The non-destructive determination of REE in fossilized bone using synchrotron radiation induced K-line X-ray microfluorescence analysis. *Fresenius Journal of Analytical Chemistry* **363** 413–420.

Janssens, K., Vittiglio, G., Deraedt, I., *et al.* (2000). Use of microscopic XRF for non-destructive analysis in art and archaeometry. *X-Ray Spectrometry* **29** 73–91.

Jarvis, K. E. (1988). Inductively coupled plasma mass spectrometry: a new technique for the rapid or ultra-trace level determination of the rare-earth elements in geological materials. *Chemical Geology* **68** 31–39.

Jarvis, K. E. and Williams, J. G. (1993). Laser ablation inductively coupled plasma mass spectrometry (LA-ICP-MS): a rapid technique for the direct, quantitative determination of major, trace and rare-earth elements in geological samples. *Chemical Geology* **106** 251–262.

Jeffrey, G. H. (ed) (1989). *Vogel's Textbook of Quantitative Chemical Analysis*. Harlow, Longman Scientific and Technical (5th edn.).

Jeffries, T. E., Pearce, N. J. G., Perkins, W. T., and Raith, A. (1996). Chemical fractionation during infrared and ultraviolet laser ablation inductively coupled plasma mass spectrometry – implications for mineral microanalysis. *Analytical Communications* **33** 35–39.

Jenkins, R. (1974). *An Introduction to X-ray Spectrometry*. Chichester, Wiley.

Jenkins, R. (1988). *X-ray Fluorescence Spectrometry*. Chichester, Wiley-Interscience.

Jenkins, R. (2002). X-ray powder methods. In *McGraw-Hill Encyclopedia of Science and Technology* 19, New York, McGraw-Hill, pp. 668–673.

Jenne, E. A. (ed.) (1979). *Chemical Modeling in Aqueous Systems*. Washington, DC, American Chemical Society Symposium Series.

Johansson, S. A. E. and Campbell, J. L. (1988). *PIXE: a novel technique for elemental analysis*. Chichester, Wiley.

Johnsen, S. J., Clausen, H. B., Dansgaard, W., *et al.* (1997). The $\delta^{18}O$ record along the Greenland Ice Core Project deep ice core and the problem of possible Eemian climatic instability. *Journal of Geophysical Research – Oceans* **102** 26397–26410.

Jones, A. M., Iacumin, P., and Young, E. D. (1999). High-resolution delta O-18 analysis of tooth enamel phosphate by isotope ratio monitoring gas chromatography mass spectrometry and ultraviolet laser fluorination. *Chemical Geology* **153** 241–248.

Jones, M. (2001). *The Molecule Hunt: archaeology and the hunt for ancient DNA*. London, Allen Lane.

Jones, R. E. (1986). *Greek and Cypriot Pottery: a review of scientific studies*. Fitch Laboratory Occasional Paper 1, Athens, British School at Athens.

Junghans, S., Sangmeister, E., and Schröder, M. (1960). *Metallanalysen kupferzeitlicher und frühbronzezeitlicher Bodenfunde aus Europa*. Berlin, Verlag Gebr. Mann.

Junghans, S., Sangmeister, E., and Schröder, M. (1968–1974). *Kupfer und Bronze in der Fruhen Metallzeit Europas*. Vol. 1. Die Materialgruppen beim Stand von 12.000 Analysen. Vol. 2. Tafeln, Tabellen und Diagramme, Karten (in 3 vols). Vol 3. Katalog der Analysen Nr. 985–10 040. Vol. 4. Katalog der Analysen Nr. 10 041–22 000 (mit Nachuntersuchungen der Analysen Nr. 1–10 040). Berlin, Verlag Gebr. Mann.

Katzenberg, M. A., Schwarcz, H. P., Knyf, M., and Melbye, F. J. (1995). Stable isotope evidence for maize horticulture and paleodiet in southern Ontario, Canada. *American Antiquity* **60** 335–350.

Kelly, J. F. (2000). Stable isotopes of carbon and nitrogen in the study of avian and mammalian trophic ecology. *Canadian Journal of Zoology* **78** 1–27.

Kempfert, K. D., Coel, B., Troost, P., and Lavery, D. S. (2001). Advancements in FTIR microscope design for faster and easier microanalysis. *American Laboratory* **33** (Nov) 22–27.

Kennett, D. J., Neff, H., Glascock, M. D., and Mason, A. Z. (2001). Interface – archaeology and technology. A geochemical revolution: inductively coupled plasma mass spectrometry. *SAA Archaeological Record* **1** 22–26.

Kilikoglou, V., Bassiakos, Y., Doonan, R. C., and Stratis, J. (1997) NAA and ICP analysis of obsidian from Central Europe and the Aegean: source characterisation and provenance determination. *Journal of Radioanalytical and Nuclear Chemistry* **216** 87–93.

Killops, S. D. and Killops, V. J. (2005). *Introduction to Organic Geochemistry*. Harlow, Longman Scientific and Technical (2nd edn.).

Kim, Y. S. and Singh, A. P. (1999). Micromorphological characteristics of compression wood degradation in waterlogged archaeological pine wood. *Holzforschung* **53** 381–385.

King, A., Hatch, J. W., and Scheetz, B. E. (1997). The chemical composition of jasper artefacts from New England and the middle Atlantic: implications for the prehistoric exchange of "Pennsylvania jasper". *Journal of Archaeological Science* **24** 793–812.

Kingston, H. M. and Walter, P. J. (1992). Comparison of microwave versus conventional dissolution for environmental applications. *Spectroscopy* **7** 20–25.

Kirchhoff, G. and Bunsen, R. (1860). Chemical analysis by observation of spectra. *Annalen der Physik und der Chemie (Poggendorff)* **110** 161–189.

Kirchner, M. T., Edwards, H. G. M., Lucy, D., and Pollard, A. M. (1997). Ancient and modern specimens of human teeth: a Fourier transform Raman spectroscopic study. *Journal of Raman Spectroscopy* **28** 171–178.

Klaproth, M. H. (1795–1815). *Beiträge zur chemischen Kenntniss der Mineralkörpe*. 6 vols. Berlin und Stettin.

Klaproth, M. H. (1798). Mémoire de numismatique docimastique. *Mémoires de l'académie royale des sciences et belles-lettres, Berlin, Classe de philosophie expérimentale* 97–113.

Knapp, A. B. and Cherry, J. F. (1994). *Provenance Studies and Bronze Age Cyprus: production, exchange and politico-economic change*. Monographs in World Archaeology 21, Madison, Prehistory Press.

Knight, D. M. (ed.) (1968). *Classical Scientific Papers: chemistry*. London, Mills and Boon.

Knight, D. M. (ed.) (1970). *Classical Scientific Papers: chemistry. Second series: papers on the nature and arrangement of the chemical elements.* London, Mills and Boon.

Koch, P. L., Heisinger, J., Moss, C., *et al.* (1995). Isotopic tracking of change in diet and habitat use in African elephants. *Science* **267** 1340–1343.

Krause, R. and Pernicka, E. (1996). SMAP – The Stuttgart Metal Analysis Project. *Archaologisches Nachrichtenblatt* **1** 274–291.

Kuczumow, A., Chevallier, P., Dillmann, P., Wajnberg, P., and Rudas, M. (2000). Investigation of petrified wood by synchrotron X-ray fluorescence and diffraction methods. *Spectrochimica Acta B* **55** 1623–1633.

Kuhn, R. D. and Sempowski, M. L. (2001). A new approach to dating the League of the Iroquois. *American Antiquity* **66** 301–314.

Kuleff, I. and Pernicka, E. (1995). Instrumental neutron activation analysis of native copper – some methodological considerations. *Journal of Radioanalytical and Nuclear Chemistry* **191** 145–161.

Kuleff, I., Djingova, R., Alexandrova, A., Vakova, V., and Amov, B. (1995). INAA, AAS and lead isotope analysis of ancient lead anchors from the Black Sea. *Journal of Radioanalytical and Nuclear Chemistry* **196** 65–76.

Kuzmin, Y. V., Popov, V. K., Glascock, M. D., and Shackley, M. S. (2002). Sources of archaeological volcanic glass in the Primorye (Maritime) province, Russian Far East. *Archaeometry* **44** 505–515.

Lajtha, K. and Michener, R. H. (1994). *Stable Isotopes in Ecology and Environmental Science.* London, Blackwell Scientific.

Lambert, J. B. (ed.) (1984). *Archaeological Chemistry III.* Advances in Chemistry Series 205, Washington, DC, American Chemical Society.

Lambert, J. B. (1997). *Traces of the Past: unraveling the secrets of archaeology through chemistry.* Reading, Mass., Addison-Wesley.

Lambert, J. B. and Grupe, G. (1993). *Prehistoric Human Bone: archaeology at the molecular level.* Berlin, Springer-Verlag.

Lambert, J. B., Simpson, S. V., Szpunar, C. B., and Buikstra, J. E. (1984a). Copper and barium as dietary discriminants – the effects of diagenesis. *Archaeometry* **26** 131–138.

Lambert, J. B., Simpson, S. V., Szpunar, C. B., and Buikstra, J. E. (1984b). Ancient human diet from inorganic analysis of bone. *Accounts of Chemical Research* **17** 298–305.

Lampadius, W. A. (1801). *Handbuch zur chemischen Analyse der Mineralkörper.* Freyberg.

Lampert, C. D., Glover, I. C., Heron, C. P., *et al.* (2002). Characterization and radiocarbon dating of archaeological resins from Southeast Asia. In *Archaeological Chemistry: materials, methods and meaning*, ed. Jakes, K. A., ACS Symposium Series 831, Washington, DC, American Chemical Society, pp. 84–109.

Langenheim, J. L. (1990). Plant resins. *American Scientist* **78** 16–24.

Larsen, C. S., Schoeninger, M. J., van der Merwe, N. J., Moore, K. M., and Lee-Thorp, J. A. (1992). Carbon and nitrogen stable isotopic signatures of human dietary change in the Georgia Bight. *American Journal of Physical Anthropology* **89** 197–214.

Lavoisier, A.-L. (1789). *Traité élémentaire de chimie, présenté dans un ordre nouveau et d'après les découvertes modernes.* Paris. (Translated (R. Kerr, Edinburgh, 1790) and reprinted New York, Dover, 1965).

Layard, A. H. (1853). *Discoveries in the ruins of Nineveh and Babylon: with travels in Armenia, Kurdistan and the desert, being the result of a second expedition undertaken for the Trustees of the British Museum*. London, J. Murray.

Leach, F. (1996). New Zealand and Oceanic obsidians: an archaeological perspective using neutron activation analysis. *Journal of the Royal Society of New Zealand* **26** 79–105.

Lee, K. M., Appleton, J., Cooke, M., Keenan, F., and Sawicka-Kapusta, K. (1999). Use of laser ablation inductively coupled plasma mass spectrometry to provide element versus time profiles in teeth. *Analytica Chimica Acta* **395** 179–185.

Lee-Thorp, J. A. and van der Merwe, N. J. (1991). Aspects of the chemistry of modern and fossil biological apatites. *Journal of Archaeological Science* **18** 343–354.

Lee-Thorp, J. A., Sealy, J. C., and van der Merwe, N. J. (1989). Stable carbon isotope ratio differences between bone collagen and bone apatite, and their relationship to diet. *Journal of Archaeological Science* **16** 585–599.

Lee-Thorp, J. A., van der Merwe, N. J., and Brain, C. K. (1994). Diet of Australopithecus-Robustus at Swartkrans from stable carbon isotopic analysis. *Journal of Human Evolution* **27** 361–372.

Leigh, G. J., Favre, H. A., and Metanomski, W. V. (1998). *Principles of Chemical Nomenclature: a guide to IUPAC recommendations*. Oxford, Blackwell Science.

Lenard, P. (1903). Über die absorption von kathoden-strahlen verscheidener Geschwindigkeit. *Annalen der Physik (Vierte Folge)* **12** 714–744.

Leung, P. L., Stokes, M. J., Li, M. T. W., Peng, Z. C., and Wu, S. C. (1998). EDXRF studies on the chemical composition of ancient porcelain bodies from Linjiang, Jiangxi, China. *X-Ray Spectrometry* **27** 11–16.

Levinson, A. A., Luz, B., and Kolodny, Y. (1987). Variations in oxygen isotope compositions of human teeth and urinary stones. *Applied Geochemistry* **2** 367–371.

Lichte, F. E., Meier, A. L., and Crock, J. G. (1987). Determination of the rare-earth elements in geological materials by inductively coupled plasma mass spectrometry. *Analytical Chemistry* **59** 1150–1157.

Lidén, K., Eriksson, G., Nordqvist, B., Götherström, A., and Bendixen, E. (2003). The wet and the wild followed by the dry and the tame – or did they occur at the same time? Diet in Mesolithic – Neolithic southern Sweden. *Antiquity* **78** 23–33.

Linderholm, J. and Lundberg, E. (1994). Chemical characterization of various archaeological soil samples using main and trace-elements determined by inductively-coupled plasma-atomic emission-spectrometry. *Journal of Archaeological Science* **21** 303–314.

Lindsay, W. L. (1979). *Chemical Equilibria in Soils*. New York, Wiley.

Linke, R. and Schreiner, M. (2000). Energy dispersive X-ray fluorescence analysis and X-ray microanalysis of medieval silver coins – an analytical approach for non-destructive investigation of corroded metallic artifacts. *Mikrochimica Acta* **133** 165–170.

Little, B., Wagner, P., and Mansfeld, F. (1991). Microbiologically influenced corrosion of metals and alloys. *International Materials Review* **36** 253–272.

Littlefield, T. A. and Thorley, N. (1979). *Atomic and Nuclear Physics: an introduction*. New York, Van Nostrand Reinhold (3rd edn.).

Lochner, F., Appleton, J., Keenan, F., and Cooke, M. (1999). Multi-element profiling of human deciduous teeth by laser ablation-inductively coupled plasma-mass spectrometry. *Analytica Chimica Acta* **401** 299–306.

Longinelli, A. (1984). Oxygen isotopes in mammal bone phosphate: a new tool for paleohydrological and paleoclimatic research? *Geochimica et Cosmochimica Acta* **48** 385–390.

Longinelli, A. (1995). Stable isotope ratios in phosphate from mammal bone and tooth as climatic indicators. In *Problems of Stable Isotopes in Tree-rings, Lake Sediments and Peat-bogs as Climatic Evidence for the Holocene*, ed. Frenzel, B., Strasbourg, European Science Foundation, pp. 57–70.

Lowenstam, H. A. and Weiner, S. (1989). *On Biomineralization*. New York, Oxford University Press.

Lowry, T. M. (1923). Uniqueness of hydrogen. *Chemical Industry – London* **42** 43–47.

Loy, T. H. (1983). Prehistoric blood residues: detection on stone tool surfaces and identification of species of interest. *Science* **220** 1269–1271.

Loy, T. H. and Dixon, E. J. (1998). Blood residues on fluted points from Eastern Beringia. *American Antiquity* **63** 21–46.

Lubell, D., Jackes, M., Schwarcz, H., Knyf, M., and Meiklejohn, C. (1994). The Mesolithic Neolithic transition in Portugal – isotopic and dental evidence of diet. *Journal of Archaeological Science* **21** 201–216.

Mallory-Greenough, L. M. and Greenough, J. D. D. (1998). New data for old pots: trace element characterization of ancient Egyptian pottery using ICP-MS. *Journal of Archaeological Science* **25** 85–97.

Mandal, S., Cooney, G., Meighan, I. G., and Jamison, D. D. (1997). Using geochemistry to interpret porcellanite stone axe production in Ireland. *Journal of Archaeological Science* **24** 757–763.

Mando, P. A. (1994). Advantages and limitations of external beams in applications to arts and archaeology, geology and environmental-problems. *Nuclear Instruments and Methods in Physics Research B* **85** 815–823.

Mano, N. and Goto, J. (2003). Biomedical and biological mass spectrometry. *Analytical Sciences* **19** 3–14.

Mansilla, J., Solis, C., Chavez-Lomeli, M. E., and Gama, J. E. (2003). Analysis of colored teeth from Precolumbian Tlatelolco: postmortem transformation or intravitam processes? *American Journal of Physical Anthropology* **120** 73–82.

Martinetto, P., Anne, M., Dooryhée, E., *et al.* (2001). Synchrotron X-ray micro-beam studies of ancient Egyptian make-up. *Nuclear Instruments and Methods in Physics Research B* **181** 744–748.

Matson, R. G. and Chisholm, B. (1991). Basketmaker II subsistence – carbon isotopes and other dietary indicators from Cedar-Mesa, Utah. *American Antiquity* **56** 444–459.

Mauk, J. L. and Hancock, R. G. V. (1998). Trace element geochemistry of native copper from the White Pine mine, Michigan (USA): implications for sourcing artefacts. *Archaeometry* **40** 97–107.

Maxwell, J. C. (1864). A dynamical theory of the electromagnetic field. *Proceedings of the Royal Society of London* **13** 531–536.

May, T. W. and Wiedmeyer, R. H. (1998). A table of polyatomic interferences in ICP-MS. *Atomic Spectroscopy* **19** 150–154.

McEvoy, J. P. and Zarate, O. (1999). *Introducing Quantum Theory*. Cambridge, Icon Books.

McGovern, P. E. (1997). Wine of Egypt's golden age: an archaeochemical perspective. *Journal of Egyptian Archaeology* **83** 69–108.

McGovern, P. E. and Michel, R. H. (1996). The analytical and archaeological challenge of detecting ancient wine: two case studies from the ancient Near East. In *The Origins and Ancient History of Wine*, eds. McGovern, P. E., Fleming, S. J., and Katz, S. H., Langhorne, PA, Gordon and Breach, pp. 57–65.

McGovern, P. E., Glusker, D. L., Exner, L. J., and Voigt, M. M. (1996). Neolithic resinated wine. *Nature* **381** 480–481.

McNeil, M. and Selwyn, L. S. (2001). Electrochemical processes in metal corrosion. In *Handbook of Archaeological Sciences*, eds. Brothwell, D. R. and Pollard, A. M., Chichester, Wiley, pp. 605–614.

Mendelejeff, D. (1869). Ueber die Beziehungen der Eigenschaften zu den Atomgewichten der Elemente. *Zeitschrift für Chemie* **12** 405–406.

Mendeleef, D. (1879, 1880). The Periodic Law of the chemical elements. *Chemical News* **40** (1879) 231–232, 243–244, 255–256, 267–268, 279–280, 291–292, 303–304. **41** (1880) 27–28.

Mester, Z. and Sturgeon, R. (eds.) (2003). *Sample Preparation for Trace Element Analysis*. Amsterdam, Elsevier.

Metcalf, D. M. and Schweizer, F. (1971). The metal contents of the silver pennies of William II and Henry I (1087–1135). *Archaeometry* **13** 177–190.

Michel, V., Ildefonse, Ph., and Morin, G. (1996). Assessment of archaeological bone and dentine preservation from Lazaret Cave (Middle Pleistocene) in France. *Palaeogeography, Palaeoclimatology, Palaeoecology* **126** 109–119.

Middleditch, B. S. (1989). *Analytical Artefacts: GC, MS, HPLC and PC*. Amsterdam, Elsevier.

Middleton, W. D. and Price, T. D. (1996). Identification of activity areas by multi-element characterization of sediments from modern and archaeological house floors using inductively coupled plasma-atomic emission spectroscopy. *Journal of Archaeological Science* **23** 673–687.

Miksic, J. N., Yap, C. T., and Younan, H. (1994). Archaeology and early Chinese glass trade in southeast-Asia. *Journal of Southeast Asian Studies* **25** 31–46.

Millard, A. R. and Hedges, R. E. M. (1996). A diffusion-adsorption model of uranium uptake by archaeological bone. *Geochimica et Cosmochimica Acta* **60** 2139–2152.

Miller, J. C. and Miller, J. N. (1993). *Statistics for Analytical Chemistry*. London, Ellis Horwood (3rd edn.).

Mills, J. S. and White, R. (1989). The identity of the resins from the Late Bronze Age shipwreck at Ulu Burun (Kaş). *Archaeometry* **31** 37–44.

Mills, J. S. and White, R. (1994). *The Organic Chemistry of Museum Objects*. Oxford, Butterworth Heinemann (2nd edn.).

Milner, N., Craig, O. E., Bailey, G. N., Pedersen, K., and Andersen, S. H. (2003). Something fishy in the Neolithic? A re-evaluation of stable isotope analysis of Mesolithic and Neolithic coastal populations. *Antiquity* **78** 9–22.

Mirti, P., Aruga, R., Zelano, V., Appolonia, L., and Aceto, M. (1990). Investigation of Roman terra-sigillata by atomic-absorption and emission-spectroscopy and multivariate-analysis of data. *Fresenius Journal of Analytical Chemistry* **336** 215–221.

Mirti, P., Lepora, A., and Sagui, L. (2000). Scientific analysis of seventh-century glass fragments from the Crypta Balbi in Rome. *Archaeometry* **42** 359–374.

Moenke-Blankenburg, L., Schumann, T., Gunther, D., Kuss, H., and Paul, M. (1992). Quantitative analysis of glass using inductively coupled plasma atomic emission and mass spectrometry, laser micro-analysis inductively coupled plasma atomic emission spectrometry and laser ablation inductively coupled plasma mass spectrometry. *Journal of Analytical Atomic Spectroscopy* **7** 251–254.

Mommsen, H. (1981). Filters to sort out pottery samples of the same provenance from a data-bank of neutron activation analyses. *Archaeometry* **23** 209–215.

Mommsen, H., Beier, Th., Dittmann, H., *et al.* (1996). X-ray fluorescence analysis on inks and papers of incunabula with synchrotron radiation. *Archaeometry* **38** 347–357.

Mommsen, H., Bier, T., and Hein, A. (2002). A complete chemical grouping of the Berkeley neutron activation analysis data on Mycenaean pottery. *Journal of Archaeological Science* **29** 613–637.

Montaser, A. (1998). *Inductively Coupled Plasma Mass Spectrometry*. New York, Wiley-VCH.

Montelius, G. O. A. (1899). *Der Orient und Europa*. Stockholm.

Moreau, J.-F. and Hancock, R. G. V. (1996). Chrono-cultural technique based on the instrumental neutron activation analysis of copper-based artifacts from the "contact" period of northeastern North America. In *Archaeological Chemistry: organic, inorganic and biochemical analysis*, ed. Orna, M. V., ACS Symposium Series 625, Washington, DC, American Chemical Society, pp. 64–82.

Morgan, M. E., Kingston, J. D., and Marino, B. D. (1994). Carbon isotopic evidence for the emergence of C_4 plants in the Neogene from Pakistan and Kenya. *Nature* **367** 162–165.

Moropoulou, A., Bisbikou, K., Van Grieken, R., Torfs, K., and Polikreti, K. (2001). Correlation between aerosols, deposits and weathering crusts on ancient marbles. *Environmental Technology* **22** 607–618.

Morrison, C. A., Lambert, D. D., Morrison, R. J. S., Ahlers, W. W., and Nicholls, I. A. (1995). Laser ablation-inductively coupled plasma-mass spectrometry: an investigation of elemental responses and matrix effects in the analysis of geostandard materials. *Chemical Geology* **119** 13–29.

Mortimer, C. (1989). X-ray fluorescence analysis of early scientific instruments. In *Archaeometry: proceedings of the 25th International Symposium*, ed. Maniatis, Y., Amsterdam, Elsevier, pp. 311–317.

Moseley, H. G. J., (1913, 1914). The high frequency spectra of the elements. *Philosophical Magazine* **26** 1024–1034 (1913), **27** 703–713 (1914).

Mottram, H. R., Dudd, S. N., Lawrence, G. J., Stott, A. W., and Evershed, R. P. (1999). New chromatographic, mass spectrometric and stable isotope approaches to the classification of degraded animal fats preserved in archaeological pottery. *Journal of Chromatography A* **833** 209–221.

Mountjoy, P.-A., Jones, R. E., and Cherry, J. F. (1978). Provenance studies of LM1B/LHIIA marine style. *Annual of the British School at Athens* **73** 143–171.

Murphy, J. and Riley, J. P. (1962). A modified single solution method for the determination of phosphate in natural waters. *Analytica Chimica Acta* **27** 31–36.

Murray, M. A., Boulton, N., and Heron, C. (2000). Viticulture and wine production. In *Ancient Egyptian Materials and Technology*, eds. Nicholson, P. T. and Shaw, I., Cambridge, Cambridge University Press, pp. 577–608.

Murrell, J. N. (2001). Avogadro and his constant. *Helvetica Chimica Acta* **84** 1314–1327.

Needham, J. (1954–2004). *Science and Civilisation in China*. 7 vols. Cambridge, Cambridge University Press.

Neff, H. (ed.) (1992). *Chemical Characterization of Ceramic Pastes in Archaeology*. Monographs in World Archaeology, Madison, Wisconsin, Prehistory Press.

Neff, H. (2000). Neutron activation analysis for provenance determination in archaeology. In *Modern Analytical Methods in Art and Archaeology*, eds. Ciliberto, E. and Spoto, G., Chemical Analysis Series 155, New York, Wiley, pp. 81–134.

Nelson, B. K., DeNiro, M. J., Schoeninger, M. J., De Paolo, D. J., and Hare, P. E. (1986). Effects of diagenesis on strontium, carbon, nitrogen and oxygen concentrations and isotopic composition of bone. *Geochimica et Cosmochimica Acta* **50** 1941–1949.

Newlands, J. A. R. (1865). On the Law of Octaves. *Chemical News* **12** 83.

Newton, I. (1671–2). New theory about light and colors. *Philosophical Transactions of the Royal Society* **6**(80) 3075–3087.

Newton, R. G. and Renfrew, C. (1970). British faience beads reconsidered. *Antiquity* **44** 199–206.

Nissenbaum, A. (1992). Molecular archaeology: organic geochemistry of Egyptian mummies. *Journal of Archaeological Science* **19** 1–6.

Nissenbaum, A. (1993). The Dead Sea – an economic resource for 10,000 years, *Hydrobiologia* **267** 127–141.

Nölte, J. (2003). *ICP Emission Spectrometry: a practical guide*. Weinheim, Wiley-VCH.

Norman, M. D., Pearson, N. J., Sharma, A., and Griffin, W. L. (1996). Quantitative analysis of trace elements in geological materials by laser ablation ICPMS: instrumental operating conditions and calibration values of NIST glasses. *Geostandards Newsletter* **20** 247–261.

Oakberg, K., Levy, T., and Smith, P. (2000). A method for skeletal arsenic analysis, applied to the chalcolithic copper smelting site of Shiqmim, Israel. *Journal of Archaeological Science* **27** 859–901.

Oakley, K. P. (1963). Fluorine, uranium and nitrogen dating of bones. In *The Scientist and Archaeology*, ed. Pyddoke, E., New York, Roy Publishers, pp. 111–119.

Oakley, K. P. (1969). Analytical methods of dating bones. In *Science in Archaeology*, eds. Brothwell, D. and Higgs, E., London, Thames and Hudson, pp. 35–45 (2nd edn.).

O'Connell, M. M., Bentley, M. D., Campbell, C. S., and Cole, B. J. W. (1988). Betulin and lupeol in bark from four white-barked birches. *Phytochemistry* **27** 2175–2176.

Oddy, A. (1983). Assaying in antiquity. *Gold Bulletin* **16** 52–59.

Oddy, A. (1986). The touchstone: the oldest colorimetric method of analysis. *Endeavour* **10** 164–166.

Olariu, A., Constantinescu, M., Constantinescu, O., *et al.* (1999). Trace analysis of ancient gold objects using radiochemical neutron activation analysis. *Journal of Radioanalytical and Nuclear Chemistry* **240** 261–267.

Olsen, S. L. (1988). *Scanning Electron Microscopy in Archaeology*. International Series 452, Oxford, British Archaeological Reports.

Orna, M. V. (ed.) (1996). *Archaeological Chemistry: organic, inorganic, and biochemical analysis*. ACS symposium series no. 625, Washington, DC, American Chemical Society.

Otto, H. and Witter, W. (1952). *Handbuch der ältesten vorgeschichtlichen Metallurgie in Mitteleuropa*. Leipzig, J. A. Barth.

Outridge, P. M., Hughes, R. J., and Evans, R. D. (1996). Determination of trace metals in teeth and bones by solution nebulization ICP-MS. *Atomic Spectroscopy* **17** 1–8.

Parr, J. F. and Boyd, W. E. (2002). The probable industrial origin of archaeological daub at an Iron Age site in northeast Thailand. *Geoarchaeology* **17** 285–303.

Parry, S. J. (1991). *Activation Spectrometry in Chemical Analysis*. New York, Wiley.

Parsons, M. L. (1997). X-ray methods. In *Analytical Instrumentation Handbook*, ed. Ewing, G. W., New York, Marcel Dekker, pp. 557–586 (2nd edn.).

Parsons, P. J. and Slavin, W. (1999). Electrothermal atomization atomic absorption spectrometry for the determination of lead in urine: results of an interlaboratory study. *Spectrochimica Acta B* **54** 853–864.

Partington, J. R. (1961–1970). *A History of Chemistry*. 4 vols. London, Macmillan.

Passi, S., Rothschild-Boros, M. C., Fasella, P., Nazzaro-Porro, M., and Whitehouse, D. (1981). An application of high performance liquid chromatography to analysis of lipids in archaeological samples. *Journal of Lipid Research* **22** 778–784.

Passi, S., Picardo, M., Deluca, A., *et al.* (1993). Saturated dicarboxylic-acids as products of unsaturated fatty-acid oxidation. *Biochimica et Biophysica Acta* **1168** 190–198.

Pate, F. D. (1994). Bone chemistry and paleodiet. *Journal of Archaeological Method and Theory* **1** 161–209.

Pauli, W. (1925). Über den Zusammenhang des Abschlusses der Elekronengruppen im Atom mit der Komplexstruktur des Spektren. *Zeitschrift für Physik* **31** 765–783.

Pearce, N. J. G., Perkins, W. T., Westgate, J. A., *et al.* (1996). A compilation of new and published major and trace element data for NIST SRM 610 and NIST SRM 612 glass reference materials. *Geostandards Newsletter* **21** 115–144.

Peltz, C., Schmid, P., and Bichler, M. (1999). INAA of Aegaean pumices for the classification of archaeological findings. *Journal of Radioanalytical and Nuclear Chemistry* **242** 361–377.

Percy, J. (1861). *Metallurgy. Volume I: Fuel; Fire-clays; Copper; Zinc; Brass*. London, Murray. Reprinted Eindhoven, Archeologische Pers Nederland (1984).

Percy, J. (1864). *Metallurgy. Volume II: Iron; Steel*. London, Murray. Reprinted Eindhoven, Archeologische Pers Nederland (1984).

Percy, J. (1870). *Metallurgy. Volume III: Lead*. London, Murray. Reprinted Eindhoven, Archeologische Pers Nederland (1984).

Percy, J. (1875). *Metallurgy. Volume IV: Silver; Gold*. London, Murray. Reprinted Eindhoven, Archeologische Pers Nederland (1984).

Perey, M. (1939). Sur un element 87, derive de l'actinium. *Comptes Rendus hebdomadaires des Séances de l'Académie des Sciences* **208** 97–99.

Perezarantegui, J., Querre, G., and Castillo, J. R. (1994). Particle-induced X-ray-emission – thick-target analysis of inorganic materials in the determination of light-elements. *Journal of Analytical Atomic Spectrometry* **9** 311–314.

Perkins, W. T., Pearce, N. J. G., and Jeffries, T. E. (1993). Laser ablation inductively coupled plasma mass-spectrometry – a new technique for the determination of trace and ultra-trace elements in silicates. *Geochimica et Cosmochimica Acta* **57** 475–482.

Perkins, W. T., Pearce, N. J. G., and Westgate, J. A. (1997). The development of laser ablation ICP-MS and calibration strategies: examples from the analysis of trace elements in volcanic glass shards and sulfide minerals. *Geostandards Newsletter* **21** 175–190.

Perlman, I. and Asaro, F. (1969). Pottery analysis by neutron activation analysis. *Archaeometry* **11** 21–52.

Perrin, J. (1909). Mouvement Brownien et réalité moléculaire. *Annales de Chimie et de Physique 8me Series* **17** 5–114.

Person, A., Bocherens, H., Saliege, J. F., *et al.* (1995). Early diagenetic evolution of bone phosphate – an X-ray diffractometry analysis. *Journal of Archaeological Science* **22** 211–221.

Petit-Dominguez, M. D., Garcia-Gimenez, R., and Rucandio, M. I. (2003). Chemical characterization of Iberian amphorae and tannin determination as indicative of amphora contents. *Mikrochimica Acta* **141** 63–68.

Pettenkoffer, M. (1850). Ueber die regemässigen Abstände der Aeguivalentzahlen der sogennanten ein fachen Radicale. *Akademie der Wissenschaften* **30** 261–272.

Pike, A. W. G., Hedges, R. E. M., and Van Calsteren, P. (2002). U-series dating of bone using the diffusion-adsorption model. *Geochimica et Cosmochimica Acta* **66** 4273–4286.

Pillay, A. E. and Punyadeera, C. (2001). An enhanced procedure for the rapid digestion of high silicate archeological specimens followed by ICP-MS determination of traces of rare earth elements (REEs). *Journal of Trace and Microprobe Techniques* **19** 225–241.

Platzner, I. T. (1997). *Modern Isotope Ratio Mass Spectrometry*. Chichester, Wiley.

Plücker, J. (1858). Ueber die Einworkung des Magneten auf die elektrischen Entladungen in verdünnten Gasen. *Annalen der Physik und Chemie* **103** 88–106, 151–157.

Polette, L. A., Meitzner, G., Yacaman, M. J., and Chianelli, R. R. (2002). Maya blue: application of XAS and HRTEM to materials science in art and archaeology. *Microchemical Journal* **71** 167–174.

Pollard, A. M. (1995). Groundwater modelling in archaeology – the need and the potential. In *Science and Site: evaluation and conservation*, eds. Beavis, J. and Barker, K., Occasional Paper 1, Bournemouth, Bournemouth University, pp. 93–98.

Pollard, A. M. (1998a). The chemical nature of the burial environment. In *Preserving Archaeological Remains in Situ*, eds. Corfield, M., Hinton, P., Nixon, T., and Pollard, A. M., London, Museum of London Archaeology Service.

Pollard, A. M. (1998b). Archaeological reconstruction using stable isotopes. In *Stable Isotopes: integration of biological, ecological and geochemical processes*, ed. Griffiths, H., Oxford, Bios, pp. 285–301.

Pollard, A. M. (in press a). What a long strange trip it's been: lead isotopes in archaeology. In *From Mine to Microscope – analysing ancient technology*, eds. Shortland, A., Freestone, I., and Rehren, T.

Pollard, A. M. (in press b). Measuring the passage of time: achievements and challenges in archaeological dating. In *Oxford Handbook of Archaeology*, eds. Cunliffe B., Gosden C., and Joyce R.

Pollard, A. M. and Hatcher, H. (1986). The chemical analysis of Oriental ceramic body compositions: part 2 – greenwares. *Journal of Archaeological Science* **13** 261–287.

Pollard, A. M. and Heron, C. (1996). *Archaeological Chemistry*. Cambridge, Royal Society of Chemistry.

Pollard, A. M. and Wilson, L. (2001). Global biogeochemical cycles and isotope systematics – how the world works. In *Handbook of Archaeological Sciences*, eds. Brothwell, D. R. and Pollard, A. M., Chichester, Wiley, pp. 191–201.

Pollard, A. M., Bussell, G. D., and Baird, D. C. (1981). The analytical investigation of Early Bronze Age jet and jet-like material from the Devizes Museum. *Archaeometry* **23** 139–167.

Pomies, M. P., Barbaza, M., Menu, M., and Vignaud, C. (1999a). Preparation of red prehistoric pigments by heating. *Anthropologie* **103** 503–518.

Pomies, M. P., Menu, M., and Vignaud, C. (1999b). TEM observations of goethite dehydration: application to archaeological samples. *Journal of the European Ceramic Society* **19** 1605–1614.

Ponting, M. and Segal, I. (1998). Inductively coupled plasma-atomic emission spectroscopy analyses of Roman military copper-alloy artefacts from the excavations at Masada, Israel. *Archaeometry* **40** 109–122.

Ponting, M., Evans, J. A., and Pashley, V. (2003). Fingerprinting of Roman mints using laser-ablation MC-ICP-MS lead isotope analysis. *Archaeometry* **45** 591–597.

Poole, C. F. (2003). *The Essence of Chromatography*. Amsterdam, Elsevier.

Potts, P. J., Webb, P. C., and Watson, J. S. (1985). Energy-dispersive X-ray fluorescence analysis of silicate rocks: comparisons with wavelength-dispersive performance. *Analyst* **110** 507–513.

Price, T. D. (ed.) (1989a). *The Chemistry of Prehistoric Human Bone*. Cambridge, Cambridge University Press.

Price, T. D. (1989b). Multi-element studies of diagenesis in prehistoric bone. In *The Chemistry of Prehistoric Human Bone*, ed. Price, T. D., Cambridge, Cambridge University Press, pp. 126–154.

Price, T. D., Blitz, J., Burton, J., and Ezzo, J. A. (1992). Diagenesis in prehistoric bone: problems and solutions. *Journal of Archaeological Science* **19** 513–529.

Price, T. D., Grupe, G., and Schrotter, P. (1994). Reconstruction of migration patterns in the Bell Beaker period by stable strontium isotope analysis. *Applied Geochemistry* **9** 413–417.

Price, W. J. (1972). *Analytical Atomic Absorption Spectrometry*. London, Heyden.

Prohaska, T., Stadlbauer, C., Wimmer, R., *et al.* (1998). Investigation of element variability in tree rings of young Norway spruce by laser-ablation-ICPMS. *Science of the Total Environment* **219** 29–39.

Pulfer, M. and Murphy, R. C. (2003). Electrospray mass spectrometry of phospholipids. *Mass Spectrometry Reviews* **22** 332–364.

Radosevich, S. C. (1993). The six deadly sins of trace element analysis: a case of wishful thinking in science. In *Investigations of Ancient Human Tissue: chemical analyses in anthropology*, ed. Sandford, M. K., Langhorne, PA, Gordon and Breach, pp. 269–332.

Raith, A., Hutton, R. C., Abell, I. D., and Crighton, J. (1995). Non-destructive sampling method of metals and alloys for laser ablation–inductively coupled plasma mass spectrometry. *Journal of Analytical Atomic Spectroscopy* **10** 591–594.

Ramsay, W. and Soddy, F. (1903). Experiments in radioactivity, and the production of helium from radium. *Proceedings of the Royal Society of London B* **72** 204–207.

Rapp, G. R. Jr. and Hill, C. L. (1998). *Geoarchaeology: the Earth-science approach to archaeological interpretation*. New Haven, Yale University Press.

Raven, A. M., van Bergen, P. F., Stott, A. W., Dudd, S. N., and Evershed, R. P. (1997). Formation of long-chain ketones in archaeological pottery vessels by pyrolysis of acyl lipids. *Journal of Analytical and Applied Pyrolysis* **40** 267–285.

Reed, S. J. B. (1993). *Electron Microprobe Analysis*. Cambridge, Cambridge University Press (2nd edn.).

Regert, M. (1997). *Les Composes Organiques en Prehistoire: nouvelles approaches analytiques.* Unpublished Ph.D. Thesis, L'Universite de Paris X.

Regert, M., Bland, H. A., Dudd, S. N., van Bergen, P. F., and Evershed, R. P. (1998). Free and bound fatty acid oxidation products in archaeological ceramic vessels. *Proceedings of the Royal Society of London Series B-Biological Sciences* **265** 2027–2032.

Rehman, I., Smith, R., Hench, L. L., and Bonfield, W. (1995). Structural evaluation of human and sheep bone and comparison with synthetic hydroxyapatite by FT-Raman spectroscopy. *Journal of Biomedical Materials Research* **29** 1287–1294.

Reiche, I., Favre-Quattropani, L., Calligaro, T., *et al.* (1999). Trace element composition of archaeological bones and postmortem alteration in the burial environment. *Nuclear Instruments and Methods in Physics Research B* **150** 656–662.

Reiche, I., Vignaud, C., and Menu, M. (2002a). The crystallinity of ancient bone and dentine: new insights by transmission electron microscopy. *Archaeometry* **44** 447–459.

Reiche, I., Vignaud, C., Favre-Quattropani, L., and Menu, M. (2002b). Fluorine analysis in biogenic and geological apatite by analytical transmission electron microscopy and nuclear reaction analysis. *Journal of Trace and Microprobe Techniques* **20** 211–231.

Renfrew, C. (1979). *Problems in European Prehistory.* Edinburgh, Edinburgh University Press.

Renfrew, C. and Bahn, P. (1996). *Archaeology: theories, methods, practice.* London, Thames and Hudson (2nd edn.).

Restelli, M., Batista, S., Bruno, M., Salceda, S., and Mendez, M. (1999). Ultrastructural study of fossil human tooth tissue. *Biocell* **23** 197–202.

Reunanen, M., Holmborn, B., and Edgren, T. (1993). Analysis of archaeological birch bark pitches. *Holzforschung* **47** 175–177.

Rice, P. M. (1987). *Pottery Analysis: a sourcebook.* Chicago, University of Chicago Press.

Richards, M. P., Schulting, R. J., and Hedges, R. E. M. (2003). Sharp shift in diet at onset of Neolithic. *Nature* **425** 366.

Richards, T. W. (1895). The composition of Athenian pottery. *American Chemical Journal* **17** 152–154.

Ringnes, A. (1989). Origin of the names of the chemical elements. *Journal of Chemical Education* **66** 731–738.

Ritz, W. (1908). Über ein neues Gesetz der Serienspektren. *Physikalische Zeitschrift* **9** 521–529.

Roberts, N. B., Walsh, H. P. J., Klenerman, L., Kelly, S. A., and Helliwell, T. R. (1996). Determination of elements in human femoral bone using inductively coupled plasma atomic emission spectrometry and inductively coupled plasma mass spectrometry. *Journal of Analytical Atomic Spectroscopy* **11** 133–138.

Robinson, N., Evershed, R. P., Higgs, J., Jerman, K., and Eglinton, G. (1987). Proof of a pine wood origin for pitch from Tudor (Mary Rose) and Etruscan shipwrecks: application of analytical organic chemistry in archaeology. *Analyst* **112** 637–644.

Robinson, S., Nicholson, R. A., Pollard, A. M., and O'Connor, T. P. (2003). An evaluation of nitrogen porosimetry as a technique for predicting taphonomic durability in animal bone. *Journal of Archaeological Science* **30** 391–403.

Rodriguez-Lugo, V., Ortiz-Velazquez, L., Miranda, J., Ortiz-Rojas, M., and Castano, V. M. (1999). Study of prehispanic wall paintings from Xochicalco, Mexico, using PIXE, XRD, SEM and FTIR. *Journal of Radioanalytical and Nuclear Chemistry* **240** 561–569.

Rutherford, E. (1899). Uranium radiation and the electrical conduction produced by it. *Philosophical Magazine* 5 **XLVII** 109–163.

Rutherford, E. (1904). *Radioactivity*. Cambridge, Cambridge University Press.

Rutherford, E. (1911). The scattering of α and β particles by matter and the structure of the atom. *Philosophical Magazine Series 6* **21** 669–688.

Rutherford, E. and Andrade, E. (1914). The wavelength of the soft gamma rays from Radium B. *Philosophical Magazine Series 6* **27** 854–868.

Rutherford, E. and Geiger, H. (1908). An electrical method of counting the number of alpha particles from radioactive substances. *Proceedings of the Royal Society* **A81** 141–161.

Rutherford, E. and Royds, T. (1909). The nature of the alpha particle from radioactive substances. *Philosophical Magazine Series 6,* **17** 281–286.

Rutherford, E. and Soddy, F. (1902). The cause and nature of radioactivity. *Philosophical Magazine Series 6* **4** 370–396.

Ruvalcaba-Sil, J. L., Salamanca, M. A. O., *et al.* (1999). Characterization of pre-Hispanic pottery from Teotihuacán, Mexico, by a combined PIXE-RBS and XRD analysis. *Nuclear Instruments and Methods in Physics Research B* **150** 591–596.

Rydberg, J. R. (1897). The new series in the spectrum of hydrogen. *Astrophysical Journal* **6** 233–238.

Sabbatini, L., Tarantino, M. G., Zambonin, P. G., and De Benedetto, G. E. (2000). Analytical characterization of paintings on pre-Roman pottery by means of spectroscopic techniques. Part II: Red, brown and black colored shards. *Fresenius Journal of Analytical Chemistry* **366** 116–124.

Salamanca, M. A. O., Ruvalcaba-Sil, J. L., Bucio, L., Manzanilla, L., and Miranda, J. (2000). Ion beam analysis of pottery from Teotihuacán, Mexico. *Nuclear Instruments and Methods in Physics Research B* **161** 762–768.

Sandford, M. K. (ed.) (1993a). *Investigations of Ancient Human Tissues: chemical analyses in anthropology*. Langhorne, PA, Gordon and Breach.

Sandford, M. K. (1993b). Understanding the biogenic-diagenetic continuum: interpreting elemental concentrations of archaeological bone. In *Investigations of Ancient Human Tissue*, ed. Sandford, M. K., Langhorne, PA, Gordon and Breach, pp. 3–57.

Sayre, E. V. (1965). Refinement in methods of neutron activation analysis of ancient glass objects through the use of lithium drifted germanium diode counters. In *Comptes Rendus VIIe Congrès International du Verre, Bruxelles, 28 Juin–3 Juillet 1965*, Charleroi, Institut National du Verre.

Sayre, E. V. and Dodson, R. W. (1957). Neutron activation study of Mediterranean potsherds. *American Journal of Archaeology* **61** 35–41.

Scaife, B., Budd, P., McDonnell, J. G., and Pollard, A. M. (1999). Lead isotope analysis, oxide ingots and the presentation of scientific data in archaeology. In *Metals in Antiquity*, eds. Young, S. M. M., Pollard, A. M., Budd, P., and Ixer, R. A. F., BAR International Series 792, Oxford, Archaeopress, pp. 122–133.

Schliemann, H. (1878). *Mykenae: Bericht über meine Forschungen und Entdeckungen in Mykenae und Tiryns*. Leipzig, F. A. Brockhaus (English translation *Mycenae: a narrative of researches and discoveries at Mycenae and Tiryns*, London, J. Murray, 1878).

Schoeninger, M. J., DeNiro, M. J., and Tauber, H. (1983). Stable nitrogen isotope ratios of bone collagen reflect marine and terrestrial components of prehistoric human diet. *Science* **220** 1381–1383.

Schofield, P. F., Cressey, G., Wren Howard, P., and Henderson, C. M. B. (1995). Origin of colour in iron and manganese containing glasses investigated by synchrotron radiation. *Glass Technology* **36** 89–94.

Schurr, M. R. (1992). Isotopic and mortuary variability in a Middle Mississippian population. *American Antiquity* **57** 300–320.

Schwarcz, H. and Schoeninger, M. (1991). Stable isotope analysis in human nutritional ecology. *Yearbook of Physical Anthropology* **34** 283–321.

Sealy, J. C. and van der Merwe, N. J. (1985). Isotope assessment of Holocene human diets in the southwestern Cape, South Africa. *Nature* **315** 138–140.

Sealy, J., Armstrong, R., and Schrire, C. (1995). Beyond lifetime averages: tracing life histories through isotopic analysis of different calcified tissues from archaeological human skeletons. *Antiquity* **69** 290–300.

Segal, I., Kloner, A., and Brenner, I. B. (1994). Multielement analysis of archaeological bronze objects using inductively coupled plasma-atomic emission spectrometry – aspects of sample preparation and spectral-line selection. *Journal of Analytical Atomic Spectrometry* **9** 737–744.

Serpico, M. and White, R. (2000). The botanical identity and transport of incense during the Egyptian New Kingdom. *Antiquity* **74** 884–897.

Shackleton, N. J. (1969). Marine mollusca in archaeology. In *Science in Archaeology*, eds. Brothwell, D. and Higgs, E., London, Thames and Hudson, pp. 407–414 (2nd edn.).

Shalev, S. (1995). Metals in ancient Israel – archaeological interpretation of chemical analysis. *Israel Journal of Chemistry* **35** 109–116.

Sheppard, B. S., Heitkemper, D. T., and Gaston, C. M. (1994). Microwave digestion for the determination of arsenic, cadmium and lead in seafood products by inductively coupled plasma-atomic emission and mass spectrometry. *Analyst* **119** 1683–1686.

Shimosaka, C. (1999). Relationship between chemical composition and crystalline structure in fish bone during cooking. *Journal of Clinical Biochemistry and Nutrition* **26** 173–182.

Sillen, A. and Parkington, J. (1996). Diagenesis of bones from Eland's bay cave. *Journal of Archaeological Science* **23** 535–542 (with correction **24** 287 1997).

Sillen, A. and Sealy, J. C. (1995). Diagenesis of strontium in fossil bone – a reconsideration of Nelson *et al.* (1986). *Journal of Archaeological Science* **22** 313–320.

Sillen, A., Sealy, J. C., and van der Merwe, N. J. (1989). Chemistry and paleodietary research: no more easy answers. *American Antiquity* **54** 504–512.

Silva, F. V., Trevizan, L. C., Silva, C. S., Nogueira, A. R. A., and Nóbrega, J. A. (2002). Evaluation of inductively coupled plasma optical emission spectrometers with axially and radially viewed configurations. *Spectrochimica Acta B* **57** 1905–1913.

Simpson, I. A., van Bergen, P. F., Perret, V., *et al.* (1999). Lipid biomarkers of manuring practice in relict anthropogenic soils. *Holocene* **9** 223–229.

Singer, C. (ed.) (1954–1984). *A History of Technology*. 8 vols. Oxford, Clarendon Press.

Skoog, D. A., Holler, F. J., and. Nieman, T. A. (1998). *Principles of Instrumental Analysis*. Philadelphia, Saunders College (5th edn.).

Smith, C., Chamberlain, A. T., Riley, M. S., *et al.* (2001). Not just old but old and cold? *Nature* **410** 771–772.

Smith, G. D. and Clark, R. J. H. (2004). Raman microscopy in archaeological science. *Journal of Archaeological Science* **31** 1137–1160.

Smith, P. R. and Wilson, M. T. (2001). Blood residues in archaeology. In *Handbook of Archaeological Sciences*, eds. Brothwell, D. R. and Pollard, A. M., Chichester, Wiley, pp. 313–322.

Sponheimer, M., Lee-Thorp, J., de Ruiter, D., *et al.* (2005). Hominins, sedges, and termites: new carbon isotope data from the Sterkfontein valley and Kruger National Park. *Journal of Human Evolution* **48** 301–312.

Spoto, G., Ciliberto, E., Allen, G. C., *et al.* (2000). Chemical and structural properties of ancient metallic artefacts: multitechnique approach to study of early bronzes. *British Corrosion Journal* **35** 43–47.

Stern, B., Heron, C., Serpico, M., and Bourriau, J. (2000). A comparison of methods for establishing fatty acid concentration gradients across potsherds: a case study using Late Bronze Age Canaanite amphorae. *Archaeometry* **42** 399–414.

Stern, B., Heron, C., Corr, L., Serpico, M., and Bourriau, J. (2003). Compositional variations in aged and heated *Pistacia* resin found in Late Bronze Age Canaanite amphorae and bowls from Amarna, Egypt. *Archaeometry* **45** 457–469.

Stevenson, C. M., Abdelrehim, I. M., and Novak, S. W. (2001). Infra-red photoacoustic and secondary ion mass spectrometry measurements of obsidian hydration rims. *Journal of Archaeological Science* **28** 109–115.

Stiner, M. C., Kuhn, S. L., Weiner, S., and Bar-Yosef, O. (1995). Differential burning, recrystallization, and fragmentation of archaeological bone. *Journal of Archaeological Science* **22** 223–237.

Stone, J. F. S. and Thomas, L. C. (1956). The use and distribution of faience in the Ancient East and Prehistoric Europe. *Proceedings of the Prehistoric Society* **22** 37–84.

Stoney, G. S. (1894). Of the "electron", or atom of electricity. *Philosophical Magazine Series 5* **38** 418–420.

Stott, A. W., Evershed, R. P., Jim, S., *et al.* (1999). Cholesterol as a new source of palaeodietary information: experimental approaches and archaeological applications. *Journal of Archaeological Science* **26** 705–716.

Streitweiser, A. Jr. and Heathcock, C. H. (1985). *Introduction to Organic Chemistry*. New York, Macmillan.

Stuart-Williams, H. L. Q., Schwarcz, H. P., White, C. D., and Spence, M. W. (1996). The isotopic composition and diagenesis of human bone from Teotihuacán and Oaxaca, Mexico. *Palaeogeography Palaeoclimatology Palaeoecology* **126** 1–14.

Svehla G. (ed.) (1996). *Vogel's Qualitative Inorganic Analysis*. Harlow, Longman (7th edn.).

Swann, C. P. (1997). Recent applications of nuclear microprobes to the study of art objects and archaeological artifacts. *Nuclear Instruments and Methods in Physics Research B* **130** 289–296.

Swann, C. P., Fleming, S. J., and Jaksic, M. (1992). Recent applications of PIXE spectrometry in archaeology. 1. Characterization of bronzes with special consideration of the influence of corrosion processes on data reliability. *Nuclear Instruments and Methods in Physics Research B* **64** 499–504.

Swann, C. P., McGovern, P. E., and Fleming, S. J. (1993). Recent applications of PIXE spectrometry in archaeology. 2. Observations on early glassmaking in the Near-East. *Nuclear Instruments and Methods in Physics Research B* **75** 445–449.

Sykes, P. (1986). *A Guidebook to Mechanism in Organic Chemistry*. London, Longman (6th edn.).

Sylvester, P. (ed.) (2001). *Laser-Ablation-ICPMS in the Earth Sciences: principles and applications*. Ottawa, Ont, Mineralogical Association of Canada.

Szabadváry, F. (1966). *History of Analytical Chemistry*. Oxford, Pergamon Press.

Talbot, J. C. and Darling, W. G. (1997). *Compilation of Stable Isotope Data for Rainfall in the United Kingdom*. Technical Report (British Geological Survey) Hydrogeology series, Keyworth, British Geological Survey.

Tamba, M. G., del M., Falciani, R., López, T. D., and Coedo, A. G. (1994). One-step microwave digestion procedures for the determination of aluminium in steels and iron ores by inductively coupled plasma atomic emission spectrometry. *Analyst* **119** 2081–2085.

Tauber, H. (1981). ^{13}C evidence for dietary habits of prehistoric man in Denmark. *Nature* **292** 332–333.

Taylor, H. P. Jr., O'Neil, J. R., and Kaplan, I. R. (eds.) (1991). *Stable Isotope Geochemistry: a tribute to Samuel Epstein*. Special Publication No. 3. San Antonio, TX, Geochemical Society.

Tennent, N. H. (ed.) (1993). *Conservation Science in the U.K.* London, James and James.

Termine, J. D. and Posner, A. S. (1966). Infrared analysis of rat bone: age dependency of amorphous and crystalline components. *Science* **153** 1523–1525.

Terry, R. E., Hardin, P. J., Houston, S. D., *et al.* (2000). Quantitative phosphorus measurement: a field test procedure for archaeological site analysis at Piedras Negras, Guatemala. *Geoarchaeology* **15** 151–166.

Thiel, B. L. (2004). Imaging and analysis in materials science by low vacuum scanning electron microscopy. *International Materials Reviews* **49** 109–122.

Thomas, G. R. and Young, T. P. (1999). The determination of bloomery furnace mass balance and efficiency. In *Geoarchaeology: exploration, environments, resources*, ed. Pollard, A. M., London, Geological Society Special Publication, pp. 155–164.

Thomas, R. G. (1990). *Studies of Archaeological Copper Corrosion Phenomena*. Unpublished Ph.D. Thesis, University of Wales, College of Cardiff, Department of Chemistry.

Thompson, M. and Walsh, J. N. (2003). *Handbook of Inductively Coupled Plasma Atomic Emission Spectrometry*. Woking, Viridian Publishing.

Thomson, J. J. (1897). Cathode rays. *Philosophical Magazine* **44** 293–316.

Thomson, J. J. (1904). On the structure of the atom: an investigation of the stability and periods of oscillation of a number of corpuscles arranged at equal intervals around the circumference of a circle; with application of the results to the theory of atomic structure. *Philosophical Magazine Series 6* **7** 237–265.

Thorpe, J. F. and Whiteley, M. A. (eds.) (1937–1956). *Thorpe's Dictionary of Applied Chemistry*. New York, Wiley (4th edn., 12 vols).

Thurlow, K. J. (ed) (1998). *Chemical Nomenclature*. Amsterdam, Kluwer Academic.

Tissot, B. P. and Welte, D. H. (1984). *Petroleum Formation and Occurrence*. Berlin, Springer-Verlag.

Tite, M. S. (1972). *Methods of Physical Examination in Archaeology*. London, Seminar Press.

Tite, M. S. (1991). Archaeological science – past achievements and future prospects. *Archaeometry* **31** 139–151.

Tiyapongpattana, W., Pongsakul, P., Shiowatana, J., and Nacapricha, D. (2004). Sequential extraction of phosphorus in soil and sediment using a continuous-flow system. *Talanta* **62** 765–771.

Topping, J. (1972). *Errors of Observation and their Treatment*. London, Chapman and Hall (4th edn.).

Totland, M., Jarvis, I., and Jarvis, K. E. (1992). An assessment of dissolution techniques for the analysis of geological samples by plasma spectrometry. *Chemical Geology* **95** 35–62.

Trickett, M., Budd, P., Montgomery, J., and Evans, J. (2003). An assessment of solubility profiling as a decontamination procedure for the $^{87}Sr/^{86}Sr$ analysis of archaeological human tissue. *Applied Geochemistry* **18** 653–658.

Trigger, B. G. (1988). Archaeology's relations with the physical and biological sciences: a historical review. In *Proceedings of the 26th International Archaeometry Symposium*, eds. Farquhar, R. M., Hancock, R. G. V., and Pavlish, L. A., Toronto, University of Toronto, pp. 1–9.

Trigger, B. G. (1989). *A History of Archaeological Thought*. Cambridge, Cambridge University Press.

Trueman, C. N. (1999). Rare earth element geochemistry and taphonomy of terrestrial vertebrate assemblages. *Palaios* **14** 555–568.

Tsalev, D. L. (2000). Vapor generation or electrothermal atomic absorption – both! *Spectrochimica Acta B* **55** 917–933.

Tsolakidou, A. and Kilikoglou, V. (2002). Comparative analysis of ancient ceramics by neutron activation analysis, inductively coupled plasma-optical emission spectrometry, inductively coupled plasma-mass spectrometry, and X-ray fluorescence. *Analytical and Bioanalytical Chemistry* **374** 566–572.

Turner, N. H. (1997). X-ray photoelectron and Auger electron spectroscopy. In *Analytical Instrumentation Handbook*, ed. Ewing, G. W., New York, Marcel Dekker, pp. 863–914 (2nd edn.).

Tykot, R. H. (1998). Mediterranean islands and multiple flows: the sources and exploitation of Sardinian obsidian. In *Archaeological Obsidian Studies: method and theory*, ed. Shackley, M. S., New York, Plenum Press, pp. 67–82.

Tykot, R. H. (2002). Contribution of stable isotope analysis to understanding dietary variation among the Maya. In *Archaeological Chemistry: materials, methods and meaning*, ed. Jakes, K. A., ACS Symposium Series 831, Washington, DC, American Chemical Society, pp. 214–230.

Tykot, R. H. and Young, S. M. M. (1996). Archaeological applications of inductively coupled plasma-mass spectrometry. In *Archaeological Chemistry: organic, inorganic and biochemical analysis*, ed. Orna, M. V., ACS Symposium Series 625, Washington, DC, American Chemical Society, pp. 116–130.

Ubelaker, D. H., Katzenberg, M. A., and Doyon, L. G. (1995). Status and diet in precontact highland Ecuador. *American Journal of Physical Anthropology* **97** 403–411.

Urem-Kotsou, D., Stern, B., Heron, C., and Kotsakis, K. (2002). Birch bark tar at Neolithic Makriyalos, Greece. *Antiquity* **76** 962–967.

van der Merwe, M. J. (1982). Carbon isotopes, photosynthesis and archaeology. *American Scientist* **70** 596–606.

van der Merwe, M. J. (1992). Light stable isotopes and the reconstruction of prehistoric diets. In *New Developments in Archaeological Science*, ed. Pollard, A. M., Proceedings of the British Academy 77, Oxford, Oxford University Press, pp. 247–264.

van der Merwe, N. J. and Vogel, J. C. (1977). ^{13}C content of human collagen as a measure of prehistoric diet in woodland North America. *Nature* **276** 815–816.

van der Merwe, N. J., Roosevelt, A. C., and Vogel, J. C. (1981). Isotopic evidence for prehistoric subsistence change at Parmana, Venezuela. *Nature* **292** 536–538.

van der Merwe, N. J., Lee-Thorp, J. A., Thackeray, J. F., *et al.* (1990). Source area determination of elephant ivory by isotopic analysis. *Nature* **346** 744–746.

Van Grieken, R. E. and Markowicz, A. A. (1993). *Handbook of X-ray Spectrometry: methods and techniques.* New York, Marcel Dekker.

van Klinken, G. J., van der Plicht, H., and Hedges, R. E. M. (1994). Bone C-13/C-12 ratios reflect (palaeo-) climatic variations. *Geophysical Research Letters* **21** 445–448.

Varma, A. (1985). *Handbook of Atomic Absorption Analysis.* Boca Raton, FLA, CRC Press.

Villard, P. (1900). Sur la réflexion et la refraction des rayons cathodiques et des rayons déviable du radium. *Comptes Rendus hebdomadaires des Séances de l'Académie des Sciences.* **130** 1010–1012.

Vogel, A. I. (1937). *A Text-book of Qualitative Chemical Analysis.* London, Longmans, Green and Co.

Vogel, A. I. (1939). *A Text-Book of Quantitative Inorganic Analysis.* London, Longmans, Green and Co.

Vogel, J. C., Eglington, B., and Auret, J. M. (1990). Isotope fingerprints in elephant bone and ivory. *Nature* **346** 747–749.

Wada, E., Mizutani, H., and Minagawa, M. (1991). The use of stable isotopes for food web analysis. *Critical Reviews in Food Science and Nutrition* **30** 361–371.

Wadsak, M., Constantinides, I., Vittiglio, G., *et al.* (2000). Multianalytical study of patina formed on archaeological metal objects from Bliesbruck-Reinheim. *Mikrochimica Acta* **133** 159–164.

Wagner, T., Boyce, A. J., and Fallick, A. E. (2002). Laser combustion analysis of δ^{34}S of sulfosalt minerals: determination of the fractionation systematics and some crystal-chemical considerations. *Geochimica et Cosmochimica Acta* **66** 2855–2863.

Walder, A. J. and Furuta, N. (1993). High-precision lead isotope ratio measurements by inductively coupled plasma multiple collector mass spectrometry. *Analytical Sciences* **9** 675–680.

Walters, M. A., Leung, Y. C., Blumenthal, N. C., Legeros, R. Z., and Konsker, K. A. (1990). A Raman and infrared spectroscopic investigation of biological hydroxyapatite. *Journal of Inorganic Biochemistry* **39** 193–200.

Wang, J. A., Sun, S. Q., Zhou, Q., *et al.* (1999). Nondestructive identification of ballpoint writing inks with Fourier transform infrared microscope. *Chinese Journal of Analytical Chemistry* **27** 697–700.

Warashina, T. (1992). Allocation of jasper archaeological implements by means of ESR and XRF. *Journal of Archaeological Science* **19** 357–373.

Ward, N. I., Abou-Shakra, F. R., and Durrant, S. F. (1990). Trace element content of biological-materials – a comparison of NAA and ICP-MS analysis. *Biological Trace Element Research* **26** 177–187.

Watling, R. J., Lynch, B. F., and Herring, D. (1997). Use of laser ablation inductively coupled plasma mass spectrometry for fingerprinting scene of crime evidence. *Journal of Analytical Atomic Spectroscopy* **12** 195–203.

Watmough, S. A., Hutchinson, T. C., and Evans, R. D. (1996). Application of laser ablation inductively coupled plasma – mass spectrometry in dendrochemical analysis. *Environmental Science and Technology* **31** 114–118.

Watmough, S. A., Hutchinson, T. C., and Evans, R. D. (1998). Development of solid calibration standards for trace elemental analyses of tree rings by laser ablation inductively coupled plasma-mass spectrometry. *Environmental Science and Technology* **32** 2185–2190.

Watts, S., Pollard, A. M. and Wolff, G. A. (1999). The organic geochemistry of jet: Pyrolosis-gas chromatography/mass spectrometry (Py-GCMS) applied to identifying jet and similar black lithic materials – preliminary results. *Journal of Archaeological Science* **26** 923–933.

Weiner, J. S., Oakley, K. P., and Le Gros Clark, W. E. (1953–6). The solution of the Piltdown problem. *Bulletin of the British Museum (Natural History) Geology* **2** 139–146.

Weiner, S. and Bar-Yosef, O. (1990). States of preservation of bones from prehistoric sites in the Near East: a survey. *Journal of Archaeological Science* **17** 187–196.

Weiner, S. and Price, P. A. (1986). Disaggregation of bone into crystals. *Calcified Tissue International* **39** 365–375.

Weiss, G. (ed.) (1980). *Hazardous Chemicals Data Book*. New Jersey, Noyes Data Corporation.

Wess, T. J., Drakopoulos, M., Snigirev, A., *et al.* (2001). The use of small-angle X-ray diffraction studies for the analysis of structural features in archaeological samples. *Archaeometry* **43** 117–129.

Wess, T. J., Alberts, I., Cameron, G., *et al.* (2002). Small angle X-ray scattering reveals changes of bone mineral habit and size in archaeological samples. *Fibre Diffraction Review* 36–43.

White, C. D. and Schwarcz, H. P. (1989). Ancient Maya diet – as inferred from isotopic and elemental analysis of human-bone. *Journal of Archaeological Science* **16** 451–474.

White, S. R. (1981). *The Provenance of Bronze Age pottery from Central and Eastern Greece*. Unpublished Ph.D. Thesis, University of Bradford, UK.

Willett, F. and Sayre, E. V. (2000). The elemental composition of Benin memorial heads. *Archaeometry* **42** 159–188.

Williams-Thorpe, O. (1995). Obsidian in the Mediterranean and the Near East: a provenance success story. *Archaeometry* **37** 217–248.

Williams-Thorpe, O. and Thorpe, R. S. (1992). Geochemistry, sources and transport of the Stonehenge bluestones. In *New Developments in Archaeological Science*, ed. Pollard, A. M., Proceedings of the British Academy 77, Oxford, Oxford University Press, pp. 133–161.

Williams-Thorpe, O., Potts, P. J., and Webb, P. C. (1999). Field-portable non-destructive analysis of lithic archaeological samples by X-ray fluorescence instrumentation using a mercury iodide detector: Comparison with wavelength-dispersive XRF and a case study in British stone axe provenancing. *Journal of Archaeological Science* **26** 215–237.

Wilson, A. S., Dixon, R. A., Dodson, H. I., *et al.* (2001). Yesterday's hair – human hair in archaeology. *Biologist* **48** 213–217.

Wilson, L. (2004). *Geochemical Approaches to Understanding In Situ Diagenesis.* Unpublished Ph.D. thesis, University of Bradford, UK.

Wilson, L. and Pollard, A. M. (2001). The provenance hypothesis. In *Handbook of Archaeological Sciences*, eds. Brothwell, D. and Pollard, A. M., Chichester, Wiley, pp. 507–517.

Wilson, L. and Pollard, A. M. (2002). Here today, gone tomorrow? Integrated experimentation and geochemical modeling in studies of archaeological diagenetic change. *Accounts of Chemical Research* **35** 644–651.

Wilson, L., Pollard, A. M., Hall, A. J., and Wilson, A. S. (in press). Assessing the influence of agrochemicals on the nature of copper corrosion in the vadose zone of arable land – Part 3: Geochemical modelling. *Conservation and Management of Archaeological Sites.*

Winkler, C. (1886). Germanium, Ge, a new nonmetallic element. *Berichte der Deutschen Chemischen Gesellschaft* **19** 210–211.

Wöhler, F. (1828). Ueber künstliche Bildung des Harnstoffs. *Annalen der Physik und Chemie* **12** 253–256.

Woldseth, R. (1973). *X-ray Energy Spectrometry.* Burlingame, CA, Kevex Corporation.

Wolff, S. R., Liddy, D. J., Newton, G. W. A., Robinson, V. J., and Smith, R. J. (1986). Classical and Hellenistic black glaze ware in the Mediterranean – a study by epithermal neutron-activation analysis. *Journal of Archaeological Science* **13** 245–259.

Wright, L. E. and Schwarcz, H. P. (1996). Infrared and isotopic evidence for diagenesis of bone apatite from Dos Pilas, Guatemala: paleodietary implications. *Journal of Archaeological Science* **23** 993–944.

Wright, S. (ed.) (1964). *Classical Scientific Papers: physics.* London, Mills and Boon.

Xu, A. W., Wang, C. S., Chi, J. Q., *et al.* (2001). Preliminary provenance research on Chinese Neolithic pottery: Huating (Xinyi County) and three Yellow River Valley sites. *Archaeometry* **43** 35–47.

Yamada, M., Tohno, S., Tohno, Y., *et al.* (1995). Accumulation of mercury in excavated bones of two natives in Japan. *Science of the Total Environment* **162** 253–256.

Yener, K. A. and Vandiver, P. B. (1993). Tin processing at Goltepe, an Early Bronze-Age site in Anatolia. *American Journal of Archaeology* **97** 207–238.

Yi, W., Budd, P., McGill, R. A. R., *et al.* (1999). Tin isotope studies of experimental and prehistoric bronzes. In *The Beginnings of Metallurgy*, eds. Hauptmann, A., Pernicka, E., Rehren, T., and Yalcin, U., Der Anschnitt Beiheft 9, Bochum, Deutschen berbau-Museum, pp. 285–290.

Yoshinaga, J., Suzuki, T., Morita, M., and Hayakawa, M. (1995). Trace-elements in ribs of elderly people and elemental variation in the presence of chronic diseases. *Science of the Total Environment* **162** 239–252.

Yoshinaga, J., Yoneda, M., Morita, M., and Suzuki, T. (1998). Lead in prehistoric, historic and contemporary Japanese: stable isotopic study by ICP mass spectrometry. *Applied Geochemistry* **13** 403–413.

Young, S. M. M., Budd, P., Haggerty, R., and Pollard, A. M. (1997). Inductively coupled plasma-mass spectrometry for the analysis of ancient metals. *Archaeometry* **39** 379–392.

Zhang, J. Z. and Chi, J. (2002). Automated analysis of nanomolar concentrations of phosphate in natural waters with liquid waveguide. *Environmental Science and Technology* **36** 1048–1053.

Zheng, J., Goessler, W., Geiszinger, A., *et al.* (1997). Multi-element determination in earthworms with instrumental neutron activation analysis and inductively coupled plasma mass spectrometry: a comparison. *Journal of Radioanalytical and Nuclear Chemistry* **223** 149–155.

Zhou, Y., Parsons, P. J., Aldous, K. M., Brockman, P., and Slavin, W. (2001). Atomization of lead from whole blood using novel tungsten filaments in electrothermal atomic absorption spectrometry. *Journal of Analytical Atomic Spectrometry* **16** 82–89.

Zong, Y. Y., Parsons, P. J., and Slavin, W. (1998). Background correction errors for lead in the presence of phosphate with Zeeman graphite furnace atomic absorption spectrometry. *Spectrochimica Acta B* **53** 1031–1039.

Zoppi, A., Signorini, G. F., Lucarelli, F., and Bachechi, L. (2002). Characterisation of painting materials from Eritrea rock art sites with non-destructive spectroscopic techniques. *Journal of Cultural Heritage* **3** 299–308.

INDEX